TO SERVE
the PRESIDENT

TO SERVE
the PRESIDENT

CONTINUITY *and* INNOVATION
in the WHITE HOUSE STAFF

BRADLEY H. PATTERSON

BROOKINGS INSTITUTION PRESS
Washington, D.C.

Copyright © 2008
THE BROOKINGS INSTITUTION
1775 Massachusetts Avenue, N.W., Washington, D.C. 20036
www.brookings.edu

Library of Congress Cataloging-in-Publication data

Patterson, Bradley H. (Bradley Hawkes), 1921–
   To serve the President : continuity and innovation in the White House staff / Bradley H. Patterson.
      p.   cm.
   Includes bibliographical references and index.
   Summary: "Opens a window onto the closely guarded Oval Office turf: the operations, offices, and people of the complete White House team. Describes its organizational structure, recent innovations made in the face of changing events, what people do, while revealing the total size and cost of the contemporary White House team"— Provided by publisher.
   ISBN 978-0-8157-6954-5 (cloth : alk. paper)
   1. Presidents—United States—Staff. I. Title.
   JK552.P368 2008
   352.23'70973—dc22   2008027114

9 8 7 6 5 4 3 2 1

Typeset in Minion

Composition by Cynthia Stock
Silver Spring, Maryland

Printed by R. R. Donnelley
Harrisonburg, Virginia

This book is dedicated to all those who,
serving the president,
serve the presidency.

Contents

Acknowledgments

While this book has one father, it has many godparents. Authors of previous books are cited in this text; this work owes much to them and is itself but one more link in a chain of continuing research on the American presidency.

Some 100 men and women, interviewed over the course of two years, were indispensable progenitors. Most were serving in the White House and made time for meeting with the author in the midst of crushing workloads; some had finished their period of service there only a few weeks or months earlier. A few were interviewed in situ, as for example the presidential pilot, on *Air Force One* itself. Almost all opened their doors with especial friendliness because, they said, of the help they had found in the author's book of 2000—published when they were first joining the White House staff.

The author cannot adequately express his debt to these public servants who shared their unmatchable experiences and unique memories with him. Many of the interviewees reviewed entire chapters, helping to guarantee accuracy and balance at a time when some writing about the White House has been overdramatic—even fanciful.

He is especially appreciative of the early support he received from chiefs of staff Andrew Card and Joshua Bolten and from deputy assistant to the president Linda Gambatesa. He much appreciates the guidance and assistance from White House executive clerk Timothy Saunders, presidential scholar Martha Kumar, journalist Alexis Simendinger, and National Park Service White House Liaison director Ann Smith.

As his research progressed, the author has become very much impressed with the innovations that the Bush administration has been making in the physical plant of the White House complex. The author is grateful indeed to have been accorded personal tours of the new White House Situation Room, the new Brady Press Briefing Room, the remodeled White House Visitor Center, and the history-revealing reconstruction in the Eisenhower Executive Office Building.

The author commends the professional skill and personal enthusiasm of transcriber Rita Hodge of HBR, Inc., and of Patty Hill, who designed the organizational charts. He is thankful for the support of the Brookings Institution Press: director Robert Faherty, acquisitions editor Chris Kelaher, copy editor Martha Gottron, as well as production manager Larry Converse, managing editor Janet Walker, and art coordinator Susan Woollen.

Like most of the author's undertakings, this book was a family enterprise. Daughter Dawn Capron, son-in-law Jim Capron, sons Bruce, Glenn, and Brian Patterson, grandson Nick Patterson, and granddaughter Kelli Phillips all either aided in the research or gave the computer the instructions that the author by himself could never master. Chief reviewer and tough critic, an experienced public administrator in her own right, and a full and energetic partner in this adventure—as in sixty-five years of marriage—was Shirley D. Patterson.

In the end the buck stops with the author; if there are mistakes, they are his. The views here are his as well, their roots growing out of fourteen years of White House service, 1954–61 and 1969–76, and from another thirty-one years of close observation of the work of the White House staff. The tone of these words stems from a deep respect for a place very few have known firsthand.

Introduction

Why a factual book about the White House staff?

Because the 135 offices of the contemporary White House staff constitute the administrative center of the executive branch of our American government. There are books—many books—about the presidency, about presidential power, and about individual presidents, but it is the men and women on the president's personal staff who first channel that power, shape it, focus it, and, on the president's instructions, help him wield it. These 135 offices are the primary units of support for the president as he exercises executive leadership.

To most Americans the White House staff and its work are nearly unknown—largely because it is usually in the president's interest to have staffers stay behind the scenes. A few senior staff members are in the public eye, but the vast majority of White House staffers do their indispensable work completely out of sight. Yet despite being curtained off from public view, staff members are public servants; in helping the nation's foremost officeholder, they do the public's business. The public thus deserves an account of why the modern staff is there, how it is organized, and what individual staff members actually do. Scandalmongering and kiss-and-tell chronicles do not meet that need.

The Surprising Unknowns

The curtain that screens most of the staff from public visibility is thick with unexpected contrasts, false stereotypes, and even paradoxes. For example:

—The Constitution includes not a word about the White House staff, and they are barely mentioned in statute. Staff members have zero legal authority in their own right, yet 100 percent of presidential authority passes through their hands.

—A president or a presidential candidate typically promises that he will have only a small White House staff and will rely predominantly on the cabinet officers for policy guidance. These pledges, if made, are rarely kept.

1

— A president's next inclination is to emphasize how few staff associates he has, when in fact they are numerous. Veterans of past administrations typically look at the current staff and cluck disapprovingly: "We did it with a third of that number." Stung by this criticism, sitting presidents try even harder to mask the size of their personal team or make a show (as did President Bill Clinton) of cutting it back by some fixed percentage.

—Despite vows to cut back, presidents typically do just the opposite: they add to the menu of White House staff services. (George W. Bush created the Office of Faith-Based and Community Initiatives, the Office of the USA Freedom Corps, and the White House Office of Homeland Security and Counterterrorism). Once instituted, many of the innovations turn out to be truly useful, and the added functions are carried over into succeeding administrations.

—Even if a cutback in staff numbers is instituted at the beginning of a president's first term, the staff's core responsibilities remain undiminished. They are met by requiring the remaining staffers to work unendurable hours, by adding detailees and consultants, and by bringing in volunteers and unpaid interns who are not included in White House budget totals. As the reelection campaign approaches, staff numbers begin to creep upward.

—From afar the White House staff appears to be a small group of broad-gauged generalists. A closer look reveals a very different scene: seventy-four principal offices engaged in specialized duties. Each of these units tells all the others to enter its guarded jurisdiction only with permission. The seventy-four are supported by twenty-one senior policy support groups.

—Supporting these ninety-five policy units, and almost totally invisible to the public, are forty additional offices that contain the three-quarters of the staff who are nonpolitical professionals. These men and women serve not just the president but the office of the president, enhancing the presidency while aiding the president. Indeed this dual loyalty—to the office as well as to the person—is found among the senior political assistants as well.

—Senior staff members are partisans of the president. But their political commitment cannot be allowed to override the intellectual integrity that they must bring to their work. Contrary to public belief, sycophants and crusaders, if tolerated briefly, are not long welcome at the White House.

—Citizens might assume that members of a White House staff are cut from the same pattern on issues of public policy. Wrong. Differences in background, experience, age, gender, race, and especially party faction arc across the White House. The environment is an intellectually electric one, which is to the president's benefit—unless the internal arguments become ad hominem or are fought out in public.

—Although the most senior White House staff members are sometimes regarded as a barrier, walling off the president from people who advocate different opinions or from papers that present unconventional ideas, they often do just the opposite, insisting that dissenters be heard and challenging memoranda that tell the president only the welcome news.

—In the midst of the coterie composed of the president's assistants, who serve entirely at his pleasure, are two key players whom the president cannot remove: the vice president and the president's spouse: Their large and energetic staffs work, on the one hand, with a sense of independence from the presidential group; on the other hand, they must be tied into the whole team, or else their principals may be embarrassingly out of step. (A third such player, of only somewhat less stature, is the vice president's spouse.)

—However intense the jurisdictions and differences within the White House may be, when a major presidential initiative is launched, each of those specialized offices has to play its role *in coordination with* every other one. Does this happen effortlessly? No, and hell no. A set of unifying offices—and especially a tough, all-seeing chief of staff—operating precisely as the president wishes, is indispensable in guaranteeing the necessary teamwork.

—Cloaked, as most of them should be, by anonymity; protected, as on occasion they must be, by executive privilege; and necessarily immersed in matters both delicate and confidential, staffers nonetheless do their work under the surveillance of an expert, unremittingly skeptical, and occasionally hostile press corps. Leaks are frequent; secrets are rare. Fortunately for our democracy, the White House is a glass house, with both light and heat streaming in.

—Within White House circles, the overriding ethical standard is so strict that it could be called unfair: the mere appearance of impropriety is itself the impropriety. A few White House incumbents, perhaps innocent in fact, have run afoul of that elevated criterion.

—The most exasperating paradox of all concerns a principle enunciated in the 1930s by Louis Brownlow, adviser to Franklin D. Roosevelt. Brownlow told President Roosevelt that White House assistants should never be "interposed" between the president and his departmental heads. But daily—yea, hourly—staff members fire questions, demand information, make pointed suggestions, summarize departmental views, add their own recommendations, convey and interpret directives—about all of which the harried cabinet recipient may complain, "Usurpation!" What is often unknown to both the recipients and the public is that these staff actions are generally, and sometimes specifically, *at the president's own instructions.* This last and most pervasive "unknown" darkly colors the view that outsiders hold of the White House staff. In the eyes of the cabinet, the bureaucracy, Congress, the press, and the public, the staff is often seen as being unaccountable, out of control, pushing its own agendas. This is almost always a false view. Let there be a White House staffer who more than once (or maybe only once) misinterprets or subverts the president's wishes, and he or she will be found on the sidewalk outside.

Shrouded in this miasma of misperceptions, the White House staff is but dimly understood. Past and present scandals and kiss-and-tell self-serving screeds published by disgruntled or avaricious former colleagues have strengthened the popular inclination to paint the staff deep purple, if not black, and to view the place as crawling with miscreants and misbehavior.

But hold on, dear readers. That's a bum rap.

Of course there have been staffers who were heavy-handed, boorish, immoral, even criminal. Some within the White House ring of power are so seduced by the privileges they are afforded and so oblivious to the public's watchful eye that they not only do foolish things but believe that their actions will go unnoticed. The nation is, and always has been, rightfully skeptical about how presidential power is used and has become, properly, ever more attentive to the behavior of the president's agents.

Greatly outnumbering the dozens whose misdeeds have sullied their surroundings, however, are the thousands who have served their presidents, and the nation, with brilliance and self-effacing commitment. The miscreants are due no apologies, but the public's very watchfulness now calls for better illumination of the White House as a whole.

The Whole White House

And it is the *whole* White House that this book describes—a concept rarely if ever employed by other presidential scholars. The White House staff community family, as the author prefers to term it, includes not just the ninety-five policy offices but the Executive Residence, *Air Force One,* Camp David, the White House Communications Agency, the *Marine One* helicopter squadron, the Situation Room, the Secret Service protective units, the Social Office, the Visitor Center, and the Commission on White House Fellows. It also includes certain elements or employees of the Office of Administration, the National Park Service, the General Services Administration, the National Archives and Records Service, and the U.S. Postal Service, plus cadres of detailees, interns, and volunteers. All of these men and women collectively make up the *whole* White House—135 separately identifiable offices working together and supporting each other in a set of such incredibly intense day-to-day relationships that they are bonded together in this one institution. (A chapter has also been added about the independent White House Historical Association.)

The "whole White House" is a part of the Executive Office of the President—the principal part. The Executive Office of the President has twelve organizational elements. Five of them (the White House Office, the Executive Residence, the Office of Policy Development, the National Security Council, and the Office of the Vice President) come under the author's definition of the "whole White House" and are the focus of this book. The other seven (six of them statutory) make up the rest of the Executive Office of the President, and while their relationships with the White House are especially close and supportive, they are not discussed here. For readers' information, the seven are:

—*The Office of Management and Budget.* OMB, a statutory organization of some 500 men and women, originated as the Bureau of the Budget in 1921, a part of the Treasury Department. It was transferred into the new Executive Office of the President in 1939 and given its current name in 1970. OMB's principal responsibility is to prepare the president's budget and to supervise and control the budgetary administration of the executive branch. OMB also works to improve management and administration throughout the executive branch, clears departmental recommendations for proposed legislation, advises the president on what action to take on bills passed by Congress, manages government procurement policies, reviews all proposed departmental regulations, oversees statistical policy, and is responsible for implementing some fifteen financial and managerial statutes.

—*The Council of Economic Advisers.* Created by Congress in 1946, the CEA is a threesome of presidentially appointed (and senatorially confirmed) advisers, with a staff of thirty. It gives professional economic advice to the president, especially relating to the nation's employment, production, and purchasing power. It drafts the annual *Economic Report of the President,* which is sent to and defended before Congress.

—*The Office of National Drug Control Policy.* First established by executive order in 1971, the ONDCP was codified in 1988; it has a presidentially appointed and senatorially confirmed director and a staff of 123. It is the president's primary source of support for development and oversight of the federal drug control program. It develops and monitors a national drug control strategy and has the authority to review departmental budgets before they are submitted to Congress and to "review the allocation of personnel to and by such departments" to ensure that those departments have the right people—and enough of them—to carry out their responsibilities under the drug control strategy.

—*The Office of the U.S. Trade Representative.* The USTR, originally created by executive order in 1963, was made statutory in 1974, supplemented by a reorganization plan in 1979. It is headed by a director and two deputy directors, one in Washington and one in Geneva, all with the rank of ambassador, appointed by the president and confirmed by the Senate. With a staff of 229, the USTR is responsible for developing and coordinating the implementation of U.S. international trade policy; the director is the chief representative of the United States in bilateral and multilateral trade negotiations.

—*The Council on Environmental Quality.* The CEQ was originally created by the Environmental Policy Act of 1969 as a board of three members, appointed by the president, with Senate confirmation, charged with reviewing any and all departmental proposals for legislative or executive action to ensure that they are consistent with the principles and standards in the act. The council conducts investigations and surveys, makes recommendations to the president on environmental policy questions, and over the years has been given responsibility for monitoring the implementation of a series of environmental statutes. The council's presidentially designated chairman is the director of the office; its staff numbers twenty-four.

—*The Office of Science and Technology Policy.* OSTP was established by statute in 1976 to advise the president on the scientific and technological aspects of important policy issues, to assist OMB in developing the federal research and development budget, and to coordinate and evaluate the effectiveness of these federal R&D programs. The director manages a staff of forty.

—*The Office of Administration.* The OA was established by a presidential executive order in 1977 to provide central administrative services—personnel, library, office supply, receiving and warehousing, duplicating, facilities management, telecommunications, and mail-messenger functions—to the Executive Office itself and to the Office of the Vice President.[1] The executive order specifies that "the Office of Administration shall, upon request, assist the White House Office in performing its role of providing those administrative services which are primarily in direct support of the President." A certain proportion of the total OA staff of 222 is allocable to the White House in support of this special responsibility.

There are significant differences between the White House part of the Executive Office of the President and these seven units that make up the rest of the Executive Office. Four functionalities differentiate them.

First, all who work at the White House (except the president's spouse) in effect serve at the pleasure of the president. (Even the vice president's status as a member of the White House staff community, and his office location on the White House campus, are at the president's discretion.) No one has tenure in his or her job *at* the White House. Many career people are assigned or detailed to the White House, but their tenure is with their positions in their home departments. In the Executive Office agencies, by contrast, most employees have civil-service tenure in their jobs.

Second, no one in the White House, including the vice president and the president's spouse, has any legal authority to *do* anything—except to assist and advise the president. (In his functions at the Capitol, the vice president, of course, has constitutional duties in the Senate.) The other Executive Office units do have statutory powers of action.

Third, there is a strong tradition that men and women who work at the White House (except the president's spouse) do not testify before congressional committees. President George W. Bush, for example, held to that tradition when former governor Tom Ridge of Pennsylvania was first appointed director of homeland security at the White House in 2001 and the Senate Appropriations Committee demanded his testimony. Ridge later went up to Capitol Hill and met with senators informally. The president may find himself forced to waive that tradition in cases of alleged scandal or criminality (such as Watergate or the Iran/Contra affair).[2] White House officers very frequently go to the Capitol and meet informally with members or staffs, but not for on-the-record testimony. (This tradition came into play when the 9/11 Commission, the independent panel investigating the al Qaeda attacks, requested testimony from National Security Adviser Condoleezza Rice. The president at first said no, but the influence of the 9/11 families who lost loved ones in the attacks was of so much weight that he finally permitted her to testify, saying, however, that this was an exception pertaining only in this instance and only to Rice.)

Fourth, the papers of those who work at the White House (including the vice president) come under the Presidential Records Act and are not subject to Freedom of Information Act (FOIA) requests.[3] The papers of the statutory units of the Executive Office (except for those of the Council of Economic Advisers) come under the Federal Records Act and are reachable pursuant to the FOIA.[4]

These distinctions undergird the author's decision to limit the focus of this book to the White House as defined above. The author cringes at the frequent fuzzing up of those differences in the news media or elsewhere by referring to the "White House Budget Office," for example, or to the "White House Science Office."

Where the Author Is Coming From

This is the author's third book about the organization and functioning of the White House staff.

The first, *The Ring of Power: The White House Staff and Its Expanding Role in Government* (Basic Books, 1988), discussed the White House staffs of Presidents Harry S. Truman, Dwight D. Eisenhower, John F. Kennedy, Lyndon B. Johnson, Richard M. Nixon, Gerald R. Ford, and Jimmy Carter. The second, *The White House Staff: Inside the West Wing and Beyond* (Brookings Institution Press, 2000), extended the coverage to include the staffs of Presidents George H. W. Bush and William J. Clinton. The principal focus of this volume is the structure and process of the White House of President George W. Bush, with emphasis on his second term. References in this book to *Bush*, therefore, are to George W. Bush unless it is clear from the context that George H. W. Bush is meant.

The purpose of all three of these works is to describe the elements of the modern White House staff, the responsibilities and functions of each element, and how they are meant to be integrated into a coordinated body of advisers and operating assistants. All three books give little attention to, and pronounce no judgments on, issues of policy, foreign or domestic; the emphasis in these books is not on what the presidents did but on how the staffs were organized to support them. The objective here is not to judge the wisdom or success of any president's policies; many other critics and historians are taking up that challenge. These three works are professional, nonpartisan, and with no first-person references whatsoever.

This book is the only known volume on the presidency that lays out the size and the budget of the whole White House (except for its classified elements)—a set of figures that have had to be pulled together from the several departments and agencies that, almost completely behind the scenes, contribute to financing the various parts of the modern White House (chapter 2).

The book contains several organization charts of the White House as it has been set up by President Bush. The charts, which portray the organizing schema of the Bush White House staff, represent a further unique compilation by the author; if the White House draws up an organization chart itself, it is never made public.

The author spent fourteen years on the White House staffs of three presidents and was close to the staff of a fourth. What follows is not a kiss-and-tell account, a personal memoir, or an exposé. It is the professional view, not of a theorist, not of an outsider looking in, but of a White House practitioner—a public administrator with intimate knowledge of how the entire White House really works. What knowledge the author has acquired from his past experience at the White House has been dramatically enriched by the nearly 100 interviews he has been privileged to have had with officers whom he has known for many years such as the vice president and the counsel to the president and with many others on or retired from the Bush staff. The president's spouse herself provided a personal commentary about her functions in the chapter describing her office. Some of the interviews were conducted in situ, such as an interview with the presidential pilot in the *Air Force One* hangar at Andrews Air Force Base (and in the plane itself) and with the commandant of the White House Communications Agency in his headquarters at Bolling Air Force Base. In the interests of accuracy, balance, and professionalism, the author not only submitted the attributed quotations for confirmation but also invited many of the interviewees to review the entire chapter(s) in which their work is described.

The author's nonpartisan aim is to illumine public administration at the apex of government, especially:

—To aid the presidential candidates in the fall of 2008, who even then are likely thinking about—or may have quietly commissioned one or two colleagues to think about—how they would structure the White House. For both of the 2008 presidential nominees, and especially for many of their advisers, 1600 Pennsylvania Avenue will be terra nova.

—To provide the 2008 president-elect with an accurate picture of the contemporary White House, so that he can make informed choices and decisions about structure and staffing. That pre-inaugural decisionmaking environment will be long on flexibility but very short on time.

—To be of help to the 1,000 or so men and women who will have been selected during the winter of 2008–09 to take their places on the afternoon of January 20, 2009, as full-time members, detailees, interns, or volunteers of the new White House staff. Most of them will have never set foot in the White House, yet will have to learn, practically overnight, how to make a White House staff function, error-free, for the new chief executive.

—To inform the other 2,500 who, during the opening months of 2009, will be appointed to noncareer positions in the departments and agencies of the executive branch—the operating leadership cadre of the new administration. To most of them, the White House staff, which will have picked them, will look like a group of strangers who seek and need their swift cooperation but who won't impart very much about how their White House is organized or what it does with the information it is given.

—To paint a factual, nonpartisan picture of the White House at work for the other indispensable participants in the Washington environment—Congress, the media, the diplomatic corps, business and think-tank leaders, and state and local politicians, many of whom have inaccurate or negative stereotypes about that institution—impressions that the White House itself is slow to correct.

—To broaden the knowledge of those who are teaching civics and political science in the nation's high schools and universities and to stimulate the interest of their students who are contemplating careers in public administration.

The White House Overall

Overall Organization of the White House

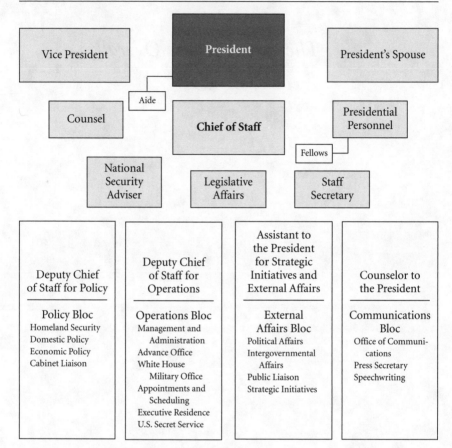

1 | *The Contemporary White House Staff*

A president-elect can be expected to ask:

How did the White House staff get to be what it is?

How much of it is fixed in statute and how much of it can a new president reshape?

What are its organizational elements? How much continuity has there been?

What innovations have been made by recent presidents?

How many men and women typically work there?

How much does it cost to operate the whole White House?

In fact, President George W. Bush did ask:

> How do you intend to get advice from people you surround yourself—who are you going to surround yourself [with]? And what process will you have in place to ensure that you get the unvarnished opinion of advisers? Because whoever sits in the Oval Office is going to find this is a complex world, with a lot of issues coming into the Oval Office—a lot—and a great expectation in the world that the United States take the lead. And so my question would be, how do you intend to set up your Oval Office so that people will come in and give you their advice?[1]

How Did the White House Staff Get to Be What It Is?

The environment out of which the modern White House staff was born, at the end of Franklin Roosevelt's first term, was, like any other difficult birth: messy and painful. At first, FDR tried to rely on his cabinet departments. "From July 1933 to September 1935," reports presidential scholar Matthew Dickinson,

> he experimented with at least five different cabinet-level coordinating councils. But, despite his repeated attempts to make their deliberations more effective, these coordinating councils proved unable to meet his

bargaining needs. By the end of 1935 he was genuinely worried that his administrative shortcomings might jeopardize his reelection chances. . . . Not surprisingly, Roosevelt spent a large portion of his waking hours soothing ruffled feathers and resolving administrative disputes. The maintenance of peace in his official family took up hours and days of Roosevelt's time that could have been used on other matters. . . . The cumulative impact of FDR's organization strategy . . . was administrative disarray.[2]

This disarray reached such proportions that consultant Louis Brownlow, on a trip to Europe, encountered pessimism abroad as to whether democracies could govern effectively when beset with economic and national security calamities. He later recalled, "It was our belief that the Presidency of the United States was the institution . . . behind which democrats might rally to repel the enemy. And, to that end, it was not only desirable but absolutely necessary that the President be better equipped for his tremendous task."[3]

Roosevelt had been meeting with several experts in public administration, including Brownlow, Charles Merriam, and Luther Gulick, to discuss government planning at the national level, and he had read a December 1935 memorandum from Merriam recommending a study of how an executive staff "should be organized, what its functions should be, and its relations to the operating agencies."[4] In February 1936, Roosevelt had an hour-long meeting with Merriam and others to discuss how such a study might be undertaken. FDR was satisfied that he had shaped the research agenda of the study to his satisfaction and was confident that he had enough personal influence on the thinking of the three leaders; on March 20, 1936, he appointed Brownlow, Merriam, and Gulick as the President's Committee on Administrative Management. He instructed them not to share their deliberations with any of his three principal White House aides, and then let the committee alone, busying himself with his reelection.

After his electoral victory the president met with the committee (Merriam was absent) on November 14, 1936. When presented with their recommendation to enhance his personal staff by six administrative assistants, of whom one would function as a kind of de facto staff director over the others, FDR balked; staff direction would remain in his own hands. "He refused to delegate staff 'coordination' to any single subordinate," Dickinson emphasized, adding "Roosevelt's administrative philosophy, as expressed in the Brownlow Committee Report, *is clearly antithetical to subsequent staff development during the last half century.*"[5]

The following January 10, Roosevelt convened an extraordinary press conference at which he unveiled the Brownlow Committee's report with its proposals for "not more than six" administrative assistants and sent Congress draft legislation to give statutory authorization to this new White House staff. For two years Congress huffed and puffed but took no final action to meet the president's request.[6] (This was the same period when FDR was pushing his failed plan to augment the membership of the Supreme Court.)

On April 3, 1939, however, Congress did enact the Reorganization Act of 1939, which began:

> SECTION I. (a) The Congress hereby declares that by reason of continued national deficits beginning in 1931, it is desirable to reduce substantially Government expenditures and that such reductions may be accomplished in some measure by proceeding immediately under the provisions of this Act. The President shall investigate the organization of all agencies of the government and shall determine what changes therein are necessary to accomplish the following purposes:
>
> . . .
>
>> (2) to increase the efficiency of the operations of the Government to the fullest extent practicable within the revenues;
>>
>> . . .
>>
>>> (b) The Congress declares that the public interest demands the carrying out of the purposes specified in subsection (a) and that such purposes may be accomplished in great measure by proceeding immediately under the provisions of this title, and can be accomplished more speedily thereby than by the enactment of specific legislation.[7]

President Roosevelt took up that invitation to "proceed immediately." On April 25, 1939, he submitted Reorganization Plan Number One, which included authorization for an institutional staff unit entitled "Executive Office of the President," but it was silent about any White House office, that is, any personal staff for the president. Congress approved the plan; it became effective on July 1, 1939.[8]

Taking these two congressional enactments together, Roosevelt saw his opportunity. On September 8, 1939, he issued his own Executive Order 8248—in effect the birth certificate for the modern White House. It begins: "By virtue of the authority vested in me by the Constitution and Statutes, and in order to effectuate the purposes of the Reorganization Act of 1939. . . and of Reorganization Plan No I . . . it is hereby ordered as follows: There shall be within the Executive Office of the President the following principal divisions, namely (1) The White House Office. . . ."

Part II, Section 1 of the order went on to specify that this new office was to be composed of "Secretaries to the President," an executive clerk, and administrative assistants to the president. These last were:

> To assist the President in such matters as he may direct, and at the specific request of the President, to get information and to condense and summarize it for his use. These Administrative Assistants shall be personal aides

to the President and shall have no authority over anyone in any department or agency, including the Executive Office of the President, other than the personnel assigned to their immediate offices. In no event shall the Administrative Assistants be interposed between the President and the head of any department or agency or between the President and any one of the divisions in the Executive Office of the President.

The originating document of the modern White House staff was thus not a statute but an executive action, amendable by any subsequent president. It set up a White House staff "with no authority over anyone in any department or agency," and it instructed White House staffers never to "interpose" themselves between the president and his cabinet. Echoes of these commands still reverberate in the White House sixty-nine years later.

The White House in Statute

Since its first appearance in the appropriations act for 1940, the term *The White House Office* appears often in statutes, but not in the sense of establishing any part of the White House staff or specifying the duties of any of its officers.

There are three exceptions to this statement. The first is the National Security Act of 1947, which created the National Security Council (NSC). The act specifies that the council "shall have a staff to be headed by a civilian executive secretary who shall be appointed by the President . . . [and who may] appoint . . . such personnel as may be necessary to perform such duties as may be prescribed by the council. . . ." The second instance of congressional creation of presidential staff is in the Homeland Security Act of 2002, which establishes the Homeland Security Council (HSC) and in similar language creates an executive secretary for the HSC. [9] Other than the president and the vice president, these are the only two positions in the entire White House that are creations of statute; to disestablish them congressional action would be required.

The third statute that prescribes any White House staff duties is the law requiring the Secret Service to protect the president, the president-elect, the vice president, and the vice president-elect, even if any of those four protectees would prefer to decline the protection. [10]

In 1978 a comprehensive statute was enacted "to clarify the authority of personnel in the White House and the Executive Residence at the White House [and] to clarify the authority for the employment of personnel by the President to meet unanticipated needs. . . ." [11] The president is "authorized to appoint and fix the pay of employees in the White House Office without regard to any other provision of law regulating the employment or compensation of personnel in the Government service." As to what the staff is to do, the statute simply says that White House employees "shall perform such official duties as the President may prescribe." In addition, the president is authorized to expend "such sums as may be necessary" for the official expenses of the Executive Residence and the White House Office. Assistance is also authorized for the domestic policy staff, the vice president, the spouse of the president, and the spouse of the vice president. The same statute does impose limits on the numbers of civil service supergrades to be employed in the White House Office, but for positions at GS-16 and below permits "such number of other employees as he [the president] may determine to be appropriate." The hiring of experts and consultants is also authorized. Finally, the 1978 statute authorizes any executive branch agency to detail employees to the White House providing that the detailing agencies are reimbursed for their detailees' salaries after 180 days and that the White House annually reports the numbers of detailees to Congress for public disclosure. Significantly, the key verb throughout this statute is "authorize," not "establish."

A 1994 act requires the White House to send to the House and Senate Governmental Affairs Committees each July 1 a list of all White House employees and detailees by name, position, and salary (excluding only individuals the naming of whom "would not be in the interest of the national defense or foreign policy.")[12]

Each year, of course, there is an appropriations statute that fixes the outlays permitted for salaries and expenses of the employees in the White House Office. In their 1998 act the Appropriations Committees inserted a provision requiring reimbursements when outside groups are invited to use the White House (chapter 2).

With the three noted exceptions, therefore, no statute of Congress by itself creates or abolishes any unit of the White House staff, prescribes organizational structure, or delineates the specific duties any staff member is to perform for the president. The new president can be assured that, legally, he or she has practically full flexibility to reshape the structure and organization of the White House staff and to fix the duties of every person serving there.

The Organizational Elements of the White House Staff

While the White House Office started with Franklin Roosevelt, the modern White House really took shape in the administration of Dwight D. Eisenhower. As World War II ended, the whole federal policymaking environment had shifted, creating new demands on White House leadership. The distinction between domestic and foreign affairs was evaporating. While cabinet agencies were still stovepiped into separate departments, the separateness of their areas of policy concern was disappearing. Diplomacy, the use of U.S. armed forces, intelligence, and the conduct of covert action were all integrated within the policy area of "national security"; economics, finance, trade, commerce, and agriculture were inseparable from one another, as were science, space, and the uses of nuclear power. New institutions appeared: the Department of Defense, the

Central Intelligence Agency, the U.S. Information Agency, the National Security Council, the Operations Coordinating Board, the Marshall Plan, the Point Four foreign assistance program, the Agency for International Development.

Eisenhower shaped his White House staff to meet these new institutional demands. He:

—Enhanced the role of the vice president by inviting Nixon to attend cabinet and NSC meetings.

—Created the positions of chief of staff and deputy chief of staff at the White House.

—Created the post of assistant to the president for national security affairs and made its holder the supervisor of the NSC staff.

—Instituted the position of staff secretary at the White House.

—Created the first cabinet secretariat, and used the cabinet regularly for the discussion of domestic policy issues.

—Enlarged the White House congressional affairs office; its head was his deputy chief of staff.

—Created the White House post of special assistant for intergovernmental affairs to enhance direct relationships with state and local governments.

—Instituted the White House position of special assistant for science and technology (which later became the Office of Science and Technology Policy in the Executive Office).

—Brought live television into his press conferences.

—Instituted a system of written reports from cabinet secretaries directly to the president to signal him about policy decisions being made at lower levels or about brewing problems. (Called "Staff Notes," this practice later became the system of weekly cabinet reports.)

—Began the use of helicopters, to and from Camp David, for instance; this facility is now managed by the Marine Corps as the HMX-One squadron (in the White House Military Office).

All of these staff enhancements instituted by Eisenhower have proved their worth to the presidency and have accordingly been continued—and expanded further—by succeeding presidents, creating a kind of baseline continuity in the staff structure of the White House.

But, reflecting their respective policy priorities, every president since Eisenhower has added innovations in the functions and staffing of the White House. President Kennedy gave his vice president a downtown office—at the White House—and, after the Bay of Pigs disaster, instituted a White House Situation Room; President Johnson added a curator to the staff; Gerald Ford began an intern program; President Carter enhanced the policy role of the vice president; Ronald Reagan created a White House Office of Management and Administration; President George H. W. Bush instituted an office of national service and a "thousand points of light" program to encourage volunteer service. President

Clinton assigned heavy policy duties to his spouse, used his vice president for all manner of assignments, foreign and domestic, created a National Economic Council, instituted the office of AIDS Policy Coordinator, and opened up a White House Visitor Center in the Malcolm Baldridge Great Hall of the Department of Commence. Several recent presidents have also greatly enhanced and expanded the communications and outreach operations of the White House.

Most of these additions (described in more detail later in the book) have become continuing elements of the modern White House. But there have been a few subtractions. President Clinton discontinued his predecessor's Points of Light office (it has become a private foundation); President George W. Bush folded President Clinton's "One America" operation and shifted Clinton's National AIDS Policy Coordination function to the Department of State.

It is not presidential whim that has brought each of the White House elements into being, but, rather, each of them has been established to meet what has been considered to be an indispensable need of the modern chief executive. Collectively almost all of them have endured from presidency to presidency for precisely that reason. If offices added last through more than one presidency (especially through a party change, such as Eisenhower's chief of staff and staff secretary, Reagan's Office of Management and Administration), expectations and traditions begin to form. The more often those offices are continued by successive presidents, the more certain it is that they will be reconfirmed as meeting the criterion of need and will become fixed elements in the White House establishment.

Thus, over the past forty-eight years, as the president's needs have expanded, step by step, function by function, White House staff elements have multiplied. The staff's growth, and its continuity, are attributable not to statutes that have accumulated but to the traditions and expectations from the years of continuous operation of the offices already there. An incoming president will find that the statutory environment allows, legally, freedom to make changes in White House structure but that those traditions and expectations are so strong that they will tend to constrict the options for instituting large-scale reshaping.

Innovations Introduced by the George W. Bush Administration

President Bush introduced three kinds of innovations at the White House—in the style of policymaking, in creating new policy offices with new responsibilities, and in impressive new physical improvements.

In Presidential Policymaking

Conditioned by the 9/11 catastrophe, and convinced that al Qaeda is determined to bring more harm to the United States, President Bush has been equally determined to strengthen the power of the presidency vis-à-vis what he considers debilitating limitations imposed by the other two branches. In this cause he has been supported—some might say egged on—by a vice president who, in 1987, had publicly subscribed to the following sentiments:

> Presidents exercised a broad range of foreign policy powers for which they neither sought nor received Congressional sanction through statute. This history speaks volumes about the Constitutional allocation of powers between the branches. It leaves little doubt that the President was expected to have the primary role of conducting the foreign policy of the United States. Congressional actions to limit the President in this area therefore should be reviewed with a considerable degree of skepticism. If they interfere with core presidential foreign policy functions, they should be struck down. Moreover, the lesson of our constitutional history is that doubtful cases should be decided in favor of the President.[13]

The president and vice president were aided in adopting this stance by the unusually broad text of Public Law 107-40, passed a week after the 9/11 disaster. In language the meaning of which has been a matter of controversy ever since, Congress wrote that "the president is authorized to use all necessary and appropriate force against those nations, organizations or persons he determines planned, authorized, committed or aided the terrorist attacks that occurred on September 11, 2001, or harbored such organizations or persons, in order to prevent any future acts of international terrorism against the United States by such nations, organizations or persons."[14]

The president was aided by the circumstance that until January 2007, the House of Representatives was controlled by his own Republican Party, which showed little interest in employing the tools Congress typically uses to counter presidential power: initiating investigations, compelling testimony of executive branch witnesses, and compelling submission of federal documents. Control of the Senate shifted back and forth between the two parties, but the extremely narrow margin between them also limited the degree of opposition interference with presidential dominance.

Within those six years, then, President Bush secretly instructed the National Security Agency to surveil telephone conversations of possible terrorists, going beyond the limitations placed on such surveillance by Congress in the Foreign Intelligence Surveillance Act of 1978. When Congress passed a statute banning "cruel, inhumane or degrading" treatment of prisoners in U.S. detention centers, the president announced that he would construe that provision "in a manner consistent with the constitutional authority of the President to supervise the unitary executive branch and as Commander in Chief."[15] Even after the changeover of power in 2007, Mr. Bush invoked executive privilege and has refused to supply requested documents or to permit his chief of staff or his former White House counsel to testify in response to House Judiciary Committee subpoenas; further he has instructed the attorney general not to prosecute the two aides even after the House had voted to cite them as being in contempt of Congress (as of this writing this issue is in litigation). Chapters 5 and 6 deal more fully with some of these issues of presidential power

Another Bush innovation affecting policy has been the discipline and order-liness both the president and the vice president have imposed on the function-ing and the relationships within and among the various White House staff offices. The handling and management of any given policy issue is in only one pair of hands, and a firm set of steps governs the progress of such issues toward the decision stage. All papers destined for Oval Office action proceed through a tightly disciplined coordination process ordained by the staff secretary and enforced by the chief of staff (see detailed discussion of these processes in chap-ters 3 and 4). The author encountered this discipline when he found out that before any interview with a White House staff member could take place, he had to write out his questions in advance and send them to a designated officer on the staff, who then had the questions reviewed by the counsel to the president. (There was very warm cooperation; only two interviews were denied, one of which was appealed and reversed, and no question was ruled out.)

A third innovation in the policymaking style of the Bush White House was the comprehensive reach of Karl Rove, Bush's chief campaign manager and political strategist. Rove, as a senior adviser to the president, was involved in every aspect of the White House policy process in addition to guiding every detail of any presidential political event (chapter 14). Readers may recall Ron Suskind's January 2003 article about White House policymaking in which he quotes John DiIulio, a former deputy assistant to the president, as saying, "What you've got is everything—and I mean everything—being run by the political arm. It's the reign of the Mayberry Machiavellis." Suskind then quotes Chief of Staff Andrew Card who "sounded an alarm about the unfettered rise of Rove in the wake of senior adviser Karen Hughes' resignation [as counselor to the pres-ident for communications]. 'I'll need designees [said Card], people trusted by the president that I can elevate for various needs to balance against Karl. . . . They are going to have to really step up, but it won't be easy. Karl is a formida-ble adversary.'"[16]

Organizational Innovations

President Bush has made important innovations in the organizational struc-ture of the White House to reflect his policy priorities. Only eight days after his inauguration, he established a program "to expand opportunities for faith-based and other community organizations to strengthen their capacity to better meet social needs in America's communities." He issued an executive order creating, in each of six cabinet departments (later expanded to six others), an Executive Center for Faith-Based and Community Initiatives.[17] In a separate executive order, he created a new White House Office for Faith-Based and Community Initiatives to "have lead responsibility in the executive branch to establish policies, priorities, and objectives for the Federal Government's comprehensive effort to enlist, equip, enable, empower, and expand the work of faith-based and other community organizations to the extent permitted by law," that is, to manage and supervise the whole interdepartmental undertaking (chapter 11).[18]

In his State of the Union Message in January 2002, President Bush called upon every American to commit 4,000 hours over his or her lifetime to volunteer some kind of service to the nation. "I invite you to join the USA Freedom Corps," he proclaimed.[19] On the same day, he signed an executive order creating the USA Freedom Corps as "an interagency initiative, bringing together executive branch departments, agencies, and offices with public service programs and components" and establishing the USA Freedom Corps Office in the White House to be the center point of this new initiative (chapter 12).[20]

The most significant structural change in the Bush White House has been the creation of the Homeland Security Council. Less than a month after the 9/11 catastrophe, on October 8, 2001, the president signed Executive Order 13228 creating a dramatically new position on the White House staff—assistant to the president for homeland security—and establishing a Homeland Security Council. Former Pennsylvania governor Tom Ridge and a staff of some 130 persons were the first incumbents. Legislation giving the Homeland Security Council statutory status took effect in January 2003. That legislation also created a cabinet-level Department of Homeland Security, leading some to ask whether a White House office was still necessary. Yes, said the president in a message to Congress on June 18, 2002. The head of the office was given the title of assistant to the president for homeland security and counterterrorism; its current staff is 48 (chapter 10).

Innovations in Physical Structures

Finally, when the subject here is innovation, the Bush administration has pioneered in instituting improvements in the physical structures of the White House that will dramatically enhance the effectiveness of the presidency. These investments will long outlast Mr. Bush's own presidency; the public can join future presidents in acknowledging—in celebrating—the value of this foresight. Chapter 36 describes them in detail. Leading the list is the transformation of the White House Situation Room together with the employment of the latest SVTCS (secure, video-teleconferencing) communications system. The president and his national security team can now meet, exchange maps, photos and papers, and converse, face to face, with an increasing number of other chiefs of state, with his military commanders, and with many of his ambassadors abroad—all in cryptologic security. SVTCS has forever changed the conduct of U.S. national security relationships; the preeminence of the president's personal participation is now routine, as is the increase in the reliance on White House–NSC staff work to support this personal presidential participation.

Paralleling this forward step in effectiveness is a new environment of beautification (as well as efficiency): the remodeling of the Eisenhower Executive Office Building. Not only are its floors, rooms, and corridors being restructured to accommodate long-needed air-conditioning, electrical, and communications equipment, but the thick, dingy layers of paint on the walls and ceilings of many of its grand salons are being peeled back to reveal magnificent nineteenth century murals and frescoes. Conservationists will be both delighted and proud to see such architectural treasures being brought back to life.

White House press facilities have been revamped: the unsightly "Pebble Beach" North Lawn press equipment area has been upgraded to a paved, National-Park-Service-quality "Stonehenge." The Brady Press Briefing Room has been thoroughly refurbished to accommodate the latest facilities and equipment and modernized to permit displays of photos or video. Permanent, in-the-wall, fiber-optic wiring has been installed in both the Residence and the West Wing, facilitating the easy use of high-definition television for presidential appearances.

The White House helicopter fleet is being massively expanded, although escalating costs have necessitated putting this initiative on hold until requirements and resources can be brought into balance. Ideas are being gathered about a new *Air Force One* (the current pair of planes are more than two decades old). A new helicopter hangar will be constructed at Camp David; a new East Visitor Entrance Building is being built. The President's Park, especially the Ellipse, has been extensively reconditioned, and the Executive Residence itself has benefited tremendously from contributions from the independent White House Historical Association for the refurbishment of the Library, the Green Room, and the Lincoln Bedroom.

How Many Men and Women Work at the Whole White House?

As adumbrated in the introduction, the contemporary White House staff can be divided into three components: policy offices, policy support offices, and professional and technical operating units. There are seventy-four separately identifiable policy offices (headed by assistants to the president, deputy assistants to the president, some special assistants, a few senior directors, and some others) that have leading policy responsibilities for the president, the vice president, or the president's spouse. As of this writing, some 459 men and women can be included in this category. (Those with the title of assistant, deputy assistant, or special assistant have formal commissions, signed by the secretary of state and the president; they are known as commissioned officers; this group numbers approximately 154.)

Twenty-one policy support offices work with or under the top seventy-four (for example, the executive secretaries of the National and Homeland Security Councils, the presidential aide, the White House social secretary); 213 men and women work in those twenty-one support offices.

By far the largest contingent of workers at the *whole White House* are in the forty professional and technical operating units, which perform their quintessential duties in complete anonymity, absolutely unknown to the public. Examples: the presidential protective units of the U.S. Secret Service, the White House Military Office (which includes *Air Force One,* the helicopter squadron, the White House Communications Agency, and Camp David), the telephone operators, the service delivery team of the General Services Administration, the chief usher and Executive Residence staff, the National Park Service White House Liaison Office and its Visitor Center, and the pool of volunteers. There are some 5,902 men and women in these forty units. While their connection to the White House is ultimately at the president's discretion, they are all nonpolitical employees, and in the words of one are "expected to serve" across administrations. Over the period of one year, there is also a corps of some 300 interns, 100 at a time; many of them do have political connections to the administration in office. Finally there is a pool of 425 volunteers, each serving a few days a week; the White House could not operate without them.

The total number of men and women typically serving in the modern White House is, thus, 6,574. Of course there are constant comings and goings, so that figure is, at any one time, an approximation. A complete listing of all of the offices in the three categories, and the number of staff in each, appears in the appendix at the end of the book.

2 | *The Cost of the Whole White House*

Introductory note: This chapter was originally entitled "The Budget of the Whole White House." Can't do that. There is no such thing. It doesn't exist. There is no sheet or document or brochure, produced by any executive or legislative author, that lays out all of the expenses of the complete White House. That will only be found here—and readers should prepare themselves for some surprises.

What are the annual dollar costs, for a typical year, of operating the modern presidency—of running the White House, the whole White House? One of the reasons that question has never been answered (and perhaps never even asked) is because the pathway to the answer is so complicated. One may start with the tab "White House Office" in the annual congressional budget submission of the Executive Office of the President, but that is only an initial fraction. In addition, twenty-two other budget accounts, thirteen of them in other departments, or parts of departments, pay the expenses, and the salaries, of men and women who are in fact members of the White House staff family. Not only are those costs scattered through those twenty-two other budgets, but in at least nine of them the dollars are not in any fashion identified as *White House.* Realistic estimates have to be made. Some of those thirteen agencies (such as the Postal Service and the National Archives) provide services directly to the White House. Sixty people in the vice president's office and one hundred seventy-eight people on the National Security Council staff work in those offices beyond the numbers publicly counted. What is the dollar value of all those services? Executive Order 12028, signed by President Carter on December 12, 1977, actually mandates that the Office of Administration (OA) "shall, upon request, assist the White House Office by performing its role of providing those administrative services which are primarily in direct support of the President." How much of the $91,745,000 appropriated to the OA in fiscal year 2008 is contributed to the White House pursuant to that provision? One former OA director told the author it would be fifty percent; a more recent director estimated one-eighth. The White House chief of management and administration says it is "difficult to quantify." The author agrees that it *is* difficult, but for the purpose of this book, uses the one-eighth estimate, which may be much too low. In addition, several of the costs and salary contributions are security-classified, with no estimates offered. The total given in this chapter, accordingly, is tens of millions too small.

Definitions

Definitions are crucial. What is meant by "the whole White House"? In this chapter, the twenty-three separate accounts that make up the costs of the "White House" are: (1) the compensation of the president, (2) the Executive Residence, (3) repair and restoration of the Residence, (4) the Office of the Vice President, (5) the residence of the vice president, (6) the White House Office, (7) the Office of Policy Development, that is, the domestic and national economic policy councils, (8) the National Security Council, (9) one-eighth of the Office of Administration, (10) the "unanticipated needs" account in the Executive Office of the President, (11) the General Services Administration White House Center Service Delivery Team, (12) the White House branch of the U.S. Postal Service, or are found in (13) the National Archives and Records Administration, (14) the Department of State, (15) the Defense Information Systems Agency (DISA) of the Department of Defense, (16) the U.S. Air Force of the Department of Defense, (17) the U.S. Marine Corps of the Department of Defense, (18) the Navy Seabees corps of the Department of Defense, (19) the presidential protective units of the U.S. Secret Service (in the Department of Homeland Security), (20) the Office of Personnel Management (which funds the President's Commission on White House Fellowships, (21) the National Park Service White House Liaison Office, (22) the White House Visitor Center (in the National Park Service). In addition (23) are the costs, scattered in various departments, of the detailees from those departments; a portion of these costs are borne by the White House.

White House in this book does *not* include the other major units of the Executive Office of the President, namely, the Office of Management and Budget, the Council of Economic Advisers, the Office of National Drug Control Policy, the Office of Science and Technology Policy, the U.S. Trade Representative, the Council on Environmental Quality, and the other seven-eighths of the Office of Administration.

The Development of the White House Expenditures

The fact that the sources of regular annual funding for the above-defined White House elements are so many—and are buried in such an array of different appropriations accounts (some of which are classified)—puts a considerable burden on the presidential scholar trying to illuminate the total, real cost of the modern White House.

The first surprise: it is not the White House staff but the Office of Administration that does the detailed preparatory work on planning the expenditures for the White House functions one through ten. (OA also provides that service for the rest of the Executive Office of the President.) The White House deputy chief of staff for operations and the chief of staff set initial targets, and the various White House staff offices involved then bring their annual budget pleas to the chief financial officer of the OA, who presents them to the OA director and finally to the deputy assistant to the president for management and administration. If any controversies arise in this process, she will get them settled with the help of the deputy chief of staff for operations and if necessary with the White House chief of staff. At the end of the process, each January, the chief of staff provides feedback on the individual sections of the Executive Office budget for the White House Office (functions one through ten, as well as the overall figure for those ten accounts) to the OA's chief financial officer. It is this office that compiles and transmits an annual combined budget presentation entitled "Executive Office of the President—Congressional Budget Submission," and it is this document that includes the budget proposals for the White House Office and those other nine accounts as well as the requests of the other Executive Office units. The table on the next page portrays the dollars appropriated for the ten accounts during the first seven years of the Bush administration. It is these ten accounts that constitute the most familiar schema of *the White House*. The principal increases have occurred in the Homeland Security Council.

The various individual departments and agencies handling accounts eleven through twenty-two go through their own internal budget-development processes and, with some consultation with the White House and with the Office of Administration, they build in agreed amounts for those functions. The commander of Camp David, for instance, inserts his dollar request into the Seabees subsection of the appropriation for the United States Navy; the U.S. Secret Service requirements are included in the budget request of the Department of Homeland Security.

The Congressional Appropriations Process

The heads of each of those requesting departments, usually accompanied by the responsible assistant secretaries, appear before their respective appropriations subcommittees. The White House (and the Executive Office of the President) budget proposal is submitted to the House and Senate Appropriations Subcommittees on Financial Services and General Government. Consistent with tradition, no one on the White House staff testifies before the committees; it is the

The Budget of Part of the White House

As enacted by Congress with applicable rescissions (except for fiscal year 2007, which is the amount requested by the president in January 2006)

Thousands of dollars

	Fiscal year						
Office	2001	2002	2003	2004	2005	2006	2007
President	390	450	450	450	450	450	450
White House Office	53,171	54,611	50,385	68,760	61,504[a]	53,292[b]	51,952
Executive Residence	10,876	11,686	12,149	12,147	12,658	12,312	12,041
Residence repair	968	8,618	1,192	4,200	1,885	1,683	1,600
Vice president	3,665	3,922	4,040	4,435	4,534	4,419	4,352
VP residence	353	318	322	329	330	322	317
Office of Policy Development	4,023	4,139	3,230	4,085	2,282	3,465	3,385
National Security Council	7,149	7,488	7,770	10,489	12,160[c]	8,618	8,405
1/8 of Office of Administration[d]	5,455	5,866	11,364	10,292[e]	11,441	11,054	12,802
Unanticipated needs	3,492	1,000	994	994	992	990	11,789[f]
Subtotal	89,540	98,098	91,896	116,461	108,236	96,596	107,093
Homeland Security Council[g]	0	26,000	19,272	(7,231)	(2,475)	( )	( )
Total[h]	89,540	123,098	111,168	116,461	108,236	96,596	107,093

Source: Prepared by the author from the series of the annual Office of Administration's *Executive Office of the President Congressional Budget Submissions,* and with the assistance of officers in OA.

a. From fiscal year 2004 for the White House Office, this figure represents $1,394,000 in personnel costs, and $1,744,000 in other expenses, but these increases were offset by some $8,411,000 in rental costs (for those White House units located in the Eisenhower Executive Office Building) and by other related charges that have been moved out of the White House Office budget into Office of Administration accounts.

b. In this account, $9,000,000 has been transferred to the Department of Defense (the Defense Information Systems Agency) for reimbursement for the White House Communications Agency for its providing the White House with nontelecommunications support (such as audiovisual services).

c. Includes a $3.3 million allocation from the fiscal year 2001 Emergency Supplemental Appropriations Act for Recovery from and Response to Terrorist Attacks on the United States (Public Law 107-38) for improvements to the White House Situation Room.

d. According to the Office of Administration, one-eighth of its staff and funds directly serve the president—akin to the White House Office—pursuant to Section 3(a) of Executive Order 12028 of December 12, 1977.

e. Some of OA's total fiscal year 2004 budget has subsequently been transferred out to the Office of Management and Budget accounts. The fiscal year 2005 OA request included $11,337,000 in incoming transfers, including the $8,411,000 referred to in note a.

f. In fiscal year 2005 Congress added to the president's Unanticipated Needs account $70,000,000 in supplemental funds specifically to be made available to the American Red Cross for "reimbursement of disaster relief associated with Hurricanes Charley, Frances, Ivan and Jeanne." At that time, this specific supplemental was not counted as part of the Executive Office of the President appropriation. There remains $10,789,000 unexpended from that supplemental. For fiscal year 2007 the Executive Office requests that this remainder be added to the regular Unanticipated Needs account of $1,000,000 that is "provided for the President to meet unanticipated needs in furtherance of national interest, security or defense."

g. Beginning with fiscal year 2004, funds for the White House Homeland Security Council have been included in the appropriation for the White House Office.

h. The components in this table, and totaled on this line, are all those elements that fit the author's definition of White House staff.

OA director who bears the responsibility for testifying in support of the combined Executive Office of the President submission. The OA director, the OA chief financial officer, and the director of the Office of Management and Budget are normally the only witnesses who actually testify in person, with the OMB director defending the budget request for OMB itself. (Occasionally the subcommittee will ask to hear from the heads of the trade, drug, and sciences offices of the Executive Office. The Secret Service testifies before the Homeland Security Appropriations Subcommittee; the director himself is the principal witness.)

Any public hearing the House subcommittee might hold on the White House requests is generally a routine affair. Few members attend because so many other committees compete for the members' time; almost no one from the public shows up. Collectively the subcommittee members may unload 150–160 questions—"administrivia" one observer termed them—that the OA director tries to answer on the spot or promises inserts for the record. In February 1992 the House Post Office and Civil Service Committee, led by Democratic Representative Paul Kanjorski, undertook an election-year vendetta against the White House then occupied by George H. W. Bush. Question after question was flung at the weary testifiers (a sample: How many floral arrangements, invitations, banners, streamers, balloons, and other decorative items were used for each event at the White House or at the residence of the vice president during 1991?) Thousands of pages were generated in response.

In recent years, a member of the subcommittee or its chief clerk may have been invited for lunch in the White House Mess; the chief usher was several times invited up to Capitol Hill to meet with members or staff informally concerning White House entertainment expenses. Appropriations staff members have come down to see the revamped Situation Room, "so they knew what the money was for," explained Deputy Chief of Staff Joseph Hagin. Another surprise: during 2005, 2006, 2007, and 2008 however, neither the House nor Senate subcommittee even scheduled testimony by the OA officials about any of the White House accounts; whatever negotiations occurred about budget figures in accounts one through eleven are handled by members and staff informally. At one point during Bush's first term, Chief of Staff Andy Card had to get on the telephone with appropriations committee staff members; they were trying to fatten the White House budget beyond the president's and Card's priorities.

Beginning with the fiscal year 2004 budget presentation, the president has, every year, asked Congress to create a consolidated appropriation account, to be called "the White House," which would be made up of elements numbered here as 1, 2, 3, 6, 7, 8, and 9, plus all of the Office of Administration plus the Council of Economic Advisers. The appropriations subcommittees have not been persuaded by this recommendation and each year have rejected it. "They don't want to weaken any oversight," commented one Appropriations staffer.[1] In the same fiscal year 2004 request, the president also asked for authority to transfer up to

10 percent of any one of the appropriations for the nine accounts and the Executive Office accounts to any of the others, providing that the transfer would not increase the receiving account by more than 50 percent and providing that he give fifteen days advance notice to both appropriations committees. Congress gave him only partial authority to shift funds among some elements but is not at all enthusiastic about conferring anything more than minimum spending flexibility to the chief executive.

In 1998 the appropriations committees became annoyed at the lateness of payments of reimbursements due the White House from political or other recognized groups that are invited to sponsor events in the Executive Residence. A requirement was written into the appropriations statute, and remains there today, that a group sponsoring a political event must pay for the estimated cost of that event in advance, must be notified about any costs beyond the estimate within sixty days of the event, must pay these charges within thirty days of the notification, and must be charged interest and penalties if the reimbursement has not been made within that deadline. The national committee of the president's political party, furthermore, must maintain a separate deposit of $25,000 to cover costs of events it sponsors in the Residence.

Floor debate on the White House budget "doesn't seem to attract much of any attention," one insider observed.

The Total Costs of the Whole White House

As already mentioned, there is no one document, except this book, that describes, or even lists, all of these twenty-three accounts together—the total expenses of the modern White House in its entirety. There is no such single, overall budget presentation made either to the Office of Management and Budget or to Congress. The several departments that contribute to the White House total keep in informal consultation with the White House deputy chief of staff for operations.

The author recognizes that some readers may take exception to the definitions used in this chapter, and in this book. Are Secret Service protective costs White House costs? From his fourteen years of service in the White House, the author is very much aware of how intense the bond of connectedness is between staffers at the White House and the uniformed and civilian-dressed men and women of the United States Secret Service. They are everywhere in the White House, warmly appreciated, and deeply respected for their professionalism and dedication. The White House staff's very lives are in their hands. Is Camp David, are the presidential helicopters, parts of the White House? Inseparable, indispensable.

A perfectionist could argue that the definitions are not broad enough. The author has omitted the costs, for example, that the Federal Bureau of Investigation contributes to the presidency by eating the expenses of its security investigations of White House employees, or that the District of Columbia contributes when D.C. fire engines are stationed on the Ellipse when the presidential helicopter lands or takes off. These definitions used in this chapter, and their consequential costs, are stated specifically and are not glossed over or hidden as may be the case with some who would claim to describe the modern presidency.

To many readers, these cost figures may seem surprisingly large. But readers should need no reminding that this is the office of the chief executive of a $3 trillion government—a government currently at war, with its security forces on duty, under the chief executive's command, in virtually every corner of the planet. The figures may seem large because this is the first time that they have been collected together in one document. They can be made to appear smaller by not talking about them, a deception in which this author will not engage.

Total Cost of the Whole White House for Fiscal Year 2008

1. Compensation of the president (including an expense
    allowance of $50,000)[2] $ 450,000
2. The Executive Residence operating expenses   12,814,000
3. The Executive Residence—repair and restoration   1,600,000
4. The vice president's downtown office   15,511,960[3]
5. Residence of the vice president—operating expenses   320,000
6. The White House Office (including the Homeland Security
    Council)   53,656,000
7. Office of Policy Development (the Domestic Policy Council
    and the National Economic Council)   3,482,000
8. National Security Council   30,300,820[4]
9. One-eighth of the Office of Administration, for direct
    services to the president pursuant to Section 3(a) of
    Executive Order 12028   11,468,125
10. The president's unanticipated needs   1,000,000
11. White House Center Service Delivery Team
    (in the GSA budget)   26,000,000
12. U.S. Postal Service, White House branch   726,000
13. National Archives professional archival support
    of the White House   1,000,000
14. Value of gifts supplied by the Department of State for
    presentation to foreign leaders at White House official
    entertainment functions   50,000
15. White House Communications Agency (in the budget of
    the Defense Information Systems Agency)   173,900,000
16. *Air Force One* (in U.S. Air Force budget)   (classified)

17. Helicopter squadron *HMX-One* (in the Marine Corps budget; this is the fiscal year 2008 appropriation segment of a fifteen-year-long procurement of twenty-eight new helicopters; but see the text on page 378)   271,000,000
18. Camp David (in the Navy/Seabees budget)   7,900,000[5]
19. Salary costs for 2,300 employees in above units 15, 16, 17, and 18 (all in the budget of the Department of Defense)[6]   151,800,000
20. U.S. Secret Service (in the budget of the Department of Homeland Security)[7]

Protection of persons and facilities	689,535,000
For protective intelligence activities	57,704,000
For handling "special security events," such as the 2009 Inaugural	1,000,000
For screening of White House mail	16,201,000
Operations of the James J. Rowley Training Center	51,954,000
Improvements at the James J. Rowley Training Center	3,725,000

21. Commission on White House Fellowships (in the budget of the Office of Personnel Management)   850,000
22. National Park Service White House Liaison Office, including the White House Visitor Center (in the budget of the National Park Service)   8,700,000
23. Cost of detailees who work more than six months in a calendar year   227,349

Total Cost of All White House Elements, for fiscal year 2008: $1,592,875,254

In reviewing that fiscal year 2008 total, readers should keep three considerations in mind.

First, the total given here does not include classified outlays. These are likely to be substantial, but they cannot be published or even estimated. The total stated here is therefore smaller than the actual total. Nor does this total include the value of gifts to the White House, especially those from the independent White House Historical Association for renovation and restoration of the public rooms (chapter 35). These of course are donated, not appropriated, funds. The total of acquisitions and renovation work for the public rooms of the White House, supported by the White House Historical Association since 2001, is $7,509,449. Finally, the author is not in a position to say that this fiscal year 2008 total is typical of each of the eight annual budgets (fiscal years 2002–09) for which the Bush administration is responsible, or that the total for the entire Bush administration is $1,592,875,254 multiplied by eight—to yield an overall total of $12.7 billion. Security outlays (Defense and Secret Service) have escalated markedly since 9/11.

Controls over Outlays

There is no person at the White House with the title of inspector general; the president depends on the deputy chief of staff for operations to see to it that the appropriated and donated funds are spent carefully; any improprieties would bring on political as well as financial damage. Most of the White House outlays listed above (for example, those of the White House Military Office and the Secret Service) are actually disbursed by the responsible departments such as Defense, Homeland Security, Interior, and the General Services Administration, where there *are* inspectors general to monitor spending.

Akin to the tradition that the president does not challenge the expenditures that Congress budgets to meet its own institutional expenses, there is a degree of comity on the part of Congress concerning the White House budget. But only a degree. In 1992, as illustrated earlier, the House subcommittee gave the president a hard time, and in 1998 the General Accounting Office went to some lengths to investigate the cost of international presidential travel.

Almost all of the billions of dollars identified here are public funds, raised by taxes. Students, scholars, and taxpayers all deserve to see where they have been invested.

The Top Crosscutting Leadership

3 | Javelin Catcher: The Chief of Staff

I started out in effect not having a chief of staff and it didn't work. So, anybody who doesn't have one and tries to run the responsibilities of the White House, I think, is putting too big a burden on the president himself. You need a filter, a person that you have total confidence in who works so closely with you that in effect he is almost an alter ego. I just can't imagine a president not having an effective chief of staff.

—Gerald R. Ford

Andy worked to make sure the policy processes ran their full course and that staffers felt included in them. He managed the president's most valued commodity—his time—in part by making sure that people saw the president only when they really needed to. Most notably, Andy managed and oversaw the White House exactly the way Bush preferred—firmly, with discipline, focus and thoughtful, deliberate planning.

—Scott McClellan

I do regard myself as having responsibility for the activities of everybody on the staff, but I don't view myself—as I think some chiefs of staff have been described—as a sort of prime minister or deputy president.

—Joshua Bolten

In 1986 presidential scholar Richard Neustadt admitted he was wrong.

I've been waiting for an opportunity to make a confession to [former Carter chief of staff] Jack Watson. For years I have tried to hold open the possibility that presidents could have White House staffs small enough so they never had to designate anybody as the administrative coordinator of the staff itself. In that respect, I think I gave Jack worse advice than Dick Cheney did. He and Rumsfeld had experienced the effort to reduce the White House staff . . . to a size . . . comparable, say, to Kennedy's time or Truman's time, and they had not succeeded. . . . I think they probably got it down to the smallest size possible, but *even at that minimum you do need some administrative coordinator.*[1]

The Necessity for Coordination

Why is coordination needed in the White House? Because the presidency—the modern White House—is a multfaceted environment of issues, people, and actions, but it is also, and always has been, a strictly singular entity: one person doing the only speaking and acting that counts. Assume that the president is going to travel to Moscow to try to persuade the Russian president to collaborate on a missile defense arrangement. The spouse plans to accompany the president. Military options and background must be elicited from Defense; diplomatic repercussions evaluated by State, assessments on Russian capabilities will come from the intelligence community; the White House national security council staff will assemble that material. When in Moscow, how many meetings will there be? What will be on the bilateral agenda? Where will the president stay? Who will be invited for dinners at the American embassy? A White House advance team will go to Moscow a month ahead of time, and the White House scheduling office will fill in dates. Because the president will speak to some large gatherings, the White House speechwriter will start some speech outlines. The world press will cover the meeting; the White House press office will work to guarantee effective arrangements. An agreement with the Russians may mean that some statutes will need to be amended, or some additional appropriations enacted; the White House legislative affairs office will prepare approaches to Congress, and the White House communications staff will set up interviews with talk-show hosts upon his return. Security will be a consideration; the Secret Service will be on the advance team and dozens of agents will accompany the delegation. What will the president's spouse want to do, visit with which groups, do which sightseeing? The spouse's staff will be in on every planning meeting. *Air Force One* will be readied; secure communications set up, helicopters needed; the White House Military Office handles these requirements.

Each of these specialized elements in the modern White House is headed by men and women possessed with inordinately strong competence, energy, jurisdictional pride, and ego. They must, however, subordinate their pride and ego to come up with an inordinately singular product: one person well prepared to carry out an action successfully. None of the elements of the White House, including the vice president, the spouse, or the National Security Council, can be allowed to work independently of the rest of the institution. The coordination and collaboration that are needed are as highly indispensable as they are highly improbable without a disciplined order preached, and, if necessary, imposed, from the top. Ideas must be exchanged, papers—even very secret ones—must be exchanged, plans must be exchanged; to draw upon all that competence means crossing all those jurisdictions.

The one at the top of the White House staff who does the preaching—and the imposing—is the chief of staff.

The White House staff for the Bush administration can be divided into five top, cross-cutting leadership officers who have an especially direct relationship to the chief of staff (the counsel, the national security adviser, the director of the legislative office, the staff secretary, and the director of the presidential personnel office) and four principal blocs of staff specializations (policy, headed by the deputy chief of staff for policy; operations, headed by the deputy chief of staff for operations; external affairs, headed by an assistant to the president; and communications, headed by a counselor to the president (see figure on page 12). The chief of staff's own responsibility is continuously to shape and mold the functioning of this nine-element corpus to fit the president's own priorities and style of work, preserving the necessary flexibility to handle problems that may have unusual dimensions. Together with the two deputy chiefs of staff, the chief of staff is the focal point for ensuring the necessary coordination on all matters needing presidential action.

The Chief of Staff's Elemental Responsibilities

Andrew Card, former chief of staff to George W. Bush, laid out three basic categories of functions that every White House staff must perform for the chief executive: manage the policy process, manage the "care and feeding" of the president, and manage the "marketing" of presidential initiatives. The policy process centers on the functioning of the four policy councils—domestic, national economic, national security, and homeland security—and on how they elevate their respective but interlinked issues for presidential decision. "Care and feeding" means organizing the president's day, supporting his movements from place to place, from city to city, from nation to nation, and making sure that the equipment and resources of the modern White House are all operating with error-free effectiveness. "Marketing" means explaining and defending the president's policy initiatives to the nation and to the world.

Overseeing the Policy Process

Each president has unique preferences for making policy decisions. For example, Dwight Eisenhower's style was consultative: the National Security Council met just about every Thursday morning; the cabinet met just about every Friday morning. Both forums had agendas and discussion papers circulated in advance, records of action circulated afterward. The discussions were lively; differences were aired, sometimes heatedly. Richard Nixon's style was solitary contemplation; he did not like meetings where divergent views were debated out loud in front of him by strong personalities. His thoughtful but controversial message to Congress on school desegregation, for example, was never circulated to the cabinet; the draft of the message and dissenting staff memos went to him in his hideaway office.

"The bureaucracy of the White House should reflect the needs and personality of the occupant of the Oval Office," Card emphasized. "It should not be cast in concrete and should not be specified by any congressional stipulation. The structure of the White House should be informed by the past, but it doesn't necessarily have to copy it. The organizational chart should reflect the needs the president has rather than the bureaucracy that he's inherited."[2]

The policy process group in the Bush organization is made up of four councils, each headed and managed by an assistant to the president supported by a deputy assistant and a White House staff unit of policy heavyweights. The four are the National Security Council (which is statutory), headed by the assistant to the president for national security affairs, commonly referred to as the national security adviser, the Homeland Security Council (also statutory), headed by the assistant to the president for homeland security affairs and counterterrorism, or homeland security adviser; the Domestic Policy Council, headed by the assistant to the president for domestic policy; and the National Economic Council, headed by the assistant to the president for economic policy. The director of the Office of Management and Budget (OMB) is de facto a fifth policy adviser, "considered as part of the White House senior staff," said Chief of Staff Joshua Bolten.[3] The Bush administration's White House rule is that each important policy issue is to have a home, and only one home, which is located in one of these five offices. Policy questions from the cabinet departments or agencies, or from the other statutory elements of the Executive Office of the President (the Office of National Drug Control Policy, the Office of the U.S. Trade Representative, the Office of Science and Technology Policy, the Council on Environmental Quality, and the Council of Economic Advisers), needing presidential decision are to come to the president only through one of these five officers.

As described in chapter 9, the chief of staff looks to his deputy chief of staff for policy to track the work of these five policy offices. "It's part of the deputy chief's job to make sure that all the right voices are being heard and that the issues are being clarified for the president," Bolten explained. "Neither the deputy chief of staff for policy nor myself was the expert in any particular policy—we were just making sure all the policy processes were done in the way they should be, and I would step in only if I thought those offices weren't performing their function as well as they could."

As Card put it: "During the day, it was meeting, meeting, meeting, meeting, settling disputes, putting sand in somebody's underwear; that was the job."

When a complicated or controversial issue comes through the policy machinery and is headed for presidential attention, the chief of staff and his policy deputy have a sensitive judgment call to make: Is it ready for the Oval Office? Are there subsidiary issues that can be settled short of the president? Vetting sessions take place around the chief of staff's table. From a perspective halfway through Bush's second term, Bolten commented:

I think this late in the administration, we have a pretty good idea of where the president stands on most issues. There were harder calls early on. They're much easier now that we have a sense of where the president is likely to come out. I often have a comfort level in saying, "I'm confident that the president would agree with that; I'll mention it to him that this is what we're doing; does anyone want to take it up to the president?"

That "comfort level" is not automatic; it is the outgrowth from months of building trust—trust on the part of the staff and among the cabinet that the chief of staff is not using his status, proximity, or ego to tip the scales of the argument and foist lopsided advice on the president. While the chief of staff may be the moderator of the debate, he is not a neuter; he is likely to have strong, independent views that the president must hear. But above all he must be an honest broker, ensuring that the whole range of arguments is presented to the chief executive. "I try not to vent my independent judgment outside the privacy of the Oval Office," said Bolten.

Bush's style is consultative but informal; "policy times" are scheduled when cabinet and senior staff members gather to discuss an issue. "While he reads whatever you give him, he rarely likes to make a decision of any significance without having had his people in front of him," Bolten commented. "We don't say, 'Here's where everybody stands; check a box.'" These meetings are held not in the stately Cabinet Room but in the Oval Office. (If the group is larger, the policy-time session moves to the Roosevelt Room.) "If there are more people than we can fit in the Roosevelt Room," Bolten added, "we shouldn't be having the meeting."

"Everybody's there together," Bolten explains, "everybody gets to talk. The president doesn't hesitate to elicit insights from somebody at a very junior level; he's glad to hear from a deputy assistant secretary as well as from the secretary." Formal paperwork is minimized. On some occasions the president's decisions are made in private and communicated to the responsible senior staff persons only confidentially. Said former chief of staff Card:

> There were some times when the president would "make a decision" during policy time, but usually [the session] was to educate the president, to let him hear the arguments about it, and then, after the meeting, he would say, "I heard the argument; this is what I am going to do." Or he would say he wanted more information. I would try to discourage the president from making a decision in a large audience.

Card added: "The president never has the luxury of making an honest, easy decision. In fact, if the president's making easy decisions, the chief of staff hasn't done his job."

In Bolten's words:

The president is a good reader but his real strength is in personal interaction, being able to bore in on what the key issue is, and forcing people to think about the implications of their own recommendations. He's also a strong decisionmaker; he tries to stay at the presidential level. He will decide the higher-order issues, and then he'll say, "You all work out the rest." And he's good at distinguishing the presidential from the nonpresidential.

"It's my job," Bolten added, "not to try to paper over controversies. I think when this White House has made mistakes, it's often been because we've failed to present clarified disagreements to the president for his choice. He's a good decisionmaker and we tend to mess up when we don't let him decide."

Meetings of the National Security Council are somewhat more formal than the policy-time sessions in the Oval Office; the paperwork is more systematic and the sessions are often held in the Situation Room, which has the capability to provide secure video teleconferencing.

One of the changes Card made involved the cabinet affairs unit, which had been used as a policy shop during the first Bush and Clinton administrations. Seeing it as being in competition with the regular policy offices of the staff, Card in 2005 turned it into the Cabinet Liaison Office with space for cabinet officers to use in the White House and to convene meetings with each other (chapter 13).

An instrument of policy coordination used by almost all chiefs of staff in recent history is the senior staff meeting, convened in the Roosevelt Room every weekday at 7:30 a.m. It is attended by the chiefs of staff to the president, to the vice president, and to the president's spouse; those at the assistant to the president level; the heads of the Office of Management and Budget, the Council of Economic Advisers, the Council on Environmental Quality; the science adviser; the deputy national security adviser; and the deputy assistant for appointments and scheduling. It is normally an information session rather than decisionmaking meeting: What are the president's plans for that day? What highly significant things are going on in Congress, in the press, and in each of the policy councils. The resulting exchange helps undergird that fundamental rule of policymaking: every major issue has a home—and just *one* home.

Care and Feeding of the President: The Administrative White House

"'Care and feeding' is a set of important responsibilities that most people don't pay attention to," commented Andy Card,

> but for the president it is still twenty-four hours in a day and you still have to pay attention to the clock and the president has to have time to eat, sleep, and be merry in addition to doing everything else. I spent a lot of time paying attention to the care and feeding of the president, making sure that his soul, body, and mind are in such a way that he can make very tough decisions when you can't predict when they will come or what they

will be. Very few people pay attention to this area of responsibility because they think what *they* are doing is most important, not what the *president* is doing.

In terms of numbers, by far the largest percentage of the White House staff family is employed in running the operational elements of the modern White House. Some 40 of its 135 offices (such as the White House Military Office, which includes the Crawford ranch and Camp David, and the protective units of the Secret Service) and 5,800 of its 6,500 staff have operational rather than policy duties. Most of the men and women who render these care and feeding services are employees of other departments (such as Defense, Interior, and Homeland Security) who are assigned to the White House staff; their vital work is done behind the scenes and out of public view. In the Bush administration, the chief of staff has a deputy chief of staff for operations to oversee and manage these indispensable and omnipresent resources. Some of them are close to the chief's own person. "I had a secure room in my house," Card mentioned. "The White House Communications Agency [WHCA] would come and certify it and the secure phone that I used. I had secure video, a safe, and all . . . kind[s] of equipment. Whenever I traveled there would be a WHCA team—the same thing with Condi Rice and Steve Hadley [then the national security adviser and deputy national security adviser]; the team would make sure that we had secure communications, including video, almost anywhere in the world."

The Marketing Function

Several White House offices are grouped into this area of activity: the communications, press, and speechwriting units support the third senior assistant, the counselor; those offices are discussed in separate chapters in this book, as are the political, public liaison, intergovernmental affairs, and strategic initiatives offices formerly supervised by Karl Rove.

Organizing before the Beginning

Despite the forty-one-day lag in officially determining the results of the 2000 presidential election, the Bush administration set up the White House, entered office, and began its legislative program remarkably smoothly. This was in part due to the group of exceptionally experienced cabinet and White House officials who led the president's team: Vice President Dick Cheney, Secretaries Colin Powell and Donald Rumsfeld, and White House aides Card, Rice, Deputy Chief of Staff Bolten, Bush legislative affairs director Nick Calio, and others. But, Bolten said,

> It wasn't just the experience—the resumes of those individuals. I think it
> was also the fact that the team that participated in the president's campaign

was in many respects transplanted into comparable government roles. . . . The president very clearly said to me when I first arrived in March of 1999 as policy director at his campaign—almost two years before the election: "I want to campaign the way I intend to govern." So, in structuring the work of the policy staff, I tried to do it in a way that would literally make it possible to say: "Okay, tomorrow we're no longer campaigning; we're actually governing."

Even before the election, candidate Bush had designated Card, who had been deputy chief of staff under his father, as his own presumptive chief of staff, "just so that Andy could start organizing." Card's instructions from Bush were: "Keep it lean," and "Don't be a funnel through which everybody had to run in order to reach me." Card said he felt

> very strongly that there should be very few constraints on people's access to the Oval Office. However, since time was critical, I didn't want people to feel as if they could just go down there on a whim. Nobody needed my permission to go to the Oval Office; nobody needed to justify what they were doing, except they had to pass their own test of *need* versus *want*. If I found that they had violated that test and had pretended that their "want" was a "need," I mean, I would rap their knuckles pretty hard."

Bolten's rule was similar: "Little goes on the president's schedule without my approval," he declared, then added: "If a cabinet officer or one of the assistants to the president needs to get in and say something to the president, I know the president and he wants me to let that person do it. It's up to me to make sure it's at a convenient time and that they don't linger. This is a president who feels that it's important that I know everything that's going on, but not that I substitute my judgment for his."

The arrangement Card had with the president was that at the end of every day the two would meet in the Oval Office and Bush would tell Card everything he had done and every person who had come in to see him during the day. "You might want to check with Mr. X," Bush would say. "I can't remember every detail, but he came to see me." To a cabinet officer requesting time with the president, Card would say, "You don't need my permission, you just have to pass the 'need vs. want' test."

Except for department heads in the national security community, who are in the White House constantly, it has been very common in recent history for some cabinet secretaries to develop a sense of alienation from the White House. The potential for this risk grows larger as formal cabinet meetings become rarer. (Exhibit A is Secretary of Labor Robert Reich, whose plaintive book from the Clinton years is entitled *Locked in the Cabinet.*)[4] Neither Card nor Bolten has been unaware of this potential. Bolten tells of going out of his way to make sure that cabinet members are invited to policy meetings with the president, so that they would come to view the policy councils as "their friends," and of giving them an organized opportunity to make coherent presentations to the president. In addition Bolten sees to it that at least twice a year every cabinet officer is scheduled for open time with the president—no agenda except what the visitor may personally bring.

Card's internal administrative supervision of the White House staff was quite exacting from the beginning.

> I would pay an awful lot of attention to the structure of the White House, the titles, how many assistants to the president, how many deputy assistants to the president, how many special assistants to the president. I'd pay attention to the budget. It was a very small budget compared to most bureaucracies and I paid very close attention to the allocation of physical space. I knew which offices had windows and which ones didn't.

The Chief of Staff's Relationship with the National Security Council

Bolten and, before him, Card, attended all NSC meetings; both believed that the chief of staff's relationship with the national security adviser must be one of "compatible personalities and mutual respect." In addition, Card suggested that the chief of staff could—and often would— be included in any conversation the national security adviser had with the president:

> I think the chief of staff—and I don't mean this out of arrogance—should be as all-knowing as the president. I'm sure that there are a handful of exceptions, but I don't think good chiefs of staff can function if they don't know everything that the president knows. The truth is, they have to know more than the president knows—which ends up being a burden because then you have to decide what the president should *not* know.

Bolten is of like mind, emphasizing that he is the chief of staff "for the whole show" but that he operates "with great deference to national security adviser Steve Hadley; certainly on any matter of substance he always includes me." Both go in to the Oval Office at the very beginning of the day; both are present for the daily 7 a.m. intelligence briefings; both discuss sensitive national security issues with the president. At 7:30 Bolten may leave to chair the senior staff meeting or, if the issue with the president is exceptionally important, he may elect to stay in the Oval Office. Hadley's deputy meanwhile attends the senior staff meetings. The president often telephones Hadley on weekends or at 6:00 a.m. to find out what is going on, calls Bolten is just as happy not being yanked into but will be filled in on later in the day.

Recognizing early in the first term that issues of international economic policy and domestic economic policy are tightly interlinked, Card, national security adviser Condoleezza Rice, and economic assistant Lawrence Lindsey instituted a new organizational arrangement to handle the linkage: they created the position of deputy national security adviser for international economic affairs, who reported to both Rice and Lindsey.

Asked to comment on the effectiveness of national security decisionmaking concerning the war in Iraq, Card recalled that as deputy chief of staff to John Sununu under President George H. W. Bush, he attended the meetings of the NSC deputies committee, which was made up of the number-two officers from the departments of State, Defense, and Justice, the CIA, and the Joint Chiefs of Staff, and was chaired by the national security adviser. During the Persian Gulf war, that NSC deputies committee was the "most valuable bureaucracy that existed," Card remembered. His own evaluation is that the corresponding group during President George W. Bush's first term did not have the "discipline" that obtained in 1990–91—"something that I wish we had done better," he commented. This experience leads Card to advise the president of 2009 to give special attention to the choice of deputy secretaries.

> You know, we think of the cabinet secretaries and you spend a lot of time with that choice. You don't spend as much time thinking about who's going to be the deputy secretary, but the deputy secretary is going to serve on the deputies committee, and that's very important. They should do the heavy lifting in a lot of policy. . . . I would counsel an incoming administration to pay attention to the bureaucracy that is one step below the principals in the White House and outside of the White House. . . . Our principals committee [a cabinet-level group meeting without the president] would have been much more valuable if we would have had a viable deputies' committee.

The Chief of Staff and Congress

Chiefs of staff, of course, never testify before congressional committees, but that stricture has not impeded their frequent sorties to the Capitol to meet with influential members of Congress on especially delicate legislative issues. In 2001 the tax reduction initiative was high on the list of presidential priorities. "I did that when the tax bill was up," recalled Card:

> I sat there with [Senators] John Breaux and Chuck Grassley and Max Baucus; I was up there sometimes all night. Much of the tax bill of 2001 was the result of me sitting in a room with Breaux, checking everybody else out and sitting there with napkins writing down numbers. Breaux shook my hand on the deal and we worked it out with Grassley and others from 10:00 at night until 3:00 in the morning.

Card also had to negotiate with members concerning the White House budget. The director of the Office of Administration is the principal witness who annually presents and defends the Executive Office and White House appropriations requests (chapter 2). Each year the president asks for wider authority to transfer monies among the several White House–related appropriations accounts, and each year the appropriations committees deny the request. "I didn't have to go to the Hill," Card recalled, "but I would call up and speak to the members. I spent quite a bit of time on the budget, both on the House and the Senate sides, and I would deal with the staffers on the appropriations committees, arguing about according the president more transfer authority. Literally at one time the amount at issue was a mere $32,000."

In 2007 Josh Bolten found himself with an assignment similar to Card's negotiations on the tax bill; the issue on this occasion was legislation authorizing supplemental funds for the Iraq war, and by this time the Democrats were running Congress. Several times Bolten convened around his table the secretaries of state and defense, the vice president, the OMB director, the national security adviser, the deputy chief of staff for policy, and the assistants for communications and legislative affairs. They hammered out the strategy to follow and created negotiating parameters within which Bolten would operate. Since the subject was money, could not the budget director do the negotiating? No. "This really wasn't a budget issue," explained Bolten. How about the national security adviser? "It will be a rough-and-tumble political horse-trading environment," warned Bolten. One of the cabinet officers? "You may not want one of your cabinet officers negotiating for the entire government, in a politically charged environment, on behalf of the president," the chief of staff cautioned. So it fell to Bolten to undertake the delicate mission at the Capitol; White House legislative assistant Candida Wolff was with him on every trip. He went first to Senator Mitch McConnell, the Republican leader, met with him several times privately, sometimes with staff. Bolten met next with House Republican leader John Boehner. Then came a session with Senate majority leader Harry Reid, where Bolten was accompanied by McConnell and Boehner. Bolten intentionally avoided meeting with Democrats if Republicans were not present. On occasion they used the telephone; if a three-way connection could not be arranged, Bolten would talk with Reid and then immediately call McConnell to keep him in the loop. McConnell knew how many votes he could count on; Reid knew how many supporters he had, and Bolten knew what the president would sign or veto.

"Everybody laid out where it ideally would come out from their standpoint, knowing that others would not agree to that, and we slowly worked our way down to fewer and fewer issues," Bolten recalled. Wolff kept in touch with a gentleman somewhat in the middle: Senator John Warner. At 6:00 every evening the cabinet–White House team would have a conference call so every one would know where the negotiations stood. At 6:45 every morning, the chief of staff would brief the president.

Looking back at having to carry assignments of this sort, Bolten summed up:

> It's not my favorite activity; I also don't favor it organizationally. I don't think that's a good role for the chief of staff, because that begins to look a little more like I'm a prime minister. But sometimes you don't have a natural person to throw into a negotiation like that, and you have some very political negotiations. . . . I do spend a fair amount of time talking to members, and I go up to the Hill whenever I get the opportunity, because I think it is a very important part of my obligations.

The Chief of Staff and the Media

Neither Card nor Bolten has been a prominent speechmaker or a frequent guest on the Sunday television talk shows. Bolten sees some of those media events as making a White House chief of staff "look like a prime minister"—a portrayal that neither he nor the president would appreciate. He emphasized:

> I think I do OK at it but I don't do something like that unless I feel that I'm well prepared. My first priority is to manage the staff and respond to the president rather than making a public figure out of myself. If it's to advance the administration's agenda and the communications people come to me and say: "You're the best spokesman to go out on Sunday on this issue," I'll of course do it, but if the issue is Iraq, I might say, "Why not use Steve Hadley or Condi Rice?" There's no benefit to me to being a public figure.

4

The Coordination Center: The Staff Secretary

In Roosevelt's White House there was no place for a Sherman Adams. [The president himself] was the recipient of staff work; he presided at the morning staff meeting; he coordinated A's report with B's (or if he did not, they went uncoordinated, and he paid a price for that).

—Richard Neustadt

The one thing that I'd recommend [incoming] people focus on is having a good system in place to really vet and check anything people want [the president] to see, so it's really scrubbed down before he says it. I think we've developed that.

—Raul Yanes

The office of staff secretary, first proposed by the Hoover Commission in 1949, was instituted by President Eisenhower in 1953 and has been a quintessential part of the White House coordinating system since 1969. The staff secretary's office has now become the switching center for all documents in the White House intended for presidential attention. Almost without exception every paper from any one of the elements of the White House staff, or from a cabinet officer, that is destined for either the attention or the action of the president must come into the staff secretary's suite as a candidate for entry into the "staffing system." Even a simple White House fact sheet that describes a matter of policy and is to be issued to the public must be entered into the staffing system and sent to the appropriate staff member for review or approval. (A few items may be purely personal or purely ceremonial, can be exempt from the staffing system, and need not be circulated around the institution.)

Once the initial decision is made that staffing is necessary, the staff secretary scrutinizes each document to identify the other offices that should see it and the reason why—merely for information, or to get comments, or to secure approval.

A prominent feature of the staff secretary's office is a very long shelf with some twenty-five upright slots—one for each of the assignments currently being made. Here is the heart of the staffing process. A memorandum, a briefing paper, a set of slides for an upcoming meeting, a proposed signing statement about an enacted bill, a draft speech, a proposed fact sheet—each is reproduced,

Sample White House Staffing Memorandum

SS/ RM NO. _____

WHITE HOUSE STAFFING MEMORANDUM

Date: _____ ACTION / CONCURRENCE / COMMENT DUE BY: _____

Subject: _____

	ACTION	FYI		ACTION	FYI
VICE PRESIDENT	☐	☐	ROVE	☐	☐
BOLTEN	☐	☐	SNOW	☐	☐
BARTLETT	☐	☐	SULLIVAN	☐	☐
CONNAUGHTON	☐	☐	TOWNSEND	☐	☐
FIELDING	☐	☐	WOLFF	☐	☐
HADLEY	☐	☐	WRIGHT	☐	☐
HAGIN	☐	☐	YANES	☐	☐
HUBBARD	☐	☐	ZINSMEISTER	☐	☐
KAPLAN	☐	☐	CLERK	☐	☐
LAZEAR	☐	☐	_____	☐	☐
MARBURGER	☐	☐	_____	☐	☐
MCBRIDE	☐	☐	_____	☐	☐
MCGURN	☐	☐	_____	☐	☐
PORTMAN	☐	☐	_____	☐	☐

REMARKS:
PLEASE FORWARD COMMENTS DIRECTLY TO — ——, EXT. ——/FAX —, BY DATE, WITH A COPY
TO THE STAFF SECRETARY. THANK YOU.

RESPONSE: _____

Assistant to the President
and Staff Secretary
Ext. 62702
FAX Ext. 62215

covered by a White House Staffing Memorandum (see opposite), and swiftly distributed to the other senior staffers whose action, concurrence, or comment is needed—and a deadline imposed. "One of our functions is to decide who needs to see it," explains staff secretary Raul Yanes. "We'll sometimes ask the author, 'Who do you think needs to see it?' We'll also often make judgments ourselves. Then we actually staff it."[1] The chief of staff's box on the staffing memorandum is the one most frequently checked; that office sees everything.

If comments are all that is required, the recipients may send them directly to the originators (with a copy to the staff secretary). Perhaps the item is just for the information of the recipient; if so, that box is checked. Every pending request requiring a response is duplicated into the corresponding slot on the long shelf; the staff secretary and his assistants watch over those deadlined slots like a mother crocodile over its hatchlings.

Are memoranda from cabinet officers treated differently? The first president Bush instituted a special cabinet in-box into which, on rare occasions, department or agency heads could deposit communications that they wanted to make sure reached the president without any White House staff intervention. In the White House of the second president Bush there is no special box, but if a cabinet officer made such a request, it would be respected, said Yanes.

> The president has a policy and the chief of staff has a policy that cabinet members can get a paper to him, so it's never stopped, but it is shared. If we get a memo from the secretary of energy, we'll decide who else in the White House needs to see it as we give it to the president. . . . If he sees some comment or information, he's likely to call one of his advisers in the White House and talk to him about it. He's assuming, in the way he operates, that the relevant people are seeing what he's seeing, so he can discuss it with them. . . . We wouldn't be staffing the document to change it. If a cabinet secretary wants to write him about something, we're not in the business of editing the memo. . . . We'll share [it] with other White House offices so they can have it, and know it's going to the president, and they can rebut it or support it if they want. But they don't change it; it's not for editing."

The president's spouse's office sometimes receives papers in the staffing process, since the spouse is often with the president at events or speaking engagements and occasionally introduces the president.

The Staffing Process in Operation

The staffing system is simple; it is universal and it has been in effect for the last several presidents. In the George W. Bush White House it is especially thorough. It has three elements: preparing the president for his meetings, drafting his speeches, and preparing him for making decisions.

Preparing the President for Meetings

The staff secretary compiles a daily briefing book to prepare the president for every activity on his schedule: meetings small and large, speeches, important telephone calls, video teleconferences in the Situation Room. The book's content is an amalgam of the outcomes of several other vital staff processes. It begins with the day's schedule, itself the product of days or weeks of analysis and debate about which schedule-proposals should be approved (see chapter 29). In here, at last, are the specifics for each meeting, event, or international telephone or video conference the president has committed himself to participate in that day. For almost all meetings, events, and calls, the book describes the scheduled item, its purpose, who will be attending, and who is the White House staff action officer. If policy issues are to be discussed, a briefing paper from the staff is often included setting forth the questions for discussion and laying out differing views, if any. Also included are any separate memoranda from cabinet officers or other agency heads. If the president is to make remarks, the briefing book includes talking points for him to use, or the text of a prepared speech—itself the product of a parallel, meticulous clearance process, which is also managed by the staff secretary. Finally the book includes information memoranda from the president's staff or others; these memos have gone through a thorough staff review and have also met the independent judgment of the staff secretary that the matter is pertinent and ripe.

If a briefing paper is lengthy and complex, does the staff secretary write a cover sheet to introduce it to the president, as was the practice in the Clinton White House? No, but the originator of the paper may be asked to summarize its basic points. "We try to make sure the memos people generate for him are in a form that is useful to him without having to have another document explaining the document," Yanes said.

Suppose there are disputes—strong differences of opinion among the staff about an issue. The president's style, commented Yanes,

> is to get memos that lay out options if there is some dispute. We work with the offices to make sure there is some kind of consensus in that kind of memo, i.e., that everyone believes that his or her respective position is fairly presented, even if they are not the author. Rather than have a cover- ing memo where we kind of add to that commentary, we make sure that the memo itself will fairly present people's views, and it doesn't need to have an explanation on top of what's already been done.

The Bush decisionmaking process is different from that of the Clinton years, where option papers were typically written out like briefs in a court case and the president was the judge. Unless the topic is one on which his advisers are divided, President Bush "usually doesn't get decision-memos; most memos to him are descriptive and informational. He likes to get background and then he likes to go to meetings and discuss things. He likes to question people. He's less of a lawyer-style; what's more useful to him is information," Yanes said.

The briefing book is sent in to the president every evening except Saturday; the boss has homework almost every night. The only papers not put in the book are especially sensitive national security items, such as operational information from the Central Intelligence Agency or the National Security Agency; these are sent directly to the president by the national security adviser. In the Bush White House, there are actually several editions of the briefing book. One version contains everything: policy, ceremonial, personal; this everything-version is also put in the hands of the chief of staff, the deputy chiefs of staff for policy and for operations, the president's personal aide, and his personal secretary. A version not including personal or ceremonial matters is given to the vice president and to the four policy council heads. None of these recipients can ever be in any doubt about "what's going on in the Oval Office."

When the president is finished with that day's briefing book, it is returned to the staff secretary and from him it goes to the White House Records Management Office.

Staffing Speeches

The process for coordinating speech drafts is similar but separate. The speechwriter prepares a draft that is then sent in two directions: to the fact-checkers who are technically on the speechwriter's staff but who do their fact-checking in minute collaboration with the staff secretary's office; and to the staff secretary so that the text of the draft speech can undergo the usual review by the White House policy officers. The staff secretary will reach out to units in the Executive Office of the President, such as the Council of Economic Advisers, if the proposed remarks discuss economic issues, or to cabinet agencies directly, such as the Department of Defense if military policy is the subject, or to the director of national intelligence if needed, and through him to the whole intelligence community. Observed Yanes:

The president really relies on the staff secretary. We see so many sets of remarks that, other than the speechwriters, nobody sees as much as we do, or looks at it as closely. . . . He's a stickler for precision and accuracy and looks to us to enforce that on the rest of the White House. . . . A big part of the job, when we're working on remarks and speeches, is to make sure that whatever someone is recommending he say is 100 percent accurate, whatever the topic is. The speechwriters have a fact-checking department under them that does research and fact-checking—three or four people. We will work pretty closely with those people to ensure that it's accurate. Every speech the president delivers has an annotation generated by them of support of all the assertions in the document. We'll police that pretty closely and make sure that it's accurate.

When the White House and the interagency reviews are completed, the staff secretary engages in a poststaffing process, whereby the White House policy officer with the principal concern for the subject of the speech inspects the draft once more to ensure that earlier word changes have not altered or weakened the overall message of the speech. No last-minute insertions or amendments are accepted without reading the entire speech through once more. The staff secretary then prepares the "speech book" with the final text in large, 24-point type for delivery. The whole speech staffing process is orderly, but it sometimes takes place under stress, as Yanes recounted.

> If you have a press conference or anything that happens quickly, it's pretty hairy at the very end, because then you have the staffing process telescoped down into a short amount of time.... You're trying to marshal the process ... [but] you have the cameras out there waiting for him. He's a pretty cool customer, but you're making changes and fixing things right to the very last moment, and then it's being put in the speech book for him to deliver. Those are some of the most hectic and dramatic moments....

Presidential Decision Documents

The daily briefing book is almost exclusively that—a briefing. In a different category are documents needing signature or formal approval; these include enrolled bills, signing statements, executive orders, proclamations, presidential determinations, commissions, memoranda to cabinet and agency heads, messages to Congress (including nominations, vetoes, and requests for ratification), and formal letters such as those to other chiefs of state, governors, members of Congress, or other national leaders. These documents go through the same staffing process. If any of them are enveloped in controversy, they will already have been the subject of White House meetings and of policy-time discussion with the president; presentation for signature is simply the last step. When space on the schedule is available, the presidential decision papers are hand-carried into the Oval Office by the staff secretary, who, being a lawyer, has studied them so that he can answer any questions the president may have. If complicated or specialized or especially probing questions are anticipated, the staff secretary invites one of the policy officers or the counsel to the president, to be present; if a significant nomination (such as naming a judge) is pending, the director of the presidential personnel office may be asked to join the staff secretary. (Enrolled bills are special: they are always accompanied by an analysis and recommendation from the Office of Management and Budget, which includes the views of the affected cabinet officers, and whatever analysis, staffing, or policy discussions are needed must have been completed within the constitutionally imposed ten-day deadline.)

The Office Close Up

The staff secretary's office numbers seven: the staff secretary, a deputy staff secretary, and five assistants. (It totaled five in the Clinton administration.) Reporting to the staff secretary are the executive clerk and the directors of the Records Management Office and of the Correspondence Office (described in chapters 25, 26, and 27).

When the president is traveling abroad, the National Security Council provides most of the material for the daily briefing book. On overnight domestic trips, the staff secretary or the deputy staff secretary plus a staff assistant travels with the presidential party, using facilities on *Air Force One* or at ground stations to pull together the same kind of daily briefing book. This procedure is also followed when the president is at his ranch in Crawford, Texas. For Camp David weekends, the weekend book is given or faxed to the president.

Looking at the Future

Yanes had some words of advice for the next president:

> All the time there's more scrutiny of the president. All over the world. The next president is going to have to deal with the war on terror too. So much of what this president talks about, and what the next president's going to be talking about, is going to be related to intelligence matters or what we think the shadowy enemy is doing. . . . [The next president] ought to have a system in place that assures, as best as possible, that before something is recommended for the president to say, it is given the kind of scrutiny that you want it to have. Because there's so much focus on what he says and things move so fast and things are so important that you want to have a process in place that gets as close as possible to 100 percent.

Staff Secretary Yanes and Deputy Staff Secretary Brent McIntosh emphasized how much of the paper flow through their office concerns legal matters or has legal consequences, which require "being careful what words are being used, of the clarity of expression. . . ." They both recommended that future staff secretaries be lawyers, noting that all three of President Bush's staff secretaries, Harriet Miers, Brett Kavanaugh, and Yanes, are attorneys. "It doesn't happen often," they warned, "but sometimes people will suggest sending him something that shouldn't be sent to him, that's not appropriate for him to get. Lawyers," they observed, "often have the right cast of mind to pick up on these things."

5 | *The National Security Adviser*

What we did not have was an integrated and open process in Washington that was organized to keep the peace, nor did we have unity of purpose and resources on the ground. Quite simply, the NSC did not do its job. . . . The president was not served well, because the NSC became too deferential to a postwar strategy that was not working. . . . The National Security Council was created in 1947 to force important decisions to be fully discussed, developed and decided on. In this case, the NSC did not fulfill its role. The NSC avoided slamming on the brakes to force the discussions with the Pentagon and everyone else that was required in the face of a deteriorating situation.

—George Tenet

In years gone by, the NSC viewed itself a little bit as an entity apart. We have a very different view. Our view is that we are part of a White House staff, in support of the president, and we have a responsibility not only to coordinate with others, but really to integrate our operations with others. So it is a single White House staff. What is the challenge? To integrate across the "stovepipes" in a coordinated strategy to achieve national objectives. So, what the NSC needs to do is to integrate across government—that's why we have an interagency process.

—Stephen Hadley

It is only George Tenet's high rank in government that distinguishes the former CIA director's book *At the Center of the Storm* from the recent blizzard of similar books, all of which have castigated the functioning of the National Security Council (NSC) during President Bush's first term.[1] In his own interviews with senior federal officials who were closely and prominently involved in national security policy decisionmaking during Bush's first term, the author has found almost unanimous concurrence with Tenet's observation that the National Security Council was dysfunctional and should have been managed differently and more effectively. One exception to that unanimity is Vice President Dick Cheney, who stated, "I don't know what you would have done differently in this building that would have led to a different outcome."[2]

The purpose of this chapter is not to cast blame on individuals; the cited books have a surfeit of personal criticism. The purpose here is to sum up the

The National Security Council

	Assistant to the President and National Security Adviser	
Special Adviser for Strategic Planning and Institutional Reform		Assistant to President and Deputy National Security Adviser for Iraq/Afghanistan
Special Adviser for Policy Implementation and Execution	Assistant to the President and Deputy National Security Adviser	

Director, Speeches	SAP/Sr. Dir. Legal Affairs	SAP/Sr. Dir. Legislative Affairs	DAP/Sr. Dir. Press	SAP/Sr. Dir. Intelligence Programs and Reform	Executive Secretary
DAP/DNSA Regional Affairs	DAP/DNSA Strategic Communications and Global Outreach	AP/DNSA International Economics	DAP/DNSA Global Democracy Strategy	DAP/DNSA Combating Terrorism	
		SAP/Sr. Dir. Defense Policy and Strategy	SAP/Sr. Dir. Counterproliferation Strategy		

"AP" means Assistant to the President; "DAP" means Deputy Assistant to the President; "SAP" means Special Assistant to the President.

Offices under Deputy National Security Adviser for Iraq/Afghanistan
Two Special Assistants to the President and Senior Directors
Senior Director for Afghanistan

Offices under Deputy National Security Adviser for Regional Affairs
Special Assistants to the President and Senior Directors for
  Russia
  East Asian Affairs
  Western Hemisphere Affairs
  South and Central Asian Affairs
  African Affairs
Senior Director for European Affairs

Offices under Deputy National Security Adviser for International Economics
Special Assistants to the President and Senior Directors for
  International Trade, Energy, and the Environment
  Relief, Stabilization, and Development

Offices under Deputy National Security Adviser for Global Democracy Strategy
Senior Directors for
  Human Rights and International Organizations
  Near East and North Africa

(notes continue)

The National Security Council (continued)

In the first, third and fourth rows, several officers there have dual reporting responsibilities.

The Assistant to the President and DNSA for Iraq and Afghanistan reports to both the National Security Adviser and to the President.

The Director for Speeches reports both to the National Security Adviser and to the Assistant to the President for Speechwriting.

The NSC Special Assistant and Senior Director for Legal Affairs reports both to the National Security Adviser and to the Counsel to the President.

The Special Assistant to the President and Senior Director for Legislative Affairs reports both to the National Security Adviser and to the Assistant to the President for Legislative Affairs.

The Deputy Assistant to the President and Deputy NSC Press Secretary reports both to the National Security Adviser and to the Press Secretary to the President.

The Special Assistant to the President and Senior Director for Intelligence programs and Reform reports both to the National Security Adviser and to the Assistant to the President for Homeland Security and Counterterrorism.

The Deputy Assistant to the President for Strategic Communications and Global Outreach reports both to the National Security Adviser and to the Director of the White House Office of Communications.

The Assistant to the President for International Economic Affairs reports both to the National Security Adviser and to the Assistant to the President for Economic Affairs.

The Deputy Assistant to the President for Combating Terrorism reports both to the National Security Adviser and to the Assistant to the President for Homeland Security and Counterterrorism.

lessons learned, particularly during the first years of the Bush presidency, describe the changes that have been made in the office of the national security adviser since 2006, and bring both the lessons and the changes to the attention of the president of 2009 and of those who will be associated with him or her in the demanding task of handling national security affairs.

The President as Chief Diplomat

Handling national security affairs, however, has become dramatically different over the last few decades because of a change in the presidency itself: the chief executive is more than commander in chief, he has also become chief diplomat.

What began with Woodrow Wilson, who traveled to Paris to join in the negotiations at the Versailles peace conference, was expanded by Franklin Roosevelt during World War II: the personal role of the American president in conducting American foreign policy affairs. Technology—secure text messages, secure telephones, secure video teleconferencing—not only has made this expanded, personal presidential role possible but has transformed it into routine. Modern presidents are constantly engaging in person-to-person communications with their combatant commanders, with their ambassadors, and with foreign chiefs of state and other world leaders.

In the first seven years of his presidency, George W. Bush had at least 748 personal telephone conversations with other chiefs of state or world leaders, participated in at least 674 face-to-face meetings with them singly or in groups, and conducted at least 15 video teleconferences with them.[3] The frequency and the substantive depth of these personal communications have placed exceptionally heavy requirements on the National Security Council staff in the White House. Readers should, therefore, not be surprised to learn that the NSC unit in the White House now numbers 249 persons.

The National Security Council itself is a body established by the National Security Act of 1947—a committee consisting of the president as chair plus the vice president and the secretaries of state and defense. The chairman of the joint chiefs of staff and the director of the Central Intelligence Agency are statutory observers. The president can designate other members at his discretion, such as the attorney general, the secretary of the Treasury, the secretary of homeland security, the director of the Office of Management and Budget, and the director of national intelligence.

The council does its work at four layers of officialdom: policy-coordinating committees made up of assistant secretaries of the member departments and usually chaired by senior directors of the NSC staff; deputies who are the under secretaries of those departments, chaired by the national security adviser, at this writing, Stephen Hadley; the principals of the member departments, meeting with Hadley; and finally the National Security Council itself, that is, the secretaries meeting with the president. The new capabilities of the recently rebuilt White House Situation Room (chapter 36) are such that any of these groups can meet with its members no matter where they are located, conducting their business via secure video teleconference and aided by all kinds of visuals—photos, drawings, maps—projected for everyone to see.

The 1947 statute mandates that "the Council shall have a staff to be headed by a civilian executive secretary to be appointed by the President." That officer, and a counterpart executive secretary of the Homeland Security Council, are the only two statutory positions in all of the White House staff, which means that an incoming president is legally free to innovate and reorganize his entire White House, other than those two posts, without any legislative involvement (see the NSC organization chart).

For fifty-five years, beginning with the Eisenhower administration, the National Security Council staff has been supervised by a person with the title of assistant to the president and national security adviser. Within that continuity, what innovations should be considered by the incoming president to avoid the dysfunctionalities of the NSC in Bush's first term and to build on the innovations that have been instituted at the NSC since 2006?

Questions of Structure

One area of innovation involves structure. There are two staff offices in the White House, both headed by assistants to the president, related to national security: the National Security Council and its staff of 249; and the Office of

Homeland Security and Counterterrorism (HSC) and its staff of 48. Many problem areas, such as the Israeli-Palestinian conflict, are the exclusive concern of the NSC; many, such as hurricanes, water quality, state and local hospital emergency capacity, are the exclusive business of the HSC. Then there are the policy issues, such as immigration or the screening of incoming airline passengers, where the expertise and jurisdictions of the two councils thoroughly overlap.

"To improve coordination at the White House," the 9/11 Commission recommended that "the existing Homeland Security Council should soon be merged into a single National Security Council." The independent commission, appointed to investigate the terrorist attacks on the United States, said such a merger "should help the NSC staff concentrate on its core duties of assisting the president and supporting interdepartmental policymaking."[4] While the two staffs have contemplated and seriously discussed such a merger on several occasions, they have decided against it, and there has been no executive or legislative action to adopt it.

The innovative arrangement that has been worked out is the appointment of a deputy national security adviser for combating terrorism, who reports both to National Security Adviser Hadley and to Deputy Homeland Security Adviser Joel Bagnal. "He is the link to make sure that Joel and I are knit up," emphasized Hadley.[5]

Problems of Communications

Beginning at least with Truman's secretary of state, Dean Acheson, information copies of significant incoming telegrams from U.S. ambassadors abroad have been sent to the White House. Since the National Security Council's Situation Room was set up in 1961, these communications have been transmitted instantly and electronically. As a consequence, NSC staff officers have been kept well informed of actions taken by U.S. diplomats. Such a system has not been replicated by the Department of Defense, however; the Situation Room does not routinely receive copies of traffic between the Pentagon and field commanders. The Department of Defense has its own secret communications system, called Secret Internet Protocol Router Network (SIPRNET), but at the start of the Bush administration that net excluded even the NSC staff.[6]

At the time of the initial occupation of Iraq, in 2003, the head of the Coalition Provisional Authority, L. Paul Bremer III, reported not to the secretary of state but directly to the secretary of defense. In May 2003 the newly arrived Bremer issued CPA Order Number One, "De-Baathification of Iraqi Society," which removed from Iraqi government office any persons who were members of Saddam Hussein's Baath Party, including 40,000 schoolteachers. In his book George Tenet declared, "Clearly this was a critical policy decision, yet there was no NSC Principals meeting to debate the move.... As bad as that was, CPA Proclamation

Number Two was worse. Again, without any formal discussion or debate back in Washington—at least any that included me or my top deputies—Bremer, on May 23, ordered the dissolution of the Iraqi army."[7] One State Department adviser subsequently described this action as "one of the greatest errors in the history of U.S. warfare."[8]

Tenet was not the only one in Washington not to know of the orders ahead of time. According to author Bob Woodward, Hadley, who was the deputy national security adviser during Bush's first term, "first learned of the orders on de-Baathification and disbanding the military as Bremer announced them to Iraq and the world. They hadn't been touched by the formal interagency process, and as far as Hadley knew there was no imprimatur from the White House. [National Security Adviser Condoleezza] Rice also had not been consulted. It hadn't come back to Washington or the NSC for a decision"[9]

Contrast the handling of that decision with the communications routine instituted in 2007: every Monday there is a secure video teleconference between the president and both the commander of U.S. forces in Iraq and the U.S. ambassador in Baghdad. That teleconference also includes the vice president, the secretaries of state and defense, the chairman of the Joint Chiefs of Staff, the director of the CIA, the director of national intelligence, and the national security adviser. Approximately every two weeks the president of Iraq joins this group near the end of a session or has a separate video session with the president.

These formal sessions are important, but it is the network of informal communication arrangements that Hadley has erected that supply the strongest yarn for "knitting up" the national security community. Every Monday, Wednesday, and Friday, Hadley has an informal 6:45 a.m. secure telephone call with the secretaries of state and defense. These three plus the vice president often meet for lunch—just the four of them. That foursome also meets informally with the president at the White House residence. About once a week the secretary of state comes over for a session with the president, the vice president, the chief of staff, and Hadley.

"We try to have flexibility and make the forum and the form of how we are going to deal with an issue reflect the character of the issue in its sensitivity. We have to do that because there are so many issues coming so fast; some of them you have time to deal with in a formal, structured interagency setting, and some you've got to get the people around the table quickly and scope them," Hadley said.

Planning for Policy Execution

Planning for policy execution was also the subject of criticism during the first years of the Iraq war. A pair of writers describe the status of planning in February 2003:

Postwar Iraq planning paralleled what happened with prewar Iraq intelligence. The work of government experts and analysts was discarded by senior Bush administration policy makers when it conflicted with or undermined their own hardened ideas about what to expect in Iraq. They were confident—or wanted to believe—that the war would go smoothly. They didn't need other views, notions or plans—not from the State Department, the CIA or the military. It was their war, and they would run it as they saw fit. . . . By February, 2003, State and Defense officials were barely on speaking terms.[10]

Four years later, the administration had learned some lessons, and Hadley introduced another innovation. He explained:

A second focus that we have brought in under this president is that we concentrate heavily on implementation and execution. The NSC has traditionally been about policy development. We still do that, on our interagency basis, but we are now very focused on: once you have a policy, what is your strategy and plan for carrying out that policy? What are the tasks? Who's responsible for each task? When are they due? And what is the mechanism for tracking performance? . . . We have a "Stoplight Chart" that says "Green: You're on track"; "Yellow": "You're at risk of going off track." And, you know, "Red": "You're off track!" If you've got a red light on your implementation/execution chart, it means that you need to get your interagency committee back together, figure out what's the problem and how to fix it.

This checklist is on the NSC's computer but is also emblazoned on a thick set of charts. "This is our tool," Hadley emphasized, "to track what each of us is doing and to support our participation in the interagency process as well."

"Strategic planning is something that is not done very well," commented Hadley in December 2007. To correct that, Hadley has initiated a plan that involves creating two new positions on the NSC staff. One has the title of special adviser for policy implementation and execution. This officer will work with Deputy National Security Adviser Jim Jeffrey to see to it that the respective NSC senior directors translate policy decisions into implementable action plans and programs. Special software will be developed so that Hadley or the council can track what actions are being undertaken and identify lags or areas that are being overlooked.

The second new post will be a special adviser for strategic planning and institutional reform. This person will have three responsibilities. First she will be part of the brainstorming within the council and, recognizing that the NSC tends to focus on immediate, tactical issues, will be the voice that says, "Wait a minute! Let's step back and ask ourselves 'What are we trying to accomplish?'"

Hadley also asked each of the NSC senior directors to put together a "Goals 2008" compilation: what specifically does each of them want to accomplish in his or her area of national security affairs before the end of the second term? Hadley is insisting that these goals be defined in objective and measurable terms, so that he and the council will know when the goal has been achieved. The special adviser will use her "stoplight" chart to alert the council as to the progress or lack of it.

In addition to this ongoing oversight function, Hadley has identified several long-term analyses and short-term studies that he believes need to be undertaken. The special adviser for strategic planning and institutional reform will assign the responsibility for taking on these studies, either within the NSC staff or to NSC member departments, or in some cases will arrange for outside consultants to complete them. The important thing, Hadley emphasized, is that the council make the intellectual investment to look beyond the immediate issues and think about problems that it will face three to five years from now. Some work, for example, has already been done to anticipate where Russia is going to be in three to five years. Similar work has also begun on China and Bangladesh.

A third responsibility of the special adviser for strategic planning and institutional reform will be to reach out to the strategic planning entities in Defense, in State (which has long had a policy planning staff), and in Treasury (where Hadley wants to get such a staff started) and meet with them weekly or biweekly to coordinate all the strategic planning in national security affairs that is being done within the administration. "We will have gotten all those bases covered," Hadley declared.

The president's daily intelligence briefing has been supplemented, on Wednesdays, by what Hadley called a "deep dive" session on any topic, as Hadley put it, "where intelligence has a direct impact on policy." The regular NSC members are usually present and special intelligence briefers explore the chosen topic in unusual depth. "Many times we've found that an intelligence briefing would provoke a policy discussion between the president and the briefers when it's the NSC principals that need to hear it. So we do a deep dive every Wednesday, and we do selective deep dives on other countries and other issues as needed—many times—in the Situation Room on Saturday mornings, so that the intelligence discussion can move seamlessly into a policy discussion in the presence of the policymakers themselves."

"Knitting Up" the White House Itself

The effectiveness of a White House staff can be damaged by internal "stovepipes"—officers who are so wrapped up inside their own specialties that coordination suffers. Hadley has made wide use of an administrative technique for mitigating that stovepiping; it is the system of dual reporting. In addition to a deputy for combating terrorism, who reports to both Hadley and the White House homeland security office, a deputy national security adviser for international economic affairs, who handles issues of trade, economic development, and the millennium challenge account, reports to Hadley and the White House National Economic Council. The deputy national security adviser for strategic communications reports to Hadley and the counselor to the president for communications, while the NSC legal adviser reports to both Hadley and the counsel to the president. The NSC legislative affairs officer reports to Hadley and the White House legislative affairs assistant, while the NSC press office reports to both Hadley and the White House press secretary. The NSC speechwriter is also part of the White House speechwriter's staff.

The emphasis Hadley and his colleagues are placing on these "knitting-up" arrangements has its foundation in the original wording of the National Security Act itself: "The function of the Council shall be to advise the president with respect to the *integration of domestic, foreign, and military policies* relating to the national security. . . ."[11] Hadley added:

> It's not only what we're going to do from a policy standpoint, but what's your latest strategy, what's your diplomatic strategy, what's your communications plan—to explain it? We have tried in this sense to do a fair amount of integration of policy and communications and legislative strategy, because in a way they are all one. You need a policy that's going to be sustainable with the public's understanding, to be funded and supported by the Congress, so if you can have that perspective as you develop your plan, your policy and then the implementation to your policy, you're better off.

Two or three weeks before the president is scheduled to give a major speech, NSC and White House policymakers sit down with the principal White House speechwriter and talk over what the themes will be and specifically what inputs the speechwriter will want from the NSC. Every weekday morning, at 6:30, just before the senior staff meeting, the White House press secretary and some of her staff come to Hadley's office, joining with the NSC press staff to discuss, as Hadley phrased it,

> What's out there in the press? What are the problems? What are the press lines we need? What issues do we need to get State and Defense on the line and make sure we're knit up on? Maybe we need to get somebody out speaking to the press? There is a rhythm to the day and I just want to say that integrating the press piece, the communications piece, and the speechwriting piece is a practice which supports the president across the White House as a whole.

The National Security Adviser and the Public

There are times, and there are issues, where members of Congress need to be kept informed of the president's priorities concerning national security matters. It was Hadley who was sent up to meet with Senator John McCain on legislation pertaining to the treatment of detainees under interrogation—the "torture" issue. "Our legislative affairs office does a great job," Hadley explained, "but every once in a while it's helpful to the legislative shop to roll me out and plunk me down in a group of legislators and talk to them. I'll have the legislative affairs director or one of her staff with me."

"I also try and do the same with press folks," Hadley added, "but again, my job is not to be prominent in the public view, not to make news, not to have my name out there. My job is to get the press in here, speaking on deep background or on background, and to get into their heads, so they understand the context of the decision. They can get quotes from other folks."

Hadley acknowledged that he is on the Sunday talk shows quite frequently, but he considers that to be one of the traditional functions of the national security adviser. "For my money," he explained, "the goal with the press is to give them an understanding of the context of a decision, so that I can affect, over time, what they bring to the stories that they write, rather than trying to be *in* the stories they write."

6

The "Just-Us" Department:
The Counsel to the President

What does a president need from the White House counsel? Find somebody that you're comfortable with, find somebody that will be a counselor, a legal counselor to you and who doesn't get cotton in the mouth when he or she walks into the Oval Office, because you need somebody who will give you his or her best judgment.

—Fred Fielding

The subpoenas and demands have just grown exponentially, and have not only caused an enormous increase in the number of people in the White House counsel's office, but this has also brought the White House counsel into a free-fire zone, where he is criticized no matter what he does. . . . That's a challenge to the professional ethic of the White House counsel and his staff—it is a new phenomenon.

—Lloyd Cutler

For nearly seven decades—since 1941—each president has established in the White House what Eisenhower counsel Gerald Morgan called the "Just-Us" Department: a personal office on his immediate staff that could give him legal advice directly—independently from the institutional resources of his Department of Justice. Over at the Justice Department, attorneys general and their associates have been skeptical. "The attorney general views *himself* as the president's lawyer," was the warning that Truman's attorney general reportedly passed on to Edward McCabe, Eisenhower's newly appointed special White House counsel.[1] "They are not equipped to do painstaking research over at the White House; they tend to skim the surface," commented a former Justice officer. "In Justice, nobody is overawed by our environment, nor are we subject to the kinds of pressures which abound at the White House. Some of those younger White House lawyers have views of their own which can color their legal judgment." Justice veterans are afraid that presidents may "shop around" for the legal advice they prefer—resulting in inconsistencies in the administration's legal judgments.

The view from the White House is different. The Department of Justice is "too remote," "twenty blocks away." White House legal staffers know that they must answer the "How do I do this?" question with a speed that matches the president's urgency. "Nothing propinqs like propinquity," former counsel Lloyd Cutler observed.[2] The attorney general, preoccupied with a department of 123,000 people, is rarely available to take part in the daily White House meetings at which the White House counsel identifies legal issues and refers them to Justice Department lawyers "who might never hear about the problem except for the White House counsel's intervention."[3]

Outer and Inner Relationships

At the beginning of an administration, one of the first steps a newly appointed White House counsel takes is negotiation of a White House-Justice "treaty": each White House counsel renegotiates it with each new attorney general.[4] Advance consultation is promised in both directions. The White House typically pledges not to exert improper pressure on Justice (especially when criminal or civil prosecutions are involved)—although allegations have been made that political officers in the George W. Bush White House improperly interfered with the removal of United States attorneys in some states. The White House counsel is eager to agree that all White House calls to the Department of Justice will come only through the counsel's office and promises to exempt the attorney general from campaign politicking.

In addition to the talents of his own immediate staff, which currently numbers over thirty-five, the White House counsel can draw upon a well of legal brainpower—and, more important, institutional memory—unique in the executive branch: the Office of Legal Counsel (OLC) in the Department of Justice. This elite staff, particularly expert in constitutional law, has the capacity not only to present recommendations on current issues to the president and the president's counsel but also to reinforce its conclusions by researching precedents from previous administrations.

White House staff, with their bookcases nearly empty at the start of an administration, cannot compete with this kind of institutional memory. The OLC, with a professional staff of twenty-six attorneys, has presented numerous memoranda of advice to the White House counsel's office during President Bush's first seven years in office. Is the counsel bound to accept the OLC advice? He is not, but Counsel Fred Fielding makes it clear that he would never present advice to the president that differed from the OLC recommendation without calling the president's attention to the existence of the difference. That such differences are rare is attributable to a practical matter: if litigation is undertaken, it is the Department of Justice that leads the courtroom argumentation, the same department that offered the original advice.

The counsel's resources are not limited to White House and Department of Justice circles: he establishes links to every executive branch agency (including the regulatory commissions at times). Each cabinet department has its own general counsel, and each of these officers, before being appointed, has an interview with the presidential legal staff. In this fashion, and through regular meetings and constant telephone calls, the White House counsel has a hand on the legal network of the entire executive branch.

The counsel's second task is to send a warning to his White House colleagues: *stay away* from any ex parte contacts whatsoever—even apparently innocent "status" inquiries—with the independent regulatory commissions and any other agencies that perform regulatory or adjudicatory functions. "White House staff members," admonished one such typical memorandum from the counsel, "should avoid even the mere appearance of interest or influence...."[5] The warning goes on to instruct staffers to stay away from investigative agencies, members of the intelligence community (unless they have the approval of the national security adviser), and offices that negotiate procurement contracts, especially if the staff member has any financial interest in a contract under negotiation. Some readers will still remember 1958 when White House chief of staff Sherman Adams made a status inquiry to the Federal Trade Commission about a case involving a person who had been a close associate in New Hampshire. The call leaked, causing so much embarrassment that Adams finally had to resign.

Ethics, and the White House Staff Manual

For a newly elected president and his new White House staff members, ethical issues connected to their employment represent a minefield with which they are likely to be unfamiliar. The counsel is the "designated agency ethics official" for the White House. Since at least the Nixon administration, the White House has had its own internal staff manual, which introduces new White House employees to the institution and lays out the rules for working there. The manual, of some 130 pages, typically has five sections: first, a listing of facilities, services, and procedures (such as where the available conference rooms and libraries are, who can use the athletic center, that the Cabinet Room is only for the use of the president, that interns and volunteers cannot clear in personal visitors, who has mess privileges, when briefing memos are due to the staff secretary); second, a listing of the different offices in the White House and what each one does; third, sample copies of the forms that are used (for schedule proposals, for example); fourth—a section overseen by the White House counsel—the statutory and administrative rules governing federal, and White House, ethical behavior (such as the specifics of the Hatch Act concerning political activities, the rules about accepting gifts and avoiding conflicts of interest); and fifth, the acronyms common in the White House (POTUS, FLOTUS, VPOTUS, among others).

Vetting Candidates for Presidential Appointment

The presidential personnel office (chapter 8) is responsible for recruiting and recommending candidates for the 1,198 full-time and 3,088 part-time presidential appointments in the executive branch (it does not recruit White House staff). For each of those candidates, two streams of data come into the White House: information about the person's qualifications and capabilities plus political considerations; and FBI reports and financial information that may evidence suitability or security problems and possible conflicts of interest. The latter stream is handled by the counsel's office, where several lawyers specialize in reviewing data on candidates' personal behavior and on financial holdings; the counsel and the presidential personnel office director are notified if problems are found. The standards for compliance here have been pushed upward in recent years to include marital faithfulness, the degree of alcohol use, and the payment of Social Security taxes for household workers—the nanny tax. Sometimes problems are curable, such as having the candidate put holdings into a blind trust or sell them, but in the end both the counsel and the personnel office director must be satisfied that nothing about the candidate would either endanger Senate confirmation or embarrass the president. (There have even been a few instances when a husband decided not to be a candidate because he did not want the extent of his wealth to be disclosed and have his wife learn of it.)

When the appointment is for U.S. attorneys, federal judges, or general counsels in the cabinet departments, the White House counsel's office is the primary player for vetting on all counts. The Bush administration does not employ "murder boards" as such, but for judicial selection the screening process is intense. The vetting is done jointly with the Department of Justice, but since 1981 it has been a White House–controlled undertaking from start to finish. (Illustrating how dramatically different this White House centralization has become, consider the viewpoint expressed by President Carter's attorney general Griffin Bell in 1977, concerning White House management of the judicial screening process: he termed it "such an outrageous intrusion into the prerogatives of the attorney general and such a politicization of the process of selection that I thought of resigning.")[6]

The judicial or counsel candidate is personally interviewed not only at the Department of Justice but at the White House, often by Justice officers coming over to the White House to hold their interviews. If the appointment is to a seat on an appeals court, the White House counsel and deputy counsel personally meet with the candidate and invite a former clerk from that circuit to sit in for the interview. The decision for the recommendation to be made to the president is made at a judicial selection meeting convened weekly by the counsel at the "principals-only" level. The meeting includes the chief of staff, the deputy chief of staff for policy, the personnel office director, the assistant for legislative affairs, and also the attorney general and comparable assistant attorneys general. The White House counsel also holds a second weekly "judicial strategy" meeting where decisions are made about the timing for sending requests for confirmation to the Senate and about issues that may be foreseen in the confirmation process itself. One issue is worked out by the counsel on a committee-by-committee basis: whether and how much of an FBI file on a candidate is to be shown to how many senators and to how many staff of the confirming Senate committee. In general, committees receive only the summary of the file; the exception is the Senate Judiciary Committee, where complete files are made available. Exceptions are negotiated by the counsel with the chair and the ranking member of other committees that are planning confirmation hearings.

After the nomination is made, both the White House counsel and the legislative affairs assistant consult with the majority (and often the minority) members of the confirming committee to work out confirmation strategy and to urge the committee to hold confirmation hearings promptly. "We want a vote." Counsel Fred Fielding emphasized, "You know the president has said, 'They're entitled to a vote under the Constitution.' You don't have to confirm the nominee, but under the Constitution the nominee is entitled to a vote and the president is entitled to have them vote."[7]

Pardons

Article II gives the president the power to grant "Reprieves and Pardons for Offenses against the United States, except in Cases of Impeachment." Justice Department regulations stipulate that in each case a "formal petition" is to be executed and delivered to the pardon attorney in the department. The pardon attorney conducts a thorough analysis, checking with the prosecuting U.S. attorney, the sentencing judge, and prison authorities, before writing up a 500-word report making a recommendation. The attorney general, at his discretion, may forward the recommendation to the White House. At the White House it is the counsel who reviews each file and, after some internal staff consultation, makes a recommendation to the president.

In his last day in office, President Clinton, in several instances bypassing these staffing procedures, granted 140 pardons and commuted 36 sentences. Judicial Watch, a private investigative organization, sued the Department of Justice to release the pardon documents. A federal district court upheld the department's refusal to supply any of those documents that were "solicited and received" by the White House (a refusal supported by the George W. Bush White House). The court stated that:

> [The president's communications privilege] must be viewed in its broader, historical context, allowing presidential advisors to provide the President

with the fullest and most candid information and advice regarding decisions to be made in many sensitive areas, including the granting or denial of pardon requests. Thus, the presidential communications privilege serves as a vitally important protection for the Presidency as an institution.[8]

Judicial Watch appealed this decision, and in May 2004 a divided Court of Appeals for the District of Columbia affirmed the district court's holding applying the presidential communications privilege to documents going to the White House; reversed the district court with respect to internal Justice Department documents that were not in the presidential category but that might be covered by a second, lesser "deliberative process privilege" set forth in the Freedom of Information Act (FOIA); and instructed the district court to determine which documents in the second category were covered under that FOIA privilege and which were not privileged at all. (The district court subsequently advised that of the 4,341 pages at issue, only 915 did not fall under either privilege, but when the Department of Justice released them, all 915 were blacked out.)

In his first seven years and two months in office, President Bush granted 157 pardons and commuted two prison sentences (one being that of I. Lewis Libby, Vice President Cheney's former top assistant).[9]

White House Review of Federal Briefs Prepared for the Supreme Court

From time to time, cases reach the Supreme Court that involve policy questions of very special concern to the president, so much so that the White House will want—will expect—will require the solicitor general and the attorney general to provide for advance White House review of the text of the government's brief. In the past such requests were rare, and the Department of Justice was reluctant to let such a text out of its hands at all. That began to change in 1977. After Solicitor General Wade H. McCree Jr. had prepared the government's brief in the case of Allan Bakke, a white man who had been denied admission to the medical school of the University of California and who was alleging reverse discrimination, Attorney General Griffin Bell termed it "the most significant civil rights controversy to come before [the Court] since the school desegregation cases of 1954."[10] He took the first draft of the brief to the White House to show the president, and it got shown to the White House counsel, the domestic policy adviser, and the vice president—whereupon days of debate and negotiation ensued. Looking back, Bell wrote that he had

> made perhaps my greatest mistake with regard to the power centers at the White House. Nowhere is the tug of power between the White House and a Cabinet department more apparent than in a dispute between the Justice Department and the President's staff over what is law and what is policy.

If the staff had its way, no doubt every major issue that naturally fell to the Justice Department would be considered policy rather than a legal matter. Then the White House would be making all the decisions, because it is the White House where policy is made.[11]

In the thirty years since this flare-up, the protocol has generally become settled: the White House reviews those briefs. Example: the solicitor general's brief in the 2008 case of the District of Columbia's ban on private possession of firearms was examined by the White House counsel and others. (The vice president joined with congressional colleagues to take a position differing from that of the administration.)

Defending Presidential Powers

Whereas throughout American history the president's Article II "executive Power" to use force was almost always exerted against armed soldiers of another country or another government, the catastrophe of 9/11 dramatically illustrated the vulnerability of the United States to terrorist attack at the hands of "nonstate actors." Providing "for the common defence" against such enemies has required the nation to think through what that historically ambiguous Article II language really means, and the usual multiplicity of players—president, courts, Congress, academics, and the press—are engaging in a historically heated discourse about it. As principal legal adviser to the president, the White House counsel is a leading participant in this dialogue.

Immediately following the 9/11 disaster, Congress and the president united in enacting Public Law 107-40, a joint resolution entitled "Authorization for Use of United States Armed Forces (AUMF)." The governing sentence reads:

That the president is authorized to use all necessary and appropriate force against those nations, organizations or persons he determines planned, authorized, committed or aided the terrorist attacks that occurred on September 11, or harbored such organizations or persons, in order to prevent any future acts of international terrorism against the United States by such nations, organizations or persons.[12]

Undergirded by language of that breadth and compass, supported by the fact that the United States is at war in Iraq, and shaken, as all Americans were, by subsequent terrorist attacks in London and Madrid, the counsel to the president had little difficulty in arguing for a broad interpretation of Article II and in consequence a very extensive use of presidential power.

Following are some examples of legal positions the Bush White House has taken "to provide for the common defence."

Article II War Power and the Courts

It supported the successful argument of Deputy Solicitor General Paul Clement before the Fourth Circuit Court of Appeals that Yaser Hamdi, a U.S. citizen captured fighting with the Taliban in Afghanistan, should continue to be held in captivity because (in the words of the court):

> The constitutional allocation of war powers affords the President extraordinarily broad authority as Commander in Chief and compels courts to assume a deferential posture in reviewing exercises of this authority. And, while the Constitution assigns courts the duty generally to review executive detentions that are alleged to be illegal, the Constitution does not specifically contemplate any role for courts in the conduct of war, or in foreign policy generally. . . . We speak . . . from the conviction that separation of powers takes on special significance when the nation itself comes under attack.[13]

In reviewing this case, the Supreme Court evaded the Article II issue, declaring: "We do not reach the question whether Article II provides such authority, however, because we agree with the Government's alternative position that Congress has in fact authorized Hamdi's detention through the AUMF." (The Court went on to strike a balance between detention and liberty and ruled that Hamdi was entitled to due process. Hamdi was freed and deported to Saudi Arabia, where he had spent most of his life before his capture.)

Military Commissions

On November 13, 2001, the White House issued a military order entitled "Detention, Treatment, and Trial of Certain Non-Citizens in the War Against Terrorism." The order, which was directly based on the AUMF, provided that captured terrorists would be tried by military commissions, appointed by the secretary of defense, with classified information protected from disclosure, and with life imprisonment or death being among the possible penalties upon conviction. An appeal could be made to the president or the secretary of defense, who would review the record and make a final decision; no other appeals (including to the courts) would be possible.

(Subsequently a Yemeni citizen named Hamdan, captured in Afghanistan and detained in Guantánamo, was charged by a military commission, but persuaded the D.C. Circuit Court of Appeals to grant habeas relief. A federal district court then stayed the commission proceedings, but the D.C. Circuit Court reversed. The Supreme Court ruled that the military commissions were not authorized by the AUMF or any other act of Congress and reversed again. Congress passed authorizing legislation, which in turn has been challenged by other detainees; in early 2008 the issue was before the Supreme Court once more.)

Interrogation Techniques

In February 2002 President Bush determined that while the Geneva Conventions provide protections to prisoners of war, members of al Qaeda, the Taliban, and associated forces are not prisoners of war but rather unlawful enemy combatants and, as such, are not entitled to the conventions' protections. The Central Intelligence Agency operates a detention and interrogation program for those unlawful enemy combatants who are captured, aiming, by the use of "enhanced interrogation techniques," to extract information that may be vital to U.S. national security. What protections, if any, should these detainees have? If the enhanced interrogation techniques go to the point of torture, the CIA agent is violating a federal law and is committing a crime. In the middle of heated controversy, Congress enacted the Military Commissions Act of 2006 (Public Law 109-366), which affirmed the authority of the president to "interpret the meaning of the Geneva Conventions."

By an executive order of July 20, 2007, the president used that authority and determined that Common Article 3 of the Geneva Conventions governing treatment of prisoners of war "shall apply" to the CIA's detention and interrogation program, providing that that program meets certain standards, which are specified in the executive order.[14] Needless to say, the White House counsel was a principal participant in drawing up this executive order and in trying to achieve, in the CIA's interrogation program, the necessary balance between methods that extract vitally needed information from detainees but that do not shock the conscience of the world.

Surveillance

The 1978 Foreign Intelligence Surveillance Act "prohibits any person from intentionally 'engag[ing]. . . in electronic surveillance under color of law except as authorized by statute.'"[15] In 2006 the attorney general, supported by the White House, argued that the AUMF was just such a statute. After eighteen months of controversy between the White House and Congress, and within the administration, a temporary statute (the Protect America Act of August, 2007, expiring February 1, 2008) was enacted permitting warrantless wiretapping "concerning individuals reasonably believed to be outside the United States." House Speaker Nancy Pelosi termed that statute "unacceptable," while Director of National Intelligence Michael McConnell defended it in a plaintive *New York Times* op-ed column entitled "Help Me Spy on Al Qaeda."[16]

As of this writing, new legislation was under consideration in which the attempt will be made to strike, again, the right balance between giving the president and his intelligence community sufficient authority to intercept and acquire information needed to "provide for the common defence" without violating the Fourth Amendment barring illegal search and seizure.

Signing Statements

Congress often enacts legislation containing provisions the president views as undercutting the chief executive's constitutional authorities. Desiring to see the major part of such an enactment become law, the president will sign the enrolled bill but issue a "signing statement" emphasizing that he will interpret the offending provision "consistent with the president's constitutional authority"—meaning he will regard the provision as merely advisory. Presidents since James Monroe have balked at what they contend are unconstitutional enactments; George H. W. Bush issued 147 such signing statements, President Reagan 105, President Clinton 80. George W. Bush, however, in his first five and a half years in office, reportedly issued 750 signing statements affecting 110 laws.[17]

A recent example: the 2006 Department of Defense Emergency Supplemental Appropriations Act contained a provision authored by Senator John McCain of Arizona banning "cruel, inhumane or degrading" treatment of prisoners at U.S. detention centers. President Bush signed the bill but added:

> The executive branch shall construe Title X in Division A of the Act, relating to detainees, in a manner consistent with the constitutional authority of the President to supervise the unitary executive branch and as Commander in Chief and consistent with the constitutional limitations on the judicial power, which will assist in achieving the shared objective of the Congress and the President, evidenced in Title X, of protecting the American people from further terrorist attacks.[18]

Not surprisingly, members of Congress, especially of the opposite party, have denounced this particular decision, and the hundreds of similar actions that President Bush has taken. Declared Democratic senator Robert Byrd of West Virginia: "Federal law is not some buffet line where the president can pick parts of some laws to follow and others to reject."[19] White House spokesman Tony Fratto responded: "The executive branch has an obligation to remain within constitutional limits. The point of the signing statement is to advise where the executive sees those limits."[20] Harvard law professor Charles Fried commented: "Congressional staff members, sometimes at the behest of interest groups, plant little stink bombs in the legislative history which then flower in later litigation. The presidential signing statements were a kind of Airwick against those stink bombs."

The counsel to the president has several times queried the Office of Legal Counsel in the Department of Justice about the president's authority to decline to execute statutory provisions that he believes are unconstitutional. In November 1994 Assistant Attorney General Walter Dellinger advised White House counsel Abner Mikva: "There are circumstances in which the President may appropriately decline to enforce a statute that he views as unconstitutional," and cited a Supreme Court case in which four justices declared that the president "has the power to veto encroaching laws . . . or even to disregard them when they are unconstitutional."[21] Dellinger went on to quote from an OLC opinion, dated November 3, 1993, that he had prepared (for White House counsel Bernard Nussbaum):

> The President may properly announce to Congress and to the public that he will not enforce a provision of an enactment he is signing. If so, then a signing statement that challenges what the President determines to be an unconstitutional encroachment on his power, or that announces the President's unwillingness to enforce (or willingness to litigate) such a provision, can be a valid and reasonable exercise of Presidential authority.

But then Dellinger added:

> We recognize that these issues are difficult ones. When the President's obligation to act in accord with the Constitution appears to be in tension with his duty to execute laws enacted by Congress, questions are raised that go to the heart of our constitutional structure. In these circumstances, a President should proceed with caution and with respect for the obligation that each of the branches shares for the maintenance of constitutional government.

In August 2006 an eleven-member task force of the American Bar Association produced a thirty-four-page report about presidential signing statements and the separation of powers doctrine and drafted a resolution that was later adopted by the ABA House of Delegates. The resolution opposed signing statements that claim a presidential authority to decline to enforce a law the president has signed; urged the president to tell Congress ahead of time if a pending bill contains a provision the president believes is unconstitutional; urged the president, if he believes a part of a bill is unconstitutional, to veto the whole bill; urged Congress to pass legislation making it a requirement that when a president signs a bill but claims the authority to decline to enforce any part of it, he must send Congress a report setting forth his reasons, and urged Congress to pass legislation enabling the president, or Congress, or "other entities" to seek judicial review in any instance where the president claims the authority to decline to enforce a law he has signed.

White House counsel Fred Fielding, to whose desk all proposed signing statements come for review, has read the ABA report and the resolution and has discussed it with the president and the staff. The White House does not intend to discontinue the issuance of presidential signing statements, but Fielding said the view is that some of the statements issued early in the Bush administration were "treatises"—overly technical and overly preachy. "We're not adopting a rule of none," Fielding stated, but added: "You really don't have to issue a signing statement, because the President can't amend the Constitution, but sometimes there is a virtue in advising the Congress and the public of the president's views."[22]

"Defending the Country" vs. Obeying the Laws

In his confirmation hearing on October 19, 2007, prospective attorney general Michael Mukasey was asked "if the president was free to violate a law enacted by Congress." His answer: "That would depend on whether what goes outside the statute nonetheless lies within the authority of the president to defend the country."[23] Yale constitutional law professor Jed Rubenfeld commented:

> It is true that a president may in rare cases disregard a federal statute—but only when Congress has acted outside its authority by passing a statute that is unconstitutional. (Who gets the last word on whether a statute is unconstitutional is something Americans have long debated and probably will always debate.) But what Judge Mukasey . . . said, and what many members of the current administration have claimed, would radically transform this accepted point of law into a completely different and un-American concept of executive power.
>
> According to Judge Mukasey's statement . . . the president's authority to "defend the nation" trumps his obligation to obey the law. . . . The president has no supreme, exclusive or trumping authority to "defend the nation."[24]

A day later, the *New York Times* quoted a statement by another player in the nation's dialogue about executive power: "Senator Hillary Clinton said Tuesday that the Bush-Cheney administration had engaged in a 'power grab' and that she would consider relinquishing some of that executive power if she followed it into the White House. . . . Asked whether a president could 'actually give up some of this power in the name of constitutional principle,' Mrs. Clinton answered, 'Absolutely.'"[25]

The Emergency Book

It was March 30, 1981. President Reagan had been shot and Press Secretary Larry Speakes was answering questions in the briefing room. Asked "who was running the government right now?" Speakes admitted, "I cannot answer that question at this time."[26] At this point, Secretary of State Alexander Haig, "out of breath and struggling to control his emotions," took the press secretary's place at the podium.[27] The question came again: "Who is making decisions for the government right now?" Haig announced to the press and to the country:

> Constitutionally, gentlemen, you have the President, the Vice President and [here Haig makes an embarrassing error] the Secretary of State, in that order, and should the President decide he wants to transfer the helm, he will do so. He has not done that. As of now, I am in control here, in the White House, pending the return of the Vice President [George H. W. Bush] and [I am] in close touch with him. If something came up, I would check with him, of course.[28]

Fred Fielding, then Reagan's presidential counsel, later stated:

To be very frank with you, that day, when I mentioned the Twenty-fifth Amendment I could see eyes glazing over in some parts of the Cabinet. They didn't even know about the Twenty-fifth Amendment.... One of the things that I had my staff working on was a book, basically an emergency book. What do you do about X, Y, Z, events concerning the president's health? . . . The book is now finished, Whenever I would travel with the president there are two copies. I would always carry a copy with me of the book. There was always one back in my office in the safe. The book basically is every situation you can imagine that has occurred to the president or the vice president: it is, for that matter, scenarios.[29]

When George H. W. Bush became president himself, Fielding's successor, C. Boyden Gray, continued to develop the emergency book. It is described as a "very comprehensive road map" that goes through "every significant hypothetical from a president being killed to having a hernia operation." It offers step-by-step guides on who should be called, by whom, in what order; who should take over what duties; at what point power should be passed temporarily to the vice president; and which procedures to follow to do all that needs to be done. Copies of it are placed in the safes of the White House chief of staff, the White House physician, the White House counsel, the vice presidential chief of staff, the head of the Secret Service, and a few others.[30]

To Fred Fielding's and Boyden Gray's everlasting credit (and Fielding at this writing is again the counsel to the president), that book still exists (it is in loose-leaf form and is updated as needed) and may be the only important, highly confidential, substantive document in the White House that has been and will be passed on from president to president. Sitting in the book, written out but undated and unsigned, are the two letters prescribed by section 3 of the Twenty-fifth Amendment. The first notifies the president pro tempore of the Senate and the Speaker of the House of Representatives that the president is "unable to discharge the powers and duties of his office"; the second notifies those two officers that the president is again able to carry out his duties.

At the very beginning, President Reagan and his staff did not invoke the Twenty-fifth Amendment; they feared its use would send one or both of two messages to the public: that the president's disability was portentously severe or that the vice president was being overly ambitious. Now that the Twenty-fifth Amendment procedure has been invoked several times (twice by George W. Bush) for routine medical procedures (a colonoscopy, for instance), the stigma of using it has just about disappeared. Let us hope that the cover-ups practiced by Grover Cleveland, Woodrow Wilson, and Franklin Roosevelt are behind us. The institution still sadly lacking a schema of emergency preparedness is

Congress, as evidenced by scholars Norman Ornstein and Thomas Mann in their book *The Broken Branch*.[31]

Guardianship of Executive Privilege

The three branches of government are in constant competition with each other for information. The president needs information to govern; Congress needs it to legislate; the courts need it for evidence in trials. Frequently the information desired by one branch has been developed in the process of subordinates in one of the other branches providing advice to their superiors—advice that would not be candid advice if it were made public. Said the Supreme Court in its famous 1974 decision, *U.S. v Nixon*:

> A President and those who assist him must be free to explore alternatives in the process of shaping policies and making decisions and to do so in a way many would be unwilling to express except privately. These are the considerations justifying a presumptive privilege for Presidential communications. The privilege is fundamental to the operation of government and inextricably rooted in the separation of powers under the Constitution.[32]

Eisenhower was the first president to use the phrase executive privilege; both Kennedy and Johnson stipulated that the privilege could be invoked only by the president; the Court of Appeals for the District of Columbia in 1997 extended executive privilege to "predecisional documents" prepared by presidential advisers even if they had not yet reached the president.

Whenever Congress is in the hands of the opposing party from the president, as in President Clinton's and President Bush's second terms, the White House can expect an especially frequent and onerous rash of demands to disclose the substance of advice and decisionmaking involving the chief executive; the motives may be political as much as (or perhaps more than) governmental.

When congressional requests are met with negative responses, the requesting committee may put them in the form of subpoenas. Negotiations are likely to ensue, and often compromises are worked out, but if not, the Senate or House committee has the option of voting to cite the affected cabinet or White House staffers for contempt of Congress, while the president has the option of formally invoking executive privilege. Controversies that have progressed to this stage in years past have almost always led to a legislative-executive compromise, often with Congress being given most of what it requested.

A landmark case, however, is pending as this book goes to press. The House Judiciary Committee had subpoenaed former White House counsel Harriet Miers and current chief of staff Joshua Bolten to try to force them to testify and produce documents about the White House decisions, in 2007, to dismiss several U.S. Attorneys. President Bush invoked executive privilege against the subpoena, but Counsel Fred Fielding then offered a compromise: Miers and Bolten could go up to Capitol Hill for private interviews with Judiciary Committee members provided that their statements would not be under oath and that no transcripts would be made. The committee rejected this offer, and on February 14, 2008, the full House, by a count of 223 to 32, voted to cite Miers and Bolten for criminal contempt of Congress—an action taken only eight times earlier in history against executive branch officials and never before against White House aides. [33]

In the case of such citations, the U.S. Attorney for the District of Columbia is expected to bring the contempt charge to a grand jury—the defendants themselves being left with the option of invoking the right of habeas corpus. There has been only one instance where an executive branch officer was actually convicted and sentenced for contempt of Congress.[34] As presidential scholar Louis Fisher recently pointed out,

> The Office of Legal Counsel wrote an opinion on May 30, 1984, concluding that . . . a U.S. Attorney is not required to bring a congressional contempt citation to a grand jury when the citation is directed against an executive official who is carrying out the President's decisions to invoke executive privilege. The memo regarded the threat of criminal prosecution from a congressional contempt citation as an "unreasonable, unwarranted, and therefore intolerable burden" on the President's exercise of constitutional authority. . . .[35]

There is another option: Congress has the right, upheld by the Supreme Court in 1821, of "inherent contempt," which means not only holding people in contempt of Congress but also bypassing the judiciary and ordering its own sergeant at arms to arrest and imprison them—in the Capitol jail. It employed this tactic in a second instance in 1827, but has not repeated such a direct action during the past 180 years, nor is it being exercised now. [36]

With respect to the Miers and Bolten citations, Attorney General Mukasey refused to refer the House action to a grand jury, stating that disobeying the subpoena "did not constitute a crime."[37] Pronouncing that "we will not allow the administration to steamroll Congress," House Judiciary Committee chairman John Conyers has brought a suit before a Federal District Court judge to force production of the documents and testimony—an action that moves this executive-congressional controversy into the hands of the judicial branch. There is a prospect that this lawsuit could reach the highest judicial levels.

An illustration of the depth of conviction concerning the prerogatives of the presidency occurred in October 2005 when Miers was nominated by the president to be an associate justice of the Supreme Court. Members of the Senate Judiciary Committee told Miers that before they would vote to confirm her, they would demand documents or testimony from her about her work in the White House advising the president. Miers refused to accede to such a demand and withdrew as a nominee. Her letter to the president contained this wording:

> The strength and independence of our three branches of government are critical to the continued success of this great nation. . . . I have steadfastly maintained that the independence of the Executive Branch must be preserved and its confidential documents and information not be released to further a confirmation process. . . . Protection of the prerogatives of the Executive Branch and continued pursuit of my confirmation are in tension. I have decided that seeking my confirmation should yield.[38]

7 | *The Office of Legislative Affairs*

> Mr. Sherman said he considered the Executive magistracy as nothing more
> than an institution for carrying the will of the Legislature into effect, that the
> person or persons ought to be appointed by and accountable to the Legislature
> only, which was the depository of the supreme will of the Society.
>
> —James Madison

> I am not going to let Congress erode the power of the executive branch. . . .
> I have an obligation to make sure that the Presidency remains robust and the
> legislative branch doesn't end up running the executive branch.
>
> —George W. Bush

The late and respected Bryce Harlow, an assistant to Eisenhower, called the
White House Office of Legislative Affairs "an ambulatory bridge across a constitutional gulf." It has been thus since 1953.

While that gulf—between the executive and the legislature, between the
president and Congress—is bridgeable, it is nonetheless wide and deep. No
major new program a president-elect may promise, such as health care or
immigration reform, can come into being without Congress enacting authorizing statutes. No dollars may be spent by the president or anyone in the executive branch without a legislative appropriation. No cabinet or near-cabinet-level
officer may be appointed, and no federal judge may sit, without Senate confirmation. No treaty the president may have negotiated may take effect without
Senate ratification. In sum, the president and Congress must work together to
govern the country.

Parallel to the constitutional gulf between branches is another gulf between
the Capitol and the White House: between the two parties. An "ambulatory
bridge" needs to be built over this chasm too, especially in a period when Congress and the White House are in different party hands. "Working together"—
building those two parallel bridges—means establishing and using hosts of relationships, some involving the president and congressional leaders personally,
thousands more at the cabinet and White House staff level. For this category of
presidential issues, it is the responsibility of the White House legislative affairs

office to manage these sets of relationships. That unit has been continuously in the White House at least since the Truman administration; it was Eisenhower who strengthened it to become a top office in the White House staff structure.

What are the relationships of this office within the White House itself? There are two guiding rules: the office has exclusive jurisdiction, and legislative assistants are policy advisers.

The Rule of Exclusive Jurisdiction

As explained in the introduction, it is an absolute necessity that the individual, specialized offices of the White House operate under a rule of jurisdictional territoriality, that is, no one else invades their respective domains. No one outside the counsel's office makes legal commitments for the president. No one besides the scheduling office makes presidential calendar commitments. No one other than the presidential personnel office makes noncareer hiring promises. Perhaps nowhere else in the whole White House environment is this rule more difficult to apply and enforce than in the area of legislative affairs. A large percentage of senior White House people have close friends in Congress or on congressional staffs—bonds forged from years of professional or campaign collegiality. For the assistant to the president for legislative affairs to insist on exclusive control over White House–Capitol deal making seems selfish and pompous—and unenforceable. But enforce it she must, because violations of this rule, in any place in the White House, invite a creep-in of chaos. Of course offices in the White House must and do share information with each other, but primary responsibilities are territorial.

"It has to be absolutely clear that the messages to the Hill, and the Hill messages coming back in, come through us," declared former deputy legislative affairs assistant Matthew Kirk.[1] Explained the current assistant to the president for legislative affairs, Candida Wolff:

> Everyone in the White House believes he or she is a legislative affairs expert, and no one is—because they don't have the same level of experience. We try to lay down the law and they get caught because we have enough contacts on the Hill that we know when somebody hasn't told us what they're doing and they're freelancing.... You don't want mixed messages going to the Hill.... If I have a policy issue, I tend to bring a policy person with me.[2]

"If we had someone who was deciding to play in our sandbox on Capitol Hill," Kirk added, he would often "make sure that the Hill folks knew that that wasn't the message from the president."

Legislative Assistants Are Policy Advisers

Having set the jurisdictional framework, a White House legislative affairs assistant's next principle of operations is to ensure that her role goes far beyond Harlow's "bridge" metaphor: she is not merely a liaison; she is a policy officer and a key participant in White House decisionmaking. With the rank of assistant to the president, Wolff attends the daily senior staff meeting and sets the agenda for sessions of the Legislative Strategy Group, which includes White House policy assistants plus the responsible cabinet officers. "We influenced policy in that forum because we could say, 'This won't fly,'" Kirk explained, "and we would walk the president out of a proposal that doesn't have a chance of passing." Added Wolff: "If we can't win the vote, then we either prepare to lose the vote or we have to figure out how we're willing to compromise." She attends all policy-time meetings with the president, or those with other White House principal officers, that have a legislative component. Policy development for the State of the Union message, for example, begins the previous fall. "We spend a lot of time in November and December reaching out to members of Congress," Wolff explains. "What is it that is kind of the *issue du jour*?" She wants legislators to give her a sense of what priorities they are feeling from their contacts back home; these recommendations are then set together with the objectives the president wants to attain. The State of the Union message is a final, exquisitely crafted amalgam of policy priorities.

The Legislative Affairs Staff, Its Techniques, and Facilities

What tools, what resources does the White House legislative assistant rely on to carry out her responsibilities? In the Bush White House, the legislative affairs office numbers twenty-four; for space reasons they are divided between the West and East wings of the White House campus. Wolff has an "inside" deputy assistant, who is with her in the West Wing and who joins in meetings with the presidential policy seniors, and two East Wing deputy assistants (one each for the House and the Senate), who in turn have nine special assistants. The eleven East Wingers spend much of their time on Capitol Hill, which is a vastly changed place from Harlow's time in the 1950s. The 535 members of Congress do their work in 218 committees and subcommittees, and Hill staffers now number over 15,000. Each congressional office has specialists—the legislative assistant, the political assistant, the scheduler, the chief of staff—and the White House representative has to keep in touch with all of them while still trying to develop a relationship with the member. Meetings proliferate; Candida Wolff's deputies attend both the Senate and the House Republican whip meetings. Matthew Kirk remembers trying to divide his time between 7 a.m. meetings with Senator Charles Grassley on Medicare, daily White House legislative strategy meetings at 8:30, and daily 9 a.m. meetings on the Hill with the Republican House leadership.

On the Senate side, the vice president's offices in the Dirksen Building and in the Capitol are traditionally bases for those of the White House legislative affairs team who cover the Senate. (The author remembers sitting in the Dirksen office in 1970 typing out a suggested speech for a senator on an item soon to be on the Senate floor.) When the Republicans controlled the House during 2001–06, the majority leader made an office in the Capitol available to the White House legislative affairs team covering the House. This arrangement, however, ended in 2007, complicating the task of White House staffers in keeping up personal contacts with representatives.

When the need to round up votes becomes critical, a well-worn technique called "the hotfoot" is employed to energize constituents in a member's home district. The White House political or public liaison offices know exactly which advocacy groups, such as the Chamber of Commerce, the National Federation of Independent Businesses, or the Farm Bureau, have a presence in the district that can be activated to contact representatives or senators from their home bases. In April 2001 President Bush's tax cut was the pending Senate business and the White House badly wanted Republican senator James Jeffords's vote. "In an unusual move," the press reported, "White House Chief of Staff Andrew H. Card Jr. called a radio station and the Associated Press bureau in Vermont earlier this week to put in a pitch for the tax cut."[3]

But this technique has risks, as former deputy Kirk recalled:

> I believe that there are issues where this is useful, and issues where it backfires immensely. . . . The tax cut was a good example. . . . A certain Democratic senator claimed he didn't like having people ginned up in his state, but it helped every time, and no matter how much he yelled at Leg. Affairs, we knew it was a useful thing. It was something run from a Senate perspective, very cautiously used, and has a huge backfire potential that you have to be aware of. The senators are smart enough to know when something starts happening, who's doing it. Your word is everything in Leg. Affairs and if the senator looks at you and asks if you're messing around in his state, you'd better give him a straight answer.

Effective persuasion means handling opponents as well as supporters; vigorous differences on today's issue can become teamwork on a different issue tomorrow; one never lets argumentation turn into permanent hostility. "There's no utility," Kirk warned, "from having either a senior person in the White House and/or the president try and dress down a senator, because you're not going to change his mind, and you are going to create an enemy. In the Senate they have long memories and they know they are going to be there long after this White House is gone."

Patronage as Leverage?

Is patronage a useful tool in the great game of eliciting votes? The two White House seniors whom the author interviewed had differing answers. Kirk recounted:

> We would have a matrix of each senator—what position they called about, who they were advocating for, how many times they advocated. We had a system to determine whether their advocating was because they had been asked to, or whether they cared. . . . We wanted to know very clearly, "Does this matter to the senator or is he just sending a letter only because he wants to show the constituent he cares about it?" We ranked that system. We would know by virtue of how they asked us, whether or not it mattered, and if there was a gray area I would follow up and say, "I am just checking on this one to see the level of importance." . . . We got requests all the time. I worked as closely with the presidential personnel office as I did with any other office in the White House. . . . This part of my job, in my view, was *as,* or *more* important than anything else. If you didn't respond to their personnel requests and handle them properly, you had an enemy for a long time. That is as important as anything we did in Leg. Affairs.

Asked if patronage was a helpful resource, Candida Wolff put it this way:

> No, not as much any more; it may have been historically. What's probably more important—it's not that you pass something; it's whether members are agreeable. If it's a matter of "You didn't let me have five people, so I don't even want to help you"—that just translates into the negative. It doesn't translate into the positive. Just because you got somebody in doesn't necessarily translate into a vote for you.

Congressional Mail

Since all postal mail to the White House is delayed because it is first run through an out-of-the-neighborhood security screening, most post-9/11 correspondence is in the form of e-mail. All congressional mail to the president flows into a unit in the legislative affairs office, known as the Legislative Correspondence Office, where each piece is put into a computerized tracking system. A judgment is made about who should respond; cabinet members or agency heads are asked to reply to regular congressional correspondence. Inquiries from majority or minority leaders are usually answered, often via telephone, by the chief of staff or one of the other White House principals. With almost no exceptions, President Bush does not sign letters to senators or representatives. He does receive, every Friday, a report on all the congressional correspondence with a brief summary of each letter.

Support from the Cabinet Departments

A vital multiplier of the White House legislative affairs director's capabilities is her network of assistants, generally at the assistant secretary level, one in every executive department and agency, all men and women selected by the White House legislative affairs director after personal interviews. This circle of associates, positioned to respond with alacrity to Wolff's queries, is de facto a part of her White House team, extending her heft throughout the executive branch. They are informally constituted into subject-matter specialists—a national security group, a Commerce-Treasury-financial group, and others similarly organized. Besides the countless hour-to-hour contacts with the White House, these associates participate with Wolff in a conference call every week, and they all meet together once a month.

"They were as much a part of our team as anyone," explained Kirk. "The relationships with them were as important as our formal meetings. . . . It was invaluable because they would let you know if the cabinet member himself was getting a little bit out of line and needed to be reined in."

Cabinet members themselves are a positive resource for the White House legislative affairs assistant. "We ask cabinet officials to make calls and outreach," said Wolff. "I'll call the cabinet secretaries directly and say, 'Here's a key agenda item and here's our strategy and here's what we need you to do.' They give us feedback from those contacts; then we used that information to determine the best moves to make."

Kirk recalled an example from January 2004, when an omnibus appropriations bill was left pending from the year before with several hot-button issues in it, one of them being a provision authorizing a two-year voucher experiment for schools in the District of Columbia that the president wanted kept in the bill. The outcome would be close. Kirk counted the likely Republican votes in the Senate, then figured out how many Democratic votes were going to be needed to reach the magic total of sixty. Because the bill was an omnibus measure, many of the cabinet departments were affected by its provisions. Kirk's office identified which departments had what interests, knew which department heads had good relationships with Democratic appropriators, mobilized the right cabinet secretaries to call the right senators, and produced sixty-one votes.

The Vice President

The vice president is of course a player on the legislative ball field. During President Bush's first term, when senators were split 50-50, Vice President Cheney had to be available on the Hill to cast tie-breaking votes. Having been a representative, secretary of defense, and White House chief of staff, Cheney brought unique expertise to the many meetings he attended, which included Republican caucus meetings and the Tuesday Republican policy luncheons. In addition to his regular office in the Dirksen Building, the vice president has a ceremonial office adjoining the Senate floor, which is especially convenient for holding ad hoc meetings of senators and White House staff in the midst of legislative sessions. Cheney has been particularly active in issues of priority interest to him: energy, national security matters, intelligence questions. He has his own legislative affairs staff of about five persons, one of whom was Candida Wolff herself before she graduated to that same position for the president.

The Presidential Spouse

Another focus of assistance on legislative affairs is the president's spouse. Laura Bush in effect has had assignments—"First Lady initiatives"—such as the No Child Left Behind education program and helping with the problems of youth gangs. "We are doing a lot of outreach with her," remarked Candida Wolff,

> meaning that she's personally spending more time with members of Congress than before. Earlier, she was doing more speeches, going into states and doing events. The members would travel with her. Then she would see members while she was in the districts. She was also doing a lot more with fundraisers. Now we're actually having her meet on issues in her office with members. That is new.

The President

Finally, of course the White House's chief legislative persuader is the president himself. Wolff sponsors two to three congressional meetings with him each week, with the Republican leadership, with the Democratic leadership, some bicameral, some bipartisan. "We talk about what the legislative agenda is," explained Wolff. "The president weighs in on what his priorities are and there is a chance to have a dialogue. We bring Democratic members in to talk about trade or other issues that we think we can get support on. . . . I do a lot of meetings in the Yellow Oval Room in the Residence."

The legislative affairs office has its antennae tuned to the importance of time with the president as it relates to achieving legislative results. "It would be rare," Kirk explained, "that a member would reach out and ask for time with the president, on an issue that mattered, that we weren't already preparing some sort of an interaction with that office." Every meeting with the president, of course, requires a briefing memo. "I'll go in ten minutes at the front of the meeting," Wolff said, " to explain who's coming in, here's why, this is what we want to talk about, and to make sure he's focused. He has the briefing memo the night before, but throughout the day he's not necessarily looking at the next event, so I go in and make sure he knows."

The president still goes up to Capitol Hill—to participate in conferences—but that happens rarely; security requirements make those arrangements much more complicated. President Bush did bend precedent by joining the Democratic leaders at their annual "issues retreat" near Williamsburg in February 2007 (right after the Democrats took control of both chambers). According to a press report,

> For nearly two hours, Mr. Bush held forth with some of the very Democrats he has spent the better part of six years sparring with. He spoke to members of Congress and their spouses, took pointed questions in a private session about Iraq, the budget deficit and immigration, and shook hands and posed for pictures. "I'm looking forward to working with you," Mr. Bush said, gesturing to those seated in the crowded ballroom. "I know you've probably heard that and you doubt whether it's true—but it's true. We're going to do big things together.[4]

In her stable of resources for approaching legislators, Wolff values a variant that she calls soft outreach. "I don't necessarily want to bring people down and demand that I need something from them," she reflected. In addition to the traditional Congressional Ball and the Congressional Picnic, Wolff sponsors presidential social events approximately once a month with bipartisan groups of legislators and staffers. "I look for more social events and venues for the president to interact—we have been able to open up the Residence . . . the Truman balcony . . . a chance to see the personal study, the Lincoln bedroom. . . ."

Every few months, Wolff sponsors a "congressional hour" with the president; representatives or senators bring in constituents who have unusual—and press-worthy—requests. After 9/11 one group brought in an enormous prayer quilt, "big enough to cover my office," she remembered. The legislative assistant makes introductions; the presentation is made; a photo is taken. "I can get five or six people through in an hour," she smiled.

Perquisites

Other traditional perquisites are not overlooked: Wolff is allotted invitation rights for members of Congress to attend formal White House dinners. Members are invited to use the presidential box at the Kennedy Center, but this turns out to be a rare occurrence because members' evening schedules are so overbooked; they have difficulty finding the time (as do the White House staffers who would join them). Representatives and senators are invited to ride along on *Air Force One* when the president is visiting the member's district or the state. "That time on *Air Force One* was very important," Kirk said, "because it is quality time with the president." If a legislator was on *Air Force One,* a legislative affairs assistant was on the plane too.

With the Democrats having taken control of Congress in 2007, a *Washington Post* reporter observed that "Bush has also been on something of a charm offensive," inviting Democrat Charles Rangel, chairman of the House Ways and Means Committee, "to ride on *Air Force One* when the president visited a charter school in Harlem. . . . Bush and Rangel seemed to get along famously, with Rangel giving the president a block-by-block account of Harlem's history as they rode through his district."[5]

What had been, before 9/11, a generalized opportunity for the public now has become a more limited perquisite, managed by legislators' offices. As is explained in chapter 33, the process for arranging White House tours changed drastically after 9/11; now members of the public must make their tour requests in advance through their senators or representative—somewhat of a burden for the congressional offices.

It was the legislative office's objective to spread these various perquisites around, "to make sure we weren't missing people," said Kirk, "that enough members had been given the chance."

Does the legislative affairs office keep score—matching the dispensation of perks with the helpfulness of the supporters—and the opposite? "I won't say I've kept score in the literal sense," explained Wolff, "but if we're having a reception coming up and we've had a tough vote, we'll thank those who supported us on the vote." And nothing is recorded. "These days everything is subject to subpoena; you don't write a lot down," she averred.

What Is New: The Changed Communications Environment

A profound difference has been caused by technology: the BlackBerry has changed the way the legislative affairs office operates. In earlier years, a secretary would hand the White House officer a slip saying that the staffer should return so-and-so's call. Now this gadget is recording and displaying for its owner perhaps two hundred e-mails every day. "Each e-mail that's sent comes over this," moaned Kirk,

> so a chief of staff, a senator—Senator Frist loved using his BlackBerry—they're sending you a note saying, "What are you guys doing about this?" and if you don't respond to that, by definition you're neglecting your people. The amount of work coming in to Leg. Affairs by virtue of these communications devices has changed a hundredfold. . . . Leg. Affairs, in order to be responsive to the Hill and to clients in the West Wing—every one of whom is e-mailing you all day long—*has to have a management system that is very disciplined* to make sure things don't slip through the cracks. There's no excuse for not responding—you can't say, "I'm sorry, I was on the Hill all day and didn't get your e-mail." There's no hiding. (Italics added)

Changes When Control of Congress Switches

Much about the way the legislative affairs office has worked in the Bush White House has been determined by which party controlled Congress. Before 2007

House Speaker Dennis Hastert and the Republican leadership vowed not to send any piece of legislation to the president that needed a veto; the veto was in effect taken out of his toolbox. Kirk pointed out that if the president did not have the veto at the back end, he "was burdened with a much deeper level of negotiation with the Hill at the front end." He had to work differences out with the congressional leadership without being able to use the veto as a threat; that required greater skill and sophistication on the part of his legislative bargainers.

Those skills, and the thoroughgoing efforts of the legislative affairs staff, paid off. In a research paper written in 2005, political scientist Andrew Rudalevige reported that the Bush White House won 80 percent of all roll-call votes during the president's first term—"more successful than any president since the heady Great Society days of the mid-1960's. . . . The average Republican House member voted with the president, on roll-call votes on which the president took a position, almost 85 percent of the time. . . . In the Senate the spread was somewhat less, but GOP loyalty topped an astonishing 90 percent on average, and 94 percent in both 2001 and 2003."[6]

Before 2007 congressional oversight of administration policies and operations was minimal. Committee chairmanships were all in Republican hands, with the result that aggressive questioning, probing investigations, and Hill subpoenas were practically nonexistent—in matters of foreign policy or domestic actions, or for intelligence issues.

But in January 2007 the lid came off. Aggressive commanding leaders Donald Rumsfeld, Paul Wolfowitz, and George Tenet were gone; national security adviser Rice left the White House for the State Department. General David Petraeus and Ambassador Ryan Crocker were flown in from Iraq in 2007 and again in 2008 to be grilled for hours by the Senate and House Armed Services committees. Accusations were hurled at the Department of Justice that some U.S. Attorneys had been fired for partisan political reasons and that the department's leaders were improperly asking political questions of career appointees; Attorney General Alberto R. Gonzales was forced from office. White House deputy chief of staff Karl Rove and his principal deputy resigned amid charges that they were involved with the U.S. Attorneys brouhaha; the Rove deputy sweated through an angry House hearing to avoid testifying about her communications with the president. The House of Representatives demanded sworn testimony and documents from former White House counsel Harriet Miers and White House chief of staff Joshua Bolten concerning the accusations about the Department of Justice. When the president invoked executive privilege to refuse to accede to the House's request, the full House voted to cite both Miers and Bolten for contempt of Congress. The House Committee on Oversight and Government Reform charged the White House with misusing and losing thousands of e-mails, then took on the vice president for evading an executive order designed to systematize the government's procedure for protecting classified information.

New talent was brought into the White House in the communications and external affairs areas, and an exceptionally experienced and respected White House veteran, Fred Fielding, was appointed counsel to the president to use his talents to make some headway in the 100 percent altered White House–congressional relationship. Fielding had his work cut out for him: that "ambulatory bridge" was studded with spikes and stink bombs.

8

Control All the Way Down: The Presidential Personnel Office

Congress and the President should work together to significantly reduce the number of executive branch political positions . . . a reduction of at least one-third is an appropriate first target.

—The 2003 National Commission on the Public Service

I disagree with the Volcker Commission recommendation. There are only about 2,500 full-time "political" positions . . . out of a total civilian workforce of 1.9 million. I do believe, however, that the Senate should be more open to having nonpolicy PAS [presidential appointees] not confirmed by the Senate, and/or ways to get the PAS confirmed faster.

—Clay Johnson

Second to none in importance and priority at the White House is the selection of the men and women whom the president wishes to employ in policymaking positions in the administration. These jobs, clearly differentiated from the positions in the career civil services, are noncareer positions, meaning they are filled by taking political factors into account, as well as considerations of merit, and that the holders serve at the pleasure of the president. How many are there?

The Noncareer Universe

There are four categories of noncareer positions—and the White House controls all selections to all of them.

1. Full-time positions, almost all established by statute, that are filled by personal presidential appointment:
   a. Presidential appointees requiring Senate confirmation (PAS)   1,177
      This subcategory includes 189 ambassadors, 94 district attorneys, 94 U.S. marshals, 15 in international organizations, and 4 in the legislative branch.
   b. Presidential appointees not requiring Senate confirmation (PA)   21
   c. Federal judges to be appointed   400
      The typical number of vacancies that need to be filled in a single presidential term, out of a total of 871 Article III and

112 non-Article III federal judges. All require Senate confirmation and most have lifetime tenure. The actual number during the first seven years of the Bush administration is 402.[1]

2. Full-time, nonpresidential, noncareer positions
   All of these appointments are approved by the White House Presidential Personnel Office.
   a. Noncareer positions in the Senior Executive Service (SES) (see accompanying box)   796
   b. Schedule C positions (see accompanying box)   1,428
3. Part-time presidential appointee positions, established in statute
   These are members of advisory boards and commissions.
   a. PAS (requiring Senate confirmation)   579
   b. PA (not requiring Senate confirmation)   2,509
   Subtotal: Categories 1, 2, and 3—the total noncareer universe of concern to the Office of Presidential Personnel   *6,910*
4. White House staff positions
   All serve at the pleasure of the president, and without Senate confirmation. The Office of Presidential Personnel does not handle White House staff appointments.
   a. Receiving formal, signed commissions from the president (assistants, deputy assistants, and special assistants to the president)   154
   b. Appointed with presidential approval (their appointments handled by the deputy chief of staff for operations on recommendations from the several assistants to the president who head the respective White House elements)   790
      This subcategory includes the White House Office plus the staffs of the vice president, the National Security, Homeland Security, National Economic, and Domestic Policy Councils, the Executive Residence, the Commission on White House Fellows, the leadership of the White House Military Office, and the staff of the Residence. It excludes employees with tenure, such as civilian and military detailees, the Secret Service, the support staffs of the Office of Administration, the General Services Administration, the Postal Service, the National Park Service, the National Archives and Records Administration, and unpaid interns and volunteers.
   Subtotal: Category 4   *944*

The total noncareer universe of positions filled by the White House.[2]   7,854

On the subject of numbers, not one but two National Commissions on the Public Service, one in 1989 and the second in 2003 (both chaired by Paul Volcker), recommended that the total full-time presidentially appointed positions, Sched-

Some Facts about Noncareer Positions

The PAS and PA positions, some federal judgeships, and the memberships on part-time advisory boards and commissions are created in statute. (Ambassadorships and most judgeships are authorized not in statute but in the Constitution itself.) The number of statutory posts can be increased or decreased only by congressional action. The president personally approves each of these appointments.

Schedule C positions are established by departments and agencies, but each such post must first be certified by the director of the Office of Personnel Management (OPM) as being "policymaking" or "confidential." Once a Schedule C job is thus authorized, the department or agency head may appoint a person to the post, but only if that person is also approved by the director of the White House Office of Presidential Personnel (OPP).

The Senior Executive Service (SES) is the corps of professional federal managers just below the level of assistant secretary. By law, only 10 percent of the positions in the SES may be filled on a noncareer basis. A department or agency head may propose a political candidate to be appointed to such a position, but the appointment must be cleared with the OPP director. Once White House approval has been signaled, the OPM grants "noncareer appointing authority" to the agency for the placement.

Both Schedule C and noncareer SES appointees are employees of the agencies in which they work, and their service is at the pleasure of the respective agency heads. The White House OPP tightly controls these appointments, sometimes pushing agencies to hire certain favored political candidates or vetoing an agency's own choices.

ule C, and noncareer SES be reduced to 2,000 from what was then approximately 3,000. Said the 1989 commission: "The operative question is not whether the current number of appointees is large or small, in absolute terms or compared to the total number of civilian employees. The real question is whether the proliferation has in fact made government more effective and responsive to presidential leadership. The Commission concludes that the answer is 'no.'"[3] Neither of the two commissions' recommendations on this matter were accepted by the administration in office, nor did Congress ever enact any implementing legislation.

The Presidential Personnel Function: Getting It Started

Candidates Ronald Reagan and George W. Bush did it right: Ronald Reagan, for example, in the fall of 1979, a year before the election, assigned E. Pendleton James to draw up a plan for identifying executive branch leadership for a possible Reagan presidency. James knew Reagan's associates well, was a professional in

the executive search business, and had served on the staff of the presidential personnel office of Richard Nixon. Bush emulated this practice: simultaneously
with his decision to run for the presidency, in June 1999, he turned to his own
gubernatorial appointments director in Austin (and friend from college years),
Clay Johnson III, to "develop a plan for what we should do after we win."

Johnson spent months digging into every book and research paper he could
find about past presidential transitions, then meeting with former cabinet secretaries James Baker, George Shultz, and Ed Meese, who had been through it all
before. From that study and from those conversations, Johnson drew several
firm conclusions about transitions generally and about presidential personnel
operations specifically:

> Campaign leaders should not be in charge of the transition. Campaigns
> are about winning while transitions are about preparing to govern. Cam-
> paign leaders are unlikely to have any time to work on the transition
> before the election, as is necessary. Also, transition leadership cannot be
> working long hours to set up a new administration if they are also recov-
> ering from the election ordeal.[4]

Johnson's advice particularly pertains to the candidate's associate who is to
be in charge of the presidential personnel process. Campaigners are ipso facto
hungry for jobs in the new administration and are thus not in a position to
make disinterested evaluations about who are and who are not qualified to be
appointed to top positions. The personnel chief must furthermore be designated early, must carry that assignment exclusively with no competitors, and
should retain that one responsibility straight through the pre- and postelection
periods. Pen James for Reagan and Clay Johnson for Bush were ideal models for
this precept.

Candidate and president-elect Jimmy Carter, in 1976, failed these tests, opening up unfortunate rivalries that wasted time and energy as the president took
office. A month after Carter's nomination, Jack Watson set up a transition planning team staff in Atlanta. Newspaper stories appeared about them; they became
publicly identified as "talent scouts"—with the result that thousands of letters
flooded in. They worked during the fall putting together a "talent inventory program" (TIP) and actually assembled lists of candidates. After the election, however, Hamilton Jordan and his own campaign staff—a different bunch with different priorities for personnel—moved in and decided they had to redo the TIP.
After the inauguration still a different person, James E. King, was appointed
director of the White House presidential personnel office.[5]

A further prescription from Clay Johnson concerned the order of selection:
the president-elect should place the highest priority on picking the new White
House staff at the same time as or even before selecting the cabinet.

An administration needs to identify the cabinet secretaries by mid-December so they can be prepared for confirmation hearings prior to Inauguration day, but it is every bit as important to select senior White House staff by this time. Cabinet officers can only receive clear direction from the White House if there are senior staff members in place to do so. . . . If the senior staff is not in place when the president is inaugurated, the value of his time and voice during the most critical "launch phase" of the administration is likely not to be maximized.[6]

The value of following Johnson's selection priority is that it permits the senior White House staff officers themselves to participate in the selection of the men and women who will be heading the departments and agencies, making it all the more probable that the relationships between the White House staff and the cabinet members will be smooth and cooperative rather than the unfortunate opposite.

Among the transition goals Johnson laid out was having "in place by inauguration day" a presidential personnel office "capable of identifying, clearing, and nominating 165 or more people by April 30." To meet that objective, the Bush team instituted a significant innovation in handling what it knew would be a flood of applications from job seekers: all résumés and applications had to be sent via the Internet, electronically instead of through the mail by the bushel. In August, three months before the election, the team set up a website and developed the software. As soon as the election had been decided, the Bush personnel team sent letters and e-mails to "donors, supporters, congressmen, senators, governors, and mayors" explaining that this new electronic system was the way to apply for or to recommend a person for an appointment. The website, which also answered commonly asked questions, was turned on. Some 90,000 applications arrived within a few weeks. Even with the truncated transition period (caused by the dispute over ballots in Florida) and the move from temporary and privately financed transition space to the government-supplied offices, "we were," in Johnson's words, "effectively managing the incoming flow of advice, requests, and job seeking from the beginning."

Identifying the Positions to Be Filled

To the Bush personnel team, the first question was not who, but what. Names came later; the more important query, Johnson said, was: "What do we want the person in this job to accomplish in the next two, three, or four years that we will be here? Given the president's priorities, what do we want this administration—this person—to accomplish?" The next preliminary question would be: "What kind of person do we think is best able to accomplish these goals, in general and in light of who else is on the team?" If a cabinet secretary was a strong policy person but new to the city, the presidential personnel office would look for a deputy secretary who was well acquainted with the decisionmaking processes of Washington, and vice versa.

"Of course politics has to be looked at, but you should look at that last," Johnson pointed out. "If you start with the political determination, it will be entirely about patronage, and not about substance." Will those who have labored in the campaign insist that their efforts be rewarded with a job in the new administration? They will, but Johnson's advice to future personnel directors is to focus on helping the president assemble the team that can help the administration be successful, not just on rewarding those who helped the president get elected. The White House Office of Political Affairs will and should be involved in the personnel selection process, and there will be tension between the political affairs office and the personnel office, but there is supposed to be. The key is for the two offices to respect each other's mission and find a good balance between competency and political perspectives.

Two publications are designed to help with recruitment. One is the *Policy and Supporting Positions* catalogue, commonly referred to as the *Plum Book*. It is published every four years just before the presidential elections; publication alternates between the House and the Senate Government Affairs Committees. The *Plum Book* covers all executive branch and legislative branch departments and agencies, identifies by title all positions GS-14 and above that "may be subject to noncompetitive appointment," shows the pay level of each and whether the appointment has a fixed term and if so its expiration, and then lists the name of each incumbent and the type of appointment he or she is holding (PAS, PA, and so forth). (If a career person happens to be holding one of those positions, he or she is identified as such.) This catalogue, however, comes out rather late in the process, and makes no mention of the duties or responsibilities of any of the positions listed; it is thus of limited usefulness to the presidential recruiter who is trying to match the substantive requirements of the job to the qualifications of an applicant or of a potential nominee.

To help meet the inadequacies of the *Plum Book*, the Council for Excellence in Government publishes the *Prune Book* (prunes being considered mature plums). Five have been printed to date covering 250 senior-level positions in the executive branch. A full paragraph states the experience, training, and skills considered necessary for each position and is followed by several pages, called Insight, laying out the statutory and executive responsibilities accompanying the position, the kinds of issues that have to be dealt with, and relationships to be managed. Candid quotations are included from previous occupants of the position, giving the reader a down-to-earth picture of what the job involves.

The process of identifying positions, therefore, can be—must be—done before the election. "I began," Johnson recalled, "in the spring of 2000 by putting together a list of what most considered the key jobs. I talked to enough people to get a sense of what kinds of people you are looking for and began do some networking around to get a list of people to start talking about. We didn't talk to any of them, but you have to begin that assemblage of names six months in advance. . . . You shouldn't start with a blank slate on election day!"

One preelectoral tactic employed to make the job of the transition leaders more doable was put into practice by the (then-named) Bureau of the Budget during the presidential campaign of 1960. Because the new president was required to produce a detailed budget proposal for the entire federal government within weeks of entering the White House, officers in the bureau gathered the candidates' press releases and scoured news reports to compile two parallel catalogues—the "Jacklopedia" and the "Dicklopedia." Each separately set forth all the public campaign promises Kennedy and Nixon were making. Immediately after the election, the deputy director of the bureau was able to present the Jacklopedia to the incoming Kennedy team and also to a group of career professionals who would be working on the proposed budget. This specific experiment has never been repeated (unfortunately, in the author's opinion). In 2001 the incoming Bush team of course worked with the Office of Management and Budget to draw up the revised budget that would reflect the new president's priorities.

In August 2000 Governor Bush chose Dick Cheney to head the transition team; in October Bush made the decision to have Andrew H. Card Jr. be his chief of staff. Vice President Al Gore did not concede the election until December 13; Card used those extra weeks to identify White House staff prospects, which meant that senior staffers could participate with Clay Johnson in identifying candidates for the cabinet posts. No actual contacts were made with potential cabinet members until after Gore's concession. Johnson's personnel staff numbered 45. In 2005 the presidential personnel office staff numbered 35; there were some 100,000 names of job applicants in the database.

Making and Clearing the Choices

As soon as Gore conceded, Bush named his key White House staffers (who began meeting as a group), and Johnson, Card, and Vice President–elect Cheney began bringing prospective cabinet secretaries to the president-elect for a decision. Each finalist was instructed to sit down with former Reagan counsel Fred Fielding to iron out any potential conflict-of-interest or security clearance issues. A "shepherd," assigned to each secretary-designate as soon as the nomination was announced, would introduce the nominee to the right senators, aid in compiling the confirmation paperwork, and prepare the candidates for their hearings.

A presidential personnel staffer also met with each secretary-designate to work out the process of choosing subcabinet officials in the respective departments. "We were going to do it *with* them, not *to* them," Johnson emphasized. Johnson said he told cabinet nominees that "we have to agree on who to recommend to the president" but "if we or you don't like them, we won't appoint them." If a cabinet secretary came in with his own list of prospective deputies, Johnson would be reassuring: "We would be glad to look at your people, and I would be shocked if some of these people aren't fantastic for the positions that you propose." But, Johnson explained, "we had to be comfortable that cabinet appointees would be implementing the president's priorities and policies, and not necessarily the secretary's."

In 1989 one cabinet secretary dug in his heels on this score. George H. W. Bush's personnel director, Chase Untermeyer, recalled that the secretary "was flabbergasted. He said, 'Do you mean to tell me that just because some people worked in a Bush campaign that I have to hire them in my department?' And the answer was: 'Had it not been for these people, and a lot of other people, George Bush would not have been elected president and you would not be the secretary of this department. That's the only way it can be!'"[7]

When the new president is of the same party as the departing one (as in the cases of Kennedy to Johnson, Nixon to Ford, Reagan to Bush), there is ambiguity and tension in this appointment process. Many veterans of the outgoing administration are still imbued with party (if not personal) loyalty, enjoy their work, represent valuable political as well as policy experience, and have settled into Washington—with friendships, mortgages, and children in school. They really don't relish being replaced. Chase Untermeyer ruefully reflected:

> The one thing I would clearly do differently was not to assume that cabinet secretaries were going to manage the firing of the Reagan Schedule Cs and the hiring of the Bush Schedule Cs in a kind and gentle way. I just assumed they would, and I assumed wrong.... Secretary [___]... who was appointed by Reagan and retained by Bush ... was basically waiting for the day when he could kick them all out. .... This happened in lots of the departments. .... The truest believers of Ronald Reagan ... were abused. They were not treated in a dignified and polite and sensitive way. ....That one area was dreadfully handled.

Upon the reelection of a sitting president, there was, at least among early twentieth century presidents, a tradition that the members of the cabinet would send in pro forma resignations, allowing the chief executive to accept one or two if he so desired without going through the embarrassing step of asking a secretary to resign. Eisenhower made this request in 1956; the author remembers Executive Clerk William Hopkins studiously collecting the set of resignation letters. In 1972 President Nixon took this practice to its extreme; he demanded that all noncareer appointees (except those serving fixed terms) send in resignations and that his White House staffers do the same (although the latter could accompany the resignation letters with a private message telling the president that their preference was to remain). This wholesale maneuver dismayed many long-term supporters; Nixon later wrote that it was "a mistake" because of its "chilling effect on the morale of people who had worked so hard during the election."[8] Presidents Reagan, Clinton, and George W. Bush did not make any such mass resignation requests upon starting their second terms; Clay Johnson termed the requests "unnecessary and disconcerting." The old tradition has apparently ceased.

Two very solid traditions have been reconfirmed, however, by the Bush administration. The first rule prohibits any office or person from making *any* personnel commitments without the advance consent of the director of the presidential personnel office. This rule applies even to the president-elect, who should never let himself be importuned to say yes to a candidate who approaches him personally. (Even a president can undermine his own system.) The second rule requires the presidential personnel office to approve all non-career appointments, including those in the Senior Executive Service and all the Schedule Cs, even though the formal appointing authority is technically in the hands of the department heads.

Preparing New Appointees to Take Over

During the 2000–2001 transition, the Bush personnel leaders eschewed the traditional practice of organizing "policy teams" of eighty to ninety people for each cabinet department, who spent most of their time assembling thick factual briefing books that turned out to be of little use to the incoming secretary. The Bush policy teams were made up of only four or five people, many from the Hill who had valuable expertise. What they looked for in each department or agency were issues approaching on the immediate horizon, important lawsuits pending, questions that needed to be acted on in the next sixty days. To accommodate a wider group of collaborators, "advisory groups" were organized as sources of support for the policy teams. As was to be expected, job seekers could be found among both sets of advisers.

Having arrived from Peoria or Pocatello, newly nominated or newly appointed senior-level men and women feel a tinge of apprehension amid their exuberance. What are they getting into? What is a "continuing resolution"? Will OMB Circular A-95 affect them? How can they fire "foot-dragging bureaucrats"? Will they ever see the president who hired them?

Assistant secretaries remain on the job an average of only twenty-two months. If their on-the-job training can be shortened, their effectiveness for the president increases. In the words of a memorandum by several fellows of the National Academy of Public Administration:

An incoming presidential administration brings in roughly 3,000 new political appointees after taking office. Many of them are extremely able people with impressive backgrounds. Typically they come to the nation's capital both mission-minded and in a hurry to make changes and to pursue new policy initiatives.

But few have any realization of what awaits them in Washington. Their new environment is very different from what they have seen in their prior careers in business or private professional life. Little in their experience has equipped newcomers to comprehend the complexity of government, the power of myriad special interest groups, and the level of increasingly intense scrutiny to which they will be subjected in both their public and private lives. The contemporary public policy and operational processes in government present to newcomers limitless chances for missteps and embarrassment.

Many incoming appointees also have been immersed only weeks before in campaigns which have been exceedingly negative about Washington, its people and its processes. They arrive, therefore, loath to listen to advice from either Washington career "bureaucrats" or former political appointees whom they either distrust as representing the other party, or believe have been captured by those entrenched denizens "inside the beltway."

Burdened by these perceptions, these new political executives, however capable and well-intentioned, are in danger of stumbling during the first crucial months of an administration—causing grief to themselves and to the president who called them here, thereby injuring the chief executive's hard-won political capital.[9]

Out of such concerns came, in October 1975, an added responsibility for the White House staff: President Gerald Ford's personnel office began an orientation program for senior political executives who were new to Washington. Groups of some thirty-six appointees were invited to the White House on three separate occasions. In the Family Theater, from Friday morning until mid-afternoon Saturday, they went to presidential appointee school.

Their "professors" included the White House chief of staff, the principal domestic policy assistant, the OMB director, and the chairman of the Civil Service Commission. The House minority leader told them "How the Congressional Leadership Looks at the Policy Executive," the president's counsel reminded them about standards of conduct, the press secretary described "Dealing with the Press." Each "student" was given a thick notebook with descriptions of the White House and Executive Office units with which he or she would be working. At 6 p.m. on Friday, the group joined President Ford in a reception in the Jacqueline Kennedy Garden. Later, within their respective departments, the appointees' preliminary education was completed with in-depth agency briefings.

The Carter White House gave little support to this program, and it faded away temporarily. The Reagan staff not only resumed the practice but also contracted with Harvard's John F. Kennedy School of Government to lead seminars based on case studies; larger conferences and briefings were hosted as well. President George H. W. Bush's personnel directors dropped the (expensive) Harvard sessions but regularly held day-long orientation conferences in the Old Executive Office Building. The Clinton White House had a three-tiered program: all-day sessions in the Old Executive Office Building for 100 or more new Schedule C appointees; similar seminars for 100 or more men and women of the Senior Executive Service (which were combined meetings of both career and noncareer officers); and larger confe ces for Senate-confirmed appointees that were managed under contract w e Center for Excellence in Government.

In 2000 a group of former public administrators associated with the National Academy of Public Administration persuaded Congress to regularize such briefings and to support them with pre-inaugural funding; Congress enacted the following amendment to the authorizing wording of the Presidential Transition Act of 1963:

> Payment of expenses during the transition for briefings, workshops, or other activities to acquaint key prospective Presidential appointees with the types of problems and challenges that most typically confront new political appointees when they make the transition from campaign and other prior activities to assuming the responsibility for governance after inauguration.
>
> Activities under this paragraph may include interchange between such appointees and individuals who—
>
> (I) held similar leadership roles in prior administrations;
>
> (II) are departmental or agency experts from the Office of Management and Budget or an Office of Inspector General of a department or agency; or
>
> (III) are relevant staff from the General Accounting Office. . . .
>
> Activities under this paragraph shall be conducted primarily for individuals the President-elect intends to nominate as department heads or appoint to key positions in the Executive Office of the President.[10]

Few if any pre-inaugural briefings of this nature were held in 2000–2001 because of the truncated inaugural period. Furthermore, Bush personnel chief Clay Johnson was, and is, skeptical of the Ford model of such briefings: "What would be a successful orientation?" he asked.

> Was it to teach them what to say and what not to say to the press? No. Is it how to deal with Congress? No, if you want to learn how to deal with Congress, go ask your legislative affairs person. If you want to learn how to deal

with the press, go ask your communications person, don't try to be a leg-islative or communications professional, or a lawyer or an ethics person. If you need teaching how to be an adult, we have picked the wrong person.

In Johnson's view, it was much more important to create and enhance team-work among the administration's new appointees: "The best thing to do to get the team oriented is . . . get them in sync with who else is on the team . . . and then give them a good, strong sense of who their leader is and what their leader expects of them. Then there should be updates about how the team is doing and what their expectations are."

The Bush White House personnel staff created a website, "Results.gov", which gave pictures and bios of all the appointees, updates on how agencies were per-forming, and videos of the annual "team meetings" the president held almost every year. (This continues as a public website, summarizing the objectives of the president's management improvement agenda and including a PowerPoint presentation of "best practices" that agencies should follow.) The first year these team meetings were held, 200 PAS appointees were invited; the second year, per-haps 500. In each of the last three years, 2,000 PAS officers and Senior Executive Service employees as well as 1,500 career civil servants joined the president at an enthusiastic session in Constitution Hall. "The message was that the president considered the assembled to be his team," explained Johnson. "The team is working great; the career folks are doing great—they are part of the team, too. And the focus needs to be on RESULTS. They loved it."

In the 2004 election year, the president told them, "You focus on your work; I'll take care of the politics." Then he gave them a virtual tour of the Oval Office and explained why it was decorated the way it was. "He helped everyone better understand what kind of person he was, why he wanted to be reminded every day of Lincoln and Washington and Churchill by means of the artwork of them in his office—and that he cared enough about connecting better with [the audi-ence] to take the time to explain this. So many of those in attendance com-mented positively about the opportunity to better connect to their leader, the president," Johnson recalled.

The Presidential Personnel Office at Work

The Office of Presidential Personnel is typically organized by category of depart-ments, with staff members specializing in the different categories, such as eco-nomic (Treasury, Commerce), national security (State, Defense), and so forth. Suggestions for candidates come from many sources—including campaign lead-ers, party headquarters, legislators, other White House colleagues, and the first lady. Personnel office staff consult with the appropriate staff in other White House offices when individual candidates are being reviewed. The appropriate personnel office staff member personally interviews every finalist. Always the question is asked: "Are there any parts of your personal, family, professional, political, civic, or financial background that, if known, would be embarrassing to you, or to the agency, or to the president?" If there were anything present that might raise a question, the candidate was told to consult a lawyer.

With the staff work completed and the case ripe for presidential decision, director Johnson's practice was to eschew memoranda and have direct, face-to-face meetings with the president—once a week or even oftener. There would be a brief discussion of "what we wanted the person to accomplish in the next several years, the type of person we were looking for (based on our goals and the others on the 'team'), . . . some of the other [candidates] we considered, and any issues (political and otherwise) that might exist."

The presidential decision is the most important, but not the only, step in the hiring process. Next come the legal and security checks—and in recent years the standards have gone up. Marital faithfulness, use of alcohol, questions like "Did you pay your nanny's Social Security tax?" are now included in the elements that count in judging a candidate's "suitability." Weeks, even months, can be consumed by these checks, with the nominees and their families kept waiting, and other would-be candidates kept wondering—assuming (wrongly) that the position in question was still available.

To assist the incoming Bush administration in 2000–01, a group of scholars and public administrators active in the Presidency Research Group of the American Political Science Association, and funded by the Pew Charitable Trust and other supporters, organized "The White House 2001 Project." The project had two parts, the first a series of interviews with past White House staffers, which resulted in a set of papers about White House organization and operations generally, and more specifically full descriptions of seven principal White House offices, including organization charts and lists of names and telephone numbers of previous incumbents. Briefing books were prepared and given to the incoming Bush staff principals.[11] The second part of the project was the development of a software package entitled Nomination Forms Online. Presidential nominees could access the White House 2001 Project's website (http://whitehouse 2001.org). The many forms that PAS nominees entering the confirmation process must fill out for the inquiring executive agencies (White House, IRS, FBI, and so forth) and for the Senate could all be downloaded and then filled out by the prospective nominees. A Pew analysis concluded that 40 percent of President Bush's 2001 nominees contacted the website and used that software.

Unless the nominee is at the cabinet or Supreme Court or federal appellate court level, he or she endures the confirmation process with little help from the overworked staff of the presidential personnel office. Courtesy calls need to be made to key senators, but the scheduling—and the tone—of the hearing likely depends on whether the Senate is or is not controlled by the party of the president.

Finally, one might wonder whether there is any resource to which spouses of new appointees can turn to get information helpful to newcomers in the city. The answer is yes, but the material comes from self-starters, not the White House in any official way. The idea began with Mrs. Sherman Adams, who invited Eisenhower White House wives on a number of get-togethers including an Easter egg hunt for White House children. In the Bush administration a group of spouses have organized a PAS Spouses Network, to which some 100 spouses of PAS-level appointees belong. They exchange information and socialize, have met with then chief of staff Andy Card, and have paid educational visits to the Secret Service, the Pentagon, and the Department of State.[12] Washington is a bureaucratic town, but it can be a friendly one, too.

The Policy Bloc

Policy Bloc

Assistant to President and Deputy Chief of Staff for Policy

Assistant to President for Homeland Security and Counterterrorism

Deputy Assistant to President for Homeland Security

Executive Secretary

For full chart, see page 121.

Special Assistant to President and Cabinet Liaison

Assistant to President for Domestic Policy

Faith-Based and Community Initiatives

USA Freedom Corps

Assistant to President for Economic Policy

9

Policymaking at the White House: Domestic and Economic Affairs

[Shortly before the inauguration] Nixon exhorted his Cabinet to work hard, seize their departments from the dastardly bureaucracies. . . . The president made it sound as if he intended to give his cabinet full freedom to run their departments without White House interference. At the time, that might have been Nixon's real intention.

—John D. Ehrlichman

[Kennedy] could not afford to accept, without seeking an independent judgment, the products and proposals of departmental advisers whose responsibilities did not require them to look, as he and his staff looked, at the government and its programs as a whole. He required a personal staff, therefore—one that represented *his* personal ways, means and purposes— to summarize and analyze those products and proposals for him, to refine the conflicting views of various agencies, to define the issues which he had to decide, to help place his personal imprint upon them, to make certain that practical political facts were never overlooked, and to enable him to make his decisions on the full range of *his* considerations and constituencies, which no cabinet member shared.

—Theodore Sorensen

Two cardinal rules govern domestic and economic policymaking in George W. Bush's administration:

Rule One: Every important policy issue will have a home—*in the White House.*

Rule Two: Even though the issue will probably be of crosscutting concern, it will still have, within the White House, *only one home.* One—and only one— assistant to the president will "own" it.

As Joel Kaplan, Bush's deputy chief of staff for policy, put it: "That was important for the president, so he knew to whom to turn to get answers and hold accountable, and also so that the rest of the government, the agencies, would know whom to talk to within the White House."[1]

Four by Four

There are four sets of policymaking machinery in the contemporary White House: the Domestic Policy Council (DPC), the National Economic Council

(NEC), the Homeland Security Council (HSC), and the National Security Council (NSC) (see page 108). (The latter two were established by statute; they are discussed in chapters 10 and 5, respectively.) The term "council," however, is misleading. It connotes a formal, plenary group of cabinet officers, the president in the chair, solemnly meeting in the Cabinet Room. That picture is decades out of date. In fact the National Economic Council has never met as a council during the Bush administration. Increasingly since the Eisenhower years, the White House practice has grown into using what has now become a pattern of four levels of policy discussants.

In ascending order of rank, the first level is the *policy coordinating councils,* or PCCs, groups of departmental assistant secretaries, chaired by a White House officer with the rank of special assistant to the president. Second are the *deputies,* deputy secretaries of departments chaired by a deputy assistant to the president. Third are the *principals,* the heads of departments and agencies, chaired by an assistant to the president but without the president in attendance. Fourth are sessions that the Bush White House calls policy time with the president, held not in the Cabinet Room but in the Roosevelt Room or the Oval Office. While the cabinet as a body may meet occasionally for information purposes, the cabinet as a collectivity is not part of George W. Bush's policymaking machinery.

Preparing and Making Domestic Policy

The calendar affects White House domestic and economic policymaking. The busiest times are in the fall, beginning as early as August, through late January, when the staff prepares options for the president's policy agenda. Everyone is aware that in January Congress assembles, the president delivers his State of the Union message, his budget, his economic report, and perhaps special messages beyond those three. The first question facing the staff is: What are the principal issues the president will have to address in those messages, and who on the staff will handle them? Responsibility for answering those questions is lodged in the chief of staff's office. An officer at that level must "set the priorities of what the president needs to decide," Deputy Chief of Staff Kaplan explained.

> An agency head can't do that kind of prioritization for the president, and neither can the head of the NEC or the DPC or the HSC; one person has to do that and that's the deputy chief of staff for policy. I direct the traffic, make sure the issues are considered and presented in a timely way, that is, in time for the president to make the decisions. If we don't do our jobs well, *time* will make more decisions than the president will.

To help Kaplan do his job, on his office wall hangs a PERT (Program Evaluation and Review Technique) chart with boxes showing each day for three months ahead. Kaplan holds a once-a-week meeting (called Joel's Anonymous—

a meeting without a name). In effect with crayons in hand, Kaplan, the chief of staff, the senior political adviser (at the time, Karl Rove), the communications chief, the legislative director, the press secretary, and the scheduler engage in what chief of staff Josh Bolten calls strategic scheduling—going over what the president's public activities will be for the next two to three months. "This is the meeting where we really think ahead," Kaplan observed. "We talk about the top-line message, and then the specific activities which will support it."

Following the rules that every issue has a home and only one home, Kaplan makes the policy "ownership" assignments—either to the assistant to the president for economic affairs (at one time Allan Hubbard, more recently Keith Hennessey, formerly Hubbard's deputy), who heads a staff of fifteen salaried officers and four interns, or to the domestic affairs assistant (Karl Zinsmeister), who has a staff of the same size. No jurisdictional "charter" is needed between the two assistants. "Any time I think I'm involved in an area that may touch Zinsmeister," Hubbard explained, "we just communicate with each other; we're very deferential; we include each other. The way it works around here, everyone assumes that their colleagues are invited to comment on anything."[2]

Starting the policy process, the White House is at the center of the action, hosting dozens of meetings, at the PPC level, at the deputy level, and then with the principals. As Hennessey emphasized,

> We run the meetings, we choose the agenda for the meetings, we gener-
> ally write the papers for the meetings—whether it is a memo or a Power-
> Point presentation. The final text always comes from us and always has
> our name on it. We will subcontract out pieces of it, so if we're going to
> be discussing auto efficiency standards, I, or our special person who han-
> dles these issues, will be working closely with the Department of Trans-
> portation folks, who might send over draft language. In all likelihood,
> however, we'll either have written the first draft of the memo or we'll have
> taken what the DOT people have done and we'll write the second draft.
> We're often tasking out to the various agencies for the analysis needed
> and for the options for necessary research, asking, "What is the back-
> ground of such-and-such? Tell us what will be the economic effects of
> doing X or Y or Z?"[3]

Added Deputy Domestic Affairs Assistant Tevi Troy: "We don't prepare a paper that affects one of the relevant agencies without sharing it with that agency."[4] If economic research is needed, the White House staff calls on the Council of Economic Advisers (CEA), right next door in the Eisenhower Executive Office Building. "They are the professional, academic economists," Hennessey observed. "They describe themselves, and we describe them, as 'our own in-house economics consulting firm.' We will rely on them to interact with the technical and economic experts in the various agencies."

Some economic issues are in large part international matters—trade policy questions being an example. Here, Hubbard and Hennessey turn to an officer on the National Security Council's staff who has the title of deputy assistant to the president for international economic affairs. While on the NSC payroll, he wears two hats: being responsible to the national security adviser for national security issues, but to Hubbard and Hennessey for international economic matters.

The makeup of a typical principals meeting—for instance on energy policy— illustrates the breadth of the Bush administration's style of policymaking. Present with the cabinet-level principals will be not only Deputy Chief of Staff Kaplan but also the CEA chairman, the director of the Office of Management and Budget, the chief of staff to the vice president, the chairman of the Council on Environmental Quality, the counselor to the president for communications, the assistant to the president for strategic initiatives, the assistant to the president for legislative affairs, the press secretary, and the deputy press secretary. Twenty to twenty-five people could be in attendance. Well in advance of the meeting, the White House economic staff would have prepared and distributed a "worksheet," a one-page paper with multiple yes-or-no questions supplementing the weightier briefing materials. The departmental staffers would brief their respective principals so that the latter could come to the White House ready to say, "Here's where we are on number four," or "number five is an option for legislative affairs." "The principals would all come in with their annotated copies of this worksheet," Hennessey said. "We worked very hard to separate out the policy questions from the legislative constraints and the other constraints, which generally are political or communications constraints. We needed to tell the president, 'Here's what we think the best policy is independent of legislative, political, or communications considerations.'"

Policy Time

Periods with the president are the acme of the policy pyramid. The president has what the Bush White House calls policy time on his calendar for every day he is in town. It does not always get used, but the deputy chief of staff for policy owns that block of time and then divvies it out. Every Friday he holds a meeting among the policy assistants or their representatives to look forward a month, spot those issues that could ripen over the next thirty days, reserve the time with the president, and assign it to the assistant who will make the presentation. "We insist on rigor in the process," Kaplan emphasized,

> to make sure there has been a deputies meeting and a principals meeting and that the issues have been properly ventilated, and the options well distilled and fully considered. I'll usually have participated in the principals meeting so I'll have a sense along the way of whether it's being done properly and whether it's actually ripe, whether they've done all the work that needs to be done to bring it to the president. We've had heads of the DPC

and the NEC who were quite good at their jobs; so a lot of times I don't need to do very much.

If the responsible cabinet member has not met the White House standard for preparation on an issue, the policy assistant who "owns" the issue will intervene to set things right and if necessary will call on the deputy chief of staff for policy for reinforcement; it is after all, the latter's clear responsibility "to make sure that what needs to be happening is happening," Kaplan commented.

A background memorandum on an issue is given to the president one or two days before the session in which that issue will be discussed. The meeting itself is held in the Roosevelt Room or the Oval Office depending on the number of attendees; the chief of staff and the vice president are always present. Policy time often begins with a PowerPoint presentation, followed by a summary of the recommendations on which the principals have reached consensus. Whether it is slides or option papers, "the president," observed Hennessey, "can handle either . . . quite easily, and was often ahead of the staff in terms of what we were discussing. . . .We'd take verbal cues from the president because he would remember things from meetings he had done several months earlier, and we could skip over those points."

Next Zinsmeister or Hubbard (or later Hennessey) lays out the pro and con arguments on the open questions and then turns to the cabinet members or other White House staff seniors, such as Candida Wolff, the head of legislative affairs, to present the differing sides of the question in their own words. "Part of what we are trying to do is encapsulate the arguments, because we've rehearsed those arguments beforehand and we run them by the people on both sides so we know that we are efficiently and clearly presenting those," Hennessey explained. "We don't have to rely on others to get the argument right the first time; they can make the emphasis wherever they want."

How are cases of serious dissent handled? Hennessey described the extra efforts that are taken to include differing points of view:

> We would make sure that we identified those dissents beforehand in the principals meetings. Then Hubbard and I, often giving Kaplan a heads-up, would figure out who were the dissenters on any particular issue. One of us would then talk with those people beforehand and say, "We're going to recognize you when we get to question four; we're going to have Secretary A lay out the almost-consensus recommendation and then recognize you to express what your dissent is." We would also, frankly, force a lot of them to rehearse their dissent with us beforehand—to push them to make sure their dissent was as clearly stated as possible.

Besides being objective honest brokers in ensuring that all the relevant arguments on an issue are fairly presented to the president, the policy assistants have a second role to play: giving the chief executive their own independent views. On an economic policy question, Hubbard and Hennessey might divide up the two roles: Hubbard brokering the group's presentation of their varying arguments, with Hennessey coming through at the end by saying, "Mr. President, our own view as *policy advisers to you* is. . . ." It was useful to have these two roles played by two separate individuals. "The credibility of your shop as an honest broker is critical to your success," Hennessey said.

> That credibility is built up over time and across multiple issues. As the various White House and cabinet officials trust in the process, then they cut you more slack as you work through those issues. A big part of that trust comes when someone is a dissenter and you treat them well and they have the opportunity to present their dissenting view to the president, and when the White House assistant neutrally and accurately handles that dissent and doesn't, in their mind, mislead the president as to what the option is.

In President Bush's own words:

> This is a job that requires crisp decisionmaking, and therefore, in order for me to make decisions, I've got to have people who bring their point of view into the Oval Office and are willing to say it. . . . People . . . walk in and get overwhelmed in the atmosphere and they say, "Man, you're looking pretty." . . . You need people to walk in on those days when you're not looking so good and saying, "You're not looking so good, Mr. President." . . . If you're the Commander in Chief and a decisionmaker, you want people to walk in and say, "I don't agree with this," or "I do agree with that, and here's what my recommendation is."[5]

Follow-Up Actions

There is a note-taker for "policy-time" sessions; if an economic issue is the subject of the meeting, Hennessey, when he was deputy assistant, made a summary of the president's decisions. These summaries were shown to Hubbard and perhaps a few other White House seniors but were not circulated outside the White House.

With presidential decisions in hand, the next task for the White House policy staffers is to compose a substantive outline of the decision that can be used as the basis for a presidential speech, an executive order or other policy communication. If the message is a speech, such as the State of the Union address, the speechwriters are often asked to sit in on the policy-time session, enabling them to comprehend not only what the policy is but the thought process behind it. For the same reason, the press secretary is kept involved throughout the process.

Contacts outside the Executive Branch

Outside interest groups typically want to give their advice and viewpoints to the White House policymakers. Kaplan made it clear that "their formal connection and way into the White House is the Office of Public Liaison, the gatekeeper. . . . On very rare occasions I'll meet with people from outside, but, again, the whole goal has been not to have this office be the issue-owner and to direct those people to the issue-owners"—meaning Zinsmeister, Hubbard, or Hennessey or their equivalents.

Consultation with members of Congress is frequent, but the White House Legislative Affairs office calls the shots, determining which senator or representative needs to be consulted. At the beginning of the Bush administration, the director of legislative affairs was Nick Calio. Bush's first domestic policy assistant, John Bridgeland, recalled:

> We'd work with Nick and his team and we'd go up to the Hill. I was constantly on the Hill advocating for legislation, advising on executive orders, giving updates to the Senate Republican and Democratic caucuses and the leadership . . . about what policy issues and legislative proposals would move forward and in what order."[6]

"I spend a lot of time on Capitol Hill," Hubbard pointed out, "working informally with the members up there." Whether it is interest groups or legislators, however, Hennessey stressed that White House staffers keep one objective firmly in mind:

> One of the things that we have to fight very hard to ensure is that we want to protect the president's options. We, the policy shop, work very hard to try to prevent people from taking options off the table. A big part of our job in the policy process is to keep options on the table for as long as possible. Even if there are options that almost everyone thinks are bad options, it sometimes helps for the president to understand, "Here's an option that your advisers considered and rejected, and here's why."

"We do consult with interest groups," Hennessey added, "but it's much more limited than people might think. We're very careful about how we do it. We need to get information from interested parties, but without tipping the president's hand." Hubbard even included Federal Reserve Chairman Ben S. Bernanke in his circle of contacts. "I have breakfast or lunch with Ben once every ten days or so," Hubbard remarked, "and I solicit his thoughts and counsel on the major issues we're addressing. He never asks my advice on what he should do about interest rates, however."

The Exception: A Policy Issue Affecting the Whole White House

Kaplan emphasized that "the role of the deputy chief of staff for policy is *almost never* to take personal ownership of a particular issue. . . ." He stuck by that rule except in the case of a single problem—one that was national in scope, that affected all three levels of government, that had been long ignored, that was at the center of attention in Congress, that was a problem about which the president was an expert, that was surrounded by a storm of controversy, that touched those affected in a deeply personal way, that involved billions of dollars, that genuinely demanded immediate action, that was festooned with interest-group dynamite, that involved almost every cabinet secretary, and that drove smack through all four of the White House policymaking mechanisms, involving homeland security and foreign policy, and having huge, combined domestic and economic consequences. The issue was immigration reform, a top priority for the president that had already been scuttled once, and Chief of Staff Joshua Bolten decided that Kaplan himself would own it.

Kaplan chaired all the rather large principals meetings, assigned Zinsmeister to produce some initial option papers, pulled in Frances Townsend from the White House Homeland Security Council, and collared Homeland Security Secretary Michael Chertoff and Commerce Secretary Carlos M. Gutierrez to take the lead in the cabinet. He enlisted Legislative Affairs Director Candi Wolff to take Zinsmeister, Chertoff, and Gutierrez up to the Capitol where they held small-group "listening sessions," many of them with perhaps 100 members, mostly Republicans at the beginning, during December 2006 and January and February 2007. The foursome would then give oral reports to the principals. The product of these sessions and meetings was not legislative language but a statement of principles laid out in a twenty-page set of charts. These in turn formed the basis of a second set of meetings with Republican senators, some conservative, some more liberal, with the message, "Here's an idea, based on what you have told us—a concept of how you might be envisioning immigration reform—and which is consistent with what the president wants to do." "We spent weeks," Kaplan recalled, "I've never seen anything like it since I've been here! We were seeing if we could find common ground that would hold for both the conservatives and the moderates."

The intent was to convince as many Republicans as possible and then approach the Democrats, led by Senators Edward M. Kennedy and Patrick J. Leahy, with a package on immigration reform that the Republicans could agree to. "If you can't corral the Republicans in the Senate," Kaplan explained, "you won't get a bill." For much of March and April, Chertoff and Gutierrez, with Kaplan and Wolff, spent two hours a day talking personally with Republican senators and keeping Kennedy informed. They gave the president weekly written progress reports. Often they had to go to the president and get his approval for modifications in the set of principles, which would allow the negotiators to get around sticking points. The president began to hear good feedback from the Republican senators, which built up his own trust in the effectiveness of his negotiating team.

With a core of Republican senators on board, the negotiators turned to the core of Democrats, and hours of three-way negotiations took place among senators from the two parties and the White House staff. This was "an exceptional, unusual role for the White House," commented Kaplan, particularly because this dialogue was taking place not in the regular congressional committee structure, and not in the form of an actual legislative markup, but privately in the Capitol. (Later some members were critical of the process, alleging that they were not sufficiently included, though this may have been partly an excuse to vote against a bill they would not have approved in any event.)

The product of this semifinal stage was the "grand bargain" on immigration reform, not yet a bill, but an overarching set of principles that conservatives, moderates, and liberals endorsed. The final stage was drafting the legislation, in Kaplan's words "an immensely contentious process." Again the White House took the lead, with Zinsmeister and his staff working on the draft with Secretary Chertoff, and Kaplan "directing the traffic," as he put it.

> We started out in December, January: weekly principals meetings that became principals phone calls. We would spend an innumerable amount of time. We'd go up to the Hill, we'd have discussions, we'd hear what the concerns were, we'd come back here and literally overnight turn new proposals and bring them back to the Hill. Once we got into the legislative dynamic, we weren't able to have the same deliberate pace of consideration; it had to happen in a much more concentrated and condensed time frame. That's why the president decided to empower me, in the chief of staff's office, to guide that and make the decisions—understanding that at times I would have to come back and check with the boss. It allowed us to move with the kind of speed that the legislative dynamic required. . . .
>
> The president is a terrific manager and delegator. He's not going to micromanage the legislative process. He set out the objectives and principles and he was going to trust his negotiators to get it done and make the judgments about where to give. Again, major issues you bring back to the president, but for the most part, his direction was clear, what he wanted out of us was clear, and we just had to make the judgment. . . . On the Hill, Chertoff would take the lead; I would not take the lead. As a cabinet member, he was our lead force. . . . Then we'd come back and I'd chair the meeting and say "Here's the work we need to turn overnight," and we'd have the discussions about where we wanted to come out and how far we were willing to give.

On other fronts, the White House was employing all its resources. Karl Rove in the political office was lobbying his old friends in the Texas congressional delegation and, beyond that, was using blogs for the first time, so that no allegation on the Internet would go unanswered. Press Secretary Tony Snow, with his skill in the radio business, got on talk radio, countering the blasts of misinformation. Legislative director Candi Wolff added up the votes in the Senate; the president had fifty-seven or perhaps fifty-eight, but not the needed sixty. When that shortfall became clear, many erstwhile supporters changed their votes and in June the "grand bargain" bill died in the Senate.

Looking Ahead to 2009

On the immigration initiative, was it right to elevate the "ownership" to the chief of staff's office? Kaplan's answer is yes.

> At the end of the day, short of the president, the chief of staff is the only person who can resolve feuds within the White House or between cabinet members. The idea of a policy process is that you try to resolve issues, compromise issues, but you don't want a policy process that discourages disagreement. Oftentimes people think they should resolve issues themselves and not involve the president. The president knows how to make decisions and he wants to know if there's disagreement. He doesn't want it to get sanded down to the lowest common denominator. The role of the policy office is not to grind away until the disagreement is gone short of the president. It is to crystallize the issue and bring disagreement to the president in a timely way.

Economic assistant Hubbard was firm about the mission of the office of a senior White House policy staffer:

> I think it's very important always to have a proactive agenda that you are working on, not just reactive. It's very easy in this job to just deal with whatever is going on at Capitol Hill or in the press. It's extremely important that the president has a clear agenda that he wants to accomplish. The part of it that's involved with economics should be led by this council and it's important that the council not get bogged down in reacting to daily and weekly events, and focus on the long-term issues that need to be solved for the American people.

The staff members interviewed by the author for this chapter were unanimous in describing the cooperativeness and friendliness of the Bush domestic and economic affairs staffs. "What's remarkable about this White House—more so than any White House of which I'm aware," Hennessey remarked, "is its remarkable collegiality. [National security adviser Stephen] Hadley and I never have conflict; we've never had one conflict—I mean, we just don't. We are deferential to each other and we work very well with [Hadley aide] Dave

McCormick, and we include each other in anything that we think the other may have an interest in."

Nonetheless, in the end, collegiality gives way to hierarchy. "I think you have to have somebody who is seen as running the operations of the White House," Kaplan observed. "I think you have to have the hierarchy to some degree, but if you can do that and still create a collegial environment—there's a balance there."

10

The Homeland Security Council

The Assistant to the President for Homeland Security shall be the official primarily responsible for advising and assisting the President in the coordination of domestic incident management activities of all departments and agencies in the event of a terrorist threat, and during and in the aftermath of terrorist attacks, major disasters, or other emergencies, within the United States.

—Executive Order 13228, as amended by Executive Order 13286

Nothing in this directive shall be construed to grant to any Assistant to the President any authority to issue orders to Federal departments and agencies, their officers or their employees.

—Homeland Security Presidential Directive 5, February 28, 2003

The catastrophe of 9/11 blew open a fourteen-month epoch of blindingly speedy change in the staid and tradition-bound world of White House and cabinet institutions. Only twenty-seven days after the 9/11 disaster, President Bush signed Executive Order 13228 creating a dramatically new element on the White House staff—the assistant to the president for homeland security—and appointed former Pennsylvania governor Tom Ridge to that position. Ridge's mission: "to develop and coordinate the implementation of a comprehensive national strategy to secure the United States from terrorist threats or attacks." The executive order went on for several pages, repeatedly instructing the new office to "coordinate and prioritize," "coordinate efforts," "ensure that," "review and assess," "facilitate," "develop criteria," and "work with"—language that gave the new presidential assistant lots of influence but zero authority to take action. He was permitted, however, to intervene in an unusual fashion in the annual budget process by being able to take a crack at the whole executive branch budget just before the director of the Office of Management and Budget sent it to the president and to "certify" to the OMB director that he " believes" that the funding levels in the budget "are necessary and appropriate for the homeland-related activities of the executive branch." The White House homeland security assistant still has that authority—and uses it.

Homeland Security Council Staff

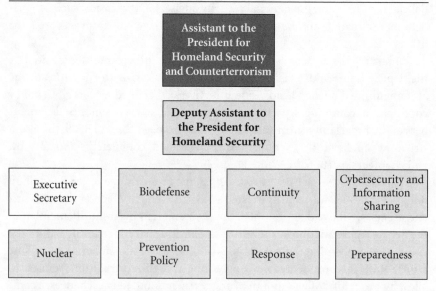

An executive order issued in February 2003 reminds the new White House assistant that he is to function "consistent with applicable law, including the statutory functions of the Secretary of Homeland Security" and that he "shall coordinate with the Assistant to the President for National Security Affairs, as appropriate."[1]

Creation of the Homeland Security Council

In the original 2001 executive order of October 8, President George W. Bush established a Homeland Security Council (HSC), with himself as chair, and specified its membership, which included the vice president, who would be chair in the president's absence. The assistant for homeland security would be responsible for "determining the agenda, ensuring that necessary papers are prepared, and recording Council actions and Presidential decisions."[2] A mere three weeks later the president issued Homeland Security Presidential Directive 1 ("Organization and Operation of the Homeland Security Council"), laying out the structure and procedure that would undergird the newly minted Homeland Security Council.[3] Under the chairmanship of the homeland security assistant, there was to be a principals committee; its membership consisted of nine cabinet or subcabinet heads (Treasury, Defense, Justice, Health and Human Services, Transportation, the Federal Emergency Management Agency, FBI, CIA, and OMB) plus three senior White House staff officers (the presidential and vice presidential chiefs of staff and the national security adviser). Other heads, such as Agriculture, Commerce, and Energy) are to be invited if relevant subjects are to be discussed.

Supporting the principals would be an HSC deputies committee, chaired by the deputy homeland security adviser and consisting of the deputies to the aforementioned agency heads. The directive also created eleven HSC policy coordination committees, each chaired by one of the seven senior policy members of the homeland security assistant's staff (see page 121) All in all, this was a structure, similar to the National Security Council, completely controlled by, and an integral part of, the White House.[4]

In his budget message of February 2002, the president requested $38 billion dollars for homeland-security-related activities in eighty federal departments and agencies, a move that prompted the chair and ranking minority member of the Senate Appropriations Committee to demand that Ridge testify before the committee concerning these outlays. Since Ridge was a member of the White House staff, the president, following a long-recognized tradition, refused to allow him to testify. After a month of angry remarks and testy exchanges, a compromise was reached in which Ridge agreed to appear behind closed doors to brief committee members and answer their questions.

Creation of the Department of Homeland Security

While the original White House Office of Homeland Security was a first step, a much broader structural task loomed. Recognizing the magnitude of the organizational sweep implied in the concept "homeland security," President Bush, in almost total secrecy, convened an inner-circle White House team that developed a strikingly bold transformation of his departments and agencies. On June 18, 2002, he lifted the curtain and asked Congress to approve the creation of a brand-new Department of Homeland Security. It involved a revolutionary reshuffling in the executive branch—pulling some twenty-two agencies out of their existing and traditional locations and combining and squeezing them into the new cabinet department. After five months of wrangling, Congress passed the pending bill and on November 25, the president signed the new Homeland Security Act, bringing into being, in fourteen months and two weeks after 9/11, a breathtakingly novel transformation of almost the entire executive branch.

The Department and the Council: Their Relationship

Would this new cabinet department obviate the need for the recently created Homeland Security Council at the White House? Not at all, asserted the president:

Even with the creation of the new Department, there will remain a strong need for a White House Office of Homeland Security. Protecting America from terrorism will remain a multidepartmental issue and will continue to require interagency coordination. Presidents will continue to require the confidential advice of a Homeland Security Advisor, and I intend for the White House Office of Homeland Security and the Homeland Security Council to maintain a strong role in coordinating our government-wide efforts to secure the homeland.[5]

In fact, besides bringing the new cabinet agency into existence, the legislation elevated the Homeland Security Council to statutory status and specified that it "shall have a staff, the head of which shall be a civilian Executive Secretary, who shall be appointed by the President." (This statutory provision was unique in that it, together with the only other similar provision, in 1947, establishing the executive secretary of the National Security Council, are the only two examples of White House officers being created by statute.) The new Homeland Security Act also authorized the new secretary of homeland security to attend meetings of the National Security Council; and permitted the president to "convene joint meetings of the Homeland Security Council and the National Security Council."[6]

At the outset, under Ridge and then his successor, General John Gordon, the White House Office of Homeland Security was authorized a fiscal 2002 budget of just under $27 million (in addition to $54.6 million for the White House Office) and a staff of 130 persons, many of whom were detailees. "It's an important point about our history," observed Joel Bagnal, deputy assistant to the president for homeland security in 2007:

A lot of folks that were here in the early days of the Office of Homeland Security were detailees or assignees from other departments and agencies; we had a need to grow very quickly, and we grabbed expertise. Now we have shifted that structure and most of the people that serve here on the Homeland Security Council are in fact full-time employees of the White House, who are appointees of the President.[7]

By fiscal year 2004, the name "office" was discontinued; the White House group was formally titled the Homeland Security Council. With the new Department of Homeland Security established and in operation, the authorized outlays for the Homeland Security Council at the White House dropped to $7.2 million and the staff numbered about thirty-five. In fiscal 2004 the Homeland Security Council budget was merged into the White House Office figure and is no longer separately identified. As of this writing the staff numbers about forty-eight.

In February 2003, as the new Department of Homeland Security was opening its doors, the president, in recognition of the fact that the Federal Emergency

Management Agency had now become a part of that department, amended the original October 2001 Executive Order by adding "major disasters, or other emergencies" to the listing of the areas about which the White House homeland security assistant would advise the president.[8] But he followed this up with Homeland Security Presidential Directive 5 specifying that the secretary of homeland security "is responsible for coordinating federal *operations* within the United States," and "shall coordinate the Federal Government's resources"(italics added).[9] These two closely interrelated sets of wording are not incompatible but, if wielded by two ego-driven personalities, could arguably lead to conflict between the White House adviser and the homeland security secretary—and at a time when conflict would be particularly unwelcome. Thanks, however, to the excellent personal relationship existing between Frances F. Townsend, at that time the White House homeland security adviser, and Homeland Security Secretary Michael Chertoff, unwelcome conflict has not occurred. "We do spend a lot of our time with the Department of Homeland Security," Joel Bagnal emphasized:

> We really do. We don't have programs, budgets, or any statutory authority to execute homeland security responsibilities. What we do . . . have [is] a responsibility to develop homeland security policy with the president, to serve as his expert staff here on homeland security policy issues and provide oversight for the implementation of those policies, which is through the Department of Homeland Security and other departments and agencies. . . . There is a desire for the White House staff not to be operational, but to leave operational matters to departments and agencies that have the funding, programs and authorities.

That "desire" is reflected in unambiguous presidential direction, as readers will note in the excerpt from the text of the president's Homeland Security Directive 5 at the beginning of this chapter.

As described elsewhere in this book, the budget requests for the policy elements of the White House are presented and defended to Congress not by any White House officer but by the director of the Office of Administration. Occasionally, the White House homeland security adviser does go up to the Hill informally to brief members of Congress and to give technical advice about pieces of legislation related to homeland security.

Are Both a Homeland Security Council and a National Security Council Needed?

In its 2005 report, the 9/11 Commission made these observations:

> The national security staff at the White House (both NSC and new Homeland Security Council staff) has already become 50% larger since 9/11. But

our impression, after talking to serving officials, is that even this enlarged staff is consumed by meetings on day-to-day issues, sifting each day's threat information and trying to coordinate everyday operations. . . . [A] . . . more serious danger is that as the NSC staff is consumed by these day-to-day tasks, it has less capacity to find the time and detachment needed to advise a president on larger policy issues. . . . To improve coordination at the White House, we believe the existing Homeland Security Council should be merged into a single National Security Council.[10]

The arguments in favor of such a merger are that it would create a single management body dealing with national security, of which homeland security is a part, a single set of voices advising the president, a single schedule of meetings. "The fact is," Bagnal commented, "that the principals and deputies and assistant secretaries of departments and agencies have both homeland security and national security responsibilities."

The counterargument is that many important homeland security issues, such as border and port security, public health and medical preparedness, critical infrastructure protection, domestic incident management, the security of domestic water supplies, and the routing of freight trains around rather than through urban areas, are not traditional national security focus areas, and the responsible officials in the interagency homeland security community do not necessarily belong at NSC meetings. On the national security adviser's plate to take to the president are urgent, if not critical, matters, such as Iraq, North Korea, Iran—situations that, every time, will outweigh homeland security problems unless imminent violence is involved. A recommendation to Congress to eliminate the Homeland Security Council would send a message throughout government that homeland security problems were of second priority. "There have been three times when we have seriously contemplated combining the two councils," Bagnal recalled, "and the decision has been made each time obviously not to do that. The president believes that he needs a dedicated staff to focus completely on homeland security issues . . . a separate assistant to the president, somebody who has the president's confidence and ear and is an equal player with the approximately twenty other persons of comparable rank in the White House who can completely focus on homeland security-counterterrorism matters."

Taking the hint from the statutory language, the president has convened joint meetings of the two councils, and the secretary of homeland security attends many NSC sessions. On average, Homeland Security Council meetings with the president occur every other month (although the president meets with individual members of the council far more frequently). The deputies convene once or twice a week, and most of the eleven policy coordination committees that the HSC administers (either exclusively or with the NSC) meet about weekly. The two council staffs work hand in glove with each other. They look at each other's agenda and make an ad hoc determination about who sits in on which meeting. The homeland security adviser attends the majority of the national security meetings conducted by the national security adviser, while the national security adviser attends somewhat fewer than half of the HSC meetings. Bagnal remembered ten or eleven meetings that the two advisers cohosted, underscoring the reality that as events or initiatives require, the pace at which principals meet can increase significantly. An intelligence program office within the National Security Council reports to both advisers jointly, as does the NSC's Combating Terrorism directorate.

The HSC executive secretary sees to it that there is an agenda for the council's meetings, that discussion papers and slides are circulated in advance, and that a "summary of conclusions" is written up afterward. The council's executive secretary, David Trulio, explained:

> We have a tremendous amount of transparency as to what meetings we're having and share broadly the pre- and postmeeting materials. What we do at least once a week is transmit to the interagency community a listing of all of our upcoming meetings—from HSC meetings with the president to policy coordination committee meetings with assistant secretaries. As a result, no one is surprised. We have a very good track record of identifying who ought to be at what meeting, but our broad notice across the federal government affords an opportunity for departments and agencies to say they'd like to come.[11]

Safety vs. Security

Melamine appears in drugs from China, glycerin in imported toothpaste; deaths have occurred. If the cause is a lack of regulatory control by Chinese authorities, it is a food safety issue, under the jurisdiction of the Food and Drug Administration. If there is any evidence of intent to harm, it is a homeland security issue.

In September 2006, for example, a small plane flew into a New York City apartment building. Officials worried—"Here we go again?" Over the next five hours an intensive intelligence review took place. What kind of aircraft? Tail number? How many passengers on board? Any of their names on the watch list? Gas tank full or not? Had the crew filed a flight plan? Was the tower giving them instructions? Information of that kind had to be seized and evaluated immediately before a judgment could be made: it was an accident. Readers will appreciate the pace, the stress, the consequences of knowing versus not knowing.

The Katrina Report

Although the Homeland Security Council was created in response to a terrorist attack, it had also been given responsibility, as recounted above, for advising the president on natural disasters as well. In late August 2005 Hurricane Katrina devastated a great swath of the Gulf Coast including New Orleans, posing a test of the federal government's newly minted homeland security arrangements. What happened? Speaking from Jackson Square in New Orleans on the evening of September 15, 2005, the president ordered "a comprehensive review of the Federal responses to Hurricane Katrina so we as a nation could make the necessary changes to be 'better prepared for any challenge of nature or act of evil men that could threaten our people.'"[12] The president's adviser for homeland security and counterterrorism, Frances Townsend, took up the assignment and assembled a group of twenty individuals, ten from the White House and ten from the agencies involved, to undertake the review. The group conducted 1,200 interviews with cabinet members and dozens of other federal officials, paid three thorough visits to New Orleans and the Gulf Coast, talked with officials, business and community leaders, and volunteers, and in five months prepared a 217-page report, which began by stating: "Individual local and State plans, as well as relatively new plans created by the Federal government . . . failed to adequately account for widespread or simultaneous catastrophes."[13] The report went on to make 125 recommendations for changes and improvements in seventeen critical areas. Four in the category of national preparedness are worthy of mention in this chapter because they are relevant to White House staff functions. Two years after the publication of this report, they have all been implemented.

The first of these recommendations: "Establish a National Operations Center to coordinate the national response and provide situational awareness and a common operating picture for the entire Federal government." A National Operations Center is located in the Department of Homeland Security. On a typical day seventy-four people are on duty there, including representatives of state and local governments, such as police officers from New York City, Los Angeles, and Chicago; fire department specialists; and representatives of corporations and sectors of American industry. The NOC is tied into the White House Situation Room.

A second recommendation calls on the federal government to "Establish a national information and knowledge management system . . . to provide a common operating picture which provides for the processing and timely provisioning of interagency information sources. . . ." Today the National Command Center at the Pentagon is connected—both electronically and through the physical presence of liaison officers—to the Department of Homeland Security's National Operations Center, as is the FBI's Strategic Information Operations Center. In an unclassified mode, state and local representatives are linked in as well.

A third recommendation called for the establishment of "a national reporting system . . . to provide a uniform information flow to senior decision makers." A system was put in place that was used in the melamine and in the New York

City airplane incidents, mentioned earlier. Alerts were circulated, and the NOC organized conference calls among all the agencies concerned.

Finally, the report called for the establishment of a disaster response group. One of the eleven policy coordination committees of the Homeland Security Council is now called the Domestic Readiness Group and is able to convene on short notice to handle incidents such as those described.

The Amended Insurrection Act

Congress has denied the president at least one expanded power that he sought in the area of homeland security. Section 333 of Chapter 15 of Title 10 of the U.S. Code is entitled "Major Public Emergencies; Interference with State and Federal Law" and reads as follows:

> The president may employ the armed forces, including the National Guard in Federal service to:
>
> (A) Restore public order and enforce the laws of the United States when, as a result of a natural disaster, epidemic or other serious public health emergency, terrorist attack or incident *or other condition* in any State or possession of the United States, the president determines that domestic violence has occurred to such an extent that the constituted authorities of the State or possession are incapable of maintaining public order."[14]

During Congress's consideration of the defense authorization bill in 2006, the Bush administration persuaded the Senate and House Armed Services committees to insert the three italicized words into Section 333, and that amendment was enacted—but, from the perspective of the National Governors Association, with little or no consultation with the nation's governors. The governors became alarmed and protested that those three words "undermine the governors' authority over the [National] Guard, [and] place the safety and welfare of citizens in jeopardy...."[15] Senators Pat Leahy of Vermont and Kit Bond of Missouri introduced an amendment to excise the three words and restore Section 333 to its long-existing, original wording, Bond stating that this provision "reduces our nation's governors' control over their Guard units and provides the President with unnecessary and unprecedented power."[16] On April 16, 2007, Leahy held a Judiciary Committee hearing with testimony from governors and National Guard representatives. The Leahy-Bond reversion was discussed between administration leaders and the governors. Deputy White House Homeland Security Assistant Bagnal emphasized the White House position: "If we have a major catastrophic event, we need quickly to mobilize our reserve and National Guard resources to provide the best relief. This is all about military support of civil authorities; what we did was give the president greater flexibility."

The senators' amendment nonetheless was put into the 2007 National Defense Authorization Act and was enacted by both chambers. Bush pocket vetoed the measure for unrelated reasons at the end of 2007, but Congress removed the offending provisions early in 2008, and Bush then signed the legislation.

Continuity of Government

It was President Eisenhower who, beginning in 1955, took the lead in creating and testing emergency relocation sites for the cabinet departments and for the White House. For three or four days in each of the several succeeding summers, he led an Operation Alert exercise in which his cabinet colleagues each went with some of their staffs to their respective relocation sites and tested their emergency plans and the communications supporting them. In 1956 Ike visited two of those sites, held a cabinet meeting on each occasion, assumed hypothetically that a massive nuclear attack on the United States had taken place, and talked out responses with the cabinet.

The Bush administration conducts similar exercises, called Pinnacle, and a new deputy assistant for continuity of government matters has been added to the staff of the Homeland Security Council. The HSC's 2007 strategy document (details below) includes these lines:

> We will continue to maintain comprehensive and effective continuity programs, including those that integrate continuity of operations and continuity of government programs, to ensure the preservation of our government under the Constitution and the continuing performance of national essential functions—those government roles that are necessary to lead and sustain the nation during and following a catastrophic emergency.[17]

There is a second office in the White House—in the Military Office—that is also concerned with issues of continuity, but the focus for that group is the continuity and safety of the chief executive.

Future Prospects for Homeland Security

In mid-July 2007 the Bush administration published an unclassified summary of a national intelligence estimate entitled *The Terrorist Threat to the U.S. Homeland*. The unanimous conclusion of the U. S. intelligence community was that "the U.S. homeland will face a persistent and evolving terrorist threat over the next three years." Looking at the innovations the president and his associates had made since 2001, the estimate's authors said: "We assess that greatly increased worldwide counterterrorism efforts over the past five years have constrained the ability of Al Qaeda to attack the U.S. homeland again and have led terrorist groups to perceive the homeland as a harder target to strike than on

9/11. These measures have helped disrupt known plots against the United States since 9/11." Nonetheless, the report continued:

> Al Qaeda is and will remain the most serious threat to the homeland, as its central leadership continues to plan high-impact plots.... [W]e judge that the United States currently is in a heightened threat environment. We assess that Al Qaeda's homeland plotting is likely to focus on prominent political, economic and infrastructure targets with the goal of producing mass casualties, visually dramatic destruction, significant economic after-shocks, and/or fear among the U.S. population.[18]

The entire homeland security community—in the remaining years of the Bush administration and in the administration that follows it—will without a doubt pay determined attention to those words. In early October 2007 President Bush issued an updated, fifty-three-page *National Strategy for Homeland Security* document. Informed by that national intelligence estimate and by the country's increased understanding of the threats confronting it since 9/11, and incorporating the lessons learned from exercises and real-world catastrophes, the Homeland Security Council at the White House developed the strategy over the course of that year, bolstering it with the insights of federal, state, local, and private sector stakeholders. Intended to guide, organize, and unify the nation's homeland security efforts, the strategy articulates the president's desire to build on the strong homeland security foundation established since 9/11. Given that the next president's team will not be fully in place until well into 2009, the strategy is likely to prioritize efforts to secure the homeland for years to come.

Helping Religion to Do Good: The Office of Faith-Based and Community Initiatives

Congress wouldn't act, so I signed an Executive Order—that means I did it on my own. It says we're going to open up billions of dollars in grant money competition to faith-based charities. And that's what's happening.

—George W. Bush

The so-called faith-based initiative was a bad idea ... the initiative turns houses of worship who receive its funds into contract employees of the federal government.

—Rev. C. Welton Gaddy

George W. Bush ... is a good man. But he is a politician. ... And if the faith-based initiative was teaching me anything, it was about the president's capacity to care about perception more than reality. He wanted it to look good. He cared less about it being good.

—David Kuo

As governor of Texas, George W. Bush believed that religious organizations could and should be close partners of government in providing social services to needy Americans. He associated himself with Marvin Olasky, known as the "godfather of compassionate conservatism," whose writings helped motivate evangelical groups to persuade private and religious charities to become more active in community service. Some of these groups were seen as having more expertise and more credibility than government agencies in meeting the needs of the underprivileged. But the First Amendment's principle of separation of church and state gave pause to religious organizations that might want to apply for, and accept, government funding, even to finance nonproselytizing social services.

In passing the welfare reform legislation in 1996, however, Congress inserted what has been called a "charitable choice" provision.[1] As one set of authors explained, under this provision

government would no longer exclude faith-based groups from receiving federal grants because of their religious character. Instead, the law said that they could retain religious symbols, scriptures and icons while delivering government social services; they could retain religious mission statements and board members with religious affiliations; they could receive federal funding without forming a separate, secularized nonprofit organization. The act also allowed them to retain their pre-existing freedom to show a preference in hiring for people who shared their faith.[2]

Governor Bush became the first governor to apply these new federal standards at the state level, issuing an executive order "directing Texas agencies to encourage faith-based organizations to provide social services to needy Texans."[3]

As early in his presidential campaign as July 1999, he pledged to institute such a partnership policy and also to establish an office of faith-based action. Nine days after entering office, President Bush fulfilled his campaign promise and, "by the authority vested in me as President of the United States and by the Constitution and the laws of the United States," issued two executive orders. The first order established the White House Office of Faith-Based and Community Initiatives (OFBCI) and enumerated eleven functions for that office, the first of which reads: "to develop, lead and coordinate the Administration's policy agenda affecting faith-based and other community programs and initiatives, expand the role of such efforts in communities, and increase their capacity, through executive action, legislation, federal and private funding and regulatory relief."[4] The new office, headed by an assistant to the president, was to have a staff "and other assistance." The office could function "through established or ad hoc committees"—a provision permitting the president to have the assistant report to him through the Domestic Policy Council. "All executive departments and agencies," said the order, "shall cooperate with the White House OFBCI and provide such information, support and assistance . . . as it may request, to the extent permitted by law," but "the agencies' actions . . . shall be carried out subject to the availability of appropriations and to the extent permitted by law."[5]

The second executive order, issued simultaneously and citing the same general presidential authority, was titled "Agency Responsibilities with Respect to Faith-Based and Community Initiatives."[6] It instructed the attorney general and the secretaries of labor, education, health and human services, and housing and urban development to "establish within their respective departments a Center for Faith-Based and Community Initiatives." Each center was to have a director appointed by the department head "in consultation with the White House OFBCI," was to be provided with "appropriate staff, administrative support, and other resources" by its home department, and was to be in operation in forty-five days.

The order laid on each center the task of conducting (in coordination with the OFBCI) an audit within its home department to identify all of the "existing barriers," that is, regulations, rules, procurement policies, and the like, that discriminated against faith-based organizations in their ability to participate in the social service programs of that department. Once the audit was complete, each center was directed to "propose initiatives" to remove those barriers. The centers were to report back to the OFBCI within 180 days. Each center was to designate an employee as the point of contact with the OFBCI and to "provide such information, support and assistance to the White House OFBCI as it may request, to the extent permitted by law."

In the early days of his administration, President Bush publicized this new program at every turn, giving forty speeches about it in as many weeks, including seven in one seventeen-day period in July of 2001.

With the results of the audits in hand, the OFBCI issued a report in August 2001 that began by declaring: "It is not Congress, but these overly restrictive Agency rules" that are "repressive" and that "actively undermine the established civil rights of these groups. Such excessive restrictions unnecessarily and improperly limit the participation of faith-based organizations that have profound contributions to make in civil society's efforts to serve the needy."[7]

The report laid out fifteen categories and examples of the barriers that needed to be removed and spurred the president to propose legislation that would accomplish most of the needed changes.[8] The bill was passed by the House, but the Democratic-controlled Senate refused to approve it. There was division, moreover, within the Christian community, with some groups viewing the president's program as involving too much governmental participation in matters of religion, while potential beneficiaries themselves were not well enough organized to exercise influence on Congress.

In the absence of congressional sanction, George Bush reached again for his presidential pen. In Executive Order 13279 of December 12, 2002, he defined specifically what he meant by federal financial assistance for faith-based organizations and the kinds of social service programs they could provide, and he set forth six "Fundamental Principles and Policymaking Criteria." They included the pronouncement that "no organization should be discriminated against on the basis of religion or religious belief in the administration or distribution of Federal financial assistance under social service programs." Bearing the Constitution's Establishment Clause in mind, the principles required that "organizations that engage in inherently religious activities, such as worship, religious instruction, and proselytization, must offer those services separately in time or location from any programs or services supported with direct Federal financial assistance" and that recipients of social services from those institutions would not be required to participate in any of those institutions' "inherently religious" activities. Agencies were told to follow these principles and amend any rules inconsistent with them.

On that same day, December 12, 2002, the president issued Executive Order 13280, adding the Department of Agriculture and the Agency for International Development to the list of agencies required to establish Centers for Faith-Based and Community Initiatives. In June 2004 and March 2006 he added the

Commerce, Veterans Affairs, and Homeland Security Departments, and the Small Business Administration to the same list.[9]

Reflecting on his exercise of executive powers, Bush commented: "I was hoping, frankly, that the Congress would pass a law. I got tired of waiting. See, I am focused on results. I want there to be positive results. I want lives to be saved as best as possible. The process got bogged down. . . . So I signed an Executive Order.[10]

Reaching Out to the Faith-Based Community

The OFBCI is located at 708 Jackson Place, a brownstone row house facing Lafayette Park. Its staff of twelve is headed by a director (currently a deputy assistant to the president). The director usually reports to the assistant to the president for domestic policy but often also to the deputy chief of staff for policy and occasionally to the president personally, since this OFBCI initiative is a personal innovation in which President Bush puts great stock. The office also has a deputy director who is a special assistant to the president. At last count, there have been three directors—John DiIulio, James Towey, and its current head, Jay Hein. The director of the OFBCI joins with the White House presidential personnel office to pick the person they want each department head to appoint as center director, which means that de facto the White House controls those appointments. "I would call it a significant influence," acknowledged Hein. Neither the center directors nor the OFBCI director is subject to Senate confirmation. The total staff in the several centers is approximately eighty.

How does the OFBCI administer these sweeping, new executive orders? The White House office has no grant-making authority or funds of its own and no legal authority to command departmental compliance. The OFBCI initiative is high on the president's management agenda, which is policed by the Office of Management and Budget, so the faith-based office has an ally in tracking progress.

Its principal job, however, is outreach—to spread the word to the operating agencies (which award the grants and have the funds), to remind them of the priority that the president gives to this initiative, and to advise the agencies about effective ways to notify the nation's faith-based community that these new opportunities exist and that they, in turn, should file applications to compete for financing. Many of the faith-based groups are local, quite small, with no representatives in Washington, and a tradition of avoiding taking government funds. The OFBCI published a sixty-seven-page catalogue of the 150-odd federal grant programs that it determined would be particularly appropriate for faith-based participation. The OFBCI group is in daily contact with the staffs of the centers, and the director meets quarterly with the center directors. He also deals directly with the policy assistant secretaries in the cabinet departments, since they are the officers who bear the accountability for the actual operation of the federal assistance programs.

The outreach effort features conferences: as of the spring of 2007, twenty-eight regional sessions of faith-based organizations had been convened; workshops are held that are in effect coaching sessions for prospective grantees, most of whom have little or no experience with seeking government support. Three national conferences have been held, and the president has appeared at all of them. Tens of thousands of religious leaders have been reached by these several categories of meetings; in addition the OFBCI has a website full of practical, procedural, and legal tips as a help to new applicants.

The OFBCI director also convenes monthly policy forums focusing on specific areas of public need, with experts on the chosen subject from the media, federal and local government, academia, and philanthropy. In February 2007, for instance, Hein organized a policy forum, called a "Compassion in Action Roundtable," that focused on curbing malaria in Africa. First Lady Laura Bush described how the Christian Children's Fund was helping teach families in rural Angola to use mosquito sprays to protect their children.

In 2002, not long after the faith-based initiative got started, the OFBCI arranged with the federal Administration for Children and Families in the Department of Health and Human Services to set aside federal funds to finance a Compassion Capital Fund. This fund concentrates on creating "intermediary organizations," which in turn help small grassroots faith-based groups working with particularly vulnerable populations such as families in poverty, prisoners reentering the community, and at-risk youth. These groups may need technical assistance in preparing grant applications, elementary capacity-building assistance in organizing their offices, even a "mini-grant" just to buy and use a computer at a headquarters. For the fiscal years 2002–06, Congress approved $231.3 million for the Compassion Capital Fund; the fiscal year 2008 appropriation request was $75 million.

The OFBCI initiative has been spreading to states and cities. Where the needs for social services are, there is where the faith-based organizations are—and there also are state and city monies available for locally rendered social services. Some of these monies are from federal block grants administered by the states and cities. Thirty-three governors and 100 mayors have established faith-based offices at their headquarters, some by executive fiat, some by legislation, some by charter, all of them with functions akin to the twelve federal centers. Do these new state and city offices look to the White House OFBCI as a model or as a leader of this now tremendously expanded initiative? "Literally, and they have told us that," said OFBCI Director Jay Hein. "They've asked us for technical support to form, to publicize, and we hold conferences with them so we can help them. We are not in the business of asking them to join us in something; we're joining them in problem-solving."[11] A few of these organizations are nondenominational or secular.

Criticism—and Legal Challenges

Has there been criticism of the faith-based initiative?

Yes. Some religious leaders believe that accepting government funds improperly entangles the receiving institution with the federal government, sapping the religious group's ability to speak out against policies of the government. "If you're bound to the government, it's very, very difficult to have that kind of prophetic voice," said Rev. Jane Holmes Dixon, a senior adviser to the Interfaith Alliance and a retired Episcopal bishop of Washington.[12]

Others consider the OFBCI initiative to be just another element of the Bush White House's unending political campaign to woo evangelicals and social conservatives. One former OFBCI staffer, himself an evangelical, wrote a self-serving book in which he reflects, "I wasn't just a Christian trying to serve God in politics. Now I was a Christian in politics looking for ways to recruit other Christians into politics so that we would have their votes."[13]

Most of the criticism of this program is based on the allegation that both the outreach and the funding actions of the faith-based initiative improperly vitiate the separation of church and state required by the First Amendment's Establishment Clause; several lawsuits have been filed raising this complaint. Especially notable was the lawsuit filed by the Wisconsin-based Freedom From Religion Foundation (FFRF) alleging that several of the regional conferences sponsored by the OFBCI and by the departments of Labor, Education, and Health and Human Services "were designed to promote, and had the effect of promoting, religious community groups over secular ones." At the conference, speeches were made, it was said, that singled out faith-based organizations as "being particularly worthy of federal funding . . . , and the belief in God is extolled as distinguishing the claimed effectiveness of faith-based social services."[14] A federal district court in Wisconsin dismissed the claims for lack of standing; a divided panel of the U.S. Court of Appeals for the Seventh Circuit reversed, "granting federal taxpayers standing to challenge Executive Branch programs on Establishment Clause grounds so long as the activities are 'financed by a congressional appropriation.'"[15]

The Supreme Court, however, in a 5-4 decision handed down in June 2007, reversed once more and denied standing to the FFRF respondents because "these appropriations did not expressly authorize, direct or even mention the expenditures of which the respondents complained. Those expenditures resulted from executive discretion, not congressional action."[16] The OFBCI was gratified by the Court's ruling, believing that it might cut off similar suits in other pending or future cases.

But it did not. In 2003 Americans United for Separation of Church and State had brought suit against an antirecidivism program being operated at the Newton state prison in Iowa by the InnerChange Freedom Initiative organization, which was part of Prison Fellowship Ministries. In June 2005, after trial, the U.S. District Court for the Southern District of Iowa found that the InnerChange program was "designed to thoroughly indoctrinate inmates in evangelical Christianity ... [and] had made no attempt to segregate religious and non-religious programming." The court declared the program unconstitutional, a violation of the Establishment Clause.[17] The plaintiffs had standing, the court found, because, in this case, unlike the Wisconsin case, "the Iowa legislature made specific appropriations from public funds." The court found the violation so serious that it ordered the Prison Fellowship Ministries to repay the state of Iowa more than $1.5 million. The defendants, while not contesting the district court's findings with respect to how the program was being operated, appealed to the U.S. Court of Appeals for the Eighth Circuit.

On December 3, 2007, a three-judge panel of that court unanimously agreed that the InnerChange program was unconstitutional, although it required repayment only for the period after June 2006. The court enumerated several reasons, concluding among other things since the program was open only to those "who agreed to participate in Christian religious transformation," it "was not allocated on neutral criteria and was not available on a nondiscriminatory basis."[18] On December 17, 2007, the defendants appealed to the 8th Circuit for a full-court review but that appeal was denied.

The Roundtable on Religion and Social Policy, an independent research project of the Rockefeller Institute of the State University of New York, published the following legal analysis in its December 2007 e-newsletter:

> The 8th Circuit's opinion ... is a landmark. ... [T]he opinion lays down a straightforward approach—backed by Supreme Court precedent coined in the far different context of aid to religious schools—for adjudicating the validity of faith-based programs in prison. Unless the Supreme Court enters the fray and changes those underlying standards, or repudiates them in the prison context, the 8th Circuit opinion is likely to remain the guidepost for prison officials, faith-based programs, and courts in evaluating other such programs.[19]

The Future of This White House Program

What has this White-House-led initiative grown to become? A *National Journal* survey in January of 2007 reported that

> thousands of small, faith-based organizations nationwide ... are using taxpayer dollars to provide social services. ... More than $2 billion in federal funding—and an untallied but growing amount of state and local support—is pouring into church-affiliated organizations around the country annually. In some cases, moreover, the government is essentially

creating faith-based organizations. . . . Amid all of the activity, a basic question has never been fully resolved: What are the limits for what faith-based organizations can do with government money? Government officials emphasize that they teach all tax-dollar recipients that the money can pay only for secular services that are clearly separate from religious activity. But sometimes that line is not so clear. . . . Krista Sisterhen, outgoing director of the Governor's Office of Faith-Based and Community Initiatives in Ohio, said that the State views the faith-based initiative as "a way to revolutionize and improve the way government purchases social services and gets social services delivered. The promise of this is only beginning to be recognized."[20]

The *Journal's* survey concluded, "billions of dollars are pouring into faith-based charities with no guarantee that the groups are providing valuable services. Promoters of the initiative argue the same is true of secular service providers. 'How do we give money to anybody when we don't know what success means?' Stanley Carlson-Thies, a former White House faith-based adviser, asked. For now, at least, the government is relying on faith."[21]

In January 2008 the first director of the OFBCI, John DiIulio, and its former deputy director, David Kuo, jointly wrote an op-ed piece in the *New York Times* entitled "The Faith to Outlast Politics." Their evaluation:

Every non-partisan study has concluded that the initiative has not delivered the grants, vouchers, tax incentives and other support for faith-based organizations that the president originally promised. In a book published last year, Michael Gerson, Mr. Bush's former speechwriter, concludes: "The faith-based initiative was not tried and found wanting. It was tried and found difficult—then tried with less and less energy." . . . Faith-based initiatives have a centrist past that can be prologue.[22]

In his State of the Union Message of January 25, 2008, President Bush lauded the work of the Office of Faith-Based and Community Initiatives, saying that "faith-based groups are bringing hope to pockets of despair with newfound support from the federal government . . . And, to help guarantee equal treatment of faith-based organizations when they compete for federal funds, I ask you [the Congress] to permanently extend [the] Charitable Choice [legislation]."

On February 25, 2008, the White House Office of Faith-Based and Community Initiatives issued a 175-page summary report entitled "The Quiet Revolution" summarizing what it thought this Bush administration innovation had accomplished in the seven years since it began. An independent analysis of the report said it

summarizes how the President implemented the initiative domestically and internationally by issuing five executive orders to spread its reach across the federal government, rewriting 16 federal rules to help faith-based organizations provide government services, providing training and assistance to more than 100,000 religious and grass-roots organizations, and encouraging similar efforts in 35 states and more than 100 cities. . . . The report spotlights the work of 50 government employees in satellite Faith-Based and Community Initiatives centers at 11 federal agencies and one independent federal office of volunteer service. It also described activities of particular programs heralded by the Initiative, including prisoner reentry programs to help offenders return to communities, mentoring children of prisoners, substance abuse treatment, health care centers in low-income communities, and assistance to homeless people.[23]

At the White House, when President Bush presented the report to a group of state leaders who had gathered in Washington for a National Governors Association meeting, he observed, "Sometimes I like to say government is not a very loving organization; it's an organization of law and justice. But there are thousands of loving people who are willing, if given help, to interface with brothers and sisters across the country that need help. And so this report is one that describes the federal-state collaboration that's taken place." The initiative "has been carried out with little fanfare," he said, adding that in 2006 alone it had funded 18,000 faith-based community organizations that provide services to at-risk youth, disaster victims, recovering drug addicts, prisoners returning to society, people with HIV/AIDS, and the homeless. "Not a final report or hard-core evaluation," commented OFBCI director Jay Hein, "the report is a progress report." Its objective was to have "the next president be aware of the initiative's purpose and accomplishments. . . . The initiative has been a deliberate, intentioned strategy to make private nonprofit work a central role in the government apparatus of delivering human services. I don't know any other president in history that has made civic service a central part of government."[24]

The report evoked both praise and criticism. A former deputy director of the OFBCI said that initiative was "a serious, substantive, careful, and significant effort to improve services, make government collaboration with grassroots and faith-based groups more fruitful, and better follow the constitutional mandate to protect religious freedom and ensure equal treatment of all."[25] But another former deputy director criticized the faith-based initiative "as being a political tool and failing to deliver a promised $8 billion in grants to faith-based organizations," saying "if they had fulfilled the President's promises, there wouldn't be any need for a glossy PR document that only proves the Initiative's great failures."[26]

A second critic said that "President Bush has spent seven years manipulating religion and twisting the Constitution. He seems obsessed with finding a 'faith-based' solution to every social problem, even it if means scrapping long-standing civil rights and civil liberties protections. Bush says he has 'leveled the playing field' for religion, but in fact he's tilted it toward religious groups, allowing them to discriminate in hiring in publicly funded programs."[27]

Illustrating the rocky road that continues to face the implementation of this initiative, the senior litigation counsel of Americans United for Separation of Church and State, on the same day the OFBCI summary report appeared, sent an eleven-page letter to the heads of four cabinet departments identifying ten fiscal year 2008 congressionally enacted earmarks mandating social service grants that he alleged "run afoul of the Constitution" and sixteen others that he found "troubling" for the same reasons. The counsel challenged the four cabinet secretaries to review *all* their fiscal year 2008 earmarks "to ensure that they comply with constitutional and regulatory requirements" and respond within fifteen days.[28]

Concluding Comment

To the presidential scholar, the White House faith-based initiative enterprise is highly significant in two ways. First, the whole, now quite vast, program is entirely executive—in concept and in administration. All of its thirteen executive branch institutional elements, in the White House and the centers in the departments and agencies, were created not by statute but by executive order. The author knows of no similar chain of executive orders by any president that, in the absence of legislation, sets up a new program and establishes so many interlinked operating bases through the federal executive branch. Some presidential scholars have commented, mostly in a negative and apprehensive tone, about the extent to which President Bush and Vice President Cheney have expanded executive power. The faith-based initiative undertaking is an expansion of executive power but rather than being accused of being deleterious, it is a program that many argue is beneficial to the social infrastructure of the nation.

Second, the OFBCI is a George W. Bush innovation—a substantive addition to the administrative corpus of the White House staff and, in the author's judgment, a strong candidate for replication in the White House of 2009—although that will be entirely up to the new president. In their *New York Times* op-ed, cited earlier, DiIulio and Kuo inserted a subhead: "One Bush initiative that will live on, no matter who becomes president."

Would the next president continue the White House Office of Faith-Based and Community Initiatives? Speaking at Messiah College, a small, private Christian college in Pennsylvania on April 13, 2008, presidential candidate Barack Obama said

> I want to keep the Office of Faith-Based Initiatives open, but I want to make sure that its mission is clear. It's not to simply build a particular faith community. The faith-based initiatives should be targeted specifically at

the issues of poverty and how to lift people up. . . . We'll make sure that it's open to everybody; it's not simply the federal government funding certain groups to be able to evangelize.[29]

Obama went on to add that "government should partner with religious organizations to provide social services as long as it is done within the requirements of the Constitution."

Volunteerism and Community Service: The USA Freedom Corps Office

The USA Freedom Corps will encourage and support those who want to serve our country. Countless Americans now serve in countless ways to improve our nation and our world. The USA Freedom Corps values this spirit and seeks to build upon it. The USA Freedom Corps will provide opportunities and create incentives for Americans to become even more involved in serving their communities and country—and in serving the peoples of other nations.

—George W. Bush

The Freedom Corps stands as a reminder of how presidential dreams can collide with Washington reality, and how promises made with fanfare can sometimes fade away. Today some of the Freedom Corps initiative's biggest early boosters, including several former Bush administration officials, say it wound up a disappointment.... "It has run out of steam," said John DiIulio.

—Sheryl Gay Stolberg, *New York Times*

Volunteering is a practice as old as America. Alexis de Tocqueville wrote that Americans' ethic of service "prompts them to assist one another and inclines them willingly to sacrifice a portion of their time and property to the welfare of the state."

In addition to the decades of private volunteer service given across the nation, government-financed volunteering began in the 1960s with the creation of the Peace Corps under President Kennedy and VISTA (Volunteers in Service to America), Foster Grandparents, and other programs started under President Johnson. In 1973 the domestically oriented programs were consolidated under ACTION, which in turn was subsumed, in 1993, under the Corporation for National and Community Service. The corporation, an independent body (and not part of the White House) now has three elements: AmeriCorps (in which half a million individuals have served), Learn and Serve America (which has funded training and education programs for more than 1 million high school students annually), and the Senior Corps (whose volunteers have already racked up 1 billion service hours). The Corporation for National and Community Service collectively is the nation's largest grant maker in support of service and volunteering. Its fiscal year 2008 budget request was $828,680.

The Bush Freedom Corps Initiative

In his 2002 State of the Union message, President Bush said:

> We have glimpsed what a new culture of responsibility could look like. We want to be a nation that serves goals larger than self. We've been offered an opportunity, and we must not let this moment pass. My call tonight is for every American to commit at least 2 years, 4,000 hours over the rest of your lifetime, to the service of your Nation. . . . I invite you to join the USA Freedom Corps. The Freedom Corps will focus on three areas of need: responding in case of crisis at home; rebuilding our communities; and extending American compassion throughout the world.[1]

Rather than delegating this new enterprise to his cabinet, or setting up a new executive branch agency, Bush turned to his own personal staff, and, on the very same day as his address, signed an executive order establishing the USA Freedom Corps as "an interagency initiative, bringing together executive branch departments, agencies and offices with public service programs and components." In that executive order he instituted a cabinet-level Freedom Corps Council, chaired by the president and also created a new office at the White House named the USA Freedom Corps Office. Among its duties, the new office was to "support the President in providing recognition to volunteers."[2] The Freedom Corps is not itself a specific body or an agency; it is simply the title for the general initiative laid out in the president's message. The "Freedom Corps Council" provision turned out to be only pro forma; the council has never met; the member agencies do their common work in constant but informal coordination.

In the State of the Union message, the president called for the existing AmeriCorps and Senior Corps to recruit more than 200,000 new volunteers and asked for a doubling of Peace Corps volunteers during the next five years, including a "new effort to encourage development and education and opportunity in the Islamic world." Since the president's call to service, the number of community volunteers leveraged by AmeriCorps state and national grantees has increased from approximately 250,000 in 2002 to approximately 850,000 in 2006, and the Peace Corps is operating at a thirty-seven-year high in the number of volunteers serving around the world.

Volunteer Number One is the president himself. At least twice a year, usually during holiday periods, such as on Martin Luther King's birthday, and during National Volunteer Week, in April, the president and First Lady Laura Bush set an example by visiting an organization that uses volunteers. In 2006 the president flew to New Orleans and pitched in helping to build a Habitat for Humanity home, then visited a volunteer camp in Biloxi, Mississippi.

After 9/11, the new Department of Homeland Security in 2002 created a Citizens Corps—a network of state, local, and tribal Citizens Corps Councils, to better prepare Americans to respond to threats of terrorism, neighborhood crime, public health issues, and disasters of all kinds. Now in its sixth year, the Citizens Corps operates nearly 2,300 Citizens Corps Councils nationwide, which serve roughly 75 percent of the U.S. population. These councils help individuals and nongovernmental organizations engage in community preparedness and response.

Operation of the USA Freedom Corps Office

The USA Freedom Corps office of six people is part of the White House Office but is located at 736 Jackson Place. It is headed by a deputy assistant to the president, supported by a special assistant to the president, two associate directors, a special assistant to the director who handles the greeter program (described below), and an executive assistant. The office reports to the president through the Domestic Policy Council.

The USA Freedom Corps initiative focuses on three areas: influencing policy by strengthening national service programs and initiatives, working with nonprofit organizations to help build their capacity, and working with individual Americans to promote more volunteer service. An example of the way volunteerism has influence on a matter of policy is the legislation that the president proposed concerning measures to meet the problem of immigration. Built into that legislation was an authorization for $300 million to help legal immigrants to assimilate into American society by using volunteers to teach them English and citizenship and reduce their feelings of isolation. The program would have been managed by the Department of Homeland Security's Office of Citizenship. The legislation did not pass, but the provisions regarding assimilation illustrate what the Freedom Corps is trying to do throughout government: "embed the principles of service and civic engagement across all the president's policies. . . . We don't conduct operations; these programs all manage themselves. What we're here to do is to influence policy, to strengthen and expand these programs. . . . We can't make voluntary service mandatory, but we can certainly do our best to incentivize it."[3]

An aspect of "incentivization" is the Freedom Corps' master database of opportunities for volunteering. The Freedom Corps office used White House Office funds to contract with some sixteen search-engine companies around the country that could reach out to nonprofit organizations such as the Points of Light Foundation and the Red Cross, and, every twenty-four hours, upload notices of volunteer opportunities into the database. A person interested in volunteer service can go into the "volunteer.gov" website, type in his or her zip code, and be presented with the volunteer opportunities pending and available in that zip code. The master list currently lists 4.2 million opportunities.

The President's Council on Service and Civic Participation

On the first anniversary of the creation of the USA Freedom Corps, President Bush issued an executive order creating, within the Corporation for National and Community Service, the President's Council on Service and Civil Participation. This council is a group of twenty-five people who are, in effect, celebrities from the nonprofit, public, and private sectors including sports, entertainment, and the media. The council's principal mission is to "encourage the recognition of outstanding volunteer service and civil participation by individuals, schools, and organizations and thereby encourage more such activity. . . ."[4] The council makes recommendations to the president, through the director of the Freedom Corps, "on ways to promote and recognize outstanding volunteer service."

One of the council's recommendations was to create a presidential award to be presented to volunteers who had rendered exceptional service. President Bush accepted this recommendation and made it official in an executive order of January 30, 2003. The award, available to all Americans, including groups, comes with a lapel pin, certificate, congratulatory letter from the president, and a letter from the President's Council on Service and Civic Participation. The organization handling the arrangements for the award is the Points of Light Foundation (originally established by President Bush's father.) As of this writing, over 655,000 President's Volunteer Service Awards have been given; the Freedom Corps office is aiming for 1 million before the end of President Bush's presidency.

Incentives for Federal Employees to Volunteer

What social service organizations say they really need is not just volunteers, but volunteers who can serve during working hours. Are federal employees able to do this? The answer is yes; the Office of Personnel Management in the Clinton administration promulgated rules permitting federal employees to volunteer during working hours and be given excused absence; they did not have to take leave to do so. The Bush Freedom Corps leadership wanted to increase the incentives for this category of volunteering, so on April 27, 2006, President Bush issued Executive Order 13401 requiring every federal agency head to establish, at the Senior Executive Service level, an "agency liaison for volunteer community service." The order specified that "the Liaison in each agency shall promote and support community service on a voluntary basis among Federal employees, including those approaching retirement; promote the use of skilled volunteers; and facilitate public recognition of volunteer community service." The liaison was to

> actively work with USA Freedom Corps to promote volunteer community service among agency employees by providing information about community service opportunities; . . . work with the USA Freedom Corps and the Director of the Office of Personnel Management (OPM) to consider any appropriate changes in agency policies or practices that are not currently consistent with OPM guidance; . . . submit an [annual] report to the USA Freedom Corps [which] shall include annual performance indicators and measurable objectives for agency action approved by the head of the agency.[5]

The Treasury Department's liaison was the treasurer of the United States, and during National Volunteer Week in 2006, she was out swinging a hammer helping to build a Habitat for Humanity house. In 2006 Secretary of Labor Elaine Chao went to Baltimore-Washington International Airport, where she handed out Care packages to soldiers boarding planes to Iraq. The 2007 National Volunteer Week found agency heads participating in fifty service-related activities; thirteen of the fifteen cabinet secretaries personally volunteered. The departmental liaison officers are trying to establish a tradition of each cabinet secretary undertaking at least two public volunteer actions each year.

There are, of course, limits to federal employees being excused from work to volunteer. The rule is that employees can be excused for volunteering during working hours if at least one of four criteria is met: the service must advance the needs of the agency, or not cause any undue harm or disruption to the agency's work flow, or provide some sort of professional development, or be approved by a supervisor. Besides applying for excused absences, federal employees also have the option of alternative work arrangements that grant them compressed work schedules, so that they have ample volunteer time each week, or flexible work scheduling so that they can build credit hours toward volunteering. For Martin Luther King's birthday (and federal holiday) in 2007, the Freedom Corps called on agency heads to encourage their employees to perform volunteer service that day, to "make it a day on, not a day off!" The D.C. Jewish Community Center, which used to need six weeks to fill its volunteer opportunities, reported in 2007 that it filled them in two weeks and had to find additional opportunities because so many government workers were volunteering.

The agency liaison officers are periodically called together for briefings by the Freedom Corps; in October 2006 they enjoyed the special privilege of a group photo with the president. "These were public servants, many of whom have worked in government for thirty-plus years, but have never met the president or been thanked by him," said an observer. "They already have full-time jobs and are taking on this liaison responsibility in addition to their regular duties."[6]

Federal Agencies Using Volunteers Who Are Not Employees

The National Park Service has long used—and depended on—volunteers in nearly every national park in the United States. It sponsors the "Take Pride in America" program in which 300,000 volunteers participate. They lead tour groups to the parks, rebuild fences, clear brush, and remove invasive species. Those who serve 500 hours in a year are qualified for an "America the Beautiful" pass giving them free entry to any national park. Forty-five volunteers help run the National Park Service's White House Visitor Center (chapter 34). Close to home, the White House itself cannot do without its pool of 425 volunteers (chaper 27).

In 2003 the president launched a new volunteer initiative through the U.S. Agency for International Development: Volunteers for Prosperity (VfP).[7] It is a federal catalyst for mobilizing highly skilled Americans such as doctors, nurses, teachers, engineers, economists, and computer specialists in new international volunteer service opportunities that help meet the U.S. government's global health and prosperity goals. It is designed for volunteers who cannot spend the two years that the Peace Corps requires. Programs that volunteers can work in include PEPFAR (President's Emergency Plan for AIDS Relief), African Global Competitiveness, Water for the Poor, Digital Freedom, and Middle East Partnership. Under the VfP initiative, those organizations that agree to take on an increased number of volunteers over what they already have are awarded a competitive advantage in their applications for USAID funding. VfP has helped USAID mobilize more than 30,000 volunteers through more than 250 partner organizations.

The Peace Corps itself, while it has not yet doubled, has reached an all-time high in the number of volunteers and has begun a supplemental initiative, called the Crisis Corps. This group is made up of returned Peace Corps volunteers able to serve in emergencies abroad or at home. Seventy-three went to the Gulf Coast in 2005 to help after the Katrina disaster.

The Greeters Program

A dramatic example of the skillful use of incentives is the greeters program, handled by a full-time staffer in the USA Freedom Corps Office. The office is given a four- or five-day advance notice of every visit the president makes within the United States. The assistant immediately contacts the volunteer center or centers and other faith-based and community organizations in the arrival city and asks for nominations: who are the several outstanding volunteers who have met the 4,000-hour level of service? The arrangement is made by the greeters officer at the White House. The result: one or more greeters are right there at the airport to receive a presidential handshake, welcome him to the city he is visiting, mention to him the projects in which the greeter is engaged and be photographed by the local press—which is eager for this type of picture.

In addition to giving these volunteers an opportunity to meet the president, the greeters program also highlights the work the volunteers are doing. In Phoenix, for example, there was a woman named Barbara MacLean whose younger sister had died of cancer in 2001. Before her sister passed away, Barbara gave her a complete beauty makeover. Seeing the joy that day of beauty brought to her sister, Barbara MacLean began Face in the Mirror, an outreach program to women with cancer. MacLean was selected to be a Freedom Corps greeter. When President Bush stepped out of *Air Force One* in Phoenix, asking his customary "Where is my Freedom Corps greeter?" he was introduced to MacLean. The resulting story, and a photo, appeared "above the fold" in at least two major Phoenix area newspapers. Afterward, MacLean received calls from people in four other states, wanting to replicate her service in their hospitals. "It's hard to measure the impact of our Freedom Corps," a close observer of the program said. As of this writing, the Freedom Corps Office has arranged over 600 presidential greeter arrivals.

Other Nations' Interest in the Freedom Corps

The American ethos of volunteer service, and especially its institutionalization in the White House, has caught the interest of other nations, some of whom have not had the same tradition or culture of responsibility, service, and citizenship. The Department of State regularly asks the Freedom Corps staff to meet with delegations from other countries. Diplomats from a number of nations—including Belgium, Denmark, Israel, the Philippines, and the United Kingdom—have come in for briefings and have been given materials describing the Freedom Corps' extensive networks of participating organizations.

Summing Up

The Corporation for National and Community Service posts the following summary on its website (www.nationalservice.org). It can be taken as an acknowledgment of, and an answer to, the criticism mentioned at the beginning of this chapter.

> Today, the ethic remains strong. Across our country, Americans of all ages, backgrounds, and abilities are devoting their time and talents to schools, churches, hospitals, and local non-profits in an effort to improve their communities and serve a purpose greater than themselves. According to data collected over the past 30 years, by the U.S. Census Bureau and the Bureau of Labor Statistics, Americans over the age of 16 are volunteering at historically high rates, with 61.2 million giving their time in 2006 to help others by mentoring students, beautifying neighborhoods, restoring

homes after disasters, and much, much more. Although the adult volunteer rate for 2006, 26.7% was down slightly from the 28.8% recorded from 2003–2005, a greater percentage of American adults are volunteering today than at any other time in the past 30 years. These include late teens, Baby Boomers, and those ages 65 and older. In addition, more and more young people are becoming involved in their communities through school-based learning and volunteering.

This increase is a critically important development, because volunteering is no longer just nice to do. It is a necessary aspect of meeting the most pressing needs facing our nation: crime, gangs, poverty, disasters and homelessness. It is also an important part of maintaining the health of our citizens, as research consistently shows that those who volunteer, especially those 65 years and older, lead healthier lives than those who do not engage in their communities.

In name, the USA Freedom Corps is a George W. Bush innovation, but in substance, in its mission, and in its institutionalization as an office within the White House, it had a predecessor: the Points of Light Movement of President George H. W. Bush. The first President Bush opened an Office of National Service in the White House, staffed it with a young man with whom he was personally close, and later gave the director the rank of assistant to the president. The creation of the Points of Light Movement, and of the office, was

> an effort to use the presidency to call people to a type of engagement in the most serious social problems of our time. To show people how they could do that should they want to respond to that call, and to support it in certain ways. We developed a basic strategy the objective of which was, ideally, to cause every American to engage in a direct and consequential way in helping to solve these serious social problems.[8]

During his four years in office the first president Bush designated 1,020 outstanding individuals, organizations, even newspapers, as Presidential Points of Light and personally met with 675 of the honorees. The private Points of Light Foundation was established at that time and continues today as a nongovernmental organization providing valuable support to the second George Bush's Freedom Corps enterprise.

The Cabinet Liaison Office

> Today the attorney general presides over a department of 95,000 people....
> [She] has a huge department to run and when the president needs her, the
> chances are she will be down on the Rio Grande looking at the fences or
> tightening up the immigration process. The whole government has grown to
> the point where the Cabinet departments, important as they are, have become
> what you might call outer moons, and the president's need for an intimate
> personal staff, who used to be the Cabinet, today requires that he create
> his own.
>
> —Lloyd Cutler

Lloyd Cutler, who had been counsel to Jimmy Carter, was counsel to President
Clinton when he made this comment on the changing relationship between the
president and the cabinet; the observation has also been true for the presidency
of George W. Bush. In the Bush administration, the cabinet has not been a pol-
icy-making body; its meetings have primarily been for information exchange.
Discussion and debate about issues of presidential policy have been centered in
the four White House councils (National Security, Domestic Policy, National
Economic, and Homeland Security) and more specifically in the hands of the
four assistants to the president who manage those councils and who work most
closely with the deputy chief of staff for policy. "Cabinet meetings are not particularly decisional meetings; they're really more informational briefings," said
one knowledgeable observer. "There hasn't been a large group debate over any
one particularly controversial issue." In that respect, not much had changed
since September 2001, when a news story summed up the status of the cabinet–
White House policy environment at that point:

> Christine Todd Whitman had been New Jersey's governor before heading
> President Bush's Environmental Protection Agency. But Bush rarely asks
> for her advice outside her area of responsibility. "Mostly we talk about the
> dog, about Barney," she said of the Scottish terrier she gave the president.
>
> Mel R. Martinez, who was chairman of Florida's Orange County before
> becoming Bush's secretary of housing and urban development, was
> recently asked if he had spoken at Cabinet meetings. "Couple of times," he
> replied. "I was asked to lead the prayer at one of them, and I did."

Bush's highly credentialed Cabinet members are finding themselves in an unaccustomed role: that of subordinates. As the administration took office, it was thought that Bush's Cabinet would be unusually powerful because of its impressive lineup of talent: former governors and senators, veterans of previous Cabinets, top business executives and a popular general. But on most of the big issues, Cabinet members have discovered that they have less clout than lesser-known White House aides. . . . In a string of politically charged decisions . . . White House aides have been the leading actors. In each case, the necessities of politics continue to pull power to Bush's inner circle in the White House.[1]

The inner circle became increasingly "innerer" during the first term of the Bush administration. In 2002 the holder of the White House position of secretary to the cabinet had the rank of assistant to the president and supervised a staff of eleven. By spring 2004 the cabinet secretary was a deputy assistant to the president and the eleven staffers were completely different people. As time went on, and it became clearer that substantive policy issues were going to be handled almost exclusively in the four policy councils, the role of the secretary to the cabinet was further amended to comport with that policymaking environment. The name of the office was accordingly changed to Cabinet Liaison, the staff was slimmed down to six persons plus two interns, and the director's title became special assistant to the president. The director attends the regular morning meetings held by the deputy chief of staff for policy, who reports on matters from the senior staff meeting, as well as the directors' meeting convened by the deputy chief of staff for political affairs.

The Cabinet Defined

Cabinet is a venerable but loose term. It has always included the heads of the statutory departments (which now include Homeland Security). President Eisenhower, who was the last president to use the cabinet systematically, included his vice president, the U.S. ambassador to the United Nations, the director of the Bureau of the Budget, and the director of the (then) Office of Defense Mobilization. Near the end of his second term, Ike invited the chairman of the Republican National Committee to sit with the cabinet. None of the presidents since Eisenhower have used the cabinet as he did—with a numbered series of papers (including a decision-summary) circulated to all the members. Clinton conferred cabinet membership on ten more agency heads: the director of the Central Intelligence Agency, the chair of the Council of Economic Advisers, the administrator of the Environmental Protection Agency, the director of the Federal Emergency Management Agency, the administrator of the General Services Administration, the director of the Office of National Drug Control

Policy, the director of the Office of Personnel Management, the administrator of the Small Business Administration, the administrator of the Social Security Administration, and the U.S. Trade Representative.

Presidents can give cabinet status to any other official they please—as Ike did with his chief and deputy chief of staff, and as Clinton did with his chiefs of domestic, national economic, and national security policy. President George W. Bush limited the additions (beyond department heads and the vice president) to the head of the Office of Management and Budget, the U.S. Trade Representative, the administrator of the Environmental Protection Agency, and the director of National Drug Control Policy. To take seats around the sides of the room, Mr. Bush invited the chair of the Council of Economic Advisers, the chair of the Council on Environmental Quality, and the director of the Office of Science and Technology, and also all his White House staff who had the rank of assistant to the president (seventeen at last count). The author's preferred definition of *cabinet member* is: any officer whom the president invites to attend cabinet meetings regularly and who sits at the table, where there are at most twenty-two chairs.

Cabinet Relationships in the Bush Administration

The cabinet met forty times in the first sixty-three months of the Bush administration.

To prepare for a cabinet meeting, the director of the Cabinet Liaison Office consults with his staff to identify issues that are ripe for reporting to the president, then takes the list to the deputy chief of staff for policy. He and the chief of staff, consulting with the president if needed, decide on the agenda, which the Cabinet Liaison Office distributes electronically the night before the meeting. The agenda is not classified but is considered "close hold."

President Bush's style is to start each cabinet meeting with a spoken prayer led by a member of the cabinet. Since the leadership's focus is so much on the wars in Iraq and Afghanistan, the president typically makes some remarks about his feelings concerning the administration's war efforts. Ross Kyle, the cabinet liaison director in the Bush White House, recalled one cabinet meeting in February 2006, where a 217-page report on "The Federal Response to Hurricane Katrina: Lessons Learned" was the topic of discussion. The report itself was the product not of any one cabinet department but of the White House Homeland Security Council staff, aided by fifteen detailees from the responsible agencies. At the meeting, each cabinet member was simply asked to summarize what his or her department had done to assist in the Katrina recovery.

The cabinet liaison director and one of his staff attend the meetings and take notes. Since cabinet meetings are informational rather than decisionmaking, no action record is compiled or distributed.

The director does make brief, ten-minute conference calls twice a week, on Mondays and Thursdays, to the chiefs of staff of all the cabinet departments; they are termed "chief of staff calls." "We'll run down the president's schedule for the next couple of weeks and sometimes we'll have announcements about upcoming events," Kyle explained.[2] Reports from cabinet meetings are included in these calls, especially when the president has asked his cabinet members to lend the support of their departments to particular presidential initiatives. If any of the four policy councils plans a principals (cabinet-level) meeting, the Cabinet Liaison Office assists in getting the right people to the right session; after a decision has been made, the liaison function is to follow up. As Kyle put it, "OK, this policy has been decided. [Now] what does this particular agency need from the White House and what does the White House need these agencies to do?" If the president will be making remarks affecting the cabinet officer's area of interest, the latter will be informed. If the cabinet member should be in an event motorcade, or in the limo with the president, or on *Air Force One,* those arrangements are made.

When a cabinet secretary asks for an appointment with the president, the chief of staff may ask the Cabinet Liaison Office to find out what is on the secretary's mind. At least once a year, each cabinet member is guaranteed a no-agenda session with the president, the chief of staff, and the deputy chief of staff for policy, where he or she can bring up any subject. If the cabinet secretary wants to discuss a policy issue, the Cabinet Liaison Office may provide some background in advance.

Keeping the President Informed

A president sits in the Oval Office knowing that he is supposed to be taking care "that the laws be faithfully executed." But what is going on out there in the far corners of his executive branch? Is anything off track? What decisions are being made that he should know about? What is coming up that may be worrisome? To answer these questions, President Eisenhower established a quiet reporting system wherein each agency head was directed to send informal notifications of such goings-on to the staff secretary, who compiled a nightly summary called Staff Notes. At times, an item in the summary would evoke a reaction of surprise from the president. In one instance Eisenhower read about a dam that was going to be built, got concerned about its cost, and demanded more information. Kennedy replicated that initiative through his cabinet secretary. From that modest beginning developed the now regular practice of cabinet reports, weekly summaries from each department to the White House. The Cabinet Liaison Office extracts the most pertinent information from these submissions and at the end of the week sends an overall report to the president.

The Bush cabinet liaison staff arranges for and prepares two cabinet reports each week, one with eight to ten pages of broad information that is circulated to the senior staff, and a shorter one made up of contributions personally authored, or signed off on, by the cabinet members—information they want the president to know. These unvarnished reports go only to the chief executive and to the chief of staff and his two deputies. Every cabinet secretary supplies something every week; a few may send in classified annexes. The departments of State and Defense of course have their own channels for classified information; trade negotiations may merit a separate classified summary.

Quite often, the cabinet reports elicit a reaction from one of the senior staff or from the chief of staff: "Get me more information about *that*," or "We need to start a policy process on this one."

When Cabinet Members Travel

The Cabinet Liaison Office asks each cabinet secretary to send the White House a schedule of his or her travel three months in advance. These itineraries are carefully studied and compared with one another and are also shared with the White House Appointments and Scheduling Office. If two cabinet secretaries are going to be in the same place at the same time, speaking on different subjects, one may be asked to change plans so the single desired "message of the week" is not diluted. Should a cabinet member be planning to visit a city that is on the president's schedule for the same time, the former may be asked to hold off. Either the cabinet liaison director or the surrogates' coordinator in the Appointments and Scheduling Office may also ask a cabinet secretary to add an extra stop to his or her planned schedule to meet with an audience the White House believes deserves special attention.

Cabinet Office Space in the White House

Heads of the agencies that make up the national security community are constantly in the Oval Office or in meetings with the White House senior staff. Cabinet department heads outside that community—Agriculture, Labor, Commerce, Interior, for example—are in the White House much less often, a situation that can lead to a sense of isolation, even alienation. Bill Clinton's secretary of labor, Robert Reich, wrote in his memoir:

> The Secretary of Transportation phones to ask me how I discover what's going on at the White House. I have no clear answer. . . . The decision-making "loop" depends on physical proximity to B—who's whispering into his ear most regularly, whose office is closest to the Oval, who's sitting or standing next to him when a key issue arises. . . . One of the best techniques is to linger in the corridors of the West Wing after a meeting, picking up gossip. Another good place is the executive parking lot between the West Wing and the Old Executive Office Building, where dozens of White

House staffers tromp every few minutes. In this administration you're either in the loop or you're out of the loop, but more likely you don't know where the loop is, or you don't even know there *is* a loop.[3]

President Clinton's chief of staff John Podesta acted to remedy this feeling of alienation by inviting groups of cabinet members, seven or eight at a time, for breakfast at the White House mess—"just to kick things around, listen to them, let them tell me what was going on."[4] In March 2005 Bush's chief of staff Andy Card instituted an innovation: he established a suite for cabinet officers to use in the Eisenhower Executive Office Building: a large conference room for meetings and an adjoining small private office. He notified each of them that they were invited, even expected, to spend at least two hours a week there. "It was important for cabinet officers to know that they were welcome in the White House," explained Card. "If they are physically present they can pick up helpful information and the White House staff can reciprocally pick up information too. The White House has a great tendency to ignore the cabinet, so I was trying to build a relationship with the cabinet that was institutional rather than personality driven."[5]

"Cabinet members are here frequently, on a daily basis," explained Cabinet Liaison Office director Kyle.

Secretary of Agriculture [Mike] Johanns and Interior Secretary [Dirk] Kempthorne have set up what they call their "Kitchen Cabinet" meetings where they bring a few senior folks from their departments and meet with White House officers weekly or biweekly here in our conference room so they can sit down and hash out whatever issues they're experiencing. The secretary will bring over his chief of staff or counselor, solicitor maybe, and meet with the White House communications staff, or policy folks, legislative affairs experts. Secretary Kempthorne is going to have a session on the Endangered Species Act here tomorrow. Secretary Johanns is using the suite a lot for the formulation of farm bills and how we all are going to feel like we have some equity in the farm bill. . . . We have told the secretaries that if they would like to meet with outside groups, governors, labor union folks, they can use this conference room for that. I think the cabinet members like to have a place to go that's theirs, so to speak, so they are not fighting for rooms when they need them. They can have a private place for phone calls. And we're here next door to support them, so they're not just on their own.

Kyle added, "Cabinet members have full White House Mess privileges, so they can come to lunch with whomever they want, whenever they want. They can bring guests to the Mess, either family or staff, so that's another way we are trying to keep them from feeling alienated."

*The Strategic Initiatives
and External Affairs Bloc*

Assistant to President for Strategic Initiatives and External Affairs

Political Affairs

Strategic Initiatives

Public Liaison

Intergovernmental Affairs

"Strategery": The White House Political Affairs Office

Bush's team did not go about this randomly. The Bush operation sniffed out potential voters with precision-guided accuracy, particularly in fast-growing suburbs. The campaign used computer models and demographic files to locate probable GOP voters. "They looked at what they read, what they watch, what they spend money on," a party official said. Once those people were identified, the RNC sought to register them, and the campaign used phone calls, mail, and front-porch visits—to encourage them to turn out for Bush. "We got a homogeneous group of new, registered voters and stayed on them like dogs," another official said.

—Dan Balz and Mike Allen, *Washington Post*

Rove has no antecedent in modern American politics, because no President before Bush thought it wise to give a political adviser so much influence. Rove wouldn't be Rove, in other words, were Bush not Bush.

—Joshua Green, *Atlantic Monthly*

Just days after the November 2004 election, Bill Clinton pulled Rove aside at the dedication ceremony of the William J. Clinton Presidential Library in Arkansas. "Hey, you did a marvelous job; it was just marvelous what you did," Clinton told Rove. "I want to get you down to the library. I want to talk politics with you. You just did an incredible job, and I'd like to really get together with you and I think we could have a great conversation."

—Peter Baker, *Washington Post*

When Ronald Reagan's political affairs director, Lyn Nofziger, was asked what in the White House he considered to be political, he reportedly replied: "Everything." That one-word answer is an accurate summation of the White House environment. Every presidential issue is political, in the broad sense that the president's decisions test the limits of consensus in the country. Politics, in the narrower sense of partisanship, colors each presidential action as well: it may excite—or threaten—support for the president's party. Policy and politics are inseparable. The president is head of his party and a domestic political leader wherever he goes, whether it's Austin or Abu Dhabi. Every two years, when congressional elections are pending, the White House is drawn deeply into those battles; every four years the White House is Political Central.

A political affairs staff has been formally a part of the White House establishment ever since June 1978; in George W. Bush's White House, politics and policy have been inextricably intertwined—in the person of senior adviser Karl Rove. Until his resignation in August 2007, Rove was de facto the agenda-setter for almost everyone in the White House. In 2001 it was said of him: "Rove has seeded the White House, and the GOP apparatus, with allies schooled in his way of thinking."[1] A 2004 account wrote that

> Rove, who holds the deceptively bland title of senior adviser to the president, has the broadest reach and most power of any official in the West Wing. But he also oversees every detail of the $259 million Bush-Cheney campaign, from staffing the campaign with his young loyalists rather than veteran Republicans, to monitoring small-newspaper clippings around the country. . . . A master of political history and minutiae, [Rove] has cultivated an aura of mystery, rarely giving on-the-record interviews and doing little to undermine the myth that he is responsible for everything that occurs in the executive branch.[2]

In February 2005 Rove was given an additional title as a third deputy chief of staff. That promotion, said Wayne Berman, a leading Republican fundraiser and friend of Rove, "gives him overt authority in a way that is recognized publicly and makes it more efficient for him to manage the intersection of politics and policy."[3] A contrary voice saw that intersection differently: "It is dangerous to put political consultants in charge of policy," said former Texas Republican Party chairman Thomas W. Pauken. "The combination of big-government conservatism and the extraordinary neoconservative influence on foreign policy has been devastating."[4] Marshall Wittmann, an aide to Senator John McCain, described Rove as "the crossing-guard at the intersection of policy and politics. He blends political hack and propeller head in a way no one has ever achieved. No one is going to question his political expertise or his policy expertise. The question for him is always hubris."[5]

Rove was almost always present at the policy-time sessions with the president, and his chief political deputy participated with the other White House deputy assistants, in the deputies level of the policy process. Rove was also a lobbyist when needed—as in May of 2006 when he met privately with House Republicans about the pending legislation on immigration, "urging them to move closer to the Senate position, which President Bush embraces."[6]

Having been closely associated with Governor Bush and with the Bush campaign of 2000, Karl Rove was a member of the first team that came into the White House in January 2001. His original title was assistant to the president and senior adviser. He had one general deputy, and then four White House offices came under his jurisdiction: the Office of Intergovernmental Affairs (chapter 15), the Office of Public Liaison (chapter 16), the Office of Strategic

Initiatives, and the Office of Political Affairs. Not counting the offices of Inter-governmental Affairs and Public Liaison, Rove and his three deputy offices had a staff of twenty plus eight interns and a flexible group of volunteers.

Office of Strategic Initiatives

The Office of Strategic Initiatives (OSI), known colloquially from a *Saturday Night Live* spoof as the "Office of Strategery," was a Rove creation, set up just after the president's election in 2000. It was in effect an in-house think tank, and it also did forward planning for the president's political activities.

In addition to directing his staff, Rove also convened a monthly or bimonthly (in 2001 it was weekly) "Strategery" group consisting of the (then) three policy council assistants (Economic Policy, Domestic Policy, National Security), the chief of staff and his policy deputy, the communications directors, the legislative affairs chief, and the staff secretary. In May 2002, Rove explained how the group worked on the planning function:

> Right now, for example, we had a strategery meeting last night; we were talking about August. We have a model for between here and the end of the year, in terms of what we are attempting to achieve, what are our goals. . . . In terms of, for example, planning the president's travels, and focusing on message, and focusing on thematic, and sort of helping make sense of our time here, we have a good handle on June. We've got the model for July; we've got the framework for August. Shortly we will have July filled out.[7]

Supporting the "Strategery" seniors was a mid-level assemblage called the Conspiracy of the Deputies, which, in the first term, met mid-week every other week "to generate ideas for the top-level group." As Rove put it, "Our ability to stay focused is how we stay in control of the agenda."[8]

"Rove told me my first job was to bug him," Peter Wehner, who became OSI director in 2003, told the *Washington Post*. Wehner hoped that the OSI "will be the inculcation of intellectual seriousness in the White House," explaining, "I'm not sure you can leave that for another [administration], but this should be an office that engages ideas in a serious way, that approaches criticisms in an intellectually honest way. . . . I think [Bush] is on the right side of history and is on the right side of the important debates of our time, and he's comfortable in that."[9]

Among the subjects the six-person OSI staff has surveyed are a study of the presidency "looking for historical patterns or analogies to guide the administration's strategic thinking," and research on second terms—"a compendium of how other presidents often went wrong in their second terms, history Bush hopes not to repeat," Wehner said. Wehner had the freedom to pepper any other offices in the White House, "analyzing current trends, highlighting issues that may be ripening or framing arguments to advance the president's policies."[10]

"There are plenty of people at the White House who write talking points," averred speechwriter Michael Gerson, "There are very few who make sustained arguments. Wehner doesn't overstate and his arguments have a lot of integrity."[11]

The Political Affairs Office: Priorities and Functions

The functions of the Bush political affairs office are integrated into one organizational cluster. To start with, however, there are some seven activities in which the Bush political office does *not* engage. First, in contrast to the Clinton practice, it does not regularly use a group of outside political consultants. Second, unlike the demands Clinton made, the Bush White House does not sign off on all the expenditures of the Republican National Committee itself, although understandings are of course reached on the RNC's overall budget priorities.[12] Campaign outlays, however, are under White House control.

Third, the political office staff does not actually do advancing. There is close coordination when a presidential political visit is being planned; the political office writes the briefing papers but it leaves the on-the-ground work to the advance professionals. Fourth, the political office does not write political speeches but reviews any that are prepared for the president. Fifth, the White House political affairs office has not been involved with the GOP's donor clubs ("Team 100," a $100 donation; "Campaign Council," $500; "President's Club," $1,000; "Chairman's Advisory Board," $5,000; "Young Eagles," $7,500; "Republican Eagles," $15,000–$20,000). These groups, and specifically the actual solicitation and collection of funds, are entirely handled by the RNC. If the president is going to do regional events and make speeches to the Eagles or one of the other donor clubs, the political office handles the event and interacts with the donor club leaders in doing so. Rove himself often spoke at Republican events where the party was raising money. In fact before the 2004 elections, Rove raised a total of $10,357,486 at seventy-five events in twenty-nine states.[13]

Sixth, similar to the Clinton and previous administrations, the White House does not do polling; the party committee handles that—and pays for it. In their public statements, presidents tend to disparage polling, asserting that their policy decisionmaking is never dependent on polling. Said political consultant Dick Morris, Clinton "never used polling to determine what position on an issue he should take. Never."[14] Declared presidential candidate George W. Bush, "I really don't care what polls and focus groups say. What I care about is doing what I think is right."[15] Sara Taylor, former director of the Bush political office, added: "President Bush was not particularly interested in polling and does not pay much attention to it. Now, if there is a message he wants to tell and the RNC is able to find out information that would allow the White House to communicate better—I believe he's pretty supportive of that."[16]

In a now-famous exchange with ABC news correspondent Martha Raddatz, Vice President Cheney also denigrated polling: "You cannot be blown off course by the fluctuations in the public opinion polls. Think about what would have happened if Abraham Lincoln had paid attention to polls, if they had had polls during the Civil War. He never would have succeeded if he hadn't had a clear objective, a vision for where he wanted to go, and he was willing to withstand the slings and arrows of the political wars in order to get there."[17]

Nonetheless, the Bush administration, like Clinton's before it, was deeply into polling. The Republican National Committee, which reports polling expenditures to the Federal Election Commission, spent $3.1 million for polling during the first two years of the Bush presidency, including $1.7 million paid out to presidential polling experts Jan van Lohuizen (voter and consumer research) and Fred Steeper (market strategies).[18] As presidential scholar Kathryn Tenpas recounted,

> The Office of Strategic Initiatives monitors and analyzes the results of numerous public surveys by major networks and news organizations as well as the findings of privately commissioned polls. And access to state surveys and other surveys conducted by GOP pollsters informs their analyses. Why does the nature of the White House political operation matter? Because no amount of polling is worthwhile unless it is properly analyzed and incorporated into White House policy and political discussions. . . . No one can dictate how presidents use polls, but denying the role of polls in the policy process is fruitless.[19]

Seventh, a departure from the Clinton practice, there is no "war room," a special facility staffed practically 24/7 as a command-message center and rapid response unit for all communications with a political edge.

The central function of the political affairs office is managing the president's political events—where he goes and whom he meets. To make recommendations on those two questions, the White House political staff draws on a function that is performed not at the White House but at campaign headquarters—a very sophisticated and intricate calculus called "microtargeting." Lists of party leaders, contributors, and registered Republicans are of course available both to the White House and to the Republican National Committee. But beyond that, where are the prospective Republican voters? Groups of prospects can be researched, not by precinct, but by interest. What are the past voting data? Who goes to church, and how regularly? Who owns homes of what valuation? Who buys books, or fishing rods? Who drives inexpensive cars, or fancy ones? Who does home schooling or reads the *National Geographic*? There are databases of every conceivable description, from snowmobile registrants to NASCAR moms. These databases can be made available to the Republican National Committee, the "Bush-Cheney Inc." Campaign Committee, or the White House, and of course much of this kind of information can be collected by local volunteers who go door-to-door in neighborhoods. From whatever source, the desired end product is the same: lists of names and e-mail addresses. The RNC lists have a total of 8 million names.

Neither microtargeting nor mass e-mailing (a Bush presidency innovation called blast e-mailing) is done *in* the White House; that would be a misuse of public funds. The campaign committee or the campaign staff sends out the messages; often the outgoing communication is simply an e-mail to supporters to tune in to the Whitehouse.gov website on the Internet to view a White House press briefing or a presidential press conference (chapter 19).

If presidential domestic travel is being considered, the microtargeted results are used to influence a whole range of choices, from the broad to the minute: How many cities? Which city of the many? Which sponsoring group? Who will be in the audience? Who on the dais? Who else will speak? In what order? For how long? Nothing—but nothing—is left to chance. It may be an event in South Bend. Ten people need to be introduced to the president; five of them will be designated "greeters." A certain representative could be nursing a grievance— that will have to be attended to. "It's all that maneuvering because it's such a big deal if the president goes anywhere," explained one observer.

In addition to supporting the political travel of the president, the vice president, and the president's spouse, the White House political office staff also reviewed the travel plans of cabinet officers to see if political duties could be added in. But more than just travel is arranged. Through coordination with the office of political affairs, the cabinet secretary comes to her destination bearing gifts: announcements that the department is making grants to the lucky state, city, or local institution. In late October 2006, for example Education Secretary Margaret Spellings was sent to Ohio where she stood next to Representative Ralph Regula in Columbus while announcing a grant of $10.4 million to the state of Ohio for teacher bonuses. An assistant administrator from the Environmental Protection Agency joined Representative Curt Weldon of Pennsylvania at a news conference announcing a $6.3 million EPA grant to a local company.[20] This kind of event is known as "strategic travel." (There is no implication here that the grant award processes have been tainted, but the timing and locale for the announcements are pure political gold of which every president has taken advantage.)

Rove himself was in demand as a speaker. In May of 2003 he went to New Hampshire (a state where candidate Bush had been defeated by John McCain in the 2000 Republican primary). The *Washington Post* described the trip:

> He is a magazine cover boy, the subject of two books and has earned a reputation as one of the most powerful and controversial advisers in this or

any White House, and so when Karl Rove came to New Hampshire, he did not come quietly. His schedule had all the trappings of a candidate rather than a mere political strategist—two public speeches, several media interviews, a private meeting with Republican contributors, a pep rally with party activists and a quiet session with the publisher of the conservative Manchester Union Leader. . . . Seven television cameras recorded his appearance at St. Anselm College and the overflow audience he attracted exceeded those drawn by two of the . . . Democratic presidential candidates. . . . Critics view Rove as the person who has made the White House one of the most political in history, a White House in which politics and policy fit hand in glove, all designed to reelect Bush to a second term. "I think there's the sense he's the driving strategic force for everything they do over there," said Steve Elmendorf, a top adviser to [Democratic Representative Richard] Gephardt's campaign.[21]

"I think this office is a little bit, perhaps, misnamed," a former political office staffer explained, "because when people hear 'political affairs' they assume that we do politics all the time. Politics is a piece of it, but it's *managing the president's politics*—it's the care and feeding of making sure his domestic initiatives and travel are being well-managed—and for that you really need to know what's going on around the country."[22] To do that, the political office has five regional divisions, each with a director responsible for ten states; through them, the White House political office reaches out to state and local party organizations. For example, suppose Mr. Bush wants to do ten presidential events in a four-month period. The regional directors work with the White House Scheduling Office to help determine how the president will spend his time and with whom; they consult with the state Republican leadership and then manage the logistics of each trip so that every detail is covered at least two months ahead of time. They make sure, for instance, that anybody who meets with the president has been checked appropriately and is not going to cause the White House embarrassment. Much of this work is done on the telephone before the advance teams are called in; the latter rely on the state party leadership to supply ten or fifteen or twenty volunteers for each event. The White House political staffers are never actually part of a local candidate's own campaign.

State Republican leaders, in turn, come to the political office for both political and official help. One may want a tour of the White House; another may ask for a letter signed by the president or for an autographed picture. The office rarely has the capacity or time to get involved in such specifics but directs them to the office that can help them.

Did this office dispense political advice? "Sometimes," said one official, "they want advice and sometimes they don't. Most state parties and most state political operatives don't want the White House telling them how to run their affairs.

I was really sensitive about that. And it was not true," he emphasized, "that we ran everything by the party. We just didn't. We talked with them a lot. We'd hear from them about some things . . . but as a general rule by the time you become the director of the political affairs office, you'd better know enough to not have to call somebody every time you need to answer a question."[23]

Nonetheless, as one party official said in 2003,

> There is total coordination. The message is coordinated, data is coordinated, the administration is coordinated. . . . The harmony between the political operation of the White House and the Republican National Committee is beyond what I've seen before. Tight coordination also means tight control by the White House, which now dictates to candidates the terms for financial assistance. In 2002, for example, the White House and the national party committees told GOP candidates that if they wanted to receive financial and other assistance, they had to include in their campaign plan a commitment, backed up with money, to bid for the Latino vote.[24]

The White House Political Affairs Office in the Personnel Business

While it is the White House presidential personnel office (PPO) that handles the recruitment, clearance, and selection of noncareer appointments, especially those made by the president (chapter 8), the PPO often turns to the political affairs office for advice and assistance. Sometimes it seeks recommendations about candidates for presidential appointments. If the position in question were at a high level, such as one requiring Senate confirmation, it was one political affairs' staffer's view that he was not the one to come to. "The irony," he said, "is that the higher on the food chain, the less we would be involved. A lot of times when you get to these assistant secretary jobs, it requires enormous technical expertise. . . . I don't mean to diminish our role because we were certainly involved in the practice, but it's pretty hard for me to argue with a straight face that somebody shouldn't be the assistant secretary of the Navy. It's not something I would do."[25]

With regard to lower-ranking jobs, however—a scheduler or an advance person—he would willingly get involved in offering advice. "Our only role in that process was to make sure that people who were serving the president supported the president, reflected his views. We would work with [the presidential personnel] office just to make sure that they were actually appointing Bush supporters to fill those jobs." It was not a matter of checking with the Republican National Committee itself but more often with state or local party sources.

When Senate confirmations were pending, the political affairs office would use some of its many close relationships with senators or with their staffs. "We would get involved in the strategy of a process," one official explained, "drumming up support, getting people to call."

Occasionally, the political affairs office would use the "hotfoot" technique of going directly to the local supporters of a member of Congress and spurring them to put grass-roots pressure on that member to go along with the president on a piece of legislation or a confirmation. "We certainly had the ability to do that, and used it very judiciously," the official commented.

As for parceling out seats on *Air Force One,* the political staffer was hesitant. "The president didn't like having people on *Air Force One* if he wasn't able to sit there and spend time with them. If he was doing a security briefing on a flight, or he was doing any number of other things that a president would do while traveling, we wouldn't always include people. But we hit all the trinket stops, you know, cuff links and that. . . ." If the trip was political and a visitor was invited, the RNC or the campaign would have to pay the going rate for a ride on *Air Force One.*

The brouhaha in 2007 concerning the firing and replacement of several U.S. district attorneys, however, revealed the very active role the White House political affairs office once played in calling the shots for the Department of Justice. The firings were widely reported in the press and resulted in the resignation of Attorney General Alberto Gonzales. The Judiciary committees of both the Senate and the House conducted investigations and demanded that they be given copies of White House e-mails concerning the controversy. Thousands of pages of e-mails were provided early in 2007; forty-six additional pages were released in June of that year, confirming that the White House political affairs office had a hand in the incident.

White House Liaison Officers

Within each cabinet department is a White House liaison officer, a noncareer appointee who has in effect been picked by the White House. These officers are channels for handling issues and problems on which the White House political affairs office might need help. Most of the liaisons' time, however, is spent in the personnel area, assisting in the recruitment and placement of noncareer appointees in their respective departments.

One instance of malfeasance on the part of a former White House liaison officer—in the Department of Justice—came to light in the spring of 2007. In testimony before the House Judiciary Committee, Monica Goodling explained how she erred when she asked political questions of applicants for career positions:

> I interviewed candidates who were to be detailed into confidential policymaking positions and attorney general appointments such as immigration judges and members of the Board of Immigration Appeals. I also interviewed requests for waivers of hiring freezes imposed on districts with an outgoing district attorney or an interim or acting U.S. attorney. . . . Nevertheless I do acknowledge that I may have gone too far in asking

political questions of applicants for career positions and I may have taken inappropriate political considerations into account on some occasions, and I regret those mistakes. . . . There were times when I crossed the line, probably in my reference calls, by asking political questions.[26]

Briefings for Departmental Political Appointees

Rove and the president wanted to have a system of keeping departmental assistant secretaries informed not only about presidential priorities and initiatives but also about the administration's political objectives—who in Congress were allies or opponents and which of them were vulnerable at the ballot box. After President Bush's reelection in 2004, arrangements were made for the leadership of the White House political affairs office to offer PowerPoint briefings to departmental political appointees; some twenty were conducted in perhaps sixteen agencies. Care was taken to avoid Hatch Act violations by not actually calling for action to help or defeat any member of Congress. On one occasion, however, the administrator of the General Services Administration (GSA), Lurita Doan, reportedly posed the question to the group, "How can this agency's actions be targeted to help our candidates?" That statement, possibly violating the Hatch Act, became public, was attacked by Democratic members of Congress, and resulted in a six-month investigation by a special counsel. In April 2007 White House spokeswoman Dana Perino issued a statement: "It is perfectly lawful for political appointees at the White House to provide information briefings to political appointees at the agencies."[27] The special counsel on June 8, 2007, however, wrote the president that the GSA administrator had engaged "in the most pernicious of political activities," and recommended that the GSA administrator "be disciplined to the fullest extent for her serious violation of the Hatch Act."[28] On April 29, 2008, the White House forced Doan to resign.

Separating Political from Official E-Mails

On February 26, 2001, Alberto Gonzales, then counsel to the president, issued a memorandum to all White House staff telling them that

e-mail is no different from other kinds of documents. Any e-mail relating to official business therefore qualifies as a Presidential record. All e-mail to your official e-mail address is automatically archived as if it were a Presidential record, and all e-mail from your official e-mail address is treated as a Presidential record unless you designate otherwise. . . . [I]f you happen to receive an e-mail on a personal e-mail account that otherwise qualifies as a Presidential record, it is your duty to ensure that it is preserved and filed as such by printing it out and saving it or by forwarding it to your White House e-mail account. . . .

Federal law and EOP [Executive Office of the President] policy require the preservation of electronic communications that relate to official business and that are sent or received by EOP staff. As a result, you must only use the authorized e-mail system for all official electronic communications.[29]

The Republican National Committee and the Bush-Cheney 2004 reelection campaign had their own, separate e-mail accounts, many of which apparently came to be used by White House officials. According to an interim report by the staff of the House Oversight and Government Reform Committee, the Republican National Committee issued BlackBerry cell phones to Karl Rove and perhaps also to others of the eighty-eight members of the White House staff (including many on the political affairs staff) who have been identified as users of those RNC accounts. In the course of a committee investigation of lobbyist Jack Abramoff, the House committee obtained copies of White House e-mails, one of which was from political affairs staffer Susan Ralston to Abramoff associate Todd Boulanger, telling Boulanger, "I now have an RNC BlackBerry which you can use to e-mail me at any time. No security issues like my WH e-mail."

The RNC did preserve some 674,367 of the e-mails from the RNC accounts used by the White House officials, including 140,216 to and from Rove, all between January 2002 and April 2007. Of the total, 240,922 were to and from government (".gov") accounts in federal agencies, and many of these concerned federal appointments and policies; in other words, they were matters of official business.

Former political affairs office director Sara Taylor told the author that she would change the name of the office. "When you say you're the 'political office,' people think all you do is politics, when in reality you do a lot more than that. You do a lot of official business—you do *mostly* official business! So I might rename it." Taylor then highlighted the problem of differentiating political e-mails from official-business e-mails. A person may have two separate accounts, but senders may not adhere to the difference and may send political or official e-mails on either account interchangeably. "There's got to be technology out there that allows you to have one e-mail account that separates stuff between official and political," Taylor exclaimed.

Rove resigned his position at the White House in August of 2007. Deputy chief of staff for policy Joel Kaplan said of him: "Basically, any important policy of the president has been something that Karl has been involved in the development of."[30] Rove's problem, said former RNC chairman Rich Bond, "is that he is inexorably linked to Bush. And the degree to which Bush is viewed favorably by history, so, too, will it view Karl Rove. The degree to which history judges George Bush harshly, so, too, will it judge Karl Rove."[31]

Partnership in Our Federal System: The Office of Intergovernmental Affairs

Congress can't do anything alone, governors can't do anything alone; Democrats, Republicans . . . no one can do anything independent of each other. We're trying to practice federalism at its best.

—Maggie Grant

Whoever gets elected . . . I just hope we get pulled in for conversations, because right now we have gained a phenomenal amount of expertise among governors and states; the hope would be that they will work pretty cooperatively with us.

—Ray Sheppach

The White House Office of Intergovernmental Affairs had its beginnings under Dwight Eisenhower. He had appointed a Commission on Intergovernmental Relations, and in transmitting its 1955 report to Congress, Ike said:

> The interests and activities of the different levels of government now impinge on each other at innumerable points, even where they may appear to be quite separable. The National Government's defense policies and programs, for example, have important repercussions on virtually every phase of State and local activity. Conversely, the effectiveness of our national defense policies depends on a myriad of State and local activities affecting the health, safety and social and economic welfare of our people.[1]

Read fifty-eight years later in an environment of resolute national concern about what is now called "homeland security," Eisenhower's words were prophetic indeed.

The commission's report included a recommendation that each president have "a Special Assistant in the Executive Office . . . to serve with a small staff as the President's chief aide and adviser on State and local relationships. He should give his exclusive attention to these matters throughout the government. He would be the coordinating center."[2] Eisenhower accepted this recommendation, established the White House Office of Intergovernmental Affairs, and appointed the commission's chairman, Meyer Kestnbaum, as its first director, assisted by former governor of Arizona Howard Pyle.

Almost every succeeding president since has had a similar office. Lyndon Johnson and Richard Nixon experimented with a variation; they put the intergovernmental affairs duties on the shoulders of their vice presidents—former mayor (and senator) Hubert Humphrey and former governor Spiro Agnew, respectively. Neither of those experiments panned out. Regarding Humphrey, Johnson told the press that "I have Hubert's balls in my pocket." As for Agnew's relationship with state and local officials, presidential aide John Ehrlichman had to keep reminding him that "his job was to sell our policy to them, not theirs to us."

President Bush's Intergovernmental Affairs Office

In the George W. Bush White House, the intergovernmental affairs office is linked together with the public liaison, political affairs, and strategic initiatives offices under an assistant to the president (formerly Karl Rove, now Barry Jackson, who had been Rove's deputy), forming a multifaceted, integrated outreach resource. The office has a staff of thirteen (including four commissioned officers), at least one working with governors, lieutenant governors, and other statewide officeholders; staff colleagues with mayors and counties, including sheriffs and other law enforcement people, many of whom are elected officials; still others with federally recognized Indian tribal governments.

The intergovernmental affairs office at the White House is supported by a circle of agency counterparts, one or more in each cabinet department, who handle intergovernmental issues at the agency level. These assistants are picked by the White House and thus work with the White House with cooperative alacrity. As Maggie Grant, the director of intergovernmental affairs in the Bush White House, explained, "The White House intergovernmental affairs role is an overall coordinator of all different departments. There are many issues, like Hurricane Katrina recovery, that touch nearly every agency. We have to make sure that we're working as seamlessly as possible and not stepping on one another and not being overly bureaucratic. It takes tight coordination."[3]

Often a governor or mayor, unhappy about a delay in response or dissatisfied with the answer he or she is getting from a cabinet department, will appeal to the White House. "We go back to that agency and ask them to review the action they have taken," Grant pointed out. "We just want to make sure we're as responsive as possible to our state and local colleagues. They definitely don't get everything they want and often they don't like to hear what we say, but I think at the end of the day they come back and say they get a fair shake."

Outside the executive branch, these White House and departmental intergovernmental affairs staffers have strong, well-organized professional associations to do business with: the "Big Seven," namely, the Council of State Governments, the National Governors Association, the U.S. Conference of Mayors, the

National Association of Counties, the National League of Cities, the National Conference of State Legislatures, and the International City/County Management Association. These associations hold national conferences—the governors, for instance, meet twice a year—and White House intergovernmental staffers attend every one of them; Grant is often on the agenda to make a formal presentation.

In May 2007 Grant called all the departmental assistants into the White House to study the total schedule of annual association meetings. "We mapped out our objectives as an administration, and I mirrored them up against what the associations' objectives are," she recounted. "Now we're working to ensure that we've got as many senior administration officials as possible going to all those meetings."

When the governors meet in Washington, they come to the White House; the president and Grant see to it that the right cabinet secretaries join in briefing the governors about issues of common interest. At a recent winter meeting, General Peter Pace, chairman of the Joint Chiefs of Staff was in attendance. Governors are commanders-in-chief of their respective National Guard forces, and by statute the Department of Defense cannot call up more than 50 percent of any state's National Guard. "The president greatly respects the fact that we have many National Guard units serving overseas," Grant pointed out, "so he wanted to be sure the governors had a direct relationship and line of communication with General Pace." Health and Human Services Secretary Michael Leavitt and Education Secretary Margaret Spellings also joined that winter meeting, since health care and education make up a very large percentage of state budgets.

Director Grant makes a note of every query that comes during such meetings. "I think equally important to organizing the meeting, if not more important, is the follow-up thereafter—making sure we close the loop and seek resolution," she said. In between the national meetings, Grant and her staff arrange monthly conference calls to the governors and send them copies of the talking points of the president's speeches.

Wherever the president travels within the United States, the governor of the state that the president is visiting is notified and invited to greet the president—"irrespective of party and out of respect and deference to that governor," Grant added. The intergovernmental affairs office aids the president's spouse as well as the president. Whenever the first lady travels, Grant gives her recommendations about what state and local officials to make contact with and about what subjects or issues are likely come up for discussion. She extends invitations to the first lady's events to state and local officials.

An important element in the intergovernmental communications network is the offices that nearly half of the states maintain in Washington. Each is headed by what is called a D.C. director, who is obviously a much-used point of personal contact with the White House and with other federal agencies that implement state-level programs. Not all the states have this facility, since it costs some $250,000 annually to keep one in business.

The advent of BlackBerries—in addition to cell phones and e-mails—has made this communications net tighter and more flexible. "It's a 24/7 operation," Grant observed. "When we were preparing to go to Virginia Tech after the unfortunate massacre there, I was speaking with the governor's chief of staff at midnight. I was fortunate enough to be doing that from my home, my car, and my computer. That has made the system more seamless, more timely, and more rapid. At the same time, it's more complicated, too."

An example of this communications network in operation took place in mid-May 2007, when the White House and congressional negotiators had reached an agreement on the shape of new immigration legislation. "Just last night," Grant explained, "we were here late for two hours. As soon as we got the bipartisan agreement up on Capitol Hill with the senators, we jumped into a communications mode and had a conference call with the 'big seven' governors, the D.C. directors, and the governors' chiefs of staff. We did absolutely all the governors, because immigration is important to every single governor, but it means something very different in every state." Even during the negotiations, Grant added,

> we'd speak to Democratic and Republican governors alike, and some border city mayors and county officials, as the deliberations were going on, so there were no surprises when the agreement came out. . . . We really try to get them as early in the game as possible, because they are our partners. . . . We had Secretary [of Homeland Security Michael] Chertoff on the call, because it is important for them to have access directly to Cabinet members.

Relations with Native American Tribal Governments

There are 560 federally recognized Indian tribal governments, and the White House intergovernmental affairs office has one or more officers specializing in this area of relationships. Besides tribes' continuing concerns for federally supported actions in the areas of education and health care, the issue of gaming looms large for both tribal and state governments. "Every one of the larger recognized tribes probably sees gaming differently," Grant commented. "Very significant amounts of money are at stake. I know a lot of tribes that are seeking land 200 to 400 miles from the reservation; they want land taken into trust at those locations because they may be close to urban areas. That may be desirable as locations for casinos, but it's not their tribal lands. These demands raise a lot of sensitivities."

The Balance Needed for White House Outreach Staffs

For all White House staff officers who are in the intergovernmental outreach business, there is a balance that must be struck between leaning over backward on some issues to be responsive to the political needs of state and local officials who are of the same party as the administration, yet acting with immediate non-partisanship when a disaster hits a state or community. President Bush's visits to Greensburg, Kansas, which was ninety-five percent obliterated by a 204-mile-an-hour tornado on May 4, 2007, or to the Virginia Tech campus after a student went on a deadly shooting spree in April 2007, demonstrate that when an emergency of that kind occurs, all governors are equal in being eligible for federal attention and assistance. "Two and a half days into the crisis post-Katrina," Grant said, "I was asked to find 40,000 beds and as many planes as possible" to evacuate people left without shelter by the hurricane. "It took me about 25 minutes. I called five governors and instantaneously they said they would take as many as needed. . . . In the end, out of 1.2 million evacuees, every single State in the Union, including Hawaii, received Katrina people."

An indispensable resource is maintained at the White House: a complete list of the home, office, and cell-phone numbers of every governor, every chief of staff, every top-level state emergency management official, and the mayors of big cities. "We keep adding to that list," Grant pointed out, "because the president does want to follow up, for instance with that Kansas mayor. He'll someday pick up the phone or get in a plane and see how they're doing."

A second kind of balance is also indispensable: on the one hand carrying into the White House the views and requests of governors or mayors, while on the other hand using those well-cultivated relationships to bring to state and local officials the policies and priorities of the president. The greatest challenge here comes "when we're in a deputies meeting," Grant said,

> and a department is laying out the policy that is being advanced, I'll ask if they understand what this will mean for a mayor or a governor, they'll ask "Whose side am I on?" It's like I'm on the president's side, but if the policy doesn't fold into what the governors' and mayors' needs, duties, and responsibilities are, then we might be "dead on arrival." We have to ensure there is some element of cooperation and ability of implementation.

A Bush Innovation: "Go-Dels"

"Co-Dels"—delegations made up of members of Congress—have long been a standard feature of U.S. diplomacy. The Bush administration has added an innovative feature to its arsenal of relationships with the nation's governors: "Go-Dels"—delegations of governors traveling to Iraq to meet with groups of soldiers from their home states. Grant instigated this practice after she received a telephone call from Governor Donald Carcieri of Rhode Island. "I am commander-in-chief of my National Guard," he said, "and I need to go see my troops, because we are starting to go to funerals, and we want to make sure the soldiers there have the equipment they need."

Six governors made the first Go-Del trip in 2004—Kathleen Blanco of Louisiana, George Pataki of New York, Tim Pawlenty of Minnesota, Linda Lingle of Hawaii, Ted Kulongoski of Oregon, and Dirk Kempthorne of Idaho. For five days, Grant led the group as they met, in Baghdad's Green Zone, with U.S. military leaders and with Ambassador L. Paul Bremer III, then went into the field to sit down at dinner with troops from their respective states. By spring of 2007, ten of these Go-Dels had been undertaken, each with six governors, a mix of Republicans and Democrats each time. On some of the trips the governors also met with their Iraqi counterparts, provincial chiefs, and found they had issues in common. "It was incredible to see young men and women from their hometowns," Grant said of that first trip. "They don't necessarily know their congressman or their senator, but they know their governor.... [The governors] all went home with their pockets stuffed with notes and messages and phone-numbers; they all called the moms and dads and wives and husbands. It was a taste of home—a very rewarding trip—something we had never done before."

Looking Forward to 2009

Grant's experience in providing leadership and coordination of the several departments in organizing outreach to state and local officials leads her to recommend the creation of a more effective common structure in the outreach organizations of the various cabinet agencies. Almost all of them have public liaison, legislative affairs, and intergovernmental relations offices—all engaged in outreach work—but often under the jurisdiction of different assistant secretaries in each department. Grant summed up: "When we have to reach out to different branches [in] a department or agency, it is cumbersome to coordinate a response for a governor. I think a cohesive structure for outreach would make tremendous sense, because then we in the White House could have a seamless interaction within our federal family and could return service with a much more rapid and more effective response."

An Independent Critique

An outside but very knowledgeable view of the White House intergovernmental affairs operation comes from Ray Sheppach, for twenty-five years the executive director of the National Governors Association, which celebrates its 100th anniversary in 2008 and currently has a staff of 110. Recalling the No Child Left Behind education initiative early in President Bush's first term, Sheppach mentioned that governors "had some problems with it . . . with some of the measurement . . . but were kind of pushed away. . . . I mean [the administration] had written the legislation, they kind of wanted to get it enacted and they really weren't willing to negotiate with outside groups. Our consultation had to be with the Congress rather than the White House."[4] He also faulted the administration for its lack of consultation concerning an amendment that gave the president more power to call up the National Guard, an amendment that most governors adamantly opposed (chapter 10).

Referring especially to health care reform, Sheppach pointed out that sometimes the states decide not to wait for action from the federal government. He noted that thirty-five states were "already doing very comprehensive reform; they are way ahead of the federal government. . . . What we will do after Vermont and Maine and Massachusetts have moved forward [on health insurance reform], is we will then convene all fifty states . . . where we'll bring in states that have done it, with outside speakers, and try to have the other states learn from them—from the ones that have actually done it, but also do a lot of papers and we will also do a lot of action grants."

Commenting that Grant was "very good and responsive," Sheppach nonetheless considered that in general the White House and the governors have had "much more of an arm's-length relationship," as compared to some past administrations. Sheppach added that the governors have been gratified to see so many former governors (John Ashcroft, Tommy Thompson, Kempthorne, Leavitt, and Mike Johanns) serving in the Bush cabinet.

A Humorous Footnote

Maggie Grant recalled her arrival in New Orleans shortly after the disaster of Katrina. With all communications down, it took a while to locate Mayor Ray Nagin for a meeting with President Bush, who had flown down to survey the damage. The hastily arranged session almost fell through, however, when Nagin, who had gone for three days without a shower, insisted on taking one before meeting with the president. Thinking quickly, Grant consulted with the president's advance team and Secret Service agents to arrange, while the president waited, a shower for the mayor—on *Air Force One*. What limits are there to the White House's intergovernmental relations services?

16

Working with Coalitions to Push the President's Agenda: The Office of Public Liaison

We have people in the White House . . . who aren't there representing the President to the country; they are representing the country to the President. That's not what White House staff should be.

Ted Sorensen

Karl Rove always said there are no permanent allies, no permanent enemies, only permanent interests. You've got to understand where all the interests lie and you better be sharing your views with them and hoping to find some common cause in as many places as possible on as many presidential priorities as possible.

Mike Meece

Out there in the public is a vast diversity of nonprofit advocacy groups that contend to represent "the general welfare." They include racial and ethnic coalitions, religious organizations of every denominational stripe, issue-advocacy collectives like the Sierra Club and the American Cetacean Society (whales), and professional and trade associations such as the National Federation of Independent Business, the American Medical Association, and the American Society of Public Administration.

Corporations knock on White House doors, too, but here a line is drawn: while the views of profit-making organizations are often invited and welcomed on issues of general public policy, White House doors are closed to any entreaties to intervene in a business firm's dispute with either a line department or a federal regulatory agency.

In this phantasmagoric cacophony of contending voices, issues arise and disappear, coalitions endlessly form and disband. Millions of dollars are amassed and spent, and skilled communicators and lobbyists wield letters, e-mails, faxes, testimony, and visits. The policy combat of the nation becomes the warfare of Washington.

The Potential Bargain

This warfare has a dual significance. To the lobbyists, the White House is a target; to the White House, interest-group power is presidential opportunity.

—*As target:* The chief executive is besieged with message carriers urging him to act on or refrain from acting on any of a thousand issues. Some message carriers sit on the sidewalk outside the White House with signs; millions send letters, e-mails, or blogs; thousands telephone the White House comment line; hundreds ask to be heard in person. All seek a sympathetic reception, and each would like to know that *someone,* if not the president himself, is paying attention to his or her entreaties. Especially expectant are the leaders of America's major nonprofit advocacy groups, who assume that the White House will receive them and give weight to their views.

—*As opportunity:* From where he sits, the president views advocacy coalitions—on issues where he and they agree—as possible extensions of his own salesmanship. The advocacy groups can amplify his influence, first to their memberships and then, through their memberships, to Congress. With skillful staff work, the president can mobilize that extramural power, enlisting organization leaders to help squeeze out just the few more House or Senate votes he needs to achieve his high-priority objectives.

Here are the makings of a bargain. In the words of a Bush administration memorandum: "This office will be organized in such a way as to allow organized groups to bring their spectrum of issues and concerns to the president but with a symbiotic relationship, so that the president has a mechanism to use to ask the groups for their help."[1]

The president, therefore, includes on his personal staff men and women who make it their business to cultivate links to all kinds of influential interest groups in America. They are usually good listeners, but they are also willing to talk and to investigate. They open doors, guaranteeing advocacy groups a fair hearing in the White House, in the departments, and on occasion in the Oval Office itself (unless, as happens on occasion, the president insists on secrecy for certain of his initiatives until they are announced.)

In the words of Tim Goeglein, deputy director of the Office of Public Liaison, who concentrated on reaching out to the politically and religiously conservative community: "One of the principal roles of public liaison is not only explaining policies that have been decided, but to faithfully and accurately report into the White House bloodstream the views of conservatives. I make sure they have a reliable access point, which is me."[2] (Access-point Goeglein, a close aide to Karl Rove, turned out to be a flawed facilitator. One of his activities was writing guest columns for his hometown newspaper, the *News-Sentinel* of Fort Wayne, Indiana. A blogger for the *News-Sentinel* discovered plagiarism in one of his columns; a subsequent investigation found that of his thirty-eight guest columns published since 2000, nineteen included plagiarized materials. The White House termed these actions "unacceptable," and Goeglein, admitting his guilt, immediately resigned from the staff in March of 2008.)[3]

For their part, interest groups, even those skeptical of the president's agenda, give the president or his representatives a chance to explain their objectives, attend briefings at the White House, and occasionally invite White House staff to their conventions. If they agree with the president, they will join his interests to their own, volunteering to do what he cannot openly request: put pressure on legislators. For over fifty-five years, the bargain has been struck; the White House Office of Public Liaison is its embodiment. As an internal memo put it, "the Office of Public Liaison will achieve these goals by mobilizing important constituency elements in ways available to no other government unit outside the White House."[4]

There is political cement in the bargain as well. As a campaigner, the president will have asked for, and received, endorsements from specific interest groups or from their leaders. Campaign contributions will have supported his bid for the White House. There is no chance that, once inaugurated, he will not have officers on his staff commissioned to be attentive to the concerns of his campaign allies.

The Purposes of the Public Liaison Function in the Bush White House

"When Karl [Rove] hired me, he said, 'Don't be an in-box! What I want you to do is just push the president's agenda,'" said Lezlee Westine, a former director of the Office of Public Liaison.[5] The Bush public liaison staffers were there to exert force in one direction: outward. Their job was to use their energies and resources to spread the word about—and further—the president's legislative program, to identify and link up with the organizations and coalitions that would help accomplish the *president's* objectives; they were not commissioned to—in fact were discouraged from—carrying the coalitions' own desiderata into the Oval Office. Westine emphasized:

> Every morning I woke up and I said, "Okay, what can I do with these constituencies for the economic package, for the energy package, for No Child Left Behind?" I was not—and I would tell people that—I'm not an in-box, and it made my job easier. That's what's different from the past. . . . But talking with [constituencies] and having a conversation about an economic package that we care about, or women's outreach—having that kind of a conversation is great and helpful and gives feedback. But not to be the place where the lobbyists come to ask for favors. That's a difference—a big difference.

This unwillingness did not mean that the public liaison staffers were completely deaf to the needs and interests of the organizations with whom they worked; those needs and interests did have to be brought to the attention of the

White House policy officers. It meant that Rove did not want his public liaison specialists being the locale for such dialogues. An outside coalition might want certain language inserted in the tax bill; it would be referred to the economic policy assistant. "I could provide them with a contact," explained Westine, "but it wasn't my job to fix their problems." At times the public liaison team had to bend the Rove instructions and be more forthcoming to listen to the views and concerns of the outside associations with which they were linked. As Michael Meece, a former deputy director of public liaison, put it:

> I think I would probably listen to almost anybody who wanted to come in and talk to me. I would be up front with them about whether or not what they were saying was going to resonate with the policymakers or was going to be something that we would devote a lot of our capital to, or time to. I would try to spend most of my time focused on the president's priorities. But if somebody wanted to come in and air a concern, I would do it. . . . If it was not a priority with me, I would make it a point to help them get connected with my counterpart in an agency.[6]

As mentioned elsewhere in this book, the White Houses of recent years make it a point to have White House liaison officers, at the political level, in the departments and agencies. Being political, these liaison officers are all picked or cleared at the White House.

Nonetheless, the public liaison team made note of the policy suggestions that their outside associations and coalitions would bring to their attention, to the extent that on January 27, 2003, for example, the director sent Karl Rove fourteen proposals for items that these outside groups wanted to see included in the forthcoming State of the Union message.

Another former director, Rhonda Keenum, added:

> In the frequent daily interaction that I had with him [Rove] the charge was to be a distant early warning system so that we could not only perform our job, but we could also keep a pulse in the legislative sphere. . . . What are the issues that are coming up . . . the legislative priorities? . . . Another was keeping a pulse on the different communities—the faith-based community, the business community . . . making sure we were communicating with them and anticipating if there was going to be a surprise. We did not want or like surprises.[7]

Keenum differentiated the role of the communications office from the role of public liaison: "Communications is tasked with taking the president's speech and talking points and putting them out. The public liaison world is to monitor what is coming in . . . knowing, for instance, who your influencers are in the blogging network. There's something we need to monitor so we can bring them in to get their opinion so we know what we need to be doing."

Some Rules of the Road

There are some no-nos that have imposed limits on public liaison activities as long as that office has been in the White House. The Anti-Lobbying Act forbids any government employee from spending federal funds to mobilize an outside group to run a lobbying campaign directed at Congress. At a cabinet meeting once, Eisenhower remarked that "he could not put a three-cent stamp on a letter to Congress" that did so. Another risk facing public liaison officers is that of falling into the "Patty Hearst syndrome," where the staffer, unwittingly or not, bonds with the cause of the outside advocacy group with which he or she is working and brings that cause into the White House. Two of President Carter's staffers, Midge Costanza and Nelson Cruikshank, let their loyalties, to women and the aging, respectively, override their loyalty to presidential policies and embarrassed both the president and themselves. When asked if he considered he held the Jewish "portfolio" in the Nixon White House, presidential Special Counsel Leonard Garment wisely responded: "No, not a portfolio; perhaps just a small manila envelope."[8]

"That's the hardest part of the job," commented Meece, the former Bush public liaison deputy director. "You can't ever have anyone inside the White House think you've gone native." He added:

> You've got to, number one, always remember you work for the president. You don't work for the outside groups; you work for the president. Your job for the president is to understand what the concerns of the outside parties are and to some degree help the policymakers in the government tap the expertise that exists outside of government. There's a lot of people of good faith, willing to provide you with their insight and their views, and it doesn't do you any good just to ignore that. You've got to reach out and find that, to know what they care about, to know what they're going to do about what they care about. To be able to access the expertise that they possess, you have to have a good relationship with them, and a lot of credibility.

Techniques of the Bush Public Liaison Office

The Bush public liaison staff uses a variety of techniques to advance the presidential agenda, some tried and true, others taking advantage of new communications technologies not available to previous presidents.

Presidential Events

The president's proposed tax bill is pending; in it are goodies for small businesses. The task is to marshal congressional support. The public liaison office would contact a frequent ally, the National Federation of Independent Business, and ask: "In Virginia, for instance, is there a congressional district whose member is on the fence and in which there are several small business firms who will benefit from that bill?" Advance work will be done; the president will visit one or two plants, take a tour of the business, have conversations with the owners, speak to the workers about how the pending bill will help both owners and workers, then he would ask questions. "The president was always adamant," said Westine. "He wanted to talk to real people; he didn't want it staged, didn't want to just stand behind a podium. . . . I had wonderful people who would do the vetting." Press and photographers would of course be on hand.

If an outside organization was moved to write a representative or senator a letter supporting the president's position on a piece of legislation, the organization knew it was expected to send a copy of the letter to the public liaison office; the file of those letters was an important database for the White House. "It was a collection," Meece commented, "not only of those who supported the president's priorities, but supported them strongly enough to take action."

Some presidential events are sorrowful. When Coretta Scott King died, President Bush and First Lady Laura Bush invited former president Bill Clinton and his wife, and former president George H. W. Bush to join them on *Air Force One*. In the motorcade in Atlanta were former president and Mrs. Jimmy Carter— four presidents at one occasion. Keenum, who was in charge of the event, recalled: "President Bush clearly wanted to participate in this event but he did not want to be intrusive; he wanted to be respectful for the King family, so I worked very closely with the [King] family to make sure that everything was done properly."

The White House itself is always the ideal setting for both intimate and large presidential events. A group of Iraqi men who had suffered amputation of one hand on orders of Saddam Hussein had been brought to the United States by a charitable group so that a doctor in Texas could fashion and equip them with artificial hands. The public liaison team heard about this generous act and invited the group to the Oval Office, where one of the men showed the president how his wedding ring could fit on his artificial hand. It was a moment filled with as much symbolism as personal emotion.

A larger event occurred on July 27, 2006, when the public liaison team invited over 3,000 people onto the South Lawn to witness the signing of the extension of the Voting Rights Act. In his eloquent statement the president included in his welcome the presidents of the Urban League and the National Association for the Advancement of Colored People, along with civil rights leaders Jesse Jackson, Benjamin Hooks, and Al Sharpton—none of them known to be cheerleaders for George Bush.

The White House South Lawn is a magnetic locale—especially when the presidential helicopter arrives or departs. The public liaison office is alerted to each flight and often invites its allies in the private sector to come and witness the plane and the president, to wave to him, greet him, and participate in a "photo-op." The

Residence's State Dining Room and its Lincoln Bedroom are magnetic too—but remembering the unfavorable publicity surrounding the Clinton coffee klatches and sleepovers, the Bush public liaison staffers avoided using those enticements. A frequently used "perk," however, was inclusion on the invitation lists for the first family's Christmas parties; the public liaison team always had a rich store of potential invitees to propose.

Some events produce an unexpected bonus for the outside groups brought in for briefings in the Roosevelt Room or in the Eisenhower Executive Building next door to the White House. On more than one occasion, President Bush asked: "You haven't seen the Oval Office?"—and then led the group on a personally conducted tour.

In Bush's second term, as the war in Iraq intensified—and public support for it diminished—the public liaison team gave increased attention to linking up with military support organizations—groups of mothers and fathers of soldiers, of brothers and sisters. Groups like this had organized to ship boxes of toiletries to the men and women on duty in Iraq, or to put up money for housing grants to military families in need. The White House paid special attention to organizations of this kind; the president met regularly in the Roosevelt Room with leaders of such associations.

Briefings at the White House

After her daily morning meeting with Karl Rove, Westine reported back to her staff: "Okay, this is what happened in the Karl meeting. These are our action items. Here are the president's five policy initiatives. What are we doing? What events do we have on the calendar? What women's groups can we bring in? Where are the Ag groups?" Briefings were scheduled in the White House—perhaps several each day. An example: 222 people were invited in from state-based family councils and "think tanks." The briefers were senior representatives from the Departments of State and Homeland Security and from the White House Economic Council. Topics: the war on terror, homeland security, the president's economic package, his domestic priorities. The U.S. Afghan Women's Council came in on July 16, 2003. The briefers were First Lady Laura Bush and Secretary of State Condoleezza Rice; the subject: women's rights in Afghanistan.

When the Central American Free Trade Agreement was pending in Congress, the White House public liaison office worked with the Department of State to make the most of visits by the presidents of El Salvador, Honduras, the Dominican Republic, and other countries of the region. The presidents came to the White House, but they also toured the country, visiting several cities where meetings were arranged with local chambers of commerce or other business and trade organizations. Their message was: "This agreement is good for our country; we think it's good for your country too." (Congress eventually approved the agreement.)

Overall Long-Range Plans

The literally hundreds of presidential events that the public liaison office arranged were by no means helter-skelter affairs. Each was part of an exquisitely detailed overall plan—and these detailed plans left nothing to chance. Here are two examples. The first: the "Public Liaison Plan for Senior Citizens," an eight-page document, was divided into "goal"; "objective"; "strategy"; "key issues" (ten are listed); "key constituencies" (forty-six groups listed, such as the National Association of Geriatric Case Managers); "recommended large group meetings" (such as Annual Senior Day at the White House); "intimate meetings with the president and the first lady" (nine, including the National Association for Hispanic Elderly Executives); "other outreach efforts"; "calendar of key events" (twenty-four, including the Wyoming Governor's Conference on Aging); "national months" (fifteen, including the National Aged Blind Persons Education Month); and "key publications" (among them, the *Journal of the American Medical Informatics Association*).

A second plan was equally detailed, and especially interesting in light of President Bush's abrupt dissolution, early on, of President Clinton's Women's Outreach Office, which had been part of the Clinton public liaison staff. There may no longer be a formal office, but there is unquestionably a multipronged White House women's outreach undertaking. The Bush seven-page "Public Liaison Plan for Women Outreach" covered the period May-September, 2001. It had the same "goal," "objectives," "strategy" format; the final sentence in the objectives section reads: "We need to maintain a strong relationship with women, not only as advocates of what have always been termed women's issues, but as advocates of the President's entire agenda."

Following the strategy paragraph, the plan went on to name six "key issues" (including tax relief for working mothers), seven "other key issues" (including Social Security), seven "key constituencies" (including women small business owners), seven "key dates" (including "April 3—Equal Pay Day—Supporters Oppose President Bush"), a group of "resources," including four websites (such as Oxygen.com), ten "magazines" (including *Sports Illustrated for Women*), twenty-one "key organizations" (including the League of Women Voters and the National Association for Girls and Women in Sport), and a list of the names and companies of seventeen women chief executive officers. The plan then included the titles and dates of eight women's events sponsored by the White House during the first President Bush's presidency, and of five women's events during President Clinton's first 180 days. The plan ended with a list of six current recommended large group meetings (including the National Women's Soccer League) and a list of eleven national women's association annual conferences scheduled to be held between April and September of 2001 (with a telephone number for each).The public liaison office developed other outreach plans; there is one for agriculture, one for Hispanics, and one for veterans, for example. These plans, determinedly and awesomely comprehensive, were the products of an enormous amount of staff research; of course each individual item listed is a flag to the public liaison staff to use it as a candidate for some kind of White House action.

Newsletters

As part of its women's outreach effort, the public liaison staff composed a series of three- or four-page newsletters, featuring stories of prime interest to women (such as "President Bush Working to Stamp Out Domestic Violence," "Women Entrepreneurs Honored at the Small Business Administration's 50th Anniversary Celebration," "Mrs. Bush Champions Women's Rights in Afghanistan and Iraq"). Each story was illustrated with a color photograph. The newsletters were attractively printed and distributed to the office's list of hundreds of "leadership groups," which in turn e-mailed the newsletters to hundreds of thousands of members who had joined the White House Women's Information Network.

Transition Arrangements: Clinton to Bush

It is especially worth noting that the first Bush public liaison Director, Lezlee Westine (who provided the author with the information in the paragraphs just above) reached out, early on, to Betsy Myers, who had been director of President Clinton's Women's Outreach program. The two of them had lunch. "She walked me through what her model was," Westine recalled, "how she operated, and she was very good and talented. Then I said, 'Let's meet with all the women that you worked with.' We had a big meeting—obviously there were probably a couple more Republicans than Democrats [one was Bobbie Kilberg, who had been director of public liaison for George H. W. Bush]—and we talked, went around the table, talked about all of their issues. And they just became a foundation for us, and for me, for the next four years."[9]

The Output of the Public Liaison Office

The public liaison office sent a weekly report to Rove, which he usually forwarded to the senior staff. A sample for the period May 26–June 6, 2003, included "Presidential Events: 4"; "Briefings: 16 – two or three each day" (for example with the Minority Small Business Women); "Outreach Meetings: 36"; "Conference Calls: 5"; "E-mail distributions: 7" (including copies of remarks by the president during a visit by Ugandan President Museveni: "300 to African-American leaders, 20 to Arab Organization leaders; 100 to small business leaders, 50 to faith-based groups").

In a typical year during the first term, the office of public liaison managed approximately 200 events, of varying sizes, that the president attended. The actual total for 2006 was 156, broken down into 40 substantive meetings with outside groups, 28 substantive meetings in the Oval Office, 10 ceremonial meetings in the Oval Office, 9 other ceremonial meetings, 41 photo-ops, 9 bill signings, 3 awards, 2 movie screenings, 3 ballgames and one egg roll.[10]

The office typically consists of some twenty staff members plus nine interns; occasionally the sheer number of events being scheduled forced the public liaison director to borrow people from other White House units.

Looking Ahead to 2009

For the next president, former director Rhonda Keenum envisioned a new set of tasks to reach out to a new audience.

> With the technological advancements coming, I would encourage the White House to blog. We are just on the forefront of utilizing blogs to brief bloggers. We did this when we did our mid-session budget review with Rob Portman in the Office of Management and Budget. We brought people who were located nearby here to the White House, and they loved it. They loved sitting there with a laptop blogging while they were getting a briefing by the OMB director and the president. We were on the cutting edge of that, and that is going to be one of the most significant, meaningful and impactful constituency groups because you are right in that niche—niche opportunities that are provided by the Internet—to brief and inform and receive feedback.

The Communications Bloc

Communications Bloc

Counselor to
the President

Offices of
Communications
and Media Affairs
Internet Director

Press Secretary

Speechwriting

"Lipstick on a Pig"?
The Office of Communications

Most people think of communications as an art. It's a convenient construction, because what it basically means is that you don't have to work hard at it, pay attention to detail, and reach into the nitty-gritty of managing people and getting things done. The truth is dramatically different. Communications isn't an art. It's a science—not rocket science, mind you, but a rigorous, detailed, painstaking endeavor that requires organization and discipline to be successful.

—Torie Clarke

To many people in the communications business, the triumph of transparency over spin is still counterintuitive. They were trained in applying lipstick to pigs. . . . Especially in politics, a whole mythology sprung up around the art of the spin: the master "spin doctor" could, or so the legend went, extract anyone from any problem by trumping substance with style. The media could be charmed, the public distracted and the story stopped. If that was ever true . . . it is no more. . . . Those who interact with the public—and today, that covers just about everyone . . . corporate executives and cabinet secretaries . . . must accept the defining feature of strategic communications in the Information Age: the death of spin.

—Torie Clarke

The White House press secretary today, and at least since 1929, has had this challenge: day to day, some fifty journalists (out of the eight hundred accredited to the White House) have their desks in her immediate neighborhood and they demand that she tell them: What is the president's view about the stories in this morning's newspapers or TV broadcasts?

The challenge to the director of the Communications Office, which first opened its doors as recently as the 1970s, is different: What should be—what is going to be—the president's policy message next week and how can we arrange to exploit every opportunity to elicit public support for it? As is obvious, those two offices are thoroughly complementary; while each has a somewhat different objective, they work hand in hand. In their respective universes, however, press relations and communications opportunities, both offices have come through enormous changes in the last thirty years.

To illustrate: In addition to his 193 press conferences, Eisenhower made "speeches and remarks" on some 700 occasions during his eight years in office, aided only by a small press office and one or two speechwriters. President Clinton gave the same number of press conferences but made speeches and remarks 4,500 times, necessitating a much larger staff with a whole new range of skills and outreach. In Reagan's time the three television networks spent the day gathering material for their early evening news broadcasts, and the White House communications planners would aim at scheduling an event a day to be featured on those half-hour programs. When George W. Bush took office, there were five networks (three broadcast and two cable); news was being broadcast 24/7, and videotape (which could be used instantaneously) had, in the 1980s, replaced film (which took time to be processed).[1] Then came the Internet, offering the eager White House literally thousands of new instantaneous opportunities for publicizing—yes, spinning—the presidential viewpoint.

Both the press operation and the communications operation have been transformed and expanded in those five and a half decades; presidential scholar Martha Joynt Kumar estimates that the White House staff contingent in both universes is now approximately 350 persons. Chapter 19 describes the contemporary White House press operation and the different world in which it functions. This chapter and chapter 18 focus on the communications responsibilities—also in a world of dramatically changed challenges and opportunities.

As Kumar wrote: "Whether it is promoting a presidential initiative or campaigning for reelection, a president must make communications part of everything he and his staff do because persuasion is so central to presidential accomplishments. A president needs supporters, and it is through effective communications that he builds winning coalitions on issues. If he is to achieve his goals, he must persuade interested groups and public officials to support them."[2]

The Formation of Communications Strategy in the Bush Administration

Bordering the White House front driveway today is "Stonehenge," a newly paved area bristling with tripods and chairs where as many as sixteen television cameras can be plugged in for immediate, stand-up news broadcasts by either reporters or White House press secretaries coming outside for interviews. The collective result is that the opportunities for the White House to make news have greatly multiplied. Competition, however, abounds in the communications environment. Washington is full of newsmakers; every congressional office has a press staff, as do most of the thousands of lobbyists and interest groups and the hundreds of foreign embassies. The White House communicators have to excel in speed, organization, and ingenuity in their fight to get their president's voice heard amid the cacophonous noise of Washington.

What gives White House communications efforts a commanding uniqueness is the president; he makes news almost automatically. When Bush is preparing a speech, however, the communications office typically arranges for policy staffers in the White House to hold an off-the-record session with reporters ahead of time to discuss not the substance of the speech but the context in which it is being given and "what the president wants to accomplish." Following the speech, a conference call may be arranged for reporters so that the press secretary can provide answers to supplementary queries. But the communications officers are careful: rarely are cabinet secretaries or staffers out front and visible. To quote former press secretary Ari Fleischer, "The president really believes . . . he's the newsmaker, not the staff."[3] It had been the Clinton practice, before an important policy announcement, to bring cabinet members over to the White House to give explanatory briefings to the press—to set the stage for the presidential state- ment. This occurs much less frequently in the Bush administration. As Martha Kumar put it, "Cabinet secretaries are viewed as part of the 'echo' of what the president has already said, rather than a voice in the initial stages of explaining the president's policies. They are used to keep a presidential theme going, rather than to go deep into policy explanations."[4]

Making plans, and sticking to them, is a first principle in the Bush White House, especially when it comes to presenting information to the press and the public. In the first term, every day started with a strategy meeting presided over by the president. Always present was Communications Counselor Karen Hughes, about whom Vice President Cheney remarked, "[She] is everywhere, into everything, and indispensable."[5] Recalled Hughes, "We . . . talk about strate- gic direction and issues and approaches. . . . This morning we covered a wide range of things . . . that's me and Andy [Card] and Karl [Rove] and the president and the vice president, and Condi [Rice] sometimes on foreign policy stuff."[6]

Immediately after the strategy session came a second meeting, chaired by the communications director, to pinpoint operational implementation of the agreed goals. There would also be biweekly communications planning meetings to schedule specific events three months in advance, and finally daily meetings to nail down what was going to take place that day or to make last-minute changes. Another Bush administration forum for planning ahead was Karl Rove's "strate- gery" group, which met monthly or bimonthly. Presidential travel, message, themes, events would be set four months in advance. The strategery group had it own supporting staff (chapter 14).

Discipline

Kumar writes that from the beginning, the Bush administration worked at developing and staying on message. She quotes deputy communications coun- selor Dan Bartlett describing the importance of discipline in the communica- tions process: "What we feel is, particularly since there is so much competition and so much news content out there, that it requires even more discipline to stay on message and stay on what you want to talk about, or you're not going to have success in getting anything across to the American people."[7]

What information to give out, when, how, and who gets it are decisions the White House communications office reserves to itself—a discipline "at the heart of the Bush communications strategies," as Kumar puts it. If the day's headlines or a television broadcast offers an opportunity for White House comment or rebuttal, it will be passed up "if it's not fulfilling or consistent with our strategic communications goal for that week, or that month, or that quarter, or whatever it may be," Bartlett told Kumar. Reporters are "in the news cycle and they're wanting to play in that and they're trying to invite you into the deep end. We tend to look at our long-term goals or our mid-term goals and say: 'Does it fit our communications priorities to do so?'"[8] Put simply, in the Bush White House, goals determine themes, and themes determine schedules, not the other way around.

Cabinetwide Coordination for Communications Effectiveness

President Bush's first chief of staff, Andy Card, "knew that it was part of his job to coordinate publicity with the departments: 'I make sure our communications team is not just a team in the White House. It is a communications team for the executive branch.'"[9] Following a White House practice widely used in recent years, the Bush communications office (like its personnel, legal, intergovernmental affairs, and legislative shops) fosters counterpart units in the cabinet departments and either actually picks these counterpart people or sees to it that they are noncareer appointees unquestionably in sync with the president's policies and priorities. Every morning there is a conference call from the counselor's office to the departmental communications teams so that they are all aware of the themes and messages the White House wants to emphasize that day. Regularly the White House communications leaders host Roosevelt Room meetings with their departmental counterparts. E-mails constantly go out to the political leadership of the cabinet departments reminding them of opportunities to spread the president's message. (One, sent to some sixty political offices of the Department of Agriculture, was leaked in 2006; it urged departmental speechmakers to include supportive "talking points," such as "President Bush has a clear strategy for victory in Iraq," in all their speech drafts.)[10] In one case, the Department of Education carried its enthusiasm too far: it commissioned a newspaper article and also paid to have a conservative columnist praise President Bush's No Child Left Behind legislation, without, in either case, revealing that they were subsidized by the government. The Government Accountability Office judged this to be a use of "covert propaganda" and Secretary Margaret Spellings terminated such purchases, calling them "stupid, wrong, and ill-advised."[11]

One very supportive use of departmental communications resources occurred in 2003 when Bartlett arranged for the Department of Agriculture to feed live audio of Bush signing the farm bill to Farm Radio stations, who could then link up and broadcast the ceremony. It was estimated that half a million farm homes listened to Bush's remarks that morning.[12] Cabinet members themselves are called upon to act as surrogates for the president in giving speeches to support presidential initiatives. In the 2005 campaign to push the president's ideas on Social Security reform, the White House designed a speechmaking program called "60 Stops in 60 Days." Bush spoke on eighteen of those stops; Vice President Cheney at five, Treasury Secretary John W. Snow at thirteen, Secretary of Commerce Carlos Gutierrez at five, Secretary of Labor Elaine Chao at ten, Secretary of Housing and Urban Development Alphonso Jackson at five, Small Business Administrator Hector Barreto at thirteen, and Social Security administrators at twenty-nine. Under secretaries and White House staff were "stoppers" as well.[13] (To no avail; the campaign did not get the support of Congress, the public, and some of the president's own party.)

A particularly enlightening (if that is the proper word to use here) example of a Bush administration communications initiative was revealed in the press in April of 2008—a "key influencer engagement strategy" concocted by the Department of Defense to stimulate public support for the war in Iraq. Even before 9/11, Assistant Secretary of Defense for Public Affairs Torie Clarke "built a system within the Pentagon to recruit 'key influentials'—movers and shakers from all walks who with the proper ministrations might be counted on to generate support for Mr. Rumsfeld's priorities."[14] More than seventy-five retired senior officers were recruited to be "message force multipliers" generating "favorable news coverage of the administration's wartime performance." As a September 2004 Pentagon memorandum explained,

> These retired senior officials provide MNF-I (Multinational Force–Iraq) a unique capability to accurately communicate with global audiences regarding current operations, as well as showcase the progress MNF-I is making in Iraq. As former U.S. Government or Department of Defense employees, [these retired officers] have first-hand experience with military doctrine and operations. They are educated, informed and ready to engage the national and international media on current issues to help deliver themes and messages, and counter enemy propaganda.[15]

These "analysts," the *New York Times* reported in April 2008,

> have been wooed in hundreds of private briefings with senior military leaders, including officials with significant influence over contracting and budget matters, records show. They have been taken on tours of Iraq and given access to classified intelligence. They have been briefed by officials from the White House, State Department and Justice Department, including Mr. Cheney, [Attorney General] Alberto Gonzales and [White House

National Security Adviser] Stephen J. Hadley. . . . To the public, these men are members of a familiar fraternity, presented tens of thousands of times on television and radio as "military analysts" whose long service has equipped them to give authoritative and unfettered judgments about the pressing issues of the post-Sept. 11 world.[16]

Clarke's "key influencer engagement" scheme was kept secret from the Pentagon's regular press office; the briefers were "a small group of political appointees," under the direction of Brent T. Krueger, a senior Clarke aide, who said that these analysts would in effect be "writing the op-ed" for the war. "Rumsfeld ultimately cleared off on all invitees," Kreuger told the *Times*. "From the start," the *Times* news story revealed, "the White House took a keen interest in which analysts had been identified by the Pentagon, requesting lists of potential recruits, and suggesting names. Ms. Clarke's team wrote summaries describing their backgrounds, business affiliations and where they stood on the war."

A *Washington Post* story quoted one of the "analysts," a retired Army colonel and Fox News military analyst, John Garrett, as being in "regular touch with the Pentagon as President Bush prepared to announce his Iraq troop surge last year. 'Please let me know if you have any specific points you want covered or that you would prefer to downplay,' Garrett wrote," the *Post* reported.[17]

The *Times* also revealed "a powerful financial dynamic":

Most of the analysts have ties to military contractors vested in the very war policies they are asked to assess on [the] air. Those business relationships are hardly ever disclosed to the viewers, and sometimes not even to the networks themselves.

Collectively, the men . . . represent more than 150 military contractors either as lobbyists, senior executives, board members or consultants. The companies include defense heavyweights, but also scores of smaller companies, all part of a vast assemblage of contractors, scrambling for hundreds of billions in military business generated by the administration's war on terror. It is furious competition, one in which inside information and easy access to senior officials are highly prized.

Records and interviews show how the Bush administration has used its control over access and information in an effort to transform the analysts into a kind of media Trojan horse – an instrument intended to shape terrorism coverage from inside the major TV and radio networks.[18]

"At least nine of the analysts," the *Times* account admitted, "have written op-ed articles for the *Times*."

A week later, a *Times* editorial excoriated the "simple deal," which was to "offer good news on Iraq, even when the news was bad," and went on to comment that "all administrations try to spin, or even manipulate, the news media, but this White House has taken that to a new low."[19]

The uproar following the press revelations brought angry congressional comment, a demand from the Senate Armed Services Committee chairman to Bob Gates, Rumsfeld's successor as defense secretary, to initiate an investigation, and, finally a Pentagon announcement that "the briefings and all other interactions with the military analysts had been suspended indefinitely, pending an internal review."[20] The Government Accountability Office began its own review of the program particularly to see "whether it violated policies barring use of government money to spread propaganda in the United States," and the Pentagon announced that the department's inspector general "would take a look at whether special access to Pentagon leaders 'may have given the contractors a competitive advantage.'"[21]

Techniques of Communication

Many presidents have been frustrated at the filtering—the controlling—effect that the networks' nightly news anchors have over the selection and presentation of news about the president in their national half-hour broadcasts. They have been equally frustrated over what little about the president and presidential activities makes it to the pages of local newspapers or into local broadcasts. The White House communications office accordingly has a director of media affairs, with subordinate "desks" for the West-Northeast, the South, the Midwest, and the Southwest, and for the Internet and specialty (including ethnic) media. The communications director made it a point to have the president meet with the editorial boards of local and regional publications when they came to Washington. "We believe local media and regional broadcasters are more interested [than the national media] in letting viewers and readers see or hear what the president has to say," Bartlett said in 2003. "It's less analytical and more reporting."[22]

"The hook and bullet crowd," as Bartlett described it—magazines for fishermen, hunters, golfers, outdoors people—shares interests with the president, who jogs and is a baseball aficionado. The White House media affairs unit gives special attention to that segment of the American press.[23]

The regional specialists in the communications office send press release material directly to the local press in their areas and ascertain how presidential initiatives are playing in the local media. For example, in May 2002 Counselor Karl Rove and Domestic Policy Assistant Margaret Spellings held an event in Wisconsin to promote the passage of the No Child Left Behind Act. White House communicators did the research to identify the state's 116 low-performing schools, and the fact that 70,000 children in them would receive supplemental services if that act passed. Rove and Spellings were thus enabled to see to it that the White House communications office sent statements with this information to local press in the appropriate cities and towns in Wisconsin. "People get their news locally," Kumar wrote, and she quoted Bartlett:

> They don't rush out and grab the *New York Times*; they rush out and grab their local paper. They don't always click on to the CBS Evening News; they click on their local newscasters that they rely on. And if you reach them through the medium in which they typically trust more often, their local newscaster, their local paper, their local reporters, the better opportunity you're going to have to get your message across.[24]

Pictures are as important as texts—perhaps more so—and the White House has some control over what is released, control that is exercised by the communications office. Since presidential events are always covered live on cable television, there are a copious set of shots so the scenes that most dramatically support the president's message can be picked out—or created. In May 2003 the president was speaking in Indianapolis promoting his economic plan. WISH-TV, the Indianapolis station, reported that "White House aides went so far as to ask people in the crowd behind Bush to take off their ties, so that they would look more like the ordinary folk the president said would benefit from his tax cut."[25] The communications operatives are in control of every detail.

"I sort of use the rule of thumb," explained communications assistant Scott Sforza, "if the sound were turned down on the television when you are just passing by, you should be able to [just] look at the TV and tell what the president's message is."[26]

A special podium, nicknamed Falcon, has been designed that has one narrow leg, permitting the best possible view of the background behind the president, which itself has been selected, often actually crafted, with exquisite care.[27]

Did the Bush White House follow the Clinton model and have a "war room" as a kind of communications command center? "I don't like the connotation of war room," said Bartlett. "I think that leads to the impression that it necessarily has to be a fight, or confrontation. . . . If something is really bad, you can set up a war room. It makes you feel as if you're on top of it. Typically I have found that the systems already in place are sufficient. Unless there is an extraordinary circumstance going on, our infrastructure is capable of handling it without setting up anything separate."[28]

In the first term, the Bush White House communications leaders, putting their emphasis on detailed long-term planning, did not have a rapid-response unit as the Clinton administration used. After the 2004 election, Bush's campaign communications director Karen Hughes returned to the White House, bringing with her the successful experience the campaign people had had with a rapid response operation. She set up a similar operation in the communications office. Its audiences are noncareer appointees in the administration, congressional staffers, party officials, television and talk-radio hosts and producers, and allies among the interest groups. Its instrument—for both defense and offense—is e-mail messages that quickly get into the news stream. As Martha Kumar explained, "In the second term, newspapers, television networks, radio programs and individuals have a variety of websites and blogs, all of which release information as soon as they get it. That puts pressure on officials in the White House and elsewhere to come up with a fast response."[29] The e-mails are one or two pages long and there are fourteen categories of them; they are sent to between 5,000 and 10,000 recipients. A morning meeting of communications leaders, headed by Bartlett and including the communications office director, the press secretary, and representatives from the media affairs office and the National Security Council, convenes to decide on the releases to issue. They take aim at inaccurate or misleading news stories, but they will also simply put out good news when that is indicated. "We don't want to be like a barking Chihuahua in the middle of the night where you are always yapping," communications director Kevin Sullivan told Kumar. "You have to pick your spots."[30] The texts of the releases are cleared through the usual internal approval process, including policy officers if appropriate. "While their efforts have gotten the president's words and explanations to the public through a variety of channels," Kumar observed, "there are limits to how much the messages can accomplish. There is no guarantee that the public will like what it hears in those messages, nor that anyone will change his or her mind. But at least the White House gets presidential words and thinking to the audiences the president and his staff want to reach."[31]

Evaluating Success

The White House press secretary typically holds a nightly "wrap-up" meeting at 6:15. "We'll gather and we'll go over everything, and then we each report on what we're picking up from the press," Fleischer told Kumar. "Staff members go over how they have been portrayed on television and report on their various media efforts during the day."[32]

To get a picture of what is going on in regional and local television, the White House uses ShadowTV, a private service that searches and records television broadcasts according to keywords, or by date and time of broadcasts, then e-mails the recorded excerpts to subscribers. "Now you have ShadowTV and things like that you can pick up on a local feed and see what the news was like there in a local market," said Scott Sforza, who runs television production for the White House.[33]

Evaluating communications success in a campaign is measurable; the goal line is election day. It is much harder when the actor is governing, Bartlett observed. "You're trying to accomplish a goal, whether it be implementing a piece of legislation or affecting public opinion over a period of time, whether it be [over] the tenure of your presidency."[34]

"In reality," Kumar summed up, "what presidents have are political and policy problems, not communications problems. The expectations of what presidential communications can deliver are much greater than what they can really do. Yet there is still much an effective communications operation can do for a president."[35]

18 | The Cyber White House: Bush Innovations in Electronic Communications

> You need to look at all of your different segments, so that when you're creating your message you factor in your online community, your print community, your radio community, your television community, and the specialty press. So you need to make sure that your message is hitting all of those touch points. We want to make sure that Americans, or anyone in the world, should have access to what the president is saying. . . . We want to present it there unfiltered and let people make up their own minds about it.
>
> —David Almacy

The Office of Communications itself has sixty staff members in some sixteen subdivisions.[1] In one of these sixteen, the Office of Media Affairs, is the White House Internet and e-communications director. The communications techniques employed using the Website "Whitehouse.gov" are quite recent—innovations unique to the administration of George W. Bush. President Bush launched the new website on August 31, 2001, saying:

> I'm very impressed. And I think the people who access this Web site will be impressed as well. . . . I appreciate so very much the Web site being available in more than one language. There are a lot of Spanish-speaking folks in America, and they'll be able to access the Web site. . . . I'm very serious about the need for all of us involved in government to do all we can to involve our citizenry in government. There's a lot of cynicism about politics in Washington, DC, and it seems to me the more accessible Washington becomes, the more likely it is people will participate in the process. And clearly, one way to do so is across the Web page. . . . We will be looking for more imaginative ways to continue people's interest in accessing the White House.[2]

The White House Online

Although the White House had a website during the Clinton and first Bush presidencies, advances in the technology as well as the public's growing familiarity with the technology have allowed George W. Bush's administration to communicate with the public using a wide range of electronic techniques.

White House "Tours"

For years, the public rooms of the Executive Residence were open to visitors during morning tours conducted Tuesdays through Saturdays. The 9/11 attacks abruptly changed tour availability. For a while all tours were canceled; later they were reinstituted with the restriction that would-be visitors must make advance reservations through the offices of their respective senators or representatives. Those not using this option had two other choices: going in person to the White House Visitor Center (chapter 34) or sitting at their computers and visiting the White House online.

Whitehouse.gov opens up to the online visitor a menu of sixteen different rooms and sites in the Residence and the West Wing, beginning with a video tour of the Oval Office conducted by President Bush himself, of the Diplomatic Reception Room by Laura Bush, of the Cabinet Room by former Chief of Staff Andy Card, of the Press Briefing Room by former press secretary Scott McClellan, of the Vice President's office by the Vice President, and of the Vice President's residence with Lynne Cheney. A click on the mouse takes the online tourist to *Air Force One*, Camp David, or the *Marine One* helicopter, lets one look at White House Gardens and Grounds, or reviews the Easter Egg Roll. There are more places to take in online than were ever included in the pre-9/11 tours!

In Focus

Under this online heading are fact sheets about some sixty-eight issues of public policy, such as energy, national security, or immigration. (The list is changed to keep it up to date.) If a reader clicks on any one of those subjects, energy, for instance, not only is a six-page fact sheet displayed but links are given to a photo of the latest presidential event about energy, a quote pulled from a recent presidential speech, a list of all the recent news articles that pertain to the administration's views on the energy issue, and another link to archives that, as White House Internet director David Almacy points out, "takes you to a page of every event the president has done about energy since the beginning of his administration."[3] The viewer can also pull up current White House news; the dates and, if desired, the full texts of all the White House press secretary's press briefings going back to January 24, 2001; the numbers, titles, and, if desired, the full text of all the executive orders President Bush has signed since January 29, 2001; and the dates and full texts of each of the president's weekly radio addresses beginning with January 27, 2001.

The White House Weekly Review

Every Saturday morning, following the president's weekly radio address, an e-mail is composed and sent to those who have subscribed to the White House website. Called the White House Weekly Review, the e-mail features the message the president had emphasized during the past week and his schedule of events supporting that message, with links to photos and quotes of the events during the week. "We had to be pretty nimble," Almacy explained. "Considering the fast pace of news and information, they really trusted me to get the message online and manage the Internet accordingly. As soon as the White House released reports, we had to make sure that they were online when readers clicked to them—there was a lot of coordination with many of the White House offices and with others throughout the administration."

Setting the Record Straight

The White House Communications Office reads or listens to every televised speech or remark that deals with any of the president's messages or initiatives. If a member of Congress or a television anchor, for instance, lets go with a charge that appears misleading, is not factually correct, or contains misinformation, the White House website has a special section called Setting the Record Straight. It quotes the offending charge and then posts a series of factual bullets giving the White House's view of the matter. The style is never ad hominem, but aims to be straightforward and factual, although journalists view this feature as one-sided, since the "facts" are those that the White House selects.

Ask the White House

Readers of "Whitehouse.gov/ask" are shown regular notices of upcoming presentations and question-and-answer sessions with senior White House staff members, cabinet secretaries, and other noteworthy figures associated with the president. Viewers are encouraged to submit online questions in advance. The questions are collected, with preference given to tough, thoughtful queries, according to Almacy. While obscenities are screened out, statements of opposing views are welcome; there are typically thirty to fifty questions to choose from. The questions are shown to the presenter ahead of time, giving the responding guest the opportunity to do any research that might be needed. During the "Ask" presentation, live questions are accepted as well, often resulting in illuminating conversations. The "Ask" periods are for sixty minutes and occur about twice a week; the aim is to cover from eight to ten questions in the hour-long period. The subjects raised usually have some connection to current news and to presidential actions. The responder gives the first (but never the last) name of the questioner, and his or her state: "Here's Ellen from Tennessee and her question is. . . ."

At the time of Hurricane Katrina, Homeland Security Secretary Chertoff was on the program by telephone from New Orleans. Some 1,200 questions were submitted, several asking, "How can we help?" "Where can we send food or money?" Both Laura Bush and Lynne Cheney have been guests on this program two or three times; so has nearly every member of the cabinet. Often the responders are important but little-known members of the White House family: the White House Chief Usher Gary Walters, the White House chef, the gardener, an agent from the U.S. Secret Service.

"Ask the White House," which began in April 2003 with an opening session with then chief of staff Andy Card, is a unique innovation of the Bush administration, providing never-before-available access to senior White House officials who are normally cloaked from public contact. It is highly popular; since it began, some 450 leaders have been brought forward to be questioned; the program even asks its audience to make suggestions about other speakers for the future. The questions come from every corner of the country; especially valued are questions and comments from military men and women stationed abroad, who see "Ask the White House" as a personal link to the leaders of their own government for which they are serving. The e-mailed queries also come in from countries all over the world—"a lot from China, a lot from the Middle East, some in different languages," explained Almacy. "It's really a unique outlet."

RSS Feeds and Podcasts

A presidential event in the East Room creates a mélange of digital signals: a text transcript, a set of still photographs (taken by the White House photo office), and audio and video files (produced by the White House Communications Agency). Beginning with President Bush's second term, users of the White House website have been offered the opportunity to subscribe to news feeds, some with the audio, called Really Simple Syndication (RSS). Viewers who have portable MC3 players such as iPods or Zunes can plug the player into the computer, click onto Whitehouse.gov, and receive an audio podcast feed of White House news, presidential speeches and remarks, presidential press briefings, or the weekly presidential radio addresses. The podcast is stored in the user's player, so that instead of being tied to a computer, the receiver can access the file anytime—while traveling or basking at the beach. Almacy recalled a reporter saying he used this feature "all the time, because it's really helpful for me as a reporter. If I'm not near a computer, I know I can download the president's speech, I can get the quote right, or I can download his radio address and write about the radio address . . . I can be at a laptop or on a plane or at a train station."

Reporters can subscribe to any of those several "feeds" including a feed in Spanish, and be electronically notified when any new item has been added. Video is an option, but because of the size of the video file, the inconvenience of the small screens, and the fact that video rapidly drains the battery life of most portable media players, this option is infrequently employed. Video however remains on the website, accessible to computers for on-demand viewing.

In a still more recent innovation, the audio of the press secretary's daily press briefings has been added to the website since 2006 and has been available for downloading. Now, also, all the "feeds" from the beginning of the Bush administration have been archived. "The value of the Internet," Almacy emphasized,

> is that if a presidential event was an hour and a half long, I know that I can go to Whitehouse.gov on my computer and listen to the whole thing and then make up my mind based on what I'm hearing. If I have an interest to learn more, beyond the sound bite, I can download the video and view the whole discussion, everything the president said. There's no filter between me and the president's words; I get his message exactly as he expressed it. There's no intermediary, no reporter, no commentator, and no blogger saying "I agree," or "I disagree!"

Links among Search Engines

Google approached the White House Internet director with an idea: the company was launching a new government search page and wanted to feature the White House RSS news feed on that page as a sample. The arrangement was consummated; Google's page would facilitate automatic links to the "Whitehouse.gov" material. Explained Almacy, "They're pulling the information from the White House website so while we're sleeping at night, the website is working on behalf of the White House as a communication tool, because it's pushing information out. It's actually interacting with other databases automatically, which is amazing."

Building on that success, Almacy worked with Apple to create a White House Room on iTunes to house the various media files that the White House was producing. TiVo, a popular digital recording company, had created a system by which subscribers could listen to podcasts via their television sets. They offered to feature the president's weekly radio addresses in a section called TiVoCast. Downloads of the president's radio addresses soared in just a few months from a few hundred to several thousand a week.

The Size of the Audience

In Almacy's judgment the best unit of measure for such traffic is the number of times a file, or page, is viewed. In an average week, the White House website receives 3 million to 4 million page views, occasionally reaching 8 million, making the White House website one of the most used websites in the world.

Blogging from the White House

A blogger is a person (or organization) who has his or her own website and uses it to set in front of the electronic public statements of personal views. Not surprisingly, many if not most of those statements are the blogger's own opinions about public affairs, representing every kind of rational or nonrational argument, and they are often aimed at opinion-leaders such as editorial writers or members of Congress. Sometimes a mainstream media outlet or a wire service will pick up a blogger screed and spread its arguments far and wide. The White House reads many of the leading public affairs blogs, and if it is decided that a White House response or rebuttal is called for and would be effective, Almacy engages with them by telephone or e-mail. As a result of those relationships, he said,

> In January of 2006, we set up a conference call with about thirty of the bloggers we knew, and we e-mailed an invitation to them to call in and hear White House press secretary do a preview of the State of the Union message—what it was going to feature that night. Bloggers would call in and, after Tony Snow finished speaking, we'd open it up for questions for half an hour. There were several instances where they, in turn, blogged about that. That was unique; no White House has ever done that.

In 2007, during the superheated public debate about immigration policy, with Congress energetically but narrowly divided, and the president trying mightily to have his proposed legislation enacted, the White House went to new tactics: it would do some live blogs of its own. Former communications director Dan Bartlett explained:

> One of the most recent things with Bush is that we are now engaging in live blogging from the White House. We have the addresses of a lot of the activists' blogs out there that are attacking us. We are empowering people inside the White House to be designated bloggers to engage in real time. ... Right now, there are only a couple of people doing this. Literally in the last couple of weeks, this has been a new thing.[4]

The latest White House blogger: the president himself. The day after his major speech on Iraq, Bush sat down in the Roosevelt Room and engaged in an hour-long round-table interview—not with the traditional journalists who cover the White House but with bloggers whose specialty was military issues. Two of them participated via video link from Baghdad. The president told them that this was the first time any president had met with bloggers.[5]

Some of the bloggers' comments:

Journalist and former Navy pilot Ward Carroll: "The president came off as more comfortable with the message than I've seen him appear on TV or in speeches. No deer-in-the-headlights stuff here. Truly unwavering and passionate. Facts on the ground notwithstanding, he believes the United States can win the Iraq War. And to be honest, being around him made me believe it at that moment too."

Former Army officer Matthew Burden: "The President was very intelligent, razor sharp, warm, focused, emotional (especially about his dad), and genuine.

Even more so than this cynical Chicago boy expected. I was overwhelmed by the sincerity—it wasn't staged."

From Bill Ardolino, who was one of those participating via video from Baghdad: "[I] asked Bush about progress in Anbar province and Fallujah and Bush's answer honestly surprised me in its length, level of detail, and grasp of events on the ground."

"All in all," added Carroll, "it was an amazing day for Military.com and one I'll never forget."

This brand-new communications activity was considered an experiment; Almacy believes it is very likely to be repeated—and to become a standard feature of a future White House communications operation.

Looking into the Future

"The Internet has really rejuvenated television," Almacy explained. "In the old days a program would air and it would be done and you'd never see it again unless you recorded it or had it in some other kind of archived format. But now, it's on YouTube fifteen minutes after it goes on the air."

An online marketing tool that is being used with increasing frequency in the business world is the practice of assembling information about an individual computer user without the person's knowledge and then exploiting that information to tailor the advertising of a product or service so that it has a special appeal to the prospective customer. Almacy gave an analogy:

> You go to your favorite restaurant—you've been going there for fifty years. You sit down and the waiter says, "Here's your pizza, here's your soda, and your onion rings are on the way." They know what you like. In the cyber world it's called a "cookie"—what the servers use to talk to each other every day saying, "This e-mailer has been here before and we know what he likes, so we're going to give him what he wants."

While private websites are using this practice, it is currently against federal e-government policy for the government to do so without the user's permission. Those concerned about online privacy are able to block cookies from their computers. "I think that there will be some evolution," Almacy predicted,

> probably with the next president. I hope that there would be, because I think it is about making it more of a unique user experience—as long as you're able to protect the user's identity, and you're not gleaning information for illicit purposes. I think that one could use it for effective assessment—so the White House staffer can say at the end of the day: "Hey, we have a thousand people on the 'energy' page, so now we know the next time we do an energy event we're going to get probably about a thousand

people." It's a good gauge as to what people are looking at. Again, we don't know who they are, we just know the numbers. . . . The beauty of doing some sort of personalized experience is that there's news that we think may be of special interest to a specific audience, as opposed to just everybody. By *not* personalizing that experience, your audience is always everybody—which is not effective, targeted communications.

Almacy drew a picture of the possible future: a person is sitting on the Metro, reading what looks like a piece of paper. It is not printed paper, however, but a metallic material and instead of producing a printed newspaper, the news publisher is sending the news out digitally, with text and images appearing on the metal sheet, which changes in real time as the news changes. Almacy ends with a word of caution: "I think there's sometimes a pressure to use technology for technology's sake. When somebody says, 'We should just start blogging!' I would say 'Why?' If the answer is, 'I just want to be out there because it's hip and everybody else is doing it,' that's probably not the best strategy. If they say, 'I really want to engage people more online and this is a new way to reach a new audience,' I would then say 'Yes!'"

Caught in the Crossfire:
The Press Secretary

The press secretary to the president stands between opposing forces—the president and the White House press corps—explaining, cajoling, begging, sometimes pushing both sides toward a better understanding of each other. It is a war of wits, both funny and sad, and it is intensely personal.

—Marlin Fitzwater

The White House press corps gathers every morning like a pride of lions. It snarls and growls, sleeps and creeps, and occasionally loves, but it is always hungry.

—Marlin Fitzwater

Seven times seven: seven rows of seven seats each: forty-nine chairs for journalists in the new James S. Brady Briefing Room. How long has the White House had a press briefing room? There was none when Herbert Hoover appointed George Akerson in March of 1929 to a new White House position called press secretary. Nor was there one until 1970, when the West Terrace area of the White House was set up as a press briefing room.

The 24/7 News Environment

Beginning with the Hoover administration, thirteen presidents have had a total of twenty-seven press secretaries. The duties and characteristics of press secretaries, as summed up in the opening quotations, above, have changed very little over those years; the nature of the news business, however, has changed enormously.[1] Eisenhower's press secretary, James Hagerty, could say, "We're locked up for the night," and everyone could go home to personal plans. In the words of Associated Press veteran Terry Hunt, there has now been a "globalization of the news." Perhaps every five minutes, all over the world, some newspaper is going to press, some news or television reporter is about to go on the air, an Internet screen is being watched by news-hungry viewers. "That globalization," Hunt explains, "has increased competition pressure in the news business. The Associated Press . . . considers itself a wire service. It used to be AP, United Press International—now closed down—Reuters, Agence France-Presse, but now every organization has got a website and they're all trying to break the same stories. It's all instantaneous; it's made the White House be much more reactive to events."[2] As a former press secretary put it:

> I appreciated the need for a clear, controlled message. In a world of twenty-four-hour news cycles, the media bombard their audiences with thousands of competing messages conveyed in countless words and images. The chances of getting any single idea through that cacophony are slim. When you wield the bully pulpit of the White House and the giant megaphone of the presidency, it is easier to set the agenda and get your ideas covered. But it still requires a coherent message and repetition of it for any concept to sink in and be fully grasped. If an administration hopes to communicate with the public effectively, it has to develop simple, straightforward, and consistent messages that connect with people's interests, concerns and needs. Then it must find a variety of ways to make those messages newsworthy so they can be hammered home to the public. Otherwise, what the president wants to say will get lost in the ether, and with it his chance to shape events, influence society and (hopefully) make a positive difference in people's lives.[3]

Hunt added that if the *Washington Post* reporter covering the White House finds out about a newsworthy item at 10:00 a.m., will he wait to put it in the next day's newspaper? No; he will post it on the *Washington Post* website immediately. Hunt summed up: "Every news service has turned into a wire service because of the Internet; everybody puts stories out there in real time. I think that the whole Internet has heightened the competition in an already fiercely competitive news town. . . . It has heightened the competition among reporters incredibly. . . . We in the Associated Press are now the biggest news suppliers to websites; I think our fastest-growing source of revenue is supplying news to Yahoo, MSNBC. . . . All the websites have to get content, and we supply the news to all of these. . . . As newspapers recede, you have the Internet."

That competition extends to sources. If White House staffers clam up, reporters will turn to outside interest groups with whom they are friendly, or to members of Congress of the opposite party. "They're going to spill the beans on anything they can," Hunt observed.

The Tightened White House

Today's press secretaries are as eager to get information as they are to give it out. One thing they want to know: What is the press—the Washington press, the national press, the world press—saying about the president, about the administration? That information and more is collected in a daily "White House News Summary" distributed to all senior members of the White House staff. (In the

Nixon years, a shorter news summary was compiled by a White House unit that was part of Pat Buchanan's office.[4] Buchanan was not above including in the summary news stories portraying some of his White House colleagues, that is, rivals, in an unfavorable light). In more recent years, the job of preparing the daily news summary has been contracted out; the current producer is the Bulletin News Service. Covering news of national import in both print and television media, a typical recent summary, marked "Produced for the Office of the White House Press Secretary," was a full 106 pages, single-spaced. Its first 20 pages included sections called Leading the News, Terrorism News, National News, International News, Editorial Wrap-Up, The Big Picture, and Washington's Schedule; these were then followed by eighty-six pages of actual news clips.

Even with the News Summary on his desk, someone in the press office was always assigned to read each of the major newspapers "the first thing each morning," former press secretary McClellan explained. "It served in part as an early warning system so that the press secretary (or his deputy) would know what matters to discuss with senior staff at the morning meeting and nothing blindsided him at the briefing."[5]

Knowing that he is commanded to "take care that the laws be faithfully executed," one of the challenges faced by every president—and every press secretary—is development of a system for being alerted if, somewhere in the far-flung executive branch, something is going off the track or if some decision is being made at lower levels about which the White House should at least be informed. A goof will become news in short order—news that can come to the White House as an embarrassing surprise. Agency heads are disinclined to report mistakes, especially to the White House, so over the years the White House has taken many different approaches to try to learn about goofs before they become news. Eisenhower initiated the practice of requiring agency heads to send Staff Secretary Andrew Goodpaster individual short memos so he could see and comment on actions being taken (or missteps being made); the White House termed them "staff notes." President Kennedy continued this mode of information gathering; subsequent presidents expanded it into a weekly "cabinet report" from each agency head. President Bush has added a requirement that cabinet members send his communications office a "night note" e-mail alerting the White House to any items that may be of special concern. The e-mails are collected and circulated to a limited number of senior staff. "It's a great tool," said Press Secretary Dana Perino. "We encourage them not to wait until the "night note"; if they have a problem they should pick up the phone fast, so we can get on top of it."[6]

Information control of a different sort is employed by press secretaries who follow a tradition used in the Johnson and Nixon White Houses: outsiders (especially journalists) who seek interviews with White House staff members have to clear their requests with the press office, and often find that it is only the press office that will speak to them.

"The Bush administration is very tightly on message," Terry Hunt commented.

There are people that I have known for years, and they join the White House staff and then say they can't talk to me, in person or on the phone. I'll get a callback from Deputy Press Secretary Tony Fratto in the press office: "Something I can help you with?" It's tougher getting to the White House staff than it has been in previous administrations—a big contrast with the Clinton administration—you could get to practically anyone. But this administration has a much tighter grip on whom reporters talk to.

Even if a journalist succeeds in contacting a senior White House staffer, the conversation may not be enlightening. "They're extraordinarily disciplined, more so than other administrations," observed Hunt. "If you talked to Karl Rove, or you talked to Dana Perino, or you talked to a Republican congressman on the Hill about a particular issue, you're going to hear the same words. They've got their talking points down. They do a good job scripting things and they do a good job in getting them out and getting people to stay on the same page. They've been remarkably successful in doing that."

Perino confirmed that this disciplined system is precisely what the George Bush White House desires.

In this White House, we work very cooperatively as a team, and I would say that if any member of the staff talks to a reporter without first coming through the press office, the staff people let us know right away. Other administrations may not like the system that we have, and that's up to them, but this system that we have works well for us. . . . I try to provide access to senior members of the staff as often as possible and when reasonable. I don't always grant those interviews for various reasons, but I think that if you were to ask the reporters, I think they might say I've been a tad bit more willing to share, and open up the curtain to the White House more often. . . . If [a reporter] were to contact Chief of Staff Josh Bolten directly, he would most often come to me or [former press secretary] Tony [Snow] . . . and say he has gotten this call and ask if he should return it. That's how Bolten wants other people in the White House to operate, and they follow that.

If an interview is approved with a senior White House staffer, a third person, a "minder," will often be added. "So nothing is unheard, unseen, or unfiltered," observed *National Journal* reporter Alexis Simendinger. "Usually the minder takes notes, and sometimes will interject in the conversation—which is a big no-no. You would be surprised; even Karl Rove would shut his lips and let the minder speak."[7]

A reporter may try to contact a potential White House interviewee by using e-mail—if he or she can discover what the staffer's e-mail address is. But then both the incoming message, and the outgoing response, if any, become part of the presidential records database. A few White House staff members are able to use an e-mail address via the Republican National Committee, but congressional investigators have criticized this practice and have attempted to have this category of messages preserved and opened for public examination. Employing the U.S. Postal Service to approach a White House staffer for timely information is next to useless; all mail addressed to "Washington, D.C. 20500" is sent to a special laboratory to be screened—for anthrax or whatever—a process that takes perhaps five weeks.

An even tougher element of the White House's disciplinary system vis-à-vis the news media is the option that almost all press secretaries, including Perino, have in reserve: to complain to editors themselves if their reporters have written or broadcast stories that are, allegedly, unfair. "I don't complain often," Perino explained. "I complain on the merits when I think it is warranted. If you nitpick a reporter to death, you're not doing yourself any favors. We complain when necessary."

Emulating its predecessors, the Bush White House uses its communications and press offices to keep close control over who in the executive branch is going to appear on the Sunday talk shows. The rule is—as it has been for years—that talk-show invitees must get a White House sign-off before accepting a spot on one of those programs. In addition the White House press secretary or deputy would give the administration representative a briefing in advance of the Sunday appearance. "It was a way to prep them for responses to likely questions and make sure everyone was on the same page," explained Scott McClellan.[8]

The tightness of the Bush White House discipline is sometimes extended to the press secretary personally. Scott McClellan tells of being excluded from the daily "communications" meetings in the Oval Office and from other private meetings. The strategy he employed was

> just showing up at a meeting you hadn't been invited to. Other times, it was possible to get complete and timely information from others who'd attended the meeting. And still other times, I could go directly to the president, who would either tell me what I needed to know himself or, if necessary, make a phone call to the necessary adviser. These word-arounds would almost always get me the information I needed . . . being kept in the dark is an uncomfortable position for any press secretary to be in.[9]

The Press Office in Operation

The Bush press office is a staff of twelve, divided into an "upper" office about fifty feet from the Oval Office, where the press secretary and her deputy sit, and a "lower" press office adjacent to the briefing room at ground level a few steps down.

The press secretary, currently Perino, keeps track of and informed about the substance of domestic policy issues being discussed in the White House by being invited to all deputy and principals meetings and to all policy-time sessions in the Oval Office. Her link to the national security policy machinery is Deputy Press Secretary Gordon Johndroe, who reports both to national security adviser Stephen Hadley and to her. Perino and her staff also attend National Security Council briefings that are held in preparation for presidential travel abroad.

Perino's other deputies and assistants each have one or more portfolios of related issues that they follow closely, such as the Energy-EPA-Interior cluster, or the Justice–Homeland Security cluster; they relate in each case to the respective policy officers on the White House staff. They are also constantly in touch with the press secretaries in the cabinet departments; every weekday at 10:30 a.m. Perino and her deputies hold conference calls with all or most of them. Not surprisingly the cabinet press secretaries respond to the White House with alacrity; the White House press secretary has a strong voice in their appointment.

The coordination between the press office and the communications staff is especially tight. The former concentrates on day-to-day issues; the latter on matters of longer range. "We just integrate seamlessly into their operation," Perino emphasized. All of these relationships are going on at warp speed. Everyone has a BlackBerry, so query and response can be managed in minutes if need be. "You're communicating all the time," Perino observed. "There's no such thing as a 5 o'clock deadline any more."

The "Gaggle"

The Bush administration has made changes in the day-to-day meetings with the collective press. The morning "gaggle"—the informal gathering of regulars with the press secretary so that both could get a feel for what the day was going to be like—had traditionally been held in the press secretary's own office. After 9/11, attendance at the gaggle soared, with the crowd sometimes spilling out into the Oval Office vicinity. Press Secretary Ari Fleischer was forced to change the locus of the gaggle to the Brady Briefing Room. The rules begun by the Clinton administration continue to apply: reporters' tapes of the sessions could be used only to make sure that the press secretary's comments are later quoted accurately; no photographs or television are permitted. The gaggle is, however, recorded and filmed, and a transcript is made by the White House Communications Agency; the film can be played and the transcript circulated for staff use anywhere in the White House. "They do that purposely because they want to make sure their spokespeople only say what they are expected to say," commented Alexis Simendinger. The reporters know that, since the early Clinton days, the film and transcript of the gaggle are passed around among the White House staff, a practice that has tended to rob the gaggle of some of the candid informality that formerly characterized that session.

The gaggle is an integrating device in a second way, as presidential scholar Martha Kumar observed:

> Because the press secretary must be familiar with all of the president's activities, plans, and policy stances as well as everything else that may be happening in the White House, every shop in the White House is responsible for updating the press secretary as he prepares for his two daily sessions with reporters. The press secretary reciprocates by distributing summaries in order to let each White House office know what the other offices are thinking. So preparing for the gaggle and the daily briefing is also a routine for distilling, integrating, and disseminating information throughout the White House.[10]

The transcript of the gaggle is not given to the press, however; doing that would undercut journalists' motivation to show up at the gaggle in the first place, and their absence would deprive the press secretary of important intelligence about what is on their minds. Unless there is hot, breaking news, the principal content of the gaggle is about the president's schedule for that day and days immediately following, allowing reporters, especially those who have strict deadlines, to adjust their own schedules accordingly. The gaggle is not an occasion for the White House to give out major announcements on policy issues; those are handled at the regular afternoon press briefing. "In addition to introducing their messages for the day, the Press Office uses the early morning gaggle to take its measure of the press corps and to learn what reporters are thinking," Kumar observed. "When they read reporters accurately, they have a sense of what to expect at that day's briefing. There are a number of reporters who are known to preview their briefing questions in the gaggle. . . . In short, the gaggle permits each side to sniff out the other.[11]

Finally, as Kumar observed, the press secretary can use the gaggle to upbraid a magazine or newspaper for a story it has run—a castigation that "would not be associated with the president's voice, face or even, in visible form anyway, his press secretary."

The Daily Press Briefing

The actual press briefing—the whole duration of it (but no cutaway shots)—was opened for C-SPAN and for cable television by President Clinton's press secretary Mike McCurry. "And McCurry now says it was his biggest mistake," Hunt said. Before that, Hunt continued, "reporters would really engage with the press secretary, have a dialogue. Now, by letting everybody broadcast it, it has turned into more of a show. It has made the press secretary become more of a celebrity. Tony Snow was adored by the White House; he was willing to debate with reporters, smack them down when he felt it was time. You know, roll his eyes, throw up his hands—he was just very theatrical." A subsequent Bush innovation has been to videostream the press briefing onto the White House website, which means it now takes place via anyone's computer in front of the whole world.

Some thought has been given to reversing the McCurry decision to put the press briefings on live video. Perino analyzed the pros and cons: "It helps the TV reporters, in the cable news, to have something to do and say, and we have a chance to get our message out. The drawback that people see every day is that sometimes the press briefing can feel more like a show than an information exchange. One network reporter prefers to skip the briefing entirely and come only to the gaggle."

Approximately 800 from the press—journalists and technicians—are accredited to the White House by their respective news organizations. After a press office review and a Secret Service check, each is issued a "hard pass," which permits entrance to the Brady Briefing Room area only. That number had been higher, 1,700, until 9/11; it is now limited to those who regularly attend press sessions.[12]

There are forty-nine journalists' seats (and six along the side for White House staff) in the Brady Briefing Room, and each seat is reserved for a specific news organization. The more prestigious (read: higher circulation) is a news organization, the closer to the front is its seat; those sitting in the first two rows are more likely to be recognized early, although the press secretary is free to begin wherever he or she wants. The briefings are brought to a close when the senior wire service reporter present judges that no more questions of consequence are pending; he or she pronounces, "Thank you, madam secretary!"

The Presidential Press Conference

It is from this duo of daily encounters with journalists—the gaggle and the press briefing—that press secretaries are in a position to prepare the president for his own news conferences. "They wouldn't be doing their job in the press office if they didn't know which reporters are really interested in which topics, and what the questions are likely to be," observed Simendinger. A presidential press conference in fact is typically preceded by two informal preparatory sessions with the president, one for half an hour in the Oval Office in the morning immediately following the intelligence briefing, the second closer to the hour of the press conference and sometimes lasting forty-five minutes. If there is to be an opening statement, the speechwriters will have written it in conjunction with the communications director. By the evening beforehand, the press secretary and his or her deputies will have prepared a set of questions that can be expected to be asked, and the proposed answers, all of which are also reviewed with the director of communications. As McClellan wrote,

> Bush would sit at his desk for these "murder board" sessions, where we'd throw the tough or killer questions at him. Bush liked bringing a little levity to the sessions, ridiculing some questions with playful responses he

would never utter in public. It was a way for him to relax and get his mind focused, in much the same way that a world-class athlete might ease nervousness ahead of a crucial contest.[13]

The seating and recognition protocol at presidential news conferences is quite firm, and the "ownership" of the specific seats, therefore, is a fiercely guarded privilege. The wire services are always in the very front row and the tradition is that the Associated Press (which services 1,500 newspapers) is called on first, Reuters (with 60) next, followed by the five television networks, then the major newspapers (*New York Times, Washington Post, Los Angeles Times, USA Today,* and *Wall Street Journal*). Bloomberg News is usually called on, and AP radio. If the president plans, ahead of time, to call on a specific reporter, his seat may be moved forward one or two rows. On the podium in front of the president is a seating chart; the press secretary highlights the names of the journalists who, in her judgment, should be recognized. The seating protocol is a helpful convenience for the president: he becomes familiar with who is sitting where. The consequence for the journalists, however, is that after the first seven or eight reporters have asked their questions, those recognized later may have to sweat to raise a query that has not already been dealt with. The experienced journalist, Hunt explained, always comes to a press briefing or presidential news conference with six or eight questions in mind, and his or her purpose in raising any of them is elemental—in Hunt's words: "I'm looking for a news lead!"

In his first six years in office, President George W. Bush held 151 press conferences, an average of 25.2 a year, compared with 24.1 for President Clinton, 35.8 for George H. W. Bush, 5.8 for Reagan, 7.1 for Nixon, and 84.1 for Roosevelt.[14] Recent presidents, beginning with George H. W. Bush, have greatly increased the number of occasions when the press conference is a joint affair, often with foreign chiefs of state with whom the president is having private meetings.

Do reporters come to presidential press conferences under instructions from their editors or bureau chiefs to ask certain questions? Not in Hunt's experience. He would typically compare notes with the bureau chief and check with perhaps the AP reporter covering the State Department or his colleague covering the Pentagon to learn what other stories were being generated. The questions he asked were based on his own professional judgment, however.

If the press conference is held in the East Room (as they often are), when it ends and the president leaves, the journalists are required to wait until a press office aide escorts them back to the press area; they are not allowed to move around the residence unescorted. Each reporter then makes up his or her own summary of the president's most newsworthy remarks. At this point, the lights and mikes are turned on at the "Stonehenge" area along the northwest driveway and each reporter hustles outdoors to his or her organization's own stand-up spot and delivers an oral report for instant live broadcast or taped for later showing.

A Bush innovation affecting the news media has been the practice of preceding a presidential address on a given subject by arranging conference calls between reporters and an appropriate senior White House staff specialist. Journalists are alerted by e-mail that a conference call is scheduled; they log on ahead of time, identify themselves, and indicate that they want to ask a question. The conference call gives background and adds emphasis to what the president is planning to say.

Personal Sessions with the President

Of special value to journalists covering the White House are the occasions when perhaps eight of them are invited up to the residence for an hour or more of candid conversation with the president. He lets his hair down, uses unpolished language, gives his opinions of other people in public life, even speculates on election outcomes. He tells the journalists, "If you ask me this in the press conference, I am going to 'fluff' you—but here's what I told Yeltsin. . . ." The information the president imparts in these sessions is always and entirely off the record—no attributed quotations allowed. Even one minor leak from such a session would have the effect of ruining the privilege for everybody.

Another variety of personal sessions with the president was the irregularly scheduled Talk-Radio Day. Recognizing the impact talk-radio hosts have on their regular listeners, the president three times invited groups of talk-radio hosts to the White House—the first group of twenty-five, in 2002, then fifty-two in 2004 and fifty-five in 2006. A big tent was set up on the North Lawn; the radio stars were seated for the whole time at folding tables. All day long, White House senior staffers, cabinet members, and the president himself came through, according to a schedule. The talk-radio hosts took back enough material for hours of broadcasts about their White House experience.

Covering the Iraq War

As the war in Iraq began, the White House communications director, with the president's approval, persuaded the Department of Defense to initiate a new system of helping the press cover the battlefield: embed them with the troops. Reflected outgoing communications chief Dan Bartlett:

> It was fundamentally different from what anyone had done before. While there were some shortcomings, I think overall it was a very positive move for us, for two reasons—I'll give you the good and the bad. The good was by giving the press corps the ability to live and work and really cover the war, right next to people, allowed them to create an emotional bond with the American people. It gave them the connectivity which is very important. The downside of the process is that it's like dealing with a very complicated war by yourself. The only perspective you are getting is the one person in this one little unit. . . . In total, though, it was very beneficial.[15]

Presidential scholar and author Martha Kumar points to another type of change that has come about in the last few years in the business of reporting war news: the fight against terrorism is in part a "war in the shadows." The battles, victories, and defeats, if any, are unseen. "What we have been doing is tracking money, finding out how funds have been shipped, digging out where diamonds were being used to finance Al Qaeda," she observed.[16] Journalists doing research on this kind of nonbattlefield war find themselves getting closer and closer to information that is security classified.

Innovation at the White House Press Facilities

George W. Bush's White House may be well known for its disciplined treatment of the press; now it is going to be well known, and applauded, for something else: the set of efficient new facilities that it created in the second term, both outdoors and indoors, to make the on-campus newsmaking-newsgathering tasks more pleasant and much more effective. Outdoors has been the redesign and upgrading of what was called the Pebble Beach area (now Stonehenge), where White House reporters give instant, stand-up reports to their respective networks. Indoors has been the complete reconstruction and reequipping of the Brady Briefing Room. Both these innovations are described in chapter 36.

The equipment upgrade has spread to the press secretary's own office. Over Assistant Press Secretary Scott Stanzel's desk, for instance, two flat screens are constantly running; one displays his incoming e-mails; the other is hooked to an internal wire arrangement that lets him tune into any of the four cable news channels (BBC, CNN, Fox News, and MSNBC) or all four at once on a split screen.

Everyone in the office has a BlackBerry, and Stanzel recounted an example of the efficiency these gadgets have added. One weekend when Stanzel was the "spokesperson on duty"—that is, the press officer to whom the White House telephone operator routed weekend or out-of-hours calls from journalists—he received a call that a member of Congress had passed away. Stanzel thus had the duty of issuing a presidential condolence statement. Did this mean that he had to suspend his weekend activities and come downtown to the office? No. Stanzel was driving a car, doing errands with a friend. He pulled the car over, moved into the passenger seat, pulled out his BlackBerry, drafted a suggested presidential statement, sent it electronically to a circle of fellow staffers (with BlackBerries) for clearance, received the return messages with the necessary approvals, and sent the text of the presidential statement, via the BlackBerry, to the news wires for issuance. The press secretary of 2007 works in a different world!

International Travel with the President

President Bush has undertaken some exceptionally unusual trips—to war-torn Iraq three times, to Pakistan, onto an aircraft carrier, to strife-scarred Israel. The trips have been both risky and newsworthy. The news organizations that regularly cover the White House identify a rotating pool of journalists available to accompany the president (the April 2007 schedule, for instance, listed thirty-one print organizations, five TV networks, nine radio outfits, and two magazine photographers). An *Air Force One* pool of no more than fifteen is selected from that larger group of eligibles, typically reporters from the Associated Press, Agence France-Presse, Reuters, and Bloomberg News, a "print pooler" from of the major newspapers, a radio correspondent, a news magazine writer, a broadcast correspondent, a TV cameraman with an assistant and perhaps four still-camera photographers. These fifteen sit at the rear of *Air Force One*, back next to the galley, behind the Secret Service compartment. Other press representatives may have the option of being added to the traveling group but they must charter a separate press plane. Anything that the pool covers is shared as promptly as possible with the larger press corps.

All of the press representatives pay the equivalent of first-class airfare, plus hotel, catering, briefing-room, and bus-charter costs, which, when totaled up, turn out to be such a major financial obligation that the number of journalists traveling with the president has been diminishing. Of course if the chartered plane is full, the per capita expenses are less. The newspapers that regularly sign up for these trips are perhaps only three: the *New York Times,* the *Washington Post,* and the *Los Angeles Times.*

On the former *Air Force One,* the press had a view down the aisle and usually could see the president and his party moving around up front. The current *Air Force One* is configured differently; there is no straight-ahead view. Unlike the first President Bush or Clinton, George W. Bush does not come back to chat with the news pool; if there is to be interplay, the reporters are invited forward to the president's conference room. "I can't complain," commented Terry Hunt of the Associated Press, a veteran of many presidential flights. "You are on *Air Force One;* if something happens, you're with the president and, you know, if something happens, it's the place to be."

The White House Correspondents Association

The dialogue between the White House press corps and the press secretary, two institutions very often at odds, has been aided over the years by the White House Correspondents Association. Founded in 1915 to give credentialing advice and thus help the White House to control unregulated requests for places on the White House beat, the association later became known for its sponsorship of the annual White House Correspondents dinner. Its nine-member board, elected from the various media constituencies, undertakes to represent the press corps in continuing negotiations with the press secretary's office about pools, passes, access, credentials, travel arrangements, and press conference rules. The association was directly involved with the deputy chief of staff for operations, Joseph

Hagin, concerning every detail of the temporary movement of the press corps out of the White House during the reconstruction of the Brady Briefing Room. (Said Hunt with a wry smile: "We had meetings with Deputy Chief of Staff Hagin, seeking assurances that we would be coming back into the building. There was always the suspicion that they were going to throw us out!")

The association of course was consulted fully about the design of the new briefing room. The association's principal source of revenue is the annual dinner; those funds also support a scholarship program.

Looking Ahead to 2009

Two veterans sum up the relationship between the president and the press. The first observation comes from Martha Kumar, a scholar who has been studying presidents for thirty-three years:

> Perhaps the governing factor in the environment within which the Press Office functions is the cooperative character of the relationship between White House officials and reporters. Their public grumbling may mask it, but reporters and officials cooperate with each other far more than they fight. The daily briefing epitomizes the symbiotic relationship between news organizations and the White House. Each side needs the other: Reporters must have information for their stories, and the White House must have publicity for its programs. Reporters may publicly complain about the amount of information they are receiving at the briefings, but they ask the questions they want answered and have found ways to make sure that the White House will answer them, one way or another.[17]

The second observation comes from Hunt, who has covered the White House for the AP for twenty-seven years:

> A president comes in and he's got a series of goals, he's got things he wants to accomplish. I think that the best way to do that is to bring everybody in on what you're trying to do and explain to them. I think that the press is ... the interlocutors—we present [the president] to the public. Sometimes there is hostility between the press and an incoming administration. They've been banged around during a campaign. My advice: "Get over it! You know, you've moved into a new stage. Now is the time to get down to business; deal with the press; don't think of them as the enemy; think of them as the medium through which you are going to convey most of your ideas." I'm an advocate of more access to the president. I think that the more interplay there is between the press and the president, the better it is for both sides. I think that it's good for us and it's good for him, because he's able to get out more of his ideas.

20 | *The Speechwriting Office*

Alas, the poor speechwriter. I knew him well. Once he was a presidential collaborator . . . a Sam Rosenman, a Clark Clifford, participating in the decisions he helped to communicate, exchanging ideas with the President as well as phrases. . . . In the last three administrations . . . he has typically not been a policy adviser but a professional wordsmith, isolated from decision-making and from personal contact with the decision-maker.

—Ted Sorensen

Speechwriters work closely with the President and the policy people on the text of the speeches. . . . Typically we will go through two or three editing sessions directly with the President in the Oval Office . . . before we go to oral rehearsal. . . . It comes down to this: President Bush spends a great deal of time on his speeches. That elevates both the speeches and the speechwriters in the policy world.

—William McGurn

Chief presidential speechwriter William McGurn sums up what the speechwriting office does: it is responsible for drafting the texts of all the formal, nonextemporaneous public utterances of the president that are covered by the press.[1] There is a wide variety in the categories of presidential speeches.

Leading the list is the State of the Union message, delivered every January. Ideas and proposals are garnered from the cabinet departments as early as the fall and are reviewed and debated in the White House policy offices during October and November, three or four months before the speech is delivered. "My speechwriters and I have regular meetings with the entire senior staff on strategy," explained McGurn. "We sit down with the policymakers . . . and we speak directly with any official who has information, experience, or policy input we can use."[2] Early drafts appear, sometimes of different sections of the message, and they are put through the staff secretary's staffing process, on a "close hold" basis, circulated only to the vice president, the chief and two deputy chiefs of staff, the principal political adviser, the communications chief, and the White House policy assistant whose subject the draft discusses. Cabinet members are shown the draft parts pertaining to their department, but the distribution of speech drafts is permitted, and closely controlled, by the staff secretary, so that he knows precisely who has copies.

By mid-December an overall draft is ready for the president. McGurn is very definite: the Sorenson description, written in 1979, does not apply at all to the White House of George W. Bush. "The president will go through it as a written document many times," he explained, "and then come the days of practice in the family theater."

> There are at least three, probably closer to six or seven oral rehearsals in the family theater. . . . The first ones are generally more editing sessions. Whenever you read aloud, you find things you didn't know were there when you were writing it. I come from journalism, and that's a very different tradition, but I find that when we read aloud, things sound differently or don't work. . . . With each reading, the president makes it more and more his speech, absorbing the logic and the lines, and making the changes he needs.

Attending the oral rehearsals are, typically, a half-dozen staff members including the chief of staff, the chief of communications, the speechwriters, and the staff secretary. The national security adviser, who sits in on any proposed speeches concerning foreign affairs, also usually attends. The president's spouse does not usually attend oral rehearsals for the State of the Union or other presidential speeches, but that office is always on the staffing list, and the spouse of course has many an opportunity privately to give personal views to the president.

Asked if his office has a hand in picking the people chosen to sit in the spouse's box at the State of Union message, McGurn said that while his staff often comes up with examples who might be mentioned by name in the address, the box holders themselves are selected by the president with the help of the scheduling office. If the president, for example, wants to have a soldier join the spouse's contingent, the speechwriting office may help in identifying one.

All of President Bush's speeches, including the weekly radio addresses, go through the same centralized drafting, staff scrutiny, and editing process as the State of the Union, although not all undergo oral dress rehearsals. Being a wartime president, Bush tends to give speeches more frequently than a peacetime chief executive, with his emphasis in recent years changing from explaining to the public why America went to war in Iraq to explaining the current situation there or defending his strategy for success. If the president flies to inspect a disaster area, where he makes two or three stops, his remarks are extemporaneous but he will have been briefed on the plane beforehand.

Either McGurn or one of his two deputies—Marc Thiessen or Chris Michel—accompanies the president on overseas trips, especially those where several speeches are planned. Typically the president delivers an address before departure, presenting an overall message that he wants to convey for the trip, followed by a full package of speeches to be given in individual countries; these speeches are supported by talking points prepared in situ.[3] "People underestimate how much he knows the policy, so he's going to want to use his own language," explained McGurn. "There's nothing worse than sticking a president with a prepared speech that does not leave him room to include ten interesting things that he sees when he is on the ground. So we give him the main principles and he can apply that to what he's just seen."

Air Force One is fully equipped to handle speech drafting, reproduction, and transmission; occasionally when time between foreign appearances is short, the speechwriter e-mails instructions to the White House to have his colleagues work on a specific topic, "and then," explained McGurn, "we will tinker with it." Such a draft usually does not require elaborate staffing in the White House because the national security adviser is also part of the group traveling with the president. "You're not inventing the wheel on the plane," McGurn added, "you're adjusting and fine-tuning." If the president gives a talk immediately after having come out of a session with a foreign leader, he handles that ad hoc because the speechwriters were not themselves in the meeting.

Speeches on foreign policy issues are sensitive, and frequent. Readers may recall that in the first President Bush's White House, there was tension between his speechwriting staff and the National Security Council staff about which office would be responsible for this category of addresses.[4] In the current Bush White House, a speechwriter on the NSC staff, Mark Busse, reports to both the NSC and McGurn. Busse handles some of the speeches the president delivers on overseas trips or in welcoming foreign visitors to the White House; the president's principal foreign policy speeches are authored by the team of McGurn, Thiessen, and Michel.

A special category of speechmaking flourishes every other year when election campaigns become priority business. The president typically aids Republican Senate or House candidates by traveling to their home states or districts and delivering vote-getting speeches. Campaign speechwriting to aid an office-seeker involves using a general outline and adapting it for the individual audience, for the issues at stake, and for the candidate who is the beneficiary of the presidential support. To ascertain the themes that will be most useful and effective, the speechwriters often consult with the candidate personally. The president himself works in the applause lines that befit the occasion and that are of proven appeal. Polling is done on behalf of the Bush White House, as for preceding presidents, but McGurn averred that "we are not involved in polling and we do not have the results sent to us; we are much more pegged to what the president wants to say." McGurn attends the so-called "strategery" meetings, where he picks up intelligence as to how recent speeches have been received.

As discussed in chapter 22, the president's spouse is an active speechmaker. When Laura Bush travels or talks about activities and priorities of the president,

McGurn and staff may assist her speechwriter (a close friend of McGurn's), whose office is located with the McGurn staff in the Eisenhower Executive Office Building.

Finally there is a category of presidential speeches that is "outsourced." These are talks featuring quips and humor, the best example of which is the annual speech to the White House Correspondents Association. Landon Parvin, who was a speechwriter on Ronald Reagan's staff and who has written for Nancy Reagan, George H. W. Bush, and Arnold Schwarzenegger, has been hired for these occasions. There is no White House "staffing" for these events.

Ceremonial Speeches

The president also presides at several different kinds of ceremonies. For example, he bestows the Congressional Medal of Honor on soldiers who have served in combat, some posthumously. Many of these presentations involve incredible stories of heroism that deeply affect the speechwriters who prepare the remarks. "That's an assignment you like," McGurn observed.

Another example is the winning sports teams that often receive presidential praise in the Rose Garden. Some authors refer to these occasions as "Rose Garden rubbish." McGurn, noting that many other events are held there, takes strong umbrage at that characterization.

> The Rose Garden is really the people's garden. Yesterday we had the commissioning ceremony for fifty ROTC (Reserve Officer Training Corps] students from around the country—people and their families who probably have never been to the White House. You have to remember—this may be routine to you, but it might be the most important event in a person's life. . . . You have an obligation to do it right for the president and to make it special for the people. I think all the speechwriters love doing those things; we really do have an obligation. We work for the people.

If the Rose Garden event is a formal ceremony like the one McGurn mentioned, the president does not want just talking points; unless it is a press conference he insists on formal texts. The winning sports teams are an exception. For those occasions "the president doesn't want to be chained to remarks," McGurn commented. "We'll give him a lot of information about the team, and some jokes, and he'll take it wherever he wants it."

Even in the most strictly managed White House, humorous accidents will occur. Just as the traditional pre-Thanksgiving turkey-pardoning ceremony was about to take place in the Rose Garden in November of 2006, the president's dog Barney bounded in, spotted the big white turkey, and made a lunge for it. At that very moment, the president appeared and, amid a chorus of squawking and barking, physically intervened to separate the Scotch terrier from the gobbler.

The Speechwriting Staff

McGurn, the chief speechwriter, carries the title of assistant to the president and heads a staff of thirteen. Two of the staff, Thiessen and Michel, serve as his deputies and core members of the team that writes or edits every speech. In addition, the office has three interns, plus an assistant who is technically on the White House staff and who helps out on special occasions, but who actually serves as the vice president's speechwriter, plus Mark Busse, who works for both McGurn and the national security adviser.

An absolutely indispensable element of the speechwriter's office is the two people who constitute its research team. Before any speech drafting is even begun, detailed material is dug up and pulled together about the site, the audience, the history of the occasion, the people who are sponsoring the event. The chosen subject is scrutinized: Has the president spoken on the same subject before? When? Where? The speechwriters' computers contain the complete archives of all the president's speeches; the previous texts may be printed out. Four fact-checkers go through a draft and verify and footnote virtually every sentence. A soldier may be quoted; the researchers go back, find the soldier, and recheck the quote. "The best way to understand the fact-checkers' role is to look at the annotated version of the speech," McGurn emphasized. "Even a speech that is only four pages can have thirty pages of annotations, backing up everything the president is to say. The fact-checkers are among the hardest workers in the White House, and they do so under severe deadlines and difficult situations."

Technology has made a difference in how the speechwriters fit into the contemporary White House. E-mail allows drafts to be sent to the offices or homes of a much larger circle of interested participants and get responses back with greater speed. BlackBerries permit colleagues to receive and send text wherever they may be. "It's like a big committee editing your work," McGurn observed. McGurn also used his top-level staff in what may be a novel mode:

> I always bring my deputies into meetings in the Oval Office about speeches. I believe the more of my people who hear the president talk about what he wants, the more likely we are to deliver it. There is no substitute for getting direction directly from the principal. It is not only the substance that we hear in these meetings—it is the president's emphasis, the way he approaches something, even offhand comments that reveal where he is going. It is invaluable—and it helps us work as a team.

McGurn's advice to the president of 2009: "If you don't invest the time and resources in explaining your policies, they will be explained by others—and probably not to your advantage."

Special Counselors to the President

21

First Special Counselor:
The Vice President

The chief embarrassment in discussing his office is, that in explaining how little there is to be said about it, one has evidently said all there is to say.
—Woodrow Wilson

Whenever possible, the vice president should serve as general adviser to the president on the full range of presidential issues and concerns. . . . The president [should] assign the vice president other responsibilities that do not conflict with the role of general adviser.
—Twentieth Century Fund Task Force on the Vice Presidency

Presidents William Clinton and George W. Bush have given their respective vice presidents, Albert Gore and Richard Cheney, a stronger and more active role than any of their antecedents and have made the vice presidential office the second most influential post in the executive branch. The vice president, once a laughingstock nobody, can now be at the right hand of the president in every area of public policy—developing national security policy, forming proposals to settle domestic issues, lobbying Congress, recruiting top-level personnel—while vigorously carrying the president's political message to the public. This is a striking transformation in American public administration.

Whatever may be readers' personal views about the Clinton-Gore or the Bush-Cheney policies abroad or at home, they should applaud this transformation of the vice presidential role. Why do we have a vice president in the first place? It is because that officer might suddenly have to become president—and he or she had better be prepared to move up and immediately function as an effective chief executive across the whole range of the president's responsibilities—and in the midst of turbulent, if not crisis, times.

The Constitution prescribes that if the president dies, resigns, or is incapacitated, the vice president takes over. Inherent in that mandate is the further requirement that the vice president should be able—and ready—in every way to fulfill all—repeat all—the duties of the presidency. Have Gore and Cheney met that criterion? The answer is yes, it was their obligation.

The country did not realize the importance of the vice presidency for 156 years, not until April 1945 when Americans woke up to learn of Franklin Roosevelt's

Office of the Vice President

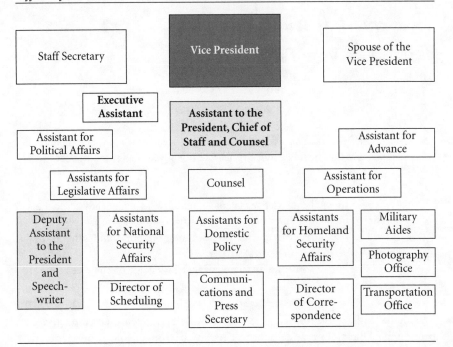

death and Harry Truman's sudden accession. Until that point, the vice presidency was often treated as almost an irrelevance. One hundred years ago, President Theodore Roosevelt, irritated at the tinkling noise a breeze was making in a White House chandelier, instructed that it be taken down and sent to the butler. "What will I do with it?" the butler asked. T. R. replied, "Give it to the vice president; he needs something to keep him awake."[1] Woodrow Wilson's demeaning view is quoted at the beginning of this chapter. Seventy-five years ago Vice President John Nance Garner declared that the job "was hardly worth a pitcher of warm spit."

From such an abysmal level of disparagement the vice presidential office has, step by escalating step, gained the recognition it must have as a preparation ground for the presidency. Not until 1918 was a vice president even invited to join cabinet meetings; Thomas Marshall was the first to do so (but after Woodrow Wilson's illness occurred, the White House staff and the first lady barred him from assuming any of the ailing president's duties). In 1937 Garner was included in legislative leadership meetings; in 1941 Henry Wallace was assigned to be head of two wartime agencies; in 1949 the vice president was made a statutory member of the new National Security Council; in 1953 Vice President Richard Nixon began a period of very extensive world travel, meeting with foreign chiefs of state (and engaging in the famous Nixon-Khrushchev "kitchen debate"); in 1961 Vice President Lyndon Johnson moved, with his staff, into the Executive Office Building (keeping his traditional Capitol Hill suite); in 1974 the vice president was provided with an official residence; only in 1978 did Congress authorize payment for an executive branch staff for the vice president in addition to his senatorial aides. Finally in 1978 Vice President Walter Mondale (while retaining his Executive Office Building space) was moved into the West Wing of the White House, a few steps from the Oval Office itself.

Aided by their new West Wing proximity, President Jimmy Carter and Vice President Mondale went on to achieve a considerably higher level of vice presidential effectiveness than had obtained during the Nixon, Johnson, Humphrey, Agnew, Ford, Rockefeller, and Quayle periods. Observed *National Journal* reporter Don Bonafede at that time: "Perhaps never before have a President and his Vice President worked on such a harmonious note. . . . Mondale is convinced that a precedent is being set that will guide succeeding administrations."[2]

Mondale was right; the model of vice presidential service that he personified has indeed become a precedent, one that was followed by George H. W. Bush (under Ronald Reagan), and, to the most striking extent ever, by Gore and now by Cheney. "It didn't just sort of happen," Vice President Cheney recalled.

> The fact was as [Governor Bush and I] . . . went through the search in the spring of 2000, when he'd asked me to head up the search for him, it was clear that he wasn't looking for sort of the traditional vice presidential pick, where you reach out and get your primary opponent or you go get the guy who's going to deliver you a big state like Florida or New York. He really had a notion, a concept in mind, of having somebody who had a lot of experience and could take on major responsibilities and be a significant part of his team. And the more he talked about it, as we went through the process of trying to find somebody to fill that job, I'd hear from him directly, as we were looking for somebody, what his concept was for the vice presidency. . . . But fact is, he had come to the conclusion of what he was looking for in a vice president long before he ever got to the convention. And that concept is, in fact, the one we've pretty much followed.[3]

The Unique Richard Cheney

Two circumstances have combined to make the Cheney vice presidency unlike any of its predecessors and to make his service especially effective for President Bush.

First, Cheney decided as long ago as 1995 that he would not try to be president. He had originally planned to run in 1996, had set up a political action committee in 1994, raised a million dollars, spent a year on the campaign trail. Then, Cheney said, after the '94 campaign, I sat down with my family over the holidays and looked at it and concluded that I did not want to run, and that I'd had a great 25 years in public service and a great career—had finished as secretary of defense and still had time to go do other things. So I went off to the private sector. And then, of course, I got pulled back into politics in 2000, but I hadn't changed my thinking about whether or not I wanted to run myself. And I also believed—and I think this may have been part of the appeal from the president's standpoint—that if I was going to play a major role for him and be an integral part of his team, it was important that I not be a candidate, that the rest of the staff, people in the building, the folks on Capitol Hill, needed to look at me as a representative of George W. Bush— and only that, as a major part of his administration, but not somebody who had his own separate agenda.

When the vice president has ambitions to be president, which is quite often the case, that mind-set inevitably colors the relationship he has with the president, and the relationship his staff has with the president's White House staff. From the beginning of his service, he is thinking, "I will be in that chair some year soon," and his advice to the president tends to be affected, perhaps slanted, by that added calculation. Members of the vice president's staff look across West Executive Avenue and salivate that they may occupy those White House offices in the near future. Such salivation can skew the candor—the thoroughness—of the information they share with their White House colleagues—or the White House staff with them. The vice president, and especially his staff, will seize every opportunity to generate favorable publicity about the vice president, potentially competing with that accruing to the president. "And when you get to the tail of an administration," Cheney added, "the vice president is thinking about his administration. People are jockeying . . . and that sets up tensions and makes it difficult for them to work together." President Bush underscored that observation in a comment to a reporter: "I'm glad my vice president is not running for president; it certainly changes the dynamics inside the White House."[4]

Such tensions were minimized during the Bush-Cheney years in office. In fact, several Cheney staffers were promoted to become members of the White House staff, for example, Candida Wolff in the legislative affairs area, and John McConnell, who is on the White House speechwriting staff and who is simultaneously the speechwriter for the vice president. Vice President Cheney commented that this unique aspect of the vice-presidential–presidential relationship "may not happen for another 200 years."

Second: the areas—and the depth—of previous governmental experience which George W. Bush and Richard Cheney brought to the presidential table were uniquely complementary. President Bush had been a governor and as such was deeply immersed in domestic matters; he had had a strong interest in educational reform in Texas, and he put the "No Child Left Behind" education initiative at the top of his to-do list when he came to Washington. Governor Bush had taken the lead in efforts to encourage religious organizations to participate more fully in providing social services to needy persons in Texas, and on his ninth day as president established the White House Office of Faith-Based and Community Initiatives, a program in which Cheney has not been involved.

Whereas many presidents had served in Congress (Nixon, Johnson, George H. W. Bush), Governor George W. Bush had not served in any position in Washington. Cheney, by contrast, was a longtime Washington hand. He had never been a governor but had uniquely strong experience at the top level of the federal executive branch, as White House chief of staff, as secretary of defense, and later, in the House of Representatives as a member of its Intelligence Committee. Thus in those areas of public life where Bush had had little experience, Cheney was a veteran, and vice versa—a "fit" almost unknown in previous American presidencies.

"There isn't any area that I've been told I can't get involved in," Cheney said. "[That is] one of the great aspects of the job. . . . If you're a junkie like I am—been involved in this business off and on for nearly 40 years—if I see an issue that's of interest, or I think I've got something to contribute, then I'm free to go stick my nose into it, obviously, ask questions, ask for studies, for briefings. I can reach down into the bureaucracy on just about any issue and find out what's going on."

At the same time, Cheney has not felt obliged to take on jobs he did not want to do. "I'm able to pass up a lot of the ceremonial stuff that I don't have to do," he said. "And I don't need any make-work projects." He has also turned down more substantive jobs. Bush and Cheney inherited Clinton Executive Order 12866 setting up a system of executive office review of departmental regulatory programs—an executive order that put the vice president in the business of handling conflicts between the departments and the Office of Management and Budget on regulatory policy issues. Cheney did not want to spend time in that area of responsibility; the executive order was amended to substitute the White House chief of staff as the officer to take on that role.

The result of these unique circumstances has been an integration in the functioning of the presidency and of the vice presidency. By no means is it a co-presidency; no one is clearer on this point than Vice President Cheney:

> The way I have operated . . . a lot of others have described it as a more significant role than perhaps any other vice president, or certainly one of the most unique vice presidencies in our history. I think that's true. But . . . in many respects it's personal. It's based on [the president's] background and on my background, and on what he wants me to do and how he conceives of the vice presidency. And he's given me a significant role, but it's very much the role of an adviser, or a counselor.

Cheney the Tiebreaker

At the very beginning of the Bush administration, with the Senate divided 50-50, the vice president's vote was needed to break any ties; whenever the Senate was in session, he had to be nearby and on call. In the first term there were six tie-breaking votes when his vote was necessary, the most important of which was in the spring of 2003 when the budget resolution on President Bush's tax package was on the floor. It was, Cheney remembered, "the key to our economic program." But more than just his vote was needed; a deadlock on substance had come up between Democrat Bill Thomas, chair of House Ways and Means, and Republican Charles Grassley, chair of Senate Finance. "I was summoned," Cheney recalled. "I got a phone call from Bill Frist, who was our leader in those days, [who] asked me to come up and try to broker the final package. . . . I ran back and forth, sort of shuttle diplomacy between the House and the Senate, and worked out the ultimate compromise. We got everybody on board for the package that finally was approved . . . with my tie-breaking vote."

It is not the intent of this chapter to catalogue the long, long list of seven years of Vice President Cheney's activities and initiatives, many of which are in the classified arena. His leadership in three important issue areas, however, does illustrate his views of the proper conduct of that office and of the powers of the presidency.

Energy Policy, and the Issue of Congressional Access to Vice Presidential Papers

Among the earliest of Vice President Cheney's specific assignments was to chair a National Energy Policy Development Group (NEPDG)—a committee of cabinet officers and agency heads that President Bush established to "develop a national energy policy designed to help the private sector, and, as necessary and appropriate, Federal, State and local governments, promote dependable, affordable, and environmentally sound protection and distribution of energy."[5] The NEPDG met during the first four months of the Bush presidency, consulted with leading private citizens who were experts in the energy business, and pulled together a package of proposals for changes in energy policy, many of which later were included in legislation.

In April 2001 John Dingell and Henry Waxman, the ranking Democrats on the House Committees on Energy and Commerce and on Government Reform, respectively, wrote the comptroller general asking the Government Accountability Office (GAO) to ascertain "the composition of the [Energy] task force; the persons with whom the vice president . . . and the task force support staff met; the notes and minutes of any such meetings and the costs incurred by the NEPDG in developing its policy recommendations." GAO (then called the General Accounting Office) said it "sought such information to determine how the NEPDG's energy policy recommendations were developed, in order to aid Congress in considering proposed legislation, assessing the need for and merits of future legislative changes, and conducting oversight of the executive branch's administration of existing laws."[6]

The vice president refused to divulge the information requested, asserting a need to "protect executive deliberations." During the spring and summer of 2001 the GAO and the vice president's office tangled with each other over this refusal. The GAO narrowed its request, eliminating its demand for "minutes and notes of meetings that NEPDG support staff and the vice president held, and for information that was presented at these meetings." Nonetheless the vice president continued to refuse to supply the information GAO was seeking, maintaining that

> If the Comptroller General's misconstruction of the statutes . . . were to prevail, his conduct would unconstitutionally interfere with the functioning of the executive branch. For example, due regard for the constitutional separation of powers requires respecting the independence of the president, the vice president and the president's other senior advisers as they execute the function of developing recommendations for policy and legislation.[7]

In February 2002, citing his statutory authority under the Budget and Accounting Act of 1921, the comptroller general filed suit in federal district court against the vice president (the first time GAO had ever filed suit against a federal official on a records-access issue). Section 716 of that 1921 statute reads that the comptroller general may "require the head of the agency to produce a record," and the statute defines "agency" as any "department, agency or instrumentality of the United States Government" (other than Congress or the Supreme Court).[8] "Indeed," wrote Comptroller General David M. Walker, "the structure and legislative history of Section 716 make unmistakably clear that the Comptroller General's authority to investigate and evaluate federal spending and activities extends to the activities of the President's closest advisers."[9]

The vice president's position, set forth in Solicitor General Theodore Olson's response brief, assailed the "virtually boundless view of the Comptroller General's own authority" and moved to dismiss the suit, giving four arguments. First, Olson said, the comptroller general lacked standing; he could not demonstrate the required "personal, particularized, concrete" injury if he failed to be given the requested information. Even if the claimed injury was "institutional" rather than "personal," that is, a diminution of legislative power, the injury was not "concrete and particularized" but "wholly abstract and widely dispersed." Second, Olson wrote, neither house of Congress and no committee of Congress made the original request; the comptroller general was "essentially acting to fulfill the curiosity of two individual members." Third, Olson argued, this was a political rather than a constitutional dispute. Olson cited an appeals court decision in an earlier case: "This dispute between the legislative and executive branches has at least some elements of the political-question doctrine. A court decision selects a victor, and tends thereafter to tilt the scales. A compromise worked out between the branches is most likely to meet their essential needs and the country's constitutional balance."[10]

Finally, the solicitor general said, Section 716 of the Budget and Accounting Act does not authorize the comptroller general to demand these records because "the vice president is not the head of [an] agency. . . . Even if the vice president or the office of the vice president might arguably fall within the nebulous phrase 'instrumentality of the United States Government,' Congress's failure to state expressly any intent to reach the vice president prevents this Court from concluding that he is an agency or head of an agency for purposes of" the Budgeting and Accounting Act.

On December 9, 2002, the court agreed with Olson and the vice president that the Comptroller General lacked standing, and dismissed the suit without reaching any of the arguments on the merits. The judge noted: "Here the record reflects that Congress as a whole has undertaken no effort to obtain the documents at issue, that no committee has requested the documents and that no congressional subpoena has been issued. Thus, an injury with respect to any congressional right to information remains wholly 'conjectural' or 'hypothetical.'"[11] The comptroller general decided not to appeal the district court's decision.[12]

Cheney's Strong Interest in Intelligence and the War on Terror

Cheney's experience as a member of the House Intelligence Committee made him as vice president immediately familiar with the legislative issues inherent in intelligence practices such as the statutory limits on surveillance, interrogation of prisoners, and presidential emergency powers. As secretary of defense, Cheney had been the supervisor of a very large portion of the U.S. intelligence community and at the same time was a consumer of the product of that community; he was especially concerned with how well intelligence operators were serving battlefield troops. Upon taking office as vice president, and with the approval of the president, Cheney explained,

> I immersed myself in what was going on in the intelligence area. . . . I'd been gone from that for eight years . . . so I took time and went out and visited the CIA and the NSA [National Security Agency] and the Defense Intelligence Agency and all the various elements of the intelligence community . . . in the spring of '01—just to get back up to speed, because I was interested in it and wanted to work it.
>
> My job is to follow intelligence carefully, everything that's in the President's Daily Brief, but then I also get a lot more than what's in the PDB, because I've a lot of other issues, and I've got the time to delve into those

issues that the president doesn't have, because he's got a lot of other things he has to worry about that I'm not involved in. And so it's an area I spend a lot of time on.

Cheney's personal visits to the nation's intelligence centers were repeated frequently, leading to newspaper stories that the vice president's "multiple trips to the CIA . . . to question analysts studying Iraq's weapons programs and alleged links to al Qaeda, [were] creating an environment in which some analysts felt they were being pressured to make their assessments fit with the Bush administration's policy objectives."[13] A presidential commission chaired by former federal appellate judge Laurence Silberman and former Democratic senator Charles Robb looked into this allegation and refuted it in 2005, saying:

> The Commission found no evidence of political pressure to influence the Intelligence Community's pre-war assessments of Iraq's weapons programs. . . . [A]nalysts universally asserted that in no instance did political pressure cause them to skew or alter any of their analytical judgments. We conclude that it was the paucity of intelligence and poor analytical tradecraft, rather than political pressure, that produced the inaccurate pre-war intelligence assessments.[14]

A difficult and controversial issue of intelligence and law took up much of the vice president's attention following the United States' first military operations in Afghanistan: limits on interrogation of captives. Should the government employ very severe methods to extract vital information? Within days after 9/11, Cheney made the following statement on *Meet the Press*:

> We've got to spend time in the shadows in the intelligence world. A lot of what needs to be done here will have to be done quietly, without any discussion, using sources and methods that are available to our intelligence agencies, if we're going to be successful. That's the world these folks operate in, and so it's going to be vital for us to use any means at our disposal, basically, to achieve our objective.[15]

The Issue of Presidential Power

Cheney also had long been on record as sympathizing with an expansive view of presidential power. He had been a member of the congressional committee that investigated the Iran-Contra affair in the Reagan presidency. That committee's minority report, which Cheney helped write and signed, affirmed that "Congress must recognize that an effective foreign policy requires and the Constitution mandates, the president to be the country's foreign policy leader." If the legislative branch places excessive constraints on the executive, the report argued, the executive had a responsibility to ignore them. "Unconstitutional statutes violate the rule of law every bit as much as do willful violations of constitutional statutes."[16]

A law on the books makes the commission of torture a federal crime.[17] To what extent would this law inhibit the president and his agents from using the interrogative methods they thought necessary? On August 2, 2002, the Office of Legal Counsel in the Department of Justice issued an opinion that it sent to the White House counsel as a guide to the conduct of the intelligence community's interrogation program. The opinion included the following language:

> As Commander in Chief, the President has the constitutional authority to order interrogations of enemy combatants to gain intelligence information concerning the military plans of the enemy.... *Any* effort by Congress to regulate the interrogation of battlefield detainees would violate the Constitution's sole vesting of the Commander-in-Chief authority in the President....[Any legal effort] that interferes with the president's direction of such core war matters as the detention and interrogation of enemy combatants would thus be unconstitutional. ... We find that in the circumstances of the current war against Al Qaeda and its allies, prosecution under Section 2340A [the torture prohibition] may be barred because enforcement of the statute would represent an unconstitutional infringement of the president's authority to conduct war.[18]

This opinion did not became public until June 2004; its revelation caused an uproar; it was "on the Internet and flying around the world," wrote Jack Goldsmith in a book published in 2007. Goldsmith was head of the Office of Legal Counsel from late 2003 until June 2004, when he persuaded Attorney General John Ashcroft to withdraw the opinion and then announced his own resignation. "This extreme conclusion has no foundation in prior OLC opinions, or in judicial decisions, or in any other source of law," Goldsmith wrote in his book. "There were no defenders of the interrogation Opinion inside the administration, either, save [the vice president's chief of staff David] Addington."[19] Elsewhere in the book, Goldsmith described Addington:

> Addington always carried a tattered copy of the Constitution in his coat pocket, and would often pull it out and quote from it with reverence. Both he and his boss Cheney seemed to care passionately about the Constitution as they understood it. That is why they fought so hard to return the presidency to what they viewed as its rightful constitutional place. It is why Cheney and the President told top aides at the outset of the first term that past presidents had "eroded" presidential power, and that they wanted "to restore" it so that they could "hand off" a much more powerful presidency.[20]

A related but separate and extremely sensitive intelligence operation is electronic surveillance, that is, eavesdropping by the National Security Agency on communications between residents of the United States and targets abroad.

Such actions are permitted by the Foreign Intelligence Surveillance Act of 1978, which mandates that warrants be obtained to keep the government in accord with the Fourth Amendment to the Constitution barring unreasonable searches and seizures. After 9/11 the president issued a directive authorizing wiretapping even without warrants; the directive was very secret, but the White House, as required, did keep the chairmen and the ranking members of the Senate and House Intelligence Committees informed. The vice president presided over these secret briefings personally, in his West Wing office. In December 2005 the *New York Times* exposed this secret presidential initiative. Again an uproar ensued, with one senator saying that the president might have committed an impeachable offense. Stephen F. Hayes, author of the book *Cheney,* wrote: "Cheney's view is simple: acts of Congress that interfere with the President's ability to carry out his functions as commander in chief violate the Constitution. Those inherent powers, Cheney believes, coupled with the authorization of force passed by Congress shortly after 9/11, place the NSA program on solid constitutional ground. He says that the NSA's lawyers and its inspector general back him up."[21]

Flying in *Air Force Two* over Oman in the Middle East later that month, Cheney called the traveling reporters into his cabin and summed up his convictions about the war on terror:

> Bottom line is, we've been very active and very aggressive defending the nation and using the tools at our disposal to do that. That ranges from everything to going into Afghanistan and closing down the terrorist camps, rounding up al Qaeda wherever we can find them in the world, to an active, robust intelligence program, putting out rewards, the capture of bad guys, and the Patriot Act. . . . Either we're serious about fighting the war on terror or we're not. Either we believe that there are individuals out there doing everything they can to try to launch more attacks, to try to get ever deadlier weapons to use against [us], or we don't. The president and I believe very deeply that there's a hell of a threat, that it's there for anybody who wants to look at it. And that our obligation and responsibility, given our job, is to do everything in our power to defeat the terrorists. And that's exactly what we're doing.[22]

In his interview with the vice president, this author showed Cheney the following quotation from former president and vice president Gerald Ford: "I personally feel that the Vice President could, very properly, be the Chief of Staff in the White House itself. . . . In that way, the Vice President is fully informed on what is . . . transpiring in the Oval Office. I feel it is better to have an elected official in that position than an appointed one."[23]

"I don't really share that view. . . . I think it's a bad idea," said Vice President Cheney.

The Vice Presidential Office

Vice President Cheney has offices in three locations: a working office a few steps away from the president on the ground floor of the West Wing, a ceremonial office in the Eisenhower Executive Office Building, and a suite in the Dirksen Senate Office Building. The vice president was authorized to have paid staff by Public Law 95-570 of November 1978, "to enable the Vice President to provide assistance to the President in connection with the performance of functions specially assigned to the Vice President by the President in the discharge of executive duties and responsibilities."

His staff is headed by a chief of staff and has eighteen units. In his national security affairs office, for instance, there are fourteen staff members—testimony to the interest the vice president has and the time he devotes to this area of public policy. The chief of staff to the vice president also carries a White House title: assistant to the president, which means that he joins in the daily senior staff meetings of the White House assistants and is fully integrated with the White House staff. The vice president's speechwriter also has White House status as a deputy assistant to the president.

The vice president's wife, Lynne Cheney, has two offices. One is in the Eisenhower Executive Office Building, where, pursuant to Section 106(c) of the above-cited statute, she has a staff of six "in connection with assistance provided . . . to the Vice President in the discharge of the Vice President's executive duties and responsibilities." Lynne Cheney is also a senior fellow of the American Enterprise Institute, where her research interests are education and the history of American culture. She is the author of nine books and of other essays, appears occasionally on the Sunday morning talk shows, and was active solo and with her husband during the 2000 and 2004 campaigns.

The total vice presidential staff group, including detailees and interns, numbers approximately ninety. Should it be bigger—or smaller? Vice President Cheney replied:

> I think it's about right. I can't recall that we ever ran into a problem where we had an issue we wanted covered or wanted to work on that we couldn't find the resources to cover. So I'd say I think it's about right. . . . I think we've been able to be involved in all those things I wanted to be involved in, and that we were not shorthanded at any time.

Those assistants who work in the vice president's Hill office are paid from a Senate appropriation; his downtown aides are paid from an Executive Office of the President appropriation which, in fiscal 2008 was $4,432,000, plus $320,000 in expenses for his residence. That sum, however, does not come anywhere near meeting the true expenses of his office, which in actuality are $16,156,800.[24] The director of the Office of Administration presents and defends the vice president's annual budget request to the appropriations subcommittees of the House and the Senate.

In his first six and one-half years as vice president, Cheney has taken perhaps 100 trips in the United States and has paid official visits to twenty-five countries.

The Residence of the Vice President

The thirty-three-room Queen Anne–style, turreted residence of the vice president on Observatory Circle was built in 1893 for the superintendent of the U.S. Naval Observatory and was later taken over by the chief of naval operations. In 1974 it was designated as the official residence for the vice president; it is still owned by the Navy, which supplies basic maintenance. In 1991 then vice president Dan Quayle and his wife established the Vice President's Residence Foundation, a nonprofit fund that could accept private donations; the fund supplements the $100,000 annually appropriated as a decoration allowance. During the Clinton administration, the Navy completed a $1.7 million rehab to upgrade the building for the Gores; for the Cheneys further basic improvements were made. After the Cheneys arrived, Lynne Cheney researched the blueprints and engaged Washington decorator Frank Rabb Randolph (who donated his professional services) to do a thorough redecoration, which was featured in the November 2001 issue of *Architectural Digest*; editor Paige Rense termed the revamped residence as "very well done; it's simple in the very best sense—as airy as a souffle."[25] The cost of nearly $400,000 was met in part by the foundation. According to a report in the *Washington Post,* Lynne Cheney herself "was deeply involved in the project, approving fabric, rugs and colors, and visiting galleries and museums before making final choices on borrowed art. 'I must have gone to the Hirshhorn three times,' she remembered. . . . Herself an author, Lynne Cheney wrote the accompanying [*Architectural Digest*] article about the project. As for their changes, she said, the design pendulum always swings. Someone else will make [the house] perfectly lovely again."[26]

Looking Ahead to 2009

After the dramatic, substantive changes that vice presidents Mondale, Gore, and Cheney have instituted in the functioning of the vice presidency, will the vice president of 2009 not bring into office the firm expectation that he or she will *not* be doing anything less? "In terms of function, it's always going to turn on the relationship between the president and the vice president," Cheney observed. He is aware that in earlier times the vice president was picked largely as part of a political calculus: would his selection help guarantee the nomination and strengthen that ticket's chances to win the general election? If that ticket won, the subsequent question of whether the new vice president should be asked to take on, and would be capable of taking on, substantive responsibilities would depend on that personal relationship between the president and the vice president—and also on the play of interests and priorities among the White House staff, the cabinet, and the Senate. "It is hard to predict that those circumstances [that pertained to Bush and Cheney] will arise again," Cheney said.

The author put the following question to the vice president: "Since the purpose of my book is to look at White House structure and process, I can't help wondering if any of our grief in Iraq is attributable to deficiencies in White House national security affairs decisionmaking processes in 2002 and 2003. What lessons have we learned which we ought to impart to the president of 2009?"

The vice president observed that it has been sixty years since America went in to Germany and Japan and put those countries back together after World War II. Because of that long lapse of time, the federal government did not, in 2003, possess a nation-building capability. The Department of Defense took it on for Iraq he said, but "probably the Department of State is more appropriate as a place for that capability to be ensconced." The president, he concluded:

> had access to everything that was available . . . [and] some of it was bad information, when you look at what the intel community produced. . . . I don't think what you would have done with the White House staff would have changed that. . . . I don't think you would have done [anything] differently in this building that would have led to a different decision. Because, as I say, I still think the decision was the right decision.

22

Second Special Counselor: The President's Spouse

I hope someday someone will take time to evaluate the true role of the wife of the President, and to assess the many burdens she has to bear and the contributions she makes.

—Harry S. Truman

I am not the one elected; I have nothing to say to the public.

—Bess Truman

America's first ladies have guided, comforted, and sustained our nation in times of trial and triumph. And since the first First Lady, each has made unique contributions to our country. Abigail Adams was a trusted adviser to President Adams in the early days of our Republic. Eleanor Roosevelt was a key author of the Universal Declaration of Human Rights. By making their bouts with breast cancer public, Betty Ford and Nancy Reagan gave women the knowledge and the courage to save their own lives. My favorite first lady— my mother-in-law, Barbara Bush—has helped children across the United States learn to read. She's brought many families together with the joy of good books—starting with our family. From Dolley Madison's heroism during the War of 1812—to Lady Bird Johnson's dedication to our natural environment—all of our first ladies have used their personal strengths and interests to improve our nation. At the same time, they have fulfilled their other very important role: the wife of the President of the United States.

—Laura Bush

Besides being a marriage partner, the president's spouse is a senior counselor to the chief executive, perhaps the president's closest and most trusted. The Constitution is silent concerning the president's spouse; the spouse is neither an elected nor an appointed officer of the federal government. She (or he) has a foot in officialdom, however, as evidenced by the following statement from a U.S. court of appeals: "We see no reason why a President could not use his or her spouse to carry out a task that the President might delegate to one of his White House aides. It is reasonable, therefore, to construe Section 105(e) [of Public Law 95-570] as treating the presidential spouse as a de facto officer or employee."[1] For years, presidents had been asking their spouses to take on certain

Office of the President's Spouse

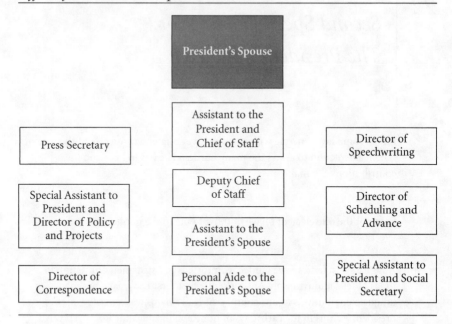

responsibilities, and by 1978 the tradition of spousal duties had become so firmly established that Congress passed a statute that finally authorized a government-paid staff for the spouse:

> Assistance and services authorized pursuant to this section to the President are authorized to be provided to the spouse of the President in connection with assistance provided by such spouse to the President in the discharge *of the President's* duties and responsibilities. If the President does not have a spouse, such assistance and services may be provided *for such purposes* to a member of the President's family whom the President designates.[2] (Italics added)

The words that the author has italicized here serve as a reminder: it is the president's duties that are being helped here, not those that may be the spouse's own.

Like other high-ranking White House assistants, the president's spouse can speak for the president with a special credibility. The past five decades have shown that the president's spouse has the broadest turf of any White House counselor. If the spouse wishes, and the president agrees, the spouse not only can be the supervisor of the residence and the manager of the events and social obligations of the first family, but she (or he) can also, in the iconoclastic tradition of Eleanor Roosevelt, crisscross the nation, journey to the most out-of-the-way places on earth, give press conferences, speak at the United Nations, deliver the president's weekly Saturday radio address to the nation, discuss matters of state with national and foreign leaders, meet and talk with ordinary folk of modest or little means, attend cabinet meetings, write books, address political rallies, write newspaper columns, have weekly business lunches with the president, convene White House assemblages, host television specials, and testify before congressional committees.

The Public Face of Laura Bush

In his two-volume work, *First Ladies: The Saga of the Presidents' Wives and Their Power: 1789–1990,* Carl Sferrazza Anthony has described comprehensively how the first ladies of those years have interpreted their roles and fulfilled those interpretations.[3] In his book *The White House Staff: Inside the West Wing and Beyond,* this author extends Anthony's description to the first ladyship of Hillary Rodham Clinton. The purpose of this chapter in a book concentrating on the George W. Bush presidency is to focus on the active role of First Lady Laura W. Bush and on the staff work that has supported her activities. The following paragraphs portray only a selective few of Mrs. Bush's activities but they illustrate the breadth and intensity of her interests and of her contributions to her husband's administration.

The Helping America's Youth Initiative

The time: February 2, 2005. The place: the U.S. House of Representatives. The occasion: The State of the Union message. President Bush announced to Congress:

> Now we need to focus on giving young people, especially young men in our cities, better options than apathy, or gangs, or jail. Tonight I propose a three-year initiative to help organizations keep young people out of gangs and show young men an ideal of manhood that respects women and rejects violence. Taking on gang life will be one part of a broader outreach to at-risk youth, which involves parents and pastors, coaches and community leaders, in programs ranging from literacy to sports. And I'm proud that the leader of this nationwide effort will be our first lady, Laura Bush.[4]

The first lady's staff took charge of this interagency effort, identifying ten federal agencies (Agriculture, Commerce, Education, Health and Human Services, Housing and Human Development, Interior, Justice, Labor, the Office of National Drug Control Policy, and the Corporation for National Community Service) plus several White House elements including the Office of Faith-Based and Community Initiatives and the USA Freedom Corps that would be involved; her project director chaired an interagency working group that met in the White House. Mrs. Bush personally attended some of the working group's sessions, then made special visits to several cities where innovative programs for urban youth were models of success: a Passport to Manhood class in the Germantown section of Philadelphia; a pilot Good Behavior Game in a hard-scrabble elementary school in Baltimore; an after-school enterprise at the Providence Family Support Center in Pittsburgh (with President Bush); "Think Detroit," a sports program for young boys; a "Cease-Fire Chicago" mentoring program for troubled youth; and a "Home Boys Industry" enterprise in a gang-infested Hispanic area of Los Angeles. Mrs. Bush explained her purpose in a television interview: "Many boys do not have many men in their lives. . . . We can change these things. We want to increase their self-esteem, their acceptance, their self-respect . . . I want to spotlight those programs around the country which are promising."[5] In addition to the visits Mrs. Bush made herself, her staff and their interagency colleagues went to some forty different cities, identifying youth programs that were solidly based on research and that exhibited real effectiveness.

Nine months after receiving her assignment, the first lady hosted a White House Conference on the Helping America's Youth Initiative. Five hundred youth program managers (and some participants) from all over the United States attended and heard presentations showing how these successful enterprises were working and how they could be replicated. President Bush introduced the first lady, saying, "She called this summit to serve as a catalyst to continue to rally decent, honorable people who are working hard to make sure young Americans have a chance to realize the promise of this country. She is a great leader of this cause."[6] After introducing her, the president described one attendee: young Michaela Huberty, whose dad had been in prison for most of Michaela's life. She was being trained to be a teacher. The conference was told about the initiative taken by a Catholic priest in Los Angeles who arranged for a group of plastic surgeons in town to remove gang tattoos from young men and women; several of these former gang members were at the conference. As Mrs. Bush's chief of staff, Anita McBride, recounted,

> There was one boy who said to Mrs. Bush, "I don't want my son to see these tattoos that I have; I want him to be proud of me." When several of those boys came here for the reception Mrs. Bush had after the conference, it was the first time they had ever worn a suit in their lives, the first time they had been at the White House. For some of them, the year before they were in jail, and now here they were, guests of the president and the first lady. It was a very dramatic moment for us.[7]

The continuing follow-up has been in the form of regional conferences on helping America's youth, in Colorado, Indiana, Minnesota, Tennessee, and Texas—each the result of detailed planning by the first lady's staff and in all of which the first lady personally has participated; still others are in the planning stage.

The National Book Festival

As first lady of Texas, beginning in 1995, Laura Bush (who has a master's degree in library science) was the honorary chairperson of the Texas Book Festival. As the first lady of the United States, and the first professional librarian to live in the White House, she and Librarian of Congress James Billington put their heads together in 2001 to create and organize a National Book Festival in Washington. Sponsored by the Library of Congress and hosted by the first lady, (fortunately just three days before September 11, 2001), some 25,000 readers and writers, old and young, crowded into tents on the East Lawn and at the Jefferson Building of the Library of Congress for what was termed a day-long "literary love-in" of readings, presentations, and book signings. Commented children's author Marc Brown, "It's the first time within memory for me that the White House has chosen to devote this kind of energy and attention to books and authors."[8] The National Book Festival has now become a major annual cultural event, having been moved to Washington's Mall to accommodate the estimated 120,000 participants who attended the festival in 2007. It begins with a gala dinner at the Library of Congress and includes a White House breakfast for distinguished authors. In 2002 fellow book-lover Lyudmila Putin, the first lady of Russia, joined the celebrations; in October 2003 the two first ladies were together again at Mrs. Putin's book festival in Moscow, inspired by Washington's National Book Festival.

A Teacher's Promotions

Mrs. Bush was an educator at the beginning of her career in Texas, a second-grade teacher for six years in public elementary schools in Austin, Dallas, and Houston. She carried her love of teaching into the White House, going with the president to visit a Washington elementary school four days after inauguration and a day later going by herself to visit a Hyattsville, Maryland, elementary school. Meanwhile she and her staff were planning a two-day White House summit conference on early education, which took place at Georgetown University in July 2002 with 450 participants attending. Mrs. Bush helped organize another education summit in Cincinnati the following October on the subject of early cognitive development. Earlier, in March 2002, the first lady met with Pakistan's education minister, Zubeda Jalal, concerning the $34 million U.S. grant that year to Pakistan for teacher training.

Throughout the Bush administration years, Mrs. Bush continued to take a lead in events and activities that highlighted needs and accomplishments in education. She was the keynote speaker at a Washington conference in May 2007 entitled "America's Silent Epidemic," which featured the release of a national online database showing parents and educators the percentage of pupils who graduate on time from high school in each of the nation's school systems.

Speechmaker

The first lady is a frequent and effective spokeswoman. Only three weeks after the tragedies of 9/11, she became the third sitting first lady to speak at the National Press Club, a talk that stressed the need for assuring the nation's children that after this experience America would be "wiser and in many ways better: more patriotic, more united, more compassionate." On November 17, 2001, she became the first White House spouse to deliver solo an entire presidential radio address as part of the weekly White House series. She spoke from the ranch at Crawford, her text reinforcing a State Department initiative to draw attention to the repression of women by the Taliban. In January 2002, Mrs. Bush joined Supreme Court Justice Anthony Kennedy and American Bar Association president Robert Hirshon in an ABA-sponsored "Dialogue on Freedom," reinforcing "principles of democracy and morality for young people . . . whether American values can be seen as offering hope, not a threat, to the rest of the world."[9]

Congressional Testimony

On the morning of September 11, 2001, Laura Bush had just taken her seat in front of Senator Edward Kennedy's Education Committee to add her support for early learning fundamentals, when the Secret Service, learning that a second plane had crashed into the World Trade Center, rushed in to whisk her out of the Russell Office Building. She and the senator promised a reappearance, which was accomplished the following January 24 (with Senator Hillary Rodham Clinton, a committee member, also present). Mrs. Bush was only the fourth first lady to appear before a congressional committee. In her testimony she combined her personal experience with her remarkable mental storehouse of scientific and statistical information to make the case "that learning must begin long before kindergarten." Asked how to end a chronic teacher shortage, Mrs. Bush said teachers should be paid more. "Certainly we can pay teachers more," she said. "That's very important."[10] According to the *Washington Post* coverage, the first lady and Senator Clinton posed for photos together, with Mrs. Clinton commenting that her successor's testimony "was terrific. . . . I'm so glad, you know, we're highlighting these programs again, because the need is so great and we've made great progress and we have a long way to go. It's good to have her voice on behalf of the needs of our most vulnerable citizens."[11]

The Arts, Design, and Preserving America

It was First Lady Laura Bush who at a special press conference in January 2004 at the National Endowment for the Arts announced a new NEA initiative: "American Masterpieces: Three Centuries of Artistic Genius." This program "will introduce Americans to the best of their cultural and artistic heritage," she said. "American arts are a reflection of our history and of the creativity of the

human spirit. An appreciation and an understanding of the arts is vitally important for every American, especially for children, who will be the painters and the
musicians of tomorrow." Simultaneously she announced that the White House
would shortly recommend that Congress appropriate an additional $18 million
to the National Endowment each year for the next three years.[12]

On July 18, 2007, Mrs. Bush presided, as she had done since her husband's
first year in office, at the White House National Design Awards assemblage,
when a series of Smithsonian-sponsored awards for architectural, product, communications, interior, and landscape design were conferred. "A day to remember
design's ability to influence the way we live," she observed.[13]

Another initiative sparked by the first lady, beginning in 2003, is the series of
Preserve America Presidential Awards, which recognize "outstanding contributions
to America's cultural and natural history."[14] The 2006 winners, for instance, were
the state of Florida, for reconstructing Mission San Luis, the former western capital of Spanish Florida, and the state of Maryland, for heightening the preservation
of Fort McHenry and Harriet Tubman's underground railroad for escaping slaves.

Aided by generous support from the White House Historical Association
(chapter 35), Mrs. Bush brought preservation close to home: redoing the Lincoln bedroom at the White House so that it now looks as it did when Lincoln
was alive; and renovating the Green Room, which had not been substantially
altered in thirty-six years. Now hanging in the Green Room is the distinctive
painting *The Builders* by a noted African American artist, the late Jacob
Lawrence.[15] She also undertook restoration in the White House Library and in
the Vermeil Room. She and the president personally paid a visit to the renovation work in progress in the Eisenhower Executive Office Building (chapter 36).

The Katrina Disaster

Laura Bush took a personal hand aiding the reconstruction of the damaged
areas of New Orleans; she made seventeen trips in the months following the hurricane, helping in opening schools, encouraging cultural preservation, even
going to a restaurant or a hotel to demonstrate the economic revitalization of the
city. She brought cabinet members such as the secretaries of labor and education
with her. As a private matter, the Laura Bush Foundation for America's Libraries
has awarded grants to 897 libraries in all fifty states, totaling $4.3 million. One of
the foundation's initiatives is the Gulf Coast School Library Recovery Initiative,
to which the foundation has made sixty-eight grants totaling $3.2 million for
Gulf Coast school libraries. Thousands of books have been made available to
students for learning, research, and enjoyment through this initiative.

The First Lady on the International Scene

Considering the position of the United States in the world, readers should not
be surprised to learn that during the first six years of the Bush administration,

the first lady visited sixty-six foreign nations, twenty-seven of them solo. (Mrs. Bush was not a beginner when it came to travel; just out of college in 1968, she "roughed it" through seventeen countries.) Some examples of the leadership she has taken in international affairs:

—In Europe in June 2001, with the president, Mrs. Bush met with disabled children in Göteborg, Sweden; lunched with NATO spouses in Brussels, toured the Prado Museum in Madrid, and encountered her first state dinner in Warsaw.

—In the Residence in November 2001, Laura met with twelve Afghan women who were forced out of law or medical school by the Taliban and who had fled the country. They had heard her recent radio address on the plight of Afghan women. "We have a future; you give us hope," said one.

—At the United Nations, on International Women's Day in March 2002, the first lady addressed the UN General Assembly, making special reference to Afghan women. "Human dignity, private property, education and health care— these rights must be guaranteed throughout the world. Together, the United States, the United Nations and our allies will prove that the forces of terror can't stop the momentum of freedom," she said.[16]

—Mrs. Bush's first solo trip was for nine days in mid-May 2002 and began with an address in Paris to the 700 delegates represented at the Organization for Economic Cooperation and Development. Dismayed by the story of children being the victims of a bombing near Chechnya, she tore up her planned speech and spoke forcefully about the responsibilities of parents, teachers, and leaders to condemn such tragedies. "Education can help children see beyond a world of hate and hopelessness," she insisted. *Washington Post* reporter Ann Gerhart commented, "Rather than being led by the West Wing, she sticks to her chief passion, education, then uses her personal empathy over public tragedies to guide her actions."[17] Next came Prague, "a city of gore and glory," wrote reporter Gerhart, and later, Budapest. The first lady's Prague visit included an official meeting with Czech President Vaclav Havel, where the two discussed issues concerning NATO, and later a half-hour session with the leader of the lower house of parliament, talking about Czech affairs. She joined representatives of twenty-five other nations in a ceremony commemorating the 1945 liberation of the Theresienstadt concentration camp, leaving a bouquet on one of the mass graves where lie 10,000 Holocaust victims—all in all, Gerhart wrote, "making a sort of field study of the age-old paradoxes that still shape the globe today."[18]

—In September 2003 Mrs. Bush undertook, solo, a third European tour that began in Paris where she presided over the raising of the American flag at the headquarters of the UN Educational, Scientific and Cultural Organization, signifying the United States' rejoining that specialized agency from which President Reagan had withdrawn the nation in 1984. In her speech at the flag raising, the first lady said that "UNESCO can now help achieve peace by spreading the values that will defeat terror and lead to a better and safer world. . . . As the civilized world stands against terror, UNESCO's work can make an enormous difference. ... We have much to offer and much to learn."[19] Her five-day trip included a visit to Moscow as the United Nations' honorary ambassador for the Decade of Literacy.

—In March 2005 the first lady, accompanied by Education Secretary Margaret Spellings, made an especially significant trip to Afghanistan. In a crowded six hours in Kabul, she met with President Hamid Karzai, then presented, at a meeting of several hundred women and girls, a $17.7 million grant to the American University of Afghanistan, remarking:

> I have watched, with great pride, as courageous women across the country have taken on leadership roles as students, teachers, judges, doctors, business and community leaders, ministers and governors. We are only a few years removed from the rule of the terrorists, when women were denied education and every basic human right. That tyranny has been replaced by a young democracy and the power of freedom is on display across Afghanistan. We must be mindful though, that democracy is more than just elections. The survival of a free society ultimately depends on the participation of all its citizens, both men and women. This is possible if institutions like this exist to give women the basic tools they need to contribute fully to society—and the most critical tool of all is an education.[20]

She went on to present a $3.5 million grant for a new English-language International School of Afghanistan, visited with grant recipients from the Artemis Program of the Afghan Women's Business Council, planted a tree at Kabul University outside a new women's dorm there, met with students and teachers, stopped by a local bakery where she talked with children, and ended her visit with a briefing by the Provisional Reconstruction Teams and a dinner with U.S. troops at Bagram Air Base. The *New York Times* reported: "Mrs. Bush was warmly received by hundreds of Afghan women gathered for the occasion, and those who met with her in small groups, from village teachers to businesswomen and ministers, said they were grateful for her support and hoped it would bring more assistance. 'It will mean a lot psychologically and mentally for us,' said Massoula Jalal, the first woman to run for president and now minister for women's affairs."[21]

—No more than two months after returning from Afghanistan, Mrs. Bush risked another sojourn into another turbulent corner of the world: Jordan, Israel, and Egypt. She addressed the World Economic Forum in a convention center in Jordan at the edge of the Dead Sea, reminding her audience that "as freedom becomes a fact of life for rising generations in the Middle East, young people need to grow up with a full understanding of freedom's rights and responsibilities: the right to discuss any issue in the public sphere, and the responsibility to respect other people and their opinions. . . . Human rights require the rights of women. And human rights are empty promises without human liberty."[22]

The audience response in the hall was polite but unenthusiastic. In Israel, when she took an outdoor walk—visiting Jerusalem's Western Wall, the Dome of the Rock, and the al-Aqsa Mosque—protesters besieged her so closely that police had to lock arms to keep them at bay, while Secret Service agents packed themselves tightly around her.

In Jericho she met with Palestinian women and in Cairo she participated in a session with some seventy Egyptian women at the U.S. ambassador's residence, speaking to them in defense of women's rights and democracy. She went out on an Egyptian political limb when she spoke approvingly of rules that Egyptian president Hosni Mubarak had proposed to govern the upcoming governmental elections; the principal opposition candidate, Ayman Nour, sarcastically called her remarks "comical." On her way home the first lady told reporters, "Other countries have totally different cultures, different traditions. They're not going to have a democracy that looks like ours."[23]

In an op-ed column a few days later, *Washington Post* columnist Eugene Robinson editorialized,

> First ladies aren't elected but can have enormous influence, both inside the White House and more broadly through use of the bully pulpit that comes with the title. Laura Bush, a former librarian, has used her visibility to push education and literacy. This remains her passion: In Egypt she appeared on the local version of "Sesame Street." That was the Laura Bush we already know. The Laura Bush we may not know so well traveled through the heart of the Arab world telling audiences and television cameras that she understands and supports women's aspirations for equality. People paid attention. In Saudi Arabia, for example, the English-language Arab News said that on her trip she "became the face of women taking on larger public roles."[24]

—In July, the Group of Eight chiefs of state, meeting in Gleneagles, Scotland, expressed their determination to upgrade the West's investment in and their assistance for Africa. Precisely as a follow-up to that determination, First Lady Laura Bush embarked for Africa (actually her second visit), stopping in Rwanda (with daughter Jenna and Cherie Blair, the wife of the British prime minister), Tanzania, South Africa, Zanzibar, and Botswana. The focus was on global health and education issues, particularly HIV/AIDS problems.

—In January 2006 Mrs. Bush visited Ghana, Liberia, and Nigeria. In February 2006 Laura Bush (and daughter Barbara) headed the U.S. government delegation at the Winter Olympic Games in Italy. In May Mrs. Bush represented the United States at the inauguration of the new president of Costa Rica, and in September she and Karen Hughes of the Department of State launched the

"Global Cultural Initiative." "One of the best ways we can deepen our friendships with the people of all countries is for us better to understand each other's culture by enjoying each other's literature, music, films and visual arts," Mrs. Bush said, describing the intent of the program. Instead of State doing its cultural exchange programs alone, the Kennedy Center, the American Film Institute, the National Endowments for the Arts and for the Humanities, the President's Committee on the Arts and Humanities, and the Institute for Museum and Library Sciences were all participating in this Global Cultural Initiative and were coordinating their offerings.[25]

—The first lady, in January 2007, addressed a day-long conference on missing and exploited children, hosted by French First Lady Bernadette Chirac and attended by First Ladies Suzanne Mubarak of Egypt and Lyudmila Putin of Russia plus Queen Silvia of Sweden and Queen Paola of Belgium.

—In June 2007 Mrs. Bush made her third visit to Africa, spending five days in Mali, Mozambique, Senegal, and Zambia. The president had just asked Congress to raise the funds supporting the President's Emergency Plan for AIDS Relief (PEPFAR) from $15 billion to $30 billion over five years, while at the same time promising $1.2 billion for a five-year initiative to halve the number of malaria deaths in Africa. Her visit, coinciding with the presidential announcement about funding increases, sent the message that the administration was putting forth serious efforts to back up its promises; malaria was a major cause of death among children in Africa.

—Mrs. Bush was one of many world leaders who were outraged at events in Burma, where a repressive military regime has imprisoned Nobel Peace Prize laureate Aung San Suu Kyi, whose party won national elections in 1990 but was shut out of power. Laura Bush met with representatives of that nation's ethnic minorities and hosted a forum about the crisis in Burma at the United Nations in September 2006. In September 2007, as new violence broke out in Burma, the exasperated first lady picked up the telephone and called UN Secretary General Ban Ki-moon, urging him to speak out against the "brutal crackdown" by the repressive leaders of that persecuted nation. Being continually briefed by the Department of State and by National Security Council staffers, Mrs. Bush kept at it. "They thumb their noses at the rest of the world," she declared in an interview with reporters. "But that doesn't mean the rest of the world shouldn't continue to speak out about these issues."

In January 2008 she followed up that remark with a formal statement on the occasion of the sixtieth anniversary of Burma's independence, saying, "Instead of celebrating their freedom, the Burmese people live in fear, poverty, and oppression under General Than Shwe and his military regime."[26] One of the reporters commented, "Mrs. Bush seems to be playing a more confident and expansive role in the past year."[27] Continuing her crescendo of criticism—and breaking tradition in doing so—Laura Bush, for the first time ever for a first lady, took the podium at the White House press briefing room and held a press conference May 5 to excoriate the Burmese leadership. "We know already that they are very inept," she declared, "that they have not been able to govern in a way that lets their . . . country, for one thing, build an economy." "An unusual foray by the president's spouse into a high-profile foreign policy crisis," commented *Washington Post* staff writer Dan Eggen.[28]

In October 2007 the first lady embarked on her fourteenth solo trip abroad, visiting Jordan, Kuwait, Saudi Arabia, and the United Arab Emirates. This trip had a very focused purpose: to raise awareness among women in the Middle East about the risks of breast cancer—a leading cause of death among women in that part of the world. She was determined, in her own way, to lessen the stigma about even discussing the subject and to stress the importance of early detection. One woman spoke up. "Thank you for caring not just about the American people, but about us as well," Umm Abdul-Rahman, forty-five, in a black cloak and a face veil revealing only her eyes, told Bush.[29]

Returning from the Middle East, Mrs. Bush was interviewed on *Fox News Sunday* on October 28; in response to a comment about the apparent increase in her policy role, she replied:

> The fact is, I've been involved for a long time in policy, and I think I just didn't get a lot of coverage on it. I mean, I really do think there's been a stereotype. And I was stereotyped as being a certain way because I was a librarian and a teacher, and you know, had the careers that traditional women have. . . . It took me a while to realize what a platform I had, and that I could be the one to go to the Middle East and talk about breast cancer and literally bring up a topic that was taboo to talk about, very much the way it was in the United States 25 or 30 years ago.[30]

"It's a noticeable difference in her role," said Michael Green, an Asia expert who provided briefing papers for Mrs. Bush when he worked at the National Security Council. "She's becoming much more public and more proscriptive. She's not following; she's leading."[31] By the first of November 2007, First Lady Laura Bush had visited seventy-two countries.

And she kept going: in early June 2008 Mrs. Bush paid another visit to Afghanistan, even though it was a war zone. She spent a day in Kabul, where she met with President Karzai, visited a police academy where female recruits were being trained, and later met with U.S. troops. She then flew by helicopter to Bamyan province where the 2,000-year-old giant statues of Buddha had been ripped from the cliffs by the Taliban. In full view of that scene of destruction, Mrs. Bush was treated to a Maori war chant by a New Zealand team that is doing reconstruction work. In Paris she was to address a conference where donor nations would be pledging as much as $15 billion for Afghan reconstruction projects through 2014.[32]

"Out of the Garden and into the Fray"

From the beginning, Laura Bush was an active player in the political arena. She addressed the Republican National Convention in the summer of 2000 and during the campaign participated in seventeen political events, including starring in seven gubernatorial or congressional fundraisers.

The 2004 presidential campaign was of course a massive undertaking. The first lady was featured on 167 political occasions. She started as early as May, with a solo appearance at a rally in Las Vegas, Nevada. A county commissioner introduced her as "a woman who has brought back dignity and grace to the White House. She has no interest in seeking her own headlines or making policy." At this assertion there were "wild cheers" from the crowd of 1,000.[33] By August her schedule was jammed; at one point, for instance, she delivered speeches in six "battleground" states in a single thirty-six-hour period. Constantly egged on to make disparaging remarks about the wife of her husband's opponent, Ms. Heinz Kerry, Laura Bush would typically comment, "She and I are actually in the same boat; I'm sure we have empathy for each other." A September 2004 report summed up the pace she was setting: "She has headlined at least 32 fundraisers, spoken at 15 rallies."

In the 2006 midterm election campaign she made sixty-seven political trips on behalf of Republican candidates. By mid-August, as one news report indicated, the first lady had "spoken at 24 political events, raising a total of $10.7 million . . . [Her] political profile has steadily grown during her tenure as first lady. . . . Said her former press secretary Susan Whitson, 'She always says, 'I am popular because I don't have to make all the hard decisions.'"[34]

"You know, this is not new for me," said the first lady, "but as I've lived here longer, I realize—I became more aware that I have more of a chance to speak out about these sorts of issues that especially concern me. And I want to take advantage of that."[35]

During the fall of 2007, when the "No Child Left Behind" reauthorization legislation was pending in Congress, Mrs. Bush added her persuasive power. She invited a series of legislators to the White House for coffee—not with the president, but with her. She later summoned the female members of the White House press corps to take a special tour, conducted by the White House curator, of the newly remodeled Lincoln Bedroom. Immediately afterward, all those on the tour were given a special briefing on the No Child Left Behind legislation by Education Secretary Spellings.

Taking a Stand on Other Public Issues

Authors and columnists typically play a dicey game with any first lady. Knowing how close she is to the center of power, they wheedle, push, egg her on to stake out positions of her own on controversial issues of the day, and then lobby the president in public. Most first ladies resist these pressures, and that is especially true of Laura Bush.

While she has made some elliptical comments such as indicating that the opposition to the Miers nomination to the Supreme Court was in part sexist, that it might not be wise to overturn *Roe* v. *Wade,* and that some stem-cell experimentation may raise false hopes, she has resolutely declined to comment on the other burning issues, such as Iraq, that have consumed the Bush White House.

In private, of course, there are few if any limits on the advice she may offer to her husband, as revealed in this exchange during an interview she had with Larry King on CNN:

> Bush: "I know that the view from outside is a lot different from the view that George and I have inside, with each other, by ourselves. And there's certainly some advice I would feel free to give him, and do. There's other advice that I really don't think I should give him."
>
> King: "Like personnel?"
>
> Bush: "Well, no, I mean, I would certainly—that's one of the things we do talk about the most, are personalities. I know everyone as well as he does, who works here. I've worked with them also. So certainly I would give him that kind of advice."[36]

When it comes to making appointments to positions in the areas of education, culture, and the arts, Mrs. Bush's views are openly sought by the presidential personnel office; they know she can help them canvass the widest possible pools of people.

In the last third of her husband's time in office, however, Mrs. Bush has become more forthright on some matters that are of high important to her, such as her above-described initiative regarding Burma. "For the first lady, Burma is providing a way to make her mark in her last 15 months in the White House," wrote *Washington Post* staff writer Peter Baker, in a story that then quoted the first lady's chief of staff, Anita McBride: "When you step into the second term, you leave campaigns behind you . . . so it does free up your time. . . . And you begin to see how fast the time moves, and you want to use it as much as possible."[37]

Another aspect of that dicey game that authors and columnists play is to compare Laura Bush with other first ladies—Nancy Reagan, Rosalyn Carter, Barbara Bush, Hillary Clinton; were they role models for what she should be? "I think," she said, "I'll just be Laura Bush."[38] Mrs. Bush does, however, keep in touch with her predecessors. She and Nancy Reagan shared a vivid interest in the Heart Truth Campaign for Women, which was started with the cooperation of the National Heart, Lung and Blood Institute of the Department of Health and Human Services—heart attacks being a leading cause of death for women. Bush and Reagan participated together in an unveiling of "red dresses" at the Kennedy Center to evoke national awareness for this campaign. Mrs. Reagan has been an overnight guest at the White House and Laura Bush has been a guest at the Reagan Library.

During the transition in 2001, Hillary Rodham Clinton expressed the hope to Mrs. Bush that she would support the "Save America's Treasures" campaign, which Mrs. Clinton had initiated; the first lady agreed and was instrumental in making sure that that enterprise did not get written out of the budget.

Laura Bush is very close to her mother-in-law, Barbara Bush. The present and former first ladies, for example, cohosted the Bush-Putin summit visit at Kennebunkport, Maine. Mrs. Carter joined Laura Bush at the funerals for former presidents Ronald Reagan and Gerald Ford.

Lynda Bird, Lady Bird Johnson's daughter, once called Mrs. Bush, inquiring whether Mrs. Johnson could drop by the White House. The thirty-minute visit turned into two-and-a-half hours; Laura escorted Lady Bird room by room through those all-too-familiar places where she and Lynda and Luci had lived, took her to view her own and LBJ's portraits, and even arranged for some of the former White House butlers to come in for a reunion. "It was really lovely to watch," exclaimed Chief of Staff McBride. On another occasion, after a signing ceremony for a Department of Education bill, the first lady invited the Johnson children and grandchildren to visit the residence, and made sure that Lynda and Luci showed their children the rooms that had been theirs.

The Social Office

For many years the social function was practically the first and only public responsibility of the first lady, and despite the new roles modern first ladies have adopted, it still ranks as one of their important duties. *Social* means much more than *entertaining*; the Social Office is responsible for all the presidential and first family events that take place in the Executive Residence or on the White House grounds—any place other than in the West Wing itself. These events range from formal state dinners and holiday receptions to awards ceremonies and informal gatherings. The social secretary forms a committee to take charge of each event, made up of representatives from the relevant White House staff offices. They meet once, or several times, depending on the size and complexity of the assemblage.

There are only a few social occasions held out of the White House for which the Social Office is responsible. One is the annual reception in New York for chiefs of state at the United Nations; another was a dinner in London hosted by President Bush for the queen; the social secretary flew over to handle it. If a VIP is being entertained at Camp David, the first lady makes suggestions for menus and flowers to the Camp David staff; for affairs at the Crawford Ranch, the social secretary makes up and sends menu cards, if appropriate. If the Bushes host a

VIP foreign visitor at the ranch, several butlers are flown down from the White House to serve the meals. Meals on *Air Force One* are cooked and served by the Air Force crew.

The Bush Social Office made several changes from the Clinton practice. The Bushes eschewed the sit-down dinners for many hundreds that required tents to be set up on the South Lawn and have instead limited dinner guests to the 134 that can be seated in the State Dining Room. The exceptions are the big parties of 750 to 800 people the Bushes threw at Christmas. They hosted fewer assemblages than the Clintons overall, but the total still added up to 350 events during 2006. In any given year during the Bush period, typically some 30,000 invitees came into the White House via invitation from the Social Office.

Draft guest lists are made up from suggestions from many sources, paying attention to requests from such VIPs as the White House chief of staff, and then presented to the president and the first lady for personal review and sign-off. But attending a White House event is a complicated process: every guest and every chauffeur must send in his or her date of birth and Social Security number, which are checked against a master security list maintained by the Secret Service. If parking is needed, very explicit instructions are issued concerning the vehicle. "So," commented former social secretary Lea Berman, "a small dinner of 134 people requires at least 75 phone calls of at least fifteen minutes in length, talking to people, explaining to them what would be the appropriate dress, answering any questions—just generally smoothing the way so the whole experience is happy and positive from the minute they get the invitation until the end of the evening; there are a lot of details to keep straight."[39] For groups that attend regularly, such as members of the press, the Social Office created a special e-mail account, permitting them to RSVP electronically.

Menus for dinners are discussed with the first lady, but Mrs. Bush and the social secretary are so much on the same wavelength here that the task of menu planning goes very smoothly. The president delegates this function (although there was one occasion when he identified a salad he didn't like—a helpful bit of intelligence for the staff to have). Flowers are suggested by the White House florist's office; for a state dinner three samples of bouquets and matching table cloths are prepared for the first lady to choose. Official gifts to foreign chiefs of state are selected by the first lady; the Department of State pays for them.

The social secretary draws up the seating plan, always with the approval of the first lady. The president and the first lady themselves choose the people they want at their own table. "I think these dinners often should be fun," commented Ms. Berman,

> including for the president and Mrs. Bush. They were always aware of that; if there was a professional sports figure or two among the guests overall, the president would enjoy it if one of those folks could sit nearby

so he could talk sports. Mrs. Bush liked to have people who were maybe from the world of culture, architects or artists—and she would engage them in their particular topic. I always had the sense that she must have prepared a little because she was so kind to people and always seemed to know their body of work and could really talk with them about it in a very specific way.

To speed up the task of arranging seating, the Bush Social Office instituted a computer software program called Seat Manager. If a dinner had ten tables, the computer drew and numbered ten tables on a big flat screen. Those invitees who accepted were numbered and the numbers entered at the appropriate table. The computer made a map of the room, ensuring that no one was left out or seated twice. As new acceptances were received, changes were instantly made on the electronic map, or if a name was entered, the computer instantly showed where the person was seated. "It was just a breeze," said Ms. Berman.

After 9/11 the tone of the first Bush term was grave; large state dinners were few. The president and first lady substituted what they called caucus dinners, which were much smaller and more intimate, and for that reason highly regarded by the foreign chiefs of state who attended. More than 100 foreign leaders were entertained in that fashion during the last two years of the first Bush term.

At every event, large or small, social aides are on duty—at least fifteen at a large function. These are single young men and women selected from the five military services who volunteer their time and pay for their own uniforms. They are expected to be knowledgeable about the history of the White House; some are fluent in a foreign language. "No 'potted plants' they," explained Ms. Berman:

> Where they were very important was at the big parties, such as at Christmas, and other events where there were receiving lines. The aides would very politely educate the people on what was expected of them in the receiving line, what to do, where to stand, where to go next. They became part of the whole push-pull of the line, and moving it. It's very important, especially at Christmastime when they're doing twenty-five events in the space of nineteen or twenty days—there's a big difference between whether or not you take three photos in a minute or two photos in a minute. It's a whole another hour at the end of the day if we can't keep it moving quickly. Those aides are very adept at moving folks through the line. It's exhausting for the first couple. On a standard day, there are two Christmas parties of at least 500 people each. That's 500 photos each session, a total of 1,000 hands to shake. I know it's like this on the campaign trail, but it's a lot to do when the aides are working all day and then coming to these parties. You want to protect them and make it as efficient as possible.

For all the pleasantness in which the Social Office is immersed, it is still a disciplined operation. In both the Clinton and the Bush years, instances arose when the leaders of an outside group that had been invited into the residence would inveigle one of the White House offices other than the Social Office to clear additional people in. At the gate, the Social Office representative would notice that these extras were not on the approved list and deny them admission. This could lead to instances of acute embarrassment.

The First Lady's Office and Staff

It is obvious that handling the range, depth, and pace of the activities described here, and handling them with no mistakes, no slip-ups, requires first-rate staff support. In her immediate office and in the first lady's correspondence office at 1800 G Street, Mrs. Bush has had a paid staff of twenty-four plus eight interns, some thirty volunteers, and perhaps four assistants detailed from other agencies. One or two White House fellows and a presidential management fellow have at times been assigned to her staff. The exact number of volunteers and these other assistants varies with the varying responsibilities that the first lady takes on in any given period.

The Social Office staff includes several calligraphers who are often helped by volunteers from the local society of professional calligraphers. "The calligraphers do a lot there," Ms. Berman explained,

> probably more than people realize. It's not just the invitations, the place cards, and menu cards, but it's all the various citations, Medal of Honor citations, Medal of Freedom, National Endowment for the Arts and National Endowment for the Humanities Awards—anything like that. They work on art for the Christmas invitations. . . . We used to spend a lot of time making sure that the menus really reflected the event. There's a place on the menu card where you have the title of the dinner and then the food list begins, and then there's a little space where you can do an interesting sketch or drawing. Often we would come up with something like that and the calligraphers would hand-paint it. In the case of the Indian official dinner, we took the wheel off the Indian flag, which is an important symbol to them. When we had the Ghanaian president for a luncheon, we found some African symbols from Ghana that said, "Good Luck, Long Life, and Good Fortune," and we hand-painted that on. What we did was to try to find things that the honoree would notice and be touched by. . . . There is a real attention to detail."

For her political appearances, care is taken not to involve detailees or volunteers who are based in the executive departments; they are governed by the Hatch Act and thus ineligible to perform partisan political functions. The Republican National Committee provides volunteers for the first lady's party-support activities.

The first lady's staff is headed by a chief of staff, who also has the title of assistant to the president. This means that she attends the morning senior staff meetings in the West Wing's Roosevelt Room presided over by the chief of staff, cabinet meetings when held, the twice-weekly National Security Council's senior staff meetings with the national security adviser, and the weekly session with the White House chief of staff on long-range scheduling. She also participates in the political strategy sessions chaired by the assistant to the president for strategic initiatives and external affairs, along with the political affairs staff. This degree of staff integration is unique to the Bush White House. As Chief of Staff Anita McBride commented,

> [National Security Adviser] Steve Hadley has senior staff meetings twice a week to which we are invited. Because the first lady does so much international travel, she is the face and voice for so many global presidential issues, that we were asked to be fully integrated. I am also invited to attend any principals meetings, meaning the "policy times" with the president, on issues in which Mrs. Bush is involved—like education or the Gulf Coast rebuilding. I would represent the interest of the first lady in those principals meetings when decisions are brought to the president. . . . This first lady's office is much more integrated into the processes of the White House than it has ever been.

Of course when solo foreign travel is being planned, the head or one of the senior directors of the NSC staff briefs the first lady and her associates; when it is a joint trip the first lady receives the same briefings as the president.

A vitally important arrangement, new with the Bush White House, is that the first lady's press secretary attends each morning's meeting of the communications specialists from every principal White House office including the vice president's. Mrs. Bush's speechwriter is physically located with the president's speechwriting team; the White House staff secretary makes sure that the first lady's office is on the checklist to review all draft presidential speeches that relate to her interests. Laura Bush's former scheduling assistant was an alumna from the presidential scheduling office and her advance officer is an alumna of the presidential advance team. The first lady's principal policy assistant has been upgraded to the level of special assistant to the president and made a member of the Domestic Policy Council staff assigned to Mrs. Bush's office. That Domestic Policy Council link is, in turn, a bridge to any of the domestic cabinet departments whose help the first lady may need. All in all, this is a remarkable meshing of skills and jurisdictions. "The first lady's participation is valued and respected," said McBride. "Coordination with our West Wing counterparts is vital; there is no longer that 'continental divide,' that sometimes existed in earlier presidencies between East and West Wings. It really doesn't exist now and I very much hope that will be true for future administrations."

23

Loyal Shadow:
The Presidential Aide

There are always two people in that Oval Office: the president and the human being who happens to be the president of the United States. I had little to do with the first, but concentrated on the second. There was such trust, that when he and I were together, the president was alone.

—Steve Bull

Immediately outside the door to the president's office sits an assistant who, because of the requirements of the job, really has to be young, energetic, unmarried, and above all possessed by what presidential adviser Louis Brownlow long ago described as a "passion for anonymity." This is the presidential aide, the loyal shadow, glued to the president's side between scheduled events. He or she in effect needs to be single because no young person holding that position has time for anything else.

The aide has custody of the daily briefing book assembled by the staff secretary (chapter 4) and is the one who sees to it that the president adheres to the schedule laid out in that compendium. Before each event begins, the aide may summon the event coordinator and do a walk-through of what is supposed to take place. Of what possible pitfalls should they be aware? What last-minute changes are being made?

If the proposed presidential remarks include mention of a VIP who is presumed to be in the audience, the aide makes sure that the dignitary is in fact present. If there is a no-show, the laudatory language is scratched, with seconds to spare. Explained former presidential aide Blake Gottesman, who held that position for four and a half years under President George W. Bush:

My view was always that my job was basically to keep all the little stuff in order, so that the president can focus on the big stuff. I can't do anything about the war or the economy, but I can do my best to make sure that that's all he has to focus on, and that he doesn't have to worry whether a speech was properly coordinated, or whether the schedule is being properly managed. To the extent that he ever has to think about such things, in my view I have not done a good job.[1]

The presidential aide reads through the entire briefing book each morning. He makes no pretense of being a policy officer but is nonetheless the last quality checkpoint for the briefing materials. "If they did not seem adequate, it was my responsibility to catch that," explained one former aide. "Based on my own knowledge of the president, he is going to ask about this, and this, so I would request the staff secretary to get supplementary information to answer those questions."[2]

The "shadow" function is indispensable. Walking to his limousine, the president might suddenly ask, "Whatever happened to such-and-such?" or "Say, remind me about so-and-so," or "Where did I put that"? or "Can you track down Mr. . . . ?" Such queries would be jotted down and taken care of.

The aide reads through speech drafts and, while not pretending to be a rewrite man, feels free to make a comment. "I probably wouldn't take it to the president, but I might say to the staff secretary or the counsel or the speechwriter: 'Hey, just a quick thought; I noticed such-and-such in the speech. Last time he was there he seemed to prefer alternative language. . . ,'" Gottesman said.

The aide does not have a role in policy sessions and does not attend the intelligence briefings or meetings where sensitive national security matters are under discussion. He does not carry the "football" (the satchel with the coded wartime commands); that is a military responsibility.

Added Gottesman, "If the aide has done a good job and if he has done it right over time, confidence will be built up enough in that way so the president feels comfortable saying anything and knowing that it would never leave the office."

One of the duties Gottesman took on was to work with the first lady to develop the ideas for and get approval of the gifts that President Bush presented to foreign leaders when they came to the United States on an official visit, when they hosted a visit by the president in their home countries, or at summit meetings. He and the president would brainstorm through a list of options, some traditional in style, others intriguingly new, like the Segway Human Transporter that President Bush presented to Japanese prime minister Koizumi. The Protocol Office in the Department of State handles (and finances) the actual procurement, but the White House end of the process is in the aide's hands.

The aide accompanies the president on every trip, domestic and international. He helps the switchboard place presidential telephone calls and keeps the minute-by-minute phone log listing the names of the people with whom the president has talked. "You kind of serve as the piece of the president's brain that he shouldn't have to use, so he can think about policy, or whatever," one aide recalled.

Before 9/11, a president arriving at an event would "go down the rope line" shaking hands with a medium-size crowd of the public before going indoors. In these encounters, folks would reach out and present the president with small gifts. The presidential aide would be right at the president's side, taking the gifts out of the president's hands, and on the spot getting the name and address of the giver so that the White House gift office could later send a note of acknowledgment. Since 9/11, there are still rope-line handshakes and the giving of gifts, but it is rarer that the general public gets close to the president. If a stranger has a question or comment for the president, the aide helps handle it.

A presidential trip has its unglamorous aspects: at a big hotel reception, the president never gets to see the front door. One aide remembered wryly:

> The president has said that he has seen more service hallways and kitchens in hotels and buildings than any other person has ever seen. The Secret Service is always bringing him in the back way—the secure way. The smell of fresh paint is overwhelming . . . because these hotels always want their service hallways to look good—and instead of coming in the grand entrances, the president of the United States is being shoved through by the garbage dumps and through the kitchens. The service elevators we take are freshly painted, and the holding rooms are usually freshly painted, and the storage rooms and the back corridors. You have to be careful where you lean up against!

"It's a fantastic experience," recalled one aide, "but your life is not your own. You have to design your daily schedule around what the president's is. You can never plan your weekends, because you don't know whether you will be there or not. . . . Things always come up—disasters, what have you—where the president has to travel at the last minute. It makes it tough to keep up with people, girlfriends. But it's been the most interesting job I will ever have."

"I'm nobody," added former aide Andrew Friendly, "and I got to follow the most powerful man on the planet around."[3] Said another aide, "You've got to be within earshot and out of camera shot."

Gottesman reflected: "You've got to be incredibly responsive, detail-oriented, unflappable—you want to look totally calm when everything else is crazy—because the principal frequently takes his or her cue from the aide and the people around him or her. If you look nervous, you make the principal think there's something to be nervous about. . . . Your role: being happy to be unrecognized."

The Operations Bloc

Operations Bloc

DAP Management and Administration	Assistant to the President and Deputy Chief of Staff for Operations	DAP Advance
AP and Staff Secretary *(reports to the Chief of Staff*	White House Military Office	DAP Apppointments and Scheduling
	United States Secret Service	The Executive Residence, Chief Usher

Offices under Deputy Assistant to the President for Management and Administration
White House Management Office
Personnel Office and Intern Coordinator
Photography Office
Visitor Office
GSA White House Center Service Delivery Team
White House Telephone Services
National Park Service White House Liaison Office
White House Visitor Center

Offices under Assistant to the President and Staff Secretary
The Executive Clerk
Director, Records Management
Presidential Correspondence Office
    Mail Analysis
    Presidential Personal Correspondence
    Proclamations
    White House Comment Line, Greetings and Volunteers
    Gift Office
    Presidential Messages
    Presidential Support
    Youth and Special Responses
    Agency Liaison
    Presidential Writers

Offices under Deputy Assistant to the President for Advance
Travel Office

Offices under Deputy Assistant to the President for Appointments and Scheduling
Presidential Diarist

Offices under the Executive Residence, Chief Usher
Curator
Calligraphy Office

White House Military Office
Director and Deputy Director
Administrative Office
Ceremonies Coordinator
Five Military Aides
Policy Plans and Requirements
Airlift Operations
General Counsel
Security Office
Information and Technology Management
Financial Management/Comptroller
Marine Helicopter Squadron One (HMX-One)
White House Communications Agency (WHCA)
Camp David
Presidential Airlift Group (*Air Force One*)
Medical Unit
White House Transportation
Presidential Food Service

United States Secret Service
Office of the Director
Office of Government and Public Affairs
Office of Legal Counsel
Office of Human Resources and Training
Office of Inspection
Office of Administration
Office of Protective Operations
Office of Protective Research
Office of Investigations

24 | *Management and Administration*

> My job. . . is like being captain of a minesweeper. As long as you're doing your job, nobody knows you're there. You make one mistake and there's a hell of an explosion.
>
> —George H. W. Bush's assistant for Management and Administration

The White House Management Office had its beginnings in 1977 in the administration of President Jimmy Carter when an officer was named special assistant to the president for administration. It continued under President Reagan; George H. W. Bush named the position assistant to the president for management and administration. In those years the White House Military Office reported to the management and administration assistant. Under George W. Bush, a new assistant to the president and deputy chief of staff for operations was created and the Military Office reported to him, as does the deputy assistant for management and administration. This deputy assistant—Linda Gambatesa in the Bush administration—heads this vital area of support services. The areas of her duties include the following.

Personnel

The personnel function within the White House Office means consulting with the heads of the several White House policy offices concerning staff levels, hiring, and salary grades within those offices. At the very beginning is the question of whom to keep from the previous administration. Reagan's management and administration assistant remembered:

> When we came in, there were some people who wanted to dismiss every single person who was on the White House payroll. Now, the President certainly has the authority to . . . do so, but there had been a time-honored group of career people within the White House who basically live from president to president, serve the presidency, were proud of that association, but kept things working. The White House telephone operators are a perfect example of that. And yet there were some in our transition who said, "Let's get rid of the White House operators." I fought those actions

and the president agreed. . . . We were successful in preventing inexperienced people from the campaign from coming over to the White House and getting jobs that might embarrass the White House or the president.[1]

The next personnel issue is detailees—how many people are to be borrowed from the departments and agencies? It is the management and administration assistant who has to sign the annual report to Congress listing the number of detailees in the various White House offices and how long they worked. Salary levels are the next area of negotiation and there is the constant pressure to push up to the top level of each category of commissioned officers: assistant, deputy assistant, and special assistant. There are some 154 commissioned officers in the George W. Bush White House.

Finally there are the perquisites: who will get what office space, mess privileges, parking spaces, television sets, BlackBerries?—who can call on White House cars for official trips in town?

The White House also makes extensive use of volunteers; a volunteer office and its volunteer coordinator operate as part of the Correspondence Office (chapter 27).

The Intern Program

One of the officers in the personnel section is the intern coordinator. Summer interns were used in the White House as early as Gerald Ford's administration. Under President Reagan, about thirty young people joined the staff each year for the summer months. There was no centrally managed procedure; each White House office did its own recruitment.

In the administration of the first President Bush, the numbers climbed, and the White House Intern Office was created to handle the recruitment and selection, do the paperwork, and manage the assignments. Opportunities were opened up for both the fall and spring semesters, in addition to the summer; between seventy and ninety interns were recruited for each of those periods. The limit for an internship was ninety days (duty in the White House beyond that requires an expensive full-field FBI investigation).

The White House offices got used to having the extra personnel—and began to depend on having them. A three-quarter-day orientation program was instituted for their first day on the job: a security lecture, a list of dos and don'ts, points about conduct and dress, and instructions on the use of White House stationery.

Under President George H. W. Bush, interns were not allowed in the East or West Wings without escort or special permission. "The minute you cross West Executive Avenue, the world changes," declared a former aide. According to one veteran of those years, most interns received college credit for their service, but they had to write a paper to do it. "There were several types of interns," recalled another. "Some were just doing it because their mothers or fathers wanted them to do it; some were serving because they truly believed in the administration, or a cause. Some were there just to get a chit on their résumé or because they wanted to get into X law school. If we got the ones who truly cared, and wanted to make a difference, we were lucky."[2]

Their reward: being invited to arrival and departure ceremonies on the South Lawn and being in a "class picture" with the president. At the end, some would apply for positions on the White House staff; the White House hired a dozen or more of them.

Much changed in the Clinton administration. The regular staff was being cut by 25 percent, and the intern program exploded—from 250 annually to 1,000 during each of the early Clinton years. Four sessions were organized: two summer sessions during which the interns worked full-time, and fall and spring sessions (to coincide with their college semesters) when the interns worked at the White House three days a week. For the first several years of the Clinton administration, 250 interns were taken in for each of the four sessions. Interns could serve in any of thirty offices in the White House or in the Office of the Vice President; applicants were invited to list their top preferences. The separate Legal Intern Program might, during each session, take in up to five full-time interns to work in the counsel's office.

In the George W. Bush administration, the intern program is smaller. One hundred interns participate in each of three sessions: fall, winter, and spring. Applicants can go to the Internet (http://whitehouse.gov/government/wh-intern.html) and find instructions for applying and also find the application forms to be filled out on line and e-mailed to the intern coordinator. Applicants must be eighteen and are limited to those who are enrolled in a graduate or undergraduate program at a college or university, or have graduated the previous semester. The questions applicants have to answer include: "Are you registered to vote?" "Did you vote in the last presidential election?" "Party affiliation?" "Why would you be a good representative of the Administration and of the White House?" "Which of the President's policies is most important to you?" "What do you consider your most significant accomplishment? Why?" A list of twenty-five White House offices is supplied, and candidates are asked to rank the four in which they would be most interested in working. (Not included as eligible assignments are the offices of advance, appointments and scheduling, press, national security and homeland security councils, and the chief of staff.) A résumé is of course required, plus three references and three letters of recommendation.

Many dozens of young men and women apply for the 100 openings. Attractive candidates are called by the White House office that takes an interest in them, and a telephone interview is conducted. If the decision is favorable, the winning interns are told to come to Washington and report for duty. Their travel and all their Washington expenses are the interns' responsibility and they receive no pay for their service. The group attends an initial half-day orientation session in the Eisenhower Executive Office Building where they are briefed on security requirements and on White House procedures and equipment. Each is subject to a random drug test.

Their duties vary but often involve doing research on upcoming projects and events. White House internship is an intensive educational program. In small groups the interns are invited to observe a daily press briefing. They meet weekly as a group to hear administration speakers on current issues and have the opportunity for Q & A exchanges with officials such as the White House chief of staff, the press secretary, other senior White House staffers, and members of the cabinet. Field trips are taken—to the Pentagon, for example, or the Holocaust Museum. The interns are also expected to participate in community service in Washington, arranged by the White House USA Freedom Corps office; perhaps twenty interns at a time will do service in a local soup kitchen. They will have Scotch during their internship—Barney and Miss Beazley, that is—and will be rewarded with a group photograph with the president. One senior White House aide remarked, "I think that to give people a glimpse of government at that level is a great experience. I have talked with parents of interns who have told me that their child spent the most wonderful three months of his or her life here."[3]

The Photography Office

Contemporary presidents have "visual diarists" as well: a staff of White House photographers who enrich the written record of each presidency by creating a photographic archive of all official presidential activities. These positions are classified as historically provided services (HPS)—these individuals perform functions that have been historically provided by their agencies to the Executive Office of the President. They have the necessary security clearances to enter any Oval Office or Cabinet Room meeting; they are treated like "just another person in the room," and their job is to record photographically almost every meeting and every event involving the chief executive. If the meetings are recurrent, one shot will do; if new faces appear, the visitors will be photographed (film is no longer used). There is close collaboration with the diarist: matching names with pictures and pictures with names.

There was a National Park Service photographer on duty in Franklin Roosevelt's time (he stayed on through the Eisenhower years), but only in the more recent presidencies have photographers taken up the role of fully documenting the president's days. "The president would walk out of his elevator in the morning and we'd be on his tail until he went back into the family quarters," explained an alumnus of the White House photo office from a previous administration. "We would review the private schedule the night before, and would assign one of our staff to cover every event of his day."

Photographers work under different schedules for each president. Daily coverage of President Bush usually begins when he arrives at the Oval Office each morning, unless he attends an event outside the White House. At major presidential events, the official photographers use a "zone" system: assistants are pre-positioned in the press stands while one photographer "comes and goes with the body." After each photography session, the discs are put into a computer in the photography office, and all photos are downloaded into a database. The images are archived by the White House photo librarian and preserved until the end of the administration. At that time, photos will be turned over to the National Archives and Records Administration for preservation. The White House photo staff selects the best shot for release to the media, use on the White House website, and so on. For most events, copies of the best photos will be printed, signed by the president, and sent to the individuals who participated in the event.

Presidential trips are prime subjects for the White House photographers; usually one (on domestic trips) or two (on foreign trips) of them will accompany the presidential party. If the president's spouse is on the trip, three photographers will be on duty. When a trip event is scheduled, the photographers make it their business to be in the most strategic spot. Usually one photographer will pre-position with the White House Press Corps, while another will stay with the president to capture backstage moments before the event actually begins. Digital photos are electronically relayed back to the White House when they are intended to be posted on the website or used for special occasions.

For international conferences of chiefs of state held overseas, the White House photo team used to set up shop and produce an exquisite photo album for presentation to each foreign head of state as the conference ended. Other governments, emulating the American preoccupation with photographic history, now bring their own photo crews with them. If the United States hosts a world leader for a state visit, the White House photo team will assemble a set of gift albums for heads of state that are then given by the President to the visiting foreign leader.

Besides its primarily archival purposes, White House photography achieves some public relations objectives as well: the foreign ambassador who presents his credentials to the president receives a letter and an accompanying photograph; every White House corridor glows with dramatic shots of recent presidential events. "Our purpose is to serve the American democracy by creating a visual record of its presidency. We are creating a legacy, not for public relations purposes, but as an archive for the future."

The GSA White House Center Service Delivery Team

The General Services Administration supports the White House in its GSA "White House Center" group, which consists of some 215 men and women who handle the tasks of maintenance and repair in the East and West Wings, the Jackson Place townhouses, and the Eisenhower and New Executive Office Buildings. (The Residence and the grounds are the responsibility of the National Park Service.) The White House pays the GSA rent for these services and the management and administration officer keeps a watchful eye on the costs and on the quality of the services performed.

One of the Jackson Place townhouses owned by GSA and rented to the White House is a minihotel for former presidents, who may arrange to stay there, without charge, when they are in the city. This modest perquisite was initiated by President Nixon. The row house at 716 Jackson Place has a bedroom, living room, dining room, and kitchen facility; the food is prepared by stewards from the White House Mess.

White House Telephone Services

In 1878 it was known as the Executive Mansion and its newly installed telephone number was 1. More than a century later, the famous number, 202-456-1414, receives many thousands of calls each day. Thanks to efficient White House telephone equipment, only a few thousand calls require personal operator assistance. Gone since 1993 is the big, old switchboard with holes and plugs: today there are only some fourteen operators on duty, in shifts, in the New Executive Office Building. Crank calls, children's calls, president's calls—all parts of the working day. One night after midnight the president's light went on; President Kennedy had one question: "Where can I find a can opener?"

The White House Staff Manual

Following a practice that has been in place since at least the Reagan administration, the Bush management and administration office has published a roughly 150-page "White House Staff Manual." Its contents includes a directory of policies, a directory of services, descriptions of the elements and offices in the White House, a summary of "legal and ethical requirements for White House employees," "administrative forms," event memoranda, policy memoranda, and emergency procedures. The manual ends with copies of the Declaration of Independence and the Constitution and attaches a map of the White House area.

The Conference Center

Experiencing the same shortage of meeting rooms in the West Wing and the Eisenhower Executive Office Building that faced their predecessors, the Bush administration has retained the Clinton initiation of a set of conference rooms at 726 Jackson Place, across the street. There are five rooms, named for Presidents Eisenhower, Jackson, Lincoln, Truman, and Wilson. The Jackson Place entrance arrangement enables officials from outside the White House to come in for meetings without having to be cleared in via the White House visitor screening system—a considerable convenience. (For a description of the responsibilities and functions of the White House Visitors Office, see page 350.)

The Executive Clerk

During his forty years in the White House, under seven Presidents, [he] has written a record of skilled and devoted service unique in the annals of the Presidency. Not only has he borne heavy responsibilities with great efficiency and uncommon good sense, but each new President in turn has learned to rely on him as a fount of wisdom, a reservoir of experience and a rock of loyalty. Guiding each new administration through its initial steps, standing as a staunch friend to all, he has been, in the best sense, a selfless partisan of the Presidency, and of the Nation that these seven Presidents have been able to serve better because of the help that he gave.

—Medal of Freedom Citation presented by President Nixon
to Executive Clerk William J. Hopkins

Every office in the White House handles presidential papers, but one category of papers is so special that it is under the exclusive care of a staff that handles nothing else: these are the original copies of the documents that, signed by the president, represent his official, public actions. Included among these documents are public laws, vetoes, instruments of ratification of treaties, executive orders, signing statements, nominations, proclamations, commissions, pardons, certificates of awards and medals, reports and messages to Congress, and public directives to executive branch departments and agencies. For all such presidential papers, the executive clerk is the next-to-last stop before the staff secretary presents them to the president for signature, and the first stop afterward, when the date is affixed and the document is transmitted.

The office has been in operation since 1865; the executive clerk and his staff of nine work in a room that is packed with history. On the walls hang pictures of Executive Clerks Rudolph Forster, who served there for forty-six years from 1897 to 1943; Maurice C. Latta, who joined the White House staff when McKinley was president and served in or at the head of the clerk's office for fifty years; and William J. Hopkins, who served there for forty years. The incumbent, G. Timothy Saunders, is already a thirty-four-year veteran. In the clerk's card file of all presidential appointees (still extant but now computerized), the opening entry is dated 1913—the appointment of William Jennings Bryan as Woodrow Wilson's secretary of state.

Nominations

The executive clerk's office does not just "handle" the cascade of presidential documents; it researches them. In the clerk's office, for example, are twenty-two loose-leaf binders of "authority sheets" (now also computerized)—one for each of the nearly 4,000 appointments the president can make. Each sheet states the title of the appointive position, the legal authority for it, its term if there is one, its purpose, method of appointment, salary, and any other key facts about the job. The executive clerk scrutinizes any new statute to ascertain if it creates a new presidentially appointed position or changes an existing one. When any proposed nomination arrives, it is checked against the corresponding authority sheet to make sure that the wording of the appointment is precisely consistent with the requirements of the statute. The presidential personnel office receives a duplicate of all the authority sheets and of all additions or changes; this collection forms the basis of its own recruitment and clearance functions. When the president has given a nomination final approval, the executive clerk collaborates with the White House press office to put together the needed press release. As of the end of 2007, President Bush had sent 3,837 civilian nominations to Congress.

Anticipating the beginning of a new administration, an adept executive clerk will have identified some of the president-elect's intended cabinet choices. In January 2001 Timothy Saunders arranged for the thirteen cabinet departments to prepare nomination forms ahead of time. No sooner was the inaugural ceremony complete than new chief executive George W. Bush was escorted into the President's Room, near the Senate chamber, and given thirteen cabinet nominations to sign. Six of them were confirmed even as the inaugural parade was in progress; the appointees took office only hours later. Saunders had made similar arrangements for Presidents George H. W. Bush and Bill Clinton.

Messages to Congress

Every draft message to Congress is compared with precedent, edited for clarity, and scrutinized for form and legality, the clerk regularly calling on the advice of the White House counsel and of experts in the Office of Management and Budget. When all the checks are completed, it is the staff of the executive clerk that prepares the document in final form to be presented, usually by the White House staff secretary, for presidential signature. Even then the very last steps, affixing the date and transmitting the paper, are the function of the executive clerk. Drawing on a tradition of considerable antiquity, the executive clerk puts the message into a special envelope, pastes it shut with a melted glob of special red wax, and—with a brass die—impresses the presidential seal: the unique imprimatur of the envelope's origin. Messages are hand-delivered to the Senate and the House by an assistant in the clerk's office. (Historical vignette: when delivering sealed messages to Congress, Forster and Latta wore formal attire—coat and tails—and rode to Capitol Hill on bicycles.)

A veto message is similarly delivered, to the chamber in which the bill originated. The aides who undertake such deliveries are the only White House staff officers permitted on the floor of either body. The aide must stand in the back of the chamber until recognized by the presiding officer. The aide is then escorted down the center aisle by the manager of the Majority Cloakroom, is introduced as "the Secretary to the President," formally bows, and announces to the presiding officer: "Mr. President, I am directed by the President of the United States to deliver a message to the Senate in writing." "The aides," Saunders recalled, "have on occasion been literally hissed and booed, usually good-naturedly, off the floor when delivering an unpopular veto."[1] In May 1986, Saunders, bearing a Reagan veto message, and arriving at the Senate in mid-afternoon, was instructed to stand "against the back wall of the chamber," according to a press account,

> clutching the president's message, while the few senators and staff aides on the floor studiously ignored him. Once Saunders was recognized, the veto would have been the Senate's pending business, and Senate GOP leaders were no longer certain that that was what they wanted. Outside the chamber, while Saunders waited, [Senator Robert] Dole fell back on his sense of humor to make the best of what was clearly an uncomfortable situation. He said the Senate would act on the veto "as soon as we find the messenger." "He's out walking around the Capitol," Dole said. "He's watering his horse." Saunders, and the veto message, were not recognized until 6:45 p.m., by which time the Senate leaders had agreed to postpone the issue.[2]

By the end of 2007, President Bush had sent 738 messages to Congress.

Executive Orders

Executive orders are a venerable category of presidential directives; George Washington issued the first one. They usually deal with actions to be taken by federal government officials and most frequently cite a specific statute as the authority for the president to promulgate them. But not always; occasionally the president uses his broad constitutional powers as chief executive as the basis for issuing an order. (This was President Roosevelt's claim when he signed Executive Order 9066 in February 1942 requiring the internment of Americans of Japanese ancestry on the West Coast.)

Drafts of executive orders typically originate in one of the cabinet departments; they are first subjected to interagency clearance under the supervision of the general counsel of the Office of Management and Budget, who also invites comments from the executive clerk and the White House staff, especially the counsel to the president and later from the Office of Legal Counsel of the Department of Justice. When signed by the president, executive orders are required by the Federal Register Act of 1935 to be delivered to the Office of the Federal Register (with less formality—the red-wax treatment is reserved for messages to Congress). That office prints each executive order in its *Weekly Compilation of Presidential Documents* and places the original in the National Archives collection. At the White House the executive clerk keeps a computerized record of all presidential executive orders as far back as 1981. The clerk can obtain orders of older vintage from the Office of the Federal Register. The total number of executive orders, since presidents began serially numbering them in Lincoln's time (October 20, 1862), had reached 13,453 by the end of 2007; President Bush had issued 257 executive orders.

Enrolled Bills

Enrolled bills and joint resolutions passed by Congress are no longer inscribed on parchment but on paper specially designed for durability. They may languish, after passage, for days or weeks or longer, before being formally sent to the president. The executive clerk's computer regularly prints out a list of all the bills and resolutions in that pending status; the clerk and the White House staff thus keep forewarned. Bills and joint resolutions are deemed to have been "presented to the president" (the Constitution's language, Article 1, Section 7) when they reach the executive clerk's doorway. A ten-day clock then begins to run. Within these unforgiving limits, the affected departments, the Office of Management and Budget, and the White House staff must complete their analyses and the president must decide whether to sign or veto the legislation. (To provide the maximum amount of time for this decisionmaking, the executive clerk and the affected officers in the administration go on line and follow the texts of the bills as they go through the legislative process.) The executive clerk tracks and polices this status-watch with minute care—a task made all the more overwhelming near the end of a congressional session, when there may be more than 200 bills at the White House being worked on simultaneously. (Once one arrived without any room at the bottom for the president's signature; it was sent back for reinscribing.)

When an enrolled bill has gone through the review process and the decision has been made that the president will sign it, the staff secretary takes it into the Oval Office. The executive clerk than transmits the signed bill to the Office of the Federal Register, which arranges for its placement in the National Archives. If the bill is of high public interest, the president may decide to have a signing ceremony. The presidents before George W. Bush used several pens to sign the bill's final page, using a different pen for each letter in the president's name, and then gave the pens as commemorative souvenirs to members of Congress or other dignitaries who had been active in getting the legislation passed. Each pen was presented in a special box bearing the presidential seal and the name of the president who did the signing. President Bush, however, decided to discontinue this practice; he uses only one pen. After signature, that pen enters a "chain of custody": the president gives it to the staff secretary, who sends it to the executive clerk, who presents it to the Office of Records Management, which holds it as part of the presidential library material.

The clerk's office is the "pocket" for pocket vetoes (bills left unsigned and thereby disapproved by the president after Congress has adjourned). The executive clerk's computer follows the progress of every enrolled bill and resolution, allowing the clerk to prepare and continuously update a tape recording announcing the presidential action on each of them. Only in this way is it possible for the executive clerk's office to answer the literally thousands of telephoned inquiries from executive and legislative staffs and from the press and public. The one-day record is 2,400 calls.

If, while Congress is in session, a veto is not received by midnight of the tenth day, the enrolled bill becomes law. On one occasion, President Lyndon Johnson, staying late at a party for his daughter, Lynda Bird, kept the executive clerk Ronald Geisler waiting—and Johnson had left a veto message, unsigned, behind at the White House. According to a press account of the incident,

> An assistant clerk was dispatched to the scene and got the President's signature at 11:30 p.m. Minutes later, en route to the Capitol, Geisler sealed the papers in an envelope with hot wax while his driver, "our best one ever," negotiated Washington traffic. Geisler delivered the veto to Congress at 11:58 p.m., two minutes before the bill would have become law. Geisler smiles as he recalls, "I've had many a hair-raising ride up Pennsylvania Avenue, trying to get presidential papers to Congress."[3]

As of the end of 2007, President George W. Bush had signed more than 1,500 bills into law and had vetoed nine.

Pardons

The Constitution gives the pardon authority to the president unqualifiedly, that is, without any requirement for congressional or judicial concurrence. Requests for pardons are all referred to the pardon attorney in the Department of Justice. This officer reviews more than 1,000 applications every year; his backlog has gone up from 2,255 in 2006 to 3,055 on October 1, 2007. He forwards those applications deemed appropriate for presidential consideration to the White House Counsel's office, where one of the assistant counsels specializes in this area of decisionmaking. If a pardon or clemency action is to be conferred on a person who is for some reason notable, the presidential action may take the form of a proclamation that, like other proclamations, is signed by the president and then transmitted by the executive clerk to the Office of the Federal Register, with a copy sent to the pardon attorney. If it is a group of individuals who are the recipients, the president can sign a "master warrant," which is dispatched to the pardon attorney. A copy of either is placed among the presidential records.

At the end of his first seven years in office, President Bush had granted 142 pardons and commuted five sentences, a rather low total when compared to most of the modern presidents (except his father, whose total was lower). The record holder is Harry S. Truman, who granted 1,913 pardons during his seven and a half years in office.[4]

Flag Lowerings

The White House executive clerk is the president's agent for changing the status of the American flag. If a person of national or worldwide repute dies, the president is likely to order that governmental buildings lower the flag to half-staff.[5] The presidential action comes in the form of a proclamation that is duly transmitted to the Office of the Federal Register. Immediately, though, the executive clerk initiates a series of a dozen or so telephone calls, the first of which is always to the White House chief usher, who accordingly lowers the flag over the Executive Residence. The next is to the Federal Protective Service in the Department of Homeland Security, which passes the word to the other federal buildings in the nation.

Instruments of Ratification of Treaties

Upon the vote of the Senate giving its consent for the president to "make" a treaty, a resolution of consent is transmitted to the White House and referred to the secretary of state.[6] The State Department's Office of Treaty Affairs drafts an Instrument of Ratification, which the executive clerk puts in the hands of the staff secretary for the president's signature. The executive clerk makes a copy of the signed instrument for the president's records and returns the original, signed document to the secretary of state, who impresses it with the Great Seal of the United States (which has its home in the State Department). State then makes the proper copies and notifications for the other party or parties to the treaty.

Reports to Congress

The president is directed by dozens of separate statutes to send reports to Congress, some of them annually. Over the years the cumulative total has come to be in the hundreds. As the staff members in the executive clerk's office research the newly enacted statutes, they identify any new requirements for reports and determine which executive agencies are responsible for their preparation. The executive clerk relies on the departments and agencies themselves to have these reports in at the White House on time; it does not play mother hen to track them all, unless the statute involved specifies an expiration of presidential authority, such as the termination date of a presidentially declared national emergency. "We absolutely ride herd on these," explained Saunders, "because the president has to file a new notice in the *Federal Register* if he wants the emergency extended."[7] After their arrival at the White House, departmental reports are circulated by the executive clerk to the policy officers on the staff; following clearance at that level, the clerk's office prepares the presidential transmittal message to Congress.

Other Functions

The executive clerk on rare occasion carries out the task of delivering a presidential notice of termination to an appointee. "One high-level government official gave me and the president holy hell for firing him," a former executive clerk recalls. "But after a while, he realized I was just delivering the message, and he invited me in for a drink."[8]

Executive clerks have long administered the oath of office to incoming cabinet members. On January 20, 2001, for example, Saunders administered the oath of office to five newly appointed cabinet officers including Secretary of State Colin Powell.

Finally, there are some twenty-five awards and medals, plus numerous certificates, citations, and commendations, that the president can issue. The processing of these is overseen by the executive clerk, who researches the legal requirements, the historical background of each, and the roster of past winners.

All in All

The executive clerk and his office are the continuing seat of White House memory about the treatment of presidential documents and are the center of expertise about the necessarily exacting processes of handling them. With typically impressive years of experience at the White House, executive clerks are expected to stay on the job to assist the newly elected chief executive and his incoming entourage. In the 143-year history of this office, there have been only ten executive clerks. All the files, papers, notebooks, and computer data in that office are retained from administration to administration; new White House staff officers go first to that office to learn some of the most essential ropes of the presidency.

26 Records Management

It is understandable that every president and his heirs wants to put the best possible face on his administration, but an uncritical or limited reconstruction of its history does nothing to serve the long-term national interest. . . . Consider what difference the release of the Kennedy, Johnson, and Nixon tapes has made in our understanding of the decision-making on Vietnam in these administrations. Consider how much we will lose if the representatives of the Reagan, Clinton, and current Bush administrations were to . . . hold back documents on the Reagan administration's decision-making relating to Iran-contra, or the Clinton administration's response to intelligence about a potential Al Qaeda attack, or the current administration's decision to fight in Iraq. . . . Current policies carry the potential for incomplete and distorted understanding of past presidential decisions, especially about controversial actions with significant consequences.

—Historian Robert Dallek

Every White House creates records—important in the present, to be sure, but even more important for the future as the building blocks for presidential history. Even amid the first day's celebrations, a wise president will think of the last day's legacy; the empty file cabinets of the inaugural afternoon will, in four or eight years, become the treasure vaults that contain the history of his presidency. In fact, the law requires preservation of the president's records.

The Legal Mandates

In brief, the Presidential Records Act of 1978[1]

—Requires the president to ensure that his "activities, deliberations, decisions and policies . . . are adequately documented and that such records are maintained."

—Insists that presidential and personal records be categorized and filed separately. *Presidential* is defined as those records, including those relating to his or his staff's activities, that "relate to or have a direct effect upon the carrying out of constitutional, statutory, or other official or ceremonial duties of the president." *Personal* is defined as "diaries, journals, or other personal notes . . . not prepared . . . in the course of transacting government business" or records that relate to "private political organizations . . . and [have] no relation" to the president's constitutional or statutory duties; also considered personal are diaries, journals, or other notes "relating exclusively to the President's own election to the . . . Presidency."

—Permits the president "to dispose of those of his Presidential records that no longer have administrative, historical, informational or evidentiary value" if he first consults the archivist and the archivist tells the president that he is not interested in them.

—Requires the president, if the archivist notifies Congress that he disagrees with the president and believes that the records "may be of special interest to the Congress," to give the appropriate congressional committees sixty days' advance notice of the disposal schedule.

—Permits the president while in office to deny public access to certain of his presidential records for up to twelve years after he leaves office, and permits the archivist to restrict public access to all the rest of the presidential records for five years (giving the archivist time to review and sort them). As soon as the five, or the twelve, years expire, requests for access, pursuant to the Freedom of Information Act, can be acted on, but eight of the nine exemptions in that Act still apply to presidential records. (The National Archives now has FOIA backlogs up to five years in length, because of the limited numbers of staff and the increased volume of requests.)

—Gives the archivist "an affirmative duty" to make the unrestricted records "available to the public as rapidly and completely as possible."

—Gives to a former president the right to instruct the archivist to deny public access to certain of *his* records for not more than twelve years.

—Specifies that both incumbent and former presidents may have constitutionally based privileges going beyond the statutory provisions, which may affect public access to their records. (The statutory twelve-year limit for the restrictions on some of the Reagan papers expired in 2000; in 2004 a request was made for some of them, but, asserting the constitutional ground of executive privilege, the Reagan representative kept sixty-four pages closed.)

The Presidential Records Act applies to the entire White House Office including the office of the vice president; later court decisions have also determined that the records of the Council of Economic Advisers, the Office of Administration, and the National Security Council are also presidential records.[2]

The Presidential Records Act was enacted in November 1978, so it applies only to the papers of President Reagan and those succeeding him. The Nixon papers are governed by special provisions; Presidents Roosevelt, Truman, Eisenhower, Kennedy, Johnson, Ford, and Carter drew up separate, unique deeds of gift to their respective presidential libraries, where they are managed under the oversight of the National Archives and Records Administration. If there are restrictions to access, they are specified in those individual deeds. Being the property of the United States, none of those collections are at present subject to Freedom of Information Act requests.

Executive Order 13233

In November 2001 President Bush issued Executive Order 13233, which spelled out his views on the constitutional privileges for restricting access that go beyond statutory provisions.[3] The order also specified the procedure that the archivist is to follow if he receives a request for access to a former president's restricted records; namely, he is to notify both the former and the incumbent president of the request. They both have to agree either to provide or to deny the requested access. The former president could take 90 days, and then more if needed, to make up his mind, and in the meantime the archivist would have no discretion to do anything but continue to block the access. In March 2007 Archivist Allen Weinstein testified to a House committee that it was currently taking 210 days to complete the typical two-president review. The American Historical Association and others, who are seeking access to Reagan administration records, brought suit challenging the executive order. The District Court for the District of Columbia dismissed part of the suit but decided that if the archivist relied on the order's requirement to continue blocking access pending the former president's decision, that delaying action of his would be "arbitrary, capricious and an abuse of discretion."[4]

A bill (HR 1255) that would negate the Bush executive order was introduced in the House of Representatives in 2007 and on March 14 was passed by a veto-proof vote of 333-93. The new bill provides that if, after a review period of not to exceed forty days, a former president, while he is still living (descendants, relatives, or assistants are not eligible) objects to the release of a presidential record, the former president must file a lawsuit claiming executive privilege, putting the decision in the hands of the courts. The same burden is put upon the incumbent president, and the bill denies this right to vice presidents. A companion bill (S 886) is, as of this writing, pending in the Senate but has been delayed by Republican objections.

The White House Office of Records Management

The White House Records Management Office reports to the staff secretary; its staff numbers twenty-three plus one intern and four volunteers. Its director, Phillip Droege, is a former officer with the presidential materials branch of the National Archives and Records Administration. Like the staff of the Executive Clerk, the records group is composed of professionals and is expected to stay from one presidency to the next. The ranks will be expanded as the transition of

2009 grows nearer; by tradition the National Archives will detail three or four trained archivists to the White House (one to the National Security Council) a year or so in advance of January 20, 2009; after a period in the White House, a few will be reassigned to the new George W. Bush presidential library in Texas to prepare the place for the some 30,000 boxes of White House papers (including 5,000 from the National Security Council) that will be trucked in after the next president is inaugurated. (The Clinton collection is reported to consist of 36,000 boxes holding 138,000,000 pages.)[5]

During a president's term in office, White House (and vice presidential) staff members are expected to preserve White House papers, including drafts, carefully; send papers not needed for current work to the records management office; and file personal (as above described) papers separately from official ones. Staffers are encouraged to seek the White House counsel's advice if they are in doubt about which is which; the counsel's staff includes lawyers who are experts in this area. Unintentional admixtures will undoubtedly occur and will be sorted out during the archivists' review months later at the presidential library. In the summer of 2008, however, director Droege or one of his staff will be paying a personal visit to each office in the White House to consult with its staff about putting their files in shape for the transfer in January and getting an idea of the quantity that will be coming from each office.

If the records management office kept every piece of paper sent to it for filing, they would need massive amounts of space; the staff constantly performs the required statutory reviews and notifies the archivist of intent to get rid of the papers that meet the test. In recent years the archivist has not entered any objections to disposals. Even with the system of constantly disposing of unwanted papers, there is not enough room in the building that the records management office occupies to contain all the boxes of records from the Bush administration's two terms in office. The National Archives and Records Administration helps out; by the end of the Bush administration's seventh year, NARA had made 22,000 cubic feet of courtesy storage available to the White House and 1,200 cubic feet available to the vice president's office. This extra space is used for storing gifts as well as papers. Six NARA employees are in effect being contributed to the White House by being engaged in managing the courtesy space.

A Bush administration improvement is technology in the White House records office that not only searches, displays, and prints copies of any document requested but also can search by keyword so that a requester need only specify a word or two or a name to permit the document to be found. The new equipment can electronically highlight the sections of interest in the document and then send the highlighted material in e-mail form to the inquirer. "Researchers are going to be extremely happy with what they get in this Bush presidential library," said Droege.[6]

A special correspondence review unit is part of the records management office; this staff inspects almost all correspondence that the president signs, after he signs it but before it is dispatched.

Presidential Libraries

Twelve presidential libraries are now in place, and the thirteenth, for George W. Bush, is coming into existence. A presidential library, sometimes with an accompanying museum, consists of land, a building, and equipment acquired and built entirely by private funds. The Presidential Libraries Act (enacted in 1955 and amended in 1987) authorizes the archivist to accept gifts of the land, the building, and the equipment necessary to create the presidential library.[7] Under the statute the library may include space the former president can use as an office. Presidential museums have been quite creative in their displays; for example, one might ask what became of the old Situation Room after the new one was installed in 2006. "We took it down; wall-to-wall paneling, the furniture, the windows—everything—is being stored so it can be reconstructed in the Bush Presidential Library," said Sharon Fawcett, the Assistant Archivist for Presidential Libraries.[8]

The act, however, requires the archivist to "promulgate architectural and design standards . . . to ensure that such depositaries preserve Presidential records . . . and contain adequate research facilities." A new edition of these standards, totaling 100 pages, was published in January 2007. The standards are quite detailed; they require, for example, that storage space not be located near loading docks, so that truck exhaust will never reach the atmosphere surrounding the stored items. As the library is being built, the construction architects and engineers are required to meet with representatives of the National Archives at the 5, 25, 50, 75, 90, and 100 percent completion points to ensure that all the standards are being followed.

The act also requires that donors who build and equip a presidential library must pay the National Archives 20 percent of the total cost as an endowment for maintaining the land, building, and equipment (more if the "usable storage space" exceeds 70,000 square feet). The library will then be staffed and managed by the Presidential Materials Branch of the National Archives and Records Administration.

Alleged Violations of the Presidential Records Act

From time to time the party out of power, the news media, or the public has questioned whether a White House was in fact retaining all official records. In the Bush administration, some eighty-eight members of the White House staff were authorized to send and receive e-mails using an account supplied by the Republican National Committee (RNC). That account being nongovernmental, messages sent through that channel would not come under the definition of "presidential records"; they were therefore not required to be preserved and were not preserved. In June 2007 the Democratic staff of the House Committee on Oversight and Government Reform issued an interim report alleging that many of the e-mails sent or received by those staff members on the RNC account in fact concerned government business and further alleging that such nonpreservation would constitute a violation of the Presidential Records Act.[9] The majority staff noted that the full committee might have to take further discovery actions to confirm the validity of the accusations.

Separately, two private advocacy organizations filed a lawsuit alleging that additional White House e-mails also had not been preserved, and a federal judge has ordered that pending the outcome of this litigation, all computer backup tapes of White House e-mail are to be kept, which the White House has promised to do.[10]

27 | *The Correspondence Office*

Write the president!

And people do. In the first six and a half years of the George W. Bush administration, the White House received over 11 million letters (a yearly average of 1,692,308). Even more people are sending e-mails, which may arrive at a rate of 850,000 *a month.* The ratio of e-mails to letters is changing dramatically. In the same period of time—six and a half years—the Clinton White House received 20,521,715 pieces of mail (yearly average 3,157,187), but only 3,876,105 e-mails. (For comparison, using yearly averages: the Eisenhower White House annually received 700,000 pieces of mail; Kennedy 1,815,000; Johnson 1,647,000; Nixon 2,687,000; Ford 2,381,000; Carter 3,532,000; Reagan 5,802,000; and George H. W. Bush 6,100,000.) Some letters come in braille and are answered in braille; many arrive in foreign languages, which are translated by helpers in the Department of State.

The inflow would be far more massive if it were not for the existence of the White House website (Whitehouse.gov), which permits online users to access, automatically, electronically, a literal encyclopedia of information about the White House (chapter 18). In fact, on the White House website a set of instructions guides would-be correspondents, including the following warnings: "Due to the large volume of e-mail received, the White House cannot respond to every message. For further up-to-date information on Presidential initiatives, current events, and topics of interest to you, please continue to use the White House website."

And further: those wanting to make an e-mail inquiry about a government program or service other than that of the White House are asked to contact "USA.gov—the official gateway to all government information. . . ." For those intending to use the old-fashioned U.S. mail the warning notice has a special reminder: "Items sent to the White House often experience a significant delivery delay, and can be irreparably harmed due to the security screening process.

Therefore, please do not send items of personal importance, such as family photographs, because items may be unable to be returned." Left unsaid is the fact that the security screening is performed in a place remote from downtown Washington.

To handle the massive flow of snail and electronic mail the White House has a full-time correspondence staff of sixty-five men and women, aided by a dozen interns and a rotating pool of fifty volunteers. While everyone at the White House serves there at the president's pleasure, some correspondence staffers, like some in the chief usher's office, are invited to stay from one administration to the next. Under its director and deputy director, the Bush Correspondence Office has several specialized subunits.

Sorting the Mail

The White House tries to respond to all the communications it receives. To do that efficiently, all incoming written or electronic mail addressed to the president goes to mail analysis—"the front line of our operation," explained Director Darren Hipp. "Everything that comes in goes there for an initial sort, based on what type of correspondence it is."[1] Much of the mail falls into a few major categories. The vice president and the first lady have their own correspondence offices.

Presidential Greetings

From sea to shining sea, Americans celebrate important passages in their lives: graduations, weddings, anniversaries, honors, special birthdays. They invite the president, as a kind of national pastor-in-chief, to be part of those celebrations. It has long been a tradition for the president and the first lady to respond, but that tradition has grown into a significant task for the correspondence office and its corps of public-spirited volunteers. A special room in the Eisenhower Executive Office Building, equipped with minidesks and walls of cubbyholes, is "greetings central" for the "pastor's" nationwide "congregation."

Incoming requests are arranged (by computer or by hand) according to the date of the upcoming celebration and then sorted, by type of event, into dozens of labeled boxes: "Eagle Scout awards," "101-and-up birthdays," and so forth. Handsome printed cards from the president and the first lady are in orderly stacks; the envelopes are addressed by the volunteers and are then stashed in precisely the order in which they will be mailed, to ensure timely arrival. (Those who are celebrating birthdays of 101 and up receive letters.)

Presidential Messages

If events, groups, or personages deserve greater recognition than a printed card bearing presidential greetings, letters or specially drafted messages are furnished; these too, are part of what can be called the pastoral role of the American presidency. Many of the thousands of nonprofit organizations in the nation send in requests (for presidential greetings that can be read aloud at their conventions, for example); the applications come in to the White House at the rate of 750 a month. The more attention a presidential letter or message is likely to attract, however, the greater is the need for careful staff checking before the presidential signature is added.

There are rules and limits: none of these presidential messages is sent to judges, for example, or to fundraisers; commercial events are taboo. The White House counsel or one of the policy assistants must often review both the request and the message itself; unfortunately some individuals or groups try to manipulate the message tradition for selfish purposes. "All our shops here in correspondence really work in concert with a lot of other offices within the White House—to make sure that the responses being generated are appropriate," explained Hipp.

The rules, of course, can be bent. A document that described the proprieties for messages under the Eisenhower administration had this paragraph at the end: "Because the White House is located on the growing fringe of precedent, and because the President is a human being—with a heart much bigger than protocol or policy, he can make exceptions to all the above rules and regulations. He can write a little girl who has lost her cat. He can write a golfer who can't control his slice. He can write anyone, anywhere, for any purpose—and the addressee is always delighted."[2]

Proclamations

Thanksgiving Day, Veterans Day, Women's Equality Day, National Farm-City Week—each year's calendar brims with occasions worthy of special national attention, and the president is the one who calls upon the populace to pay heed. He issues a proclamation for each such notification. The celebratory ones are drafted in the proclamations unit of the Correspondence Office. Another variety of proclamation is the lengthy, detailed, and highly technical instrument a president issues to implement the terms of an international trade agreement or treaty, for example. A document of this complexity would be drafted by the lawyers in the Commerce or State Department. Presidents issue about 100 proclamations a year; President Bush issued 636 of them in his first six and a half years in office.

Other Types of Correspondence

The president corresponds on personal matters, for instance to other members of his family. A special correspondence unit handles this category of mail. Another category is mail from schoolchildren. Not only do individual students write in, but whole classes will come in with a collective request.

The Volunteer Office

Approximately 525 men and women, many of them senior citizens, come into the White House on a part-time basis to help out as volunteers. They work from one to three days a week; the minimum commitment is sixteen hours a month. Other than a compulsory briefing on ethics (behavior in the White House, the use of White House stationery, and so on), volunteers receive very little orientation. They work in several different offices; some fifty of them are in the Correspondence Office, helping to sort and handle the thousands of letters and e-mails to the president that arrive daily.

A few volunteers rotate in and out of the first lady's office; another group serves in the social secretary's domain. They answer telephone calls on the Comment Line; they address the thousands of cards that the president and the first lady send out as greetings to folks who are celebrating golden wedding anniversaries and other similar special events in their lives. Volunteers hand out programs at South Lawn receptions and help (some in costumes) at the Easter Egg Roll. At Christmastime, extra volunteers—some coming (at their own expense) from distant parts of the country—help "deck the halls" of the White House during a three-day, dawn-to-midnight decorating marathon. One couple, while trimming the White House Christmas tree in the mid-1980s, fell in love, courted, and later married; she continued to work at the White House; he continued to be a volunteer.

The volunteers are given a "national agency" check by the Secret Service, then put on the access list with a daily "V" pass for entry. The selection (from a long waiting list) of volunteers, their assignments, and the backup paperwork are handled by the White House Volunteer Office, a part of the Correspondence Office. Besides the pride they have in serving such a revered institution, the volunteers receive modest rewards: the Volunteer Office sponsors special local trips (for example, a behind-the-scenes tour of the National Archives, or a lecture on the history and preservation of the Eisenhower Executive Office Building), and there are special thank-you appearances (for instance by the president and the chief of staff). The president and the first lady sponsor an annual Volunteer Appreciation Day in the Rose Garden.

The nation, as well as the first family, can be grateful for these thousands of hours of public-spirited dedication. Said a senior White House aide: "We could not operate without the volunteers; there is no way around it."

The Comment Line

As chief of state, the president is "president of all the people," say the textbooks, and it appears that more and more of the people themselves are discovering this axiom. By the 1970s the White House switchboard operators were being swamped with calls from the general public. A supplementary answering system was designed, and volunteers were invited to come into the White House to help answer the thousands of public queries. The idea worked; like other White House innovations, the Comment Line has been continued from presidency to presidency.

A separate telephone number, 202-456-1111, leads directly to the Comment Line responders. Some interest groups and radio stations broadcast the Comment Line number and urge their members or listeners to call the White House. Special cubicles have been built into a room in the Eisenhower Executive Office Building and are staffed daily by volunteers, who donate one or two days a week of their time. On nights of presidential speeches or press conferences, extra phones are set up and Greetings Office volunteers are recruited to handle the avalanche of comments. The calls average a thousand a day, with as few as five hundred or as many as several thousand.

Most of the callers comment on current issues, supporting or disagreeing with the president. "We are delighted to have your opinion," they are told, and the calls are carefully noted: from what state, on what issue, and whether pro or con. Calls come in from Americans living abroad; foreigners phone in as well. Both a daily and a weekly report are forwarded to the president with copies to other senior staff members, and it is this kind of assurance that most of the callers want. If the comment is particularly illuminating, the volunteer may write out a comment message and send it to the White House policy staff officer for whom it would be most useful.

Some callers ask questions—"Why is the flag at half-staff today?" "Has the White House always been white?"—but the volunteers diplomatically explain that their responsibility is to receive and relay comments, not to answer questions. A few calls threaten the president; the Secret Service handles those.

On some issues, hundreds of calls use identical wording—evidence that a lobbying campaign is being mounted. Many of the callers ask to speak with the president; he *is* the White House; he is *their* president. "I gave my dollar to his campaign—surely he can talk with me!"

Quite a few of the calls are from people with personal problems. They may be elderly or lonely, confused by what they perceive as a complicated and impersonal society. They telephone the White House and, fortunately, find themselves talking to a friendly voice. Some of their requests are simple: who is their congressperson? What number can they call to report a lost Social Security card? The volunteers give them referral information, but the cardinal rule is: Comment Line staffers are not there to offer callers advice on how to handle their personal problems. Nevertheless, if the caller seems desperate and if the emergency can be identified as legitimate (a few are recognized as "repeaters"), the volunteers, making no promises, write up a "hardship case" note, which is passed on to the Agency Liaison staffers (described in the next section). Each day, typically, several cases are passed on.

Occasionally there are calls from people who are mentally ill; one volunteer commented that the number of such calls increases measurably when the moon is full. "I just talked with God!" one staffer reports, or "to Jesus!" Several callers are in tears, emotionally ravaged, "If you don't help me, I am going to kill myself!" Most of the callers, however, are citizens who telephone the White House in the good faith that they are letting the federal government know their opinions and that their views may have an influence on government action.

The volunteers are given careful training that stresses the rules they need to follow. Issues that are current are summarized for them so that volunteers will be alert to the likelihood of questions on those subjects. Volunteers are also taught to anticipate the stress they will be under at times—handling the tears, the emotions, the calls from those who are having personal problems or who are mentally ill. The volunteers never give out even their first names, identifying themselves only with an "operator number." This somewhat impersonal technique had to be instituted after a person from California somehow discovered a Comment Line staffer's name and came straightaway to Washington from Beverly Hills looking for her. The workers also do not say that they are volunteers, with the result that some citizens upbraid them: "Why are they paying you if you can't help me?"

Comment Line staffers are proud of the service they render. "But it's not like mail!" exclaimed former Comment Line supervisor Judithanne Scourfield. "A caller is very much there—a real person with a real problem!"

The Comment Line is a unique part of the pastoral role of the modern presidency.

Agency Liaison

Masked under the prosaic label of Agency Liaison, four staff members in a room in the Eisenhower Executive Office Building personify a particularly empathetic extension of the pastoral presidency. To them are given the hardship cases: those scrawled in letters, those referred from the Comment Line office. A veteran from the war in Iraq asks about how she can get all of her service-connected benefits; a school inquires about obtaining computers for classrooms; an individual needing a living transplant wonders about medical insurance; someone who wants to start up a small business needs to know where a loan can be obtained. Where there is federal jurisdiction, Agency Liaison staff refer cases to the appropriate federal agency, which can investigate and possibly assist.

Some writers or callers have legal problems; if a person fits within the low-income guidelines, a referral may be made to the local Legal Services Corporation (which is federally funded). Others are elderly people, and the local agency on aging (also federally funded in part) can be contacted by the Agency Liaison staff to see about assistance. Hundreds of desperate people write or call the president; for them he is the ultimate ombudsman. These are the toughest of all to handle: people in urgent need, men and women who are sick, jobless, homeless; who have no food for hungry children. They call the White House, the nation's parsonage of last resort. In these situations the Agency Liaison staffers refer the case to the local Salvation Army or try to identify other possible sources of emergency assistance, such as churches, charities, or the local government.

Each case is registered into a computer, as is every departmental or White House action taken. White House aides may often locate and telephone the individual citizens to get more of their stories firsthand and to find out what efforts they have already made to help themselves. Those who write or call repeatedly and who are attempting to milk the system are easily identified, but the cases of real need are kept current until some answer is provided. Agency Liaison staffers have handled thousands of cases since the Bush administration took office.

The Gift Office

Article I, Section 9 of the Constitution stipulates that "No Person holding any Office or Profit or Trust . . . shall, without the consent of Congress, accept of any present, Emolument, Office, or Title, of any kind whatever, from any King, Prince or foreign state." In Public Law 90-83 of September 11, 1967, Congress did allow a federal official, while prohibited from ever requesting or otherwise encouraging the tender of a gift, to accept and retain "a gift of minimal value tendered or received as a souvenir or mark of courtesy." Federal officials, including the first family, could also accept "a gift of more than minimal value when it appears that to refuse the gift would be likely to cause offense or embarrassment or otherwise adversely affect the foreign relations of the United States." The statute stipulated, however, that "a gift of more than minimal value is deemed to have been accepted on behalf of the United States and shall be deposited by the donee for use and disposal as the property of the United States under regulations prescribed under this section." "Minimal value" is currently set at $305. This decision is made by the president; it can be and has been revised upward since 1967.

(Along with other federal employees) the first family may accept—and retain for personal use—foreign gifts valued under $305. If the foreign gift is valued over $305, and the federal donee, including the first family, wishes to retain it for personal use, the gift, which has become the property of the federal government, must, by law, be commercially appraised and the donee must purchase it from the government.

All gifts, both foreign and domestic, to the first family must be registered with the White House Gift Office (a section of the Correspondence Office) along with its value and disposition. At the White House, the counsel to the president may rule that certain gifts, such as those tendered for commercial purposes, are inappropriate for acceptance by the first family. Such gifts are returned; others not desired by the first family may be sent to the General Services Administration, which can offer them to other federal agencies or to charities or can auction them off. A separate statute requires the Department of State's Office of Protocol annually to publish a list of all gifts from all foreign governments to all federal employees, including those given to the first family.

Under current law the first family has four choices for disposal of gifts that are accepted by the White House. The gift may be deposited in a presidential library or given to the Smithsonian Institution or to one of the cabinet departments, for example, the Department of State, or if it is an animal, to the National Zoo, for display. The gift may be placed in the custody of the National Archives and Records Administration to be held for possible future personal retention by the first family. It may be added to the permanent collection of the Executive Residence, which is in the custody of the National Park Service, or it may be retained immediately for personal use. Gifts so retained that are valued in excess of $305 must be reported to the Office of Government Ethics (if it is a foreign gift, it must be commercially appraised).[3] The Office of Government Ethics then annually includes notice of the gift, and the donor, in its *Public Financial Disclosure Report.*

In addition to the legal hurdles, the sending of gifts to the White House runs a practical gauntlet: the post-9/11 security screening process. This takes place far from Washington and uses equipment that can rough up packages of any size. The e-mail warning on the White House website ends with this instruction: "We also request that gifts of a consumable nature, such as food, flowers and other perishable items, not be sent to the White House due to the security screening process. While the President and Mrs. Bush and Vice President and Mrs. Cheney appreciate your thoughtfulness, they request that you look to your local community for opportunities to assist your neighbors in need."

Nonetheless, President and Mrs. Bush have received over 50,000 gifts since his inauguration in 2001. On May 13, 2008, as required by law, President Bush sent the Office of Government Ethics a report (which was made public) that during 2007 he had received, and was retaining, ten domestic gifts each valued in excess of $305. They included a self-propelled trimmer-mower and accessories (from the White House staff, valued at $1,185), a custom Hawaiian shirt (from the White House Staff, $400), and from a bicycle store in Wisconsin, a trek bike (valued at $6,160).

The Calligrapher

Here is a Bush administration innovation: a calligrapher in the Correspondence Office. There are two calligraphy offices: one in the chief usher's domain who prepares invitations and menus for events like state dinners; and, beginning in 2007, one in the Correspondence Office. If the president makes a trip abroad and the White House photographer takes a camera shot of the president with the foreign chief of state he is visiting, the president will send his host a thank-you note with an autographed picture. The letter will be prepared, the calligrapher will inscribe (but not sign) the photograph, and the two pieces of paper will be handled together in the review and dispatch process.

The Correspondence Support Office

The support unit is the final gateway for outgoing presidential correspondence. At the last step before signature, the piece of paper is scrutinized with exacting care—checked for spelling, citations if they are given, the White House photographer's photos to be autographed. Every detail has to be right.

It is never discussed publicly, but every White House has and uses an autopen. The extremely strict rules about its use are set and enforced by the staff secretary.

The president is kept informed about incoming mail. As his predecessor in the Clinton White House did, Director Hipp sends the president not only statistics about e-mails and letters pro and con but also passes on a few samples and occasionally a piece of incoming mail of unusual human interest. The president on occasion handwrites his own responses directly.

Looking into 2009, Hipp emphasized accountability as the principal virtue to be pursued. In his words: "making sure that things are done efficiently, of highest quality—but also that we are generating it as quickly as we can, in a time-efficient manner. One thing we do that helps us stress accountability is that we date-stamp things as they come in, so we know we're moving things along—not holding anything for a lengthy period of time."

Paving the Way:
The Advance Office

Advancing is an art! It is the exhausting, detailed planning that makes each presidential trip and event appear to be an *effortless* success. An incredible diversity of activities . . . is involved. . . . The advance person is manager, integrating and coordinating. . . . The lead advance is the head of a highly professional and dedicated team of White House experts. The advance group must accomplish these things in an anonymous fashion—giving gladly the credit for a successful visit to the local people or event sponsors.

—Clinton White House Advance Manual

. . .dropping down onto the four-and-a-half-acre deck of the mighty USS *Lincoln,* with its five thousand inhabitants cheering wildly as their commander in chief stepped out of the plane with his helmet cradled under his arm, the crinkled eyes and gray-flecked hair and form-fitting flight suit summoning up a Paul Newmanesque virility. . . .

—Robert Draper in *Dead Certain*

Presidents never stay home. From Sarasota's Emma E. Booker Elementary School to Baghdad, Iraq, from Katrina to the Kremlin, the president of the United States is visitor in chief, representing now his government, now his party, now all the people of the nation. As chief of state he greets the National Hispanic Prayer Breakfast; as chief partisan he addresses a Senate candidate's final rally; as chief executive he stands in New Orleans' Jackson Square and promises help; as chief diplomat he joins the Asia Pacific Economic Cooperation forum in Sydney, Australia; as commander-in-chief he secretly flies to Iraq to meet with the sheiks of the Anbar Salvation Council. The lines between his roles are, of course, never quite that distinct: in each place he travels the president is all these "chiefs" at once.

His national and political roles are public and he wants them to be so; cameras and the press are invited to witness every handshake, film each ceremony, record all the ringing words. A presidential trip is usually substantive, but it is also theater: each city an act, every stop a scene. As the Secret Service recognizes, however, in any balcony can lurk a John Wilkes Booth, at any window a Lee Harvey Oswald; a Sara Jane Moore or a John Hinckley may emerge from any crowd. One other presidential role is quintessential but usually more concealed: as commander-in-chief of a nation at war, the American president—no matter where he is in the world—must be able to be in instant contact with his national security command centers.

A presidential trip, therefore, is not a casual sojourn: it is a massive expedition, its every mile planned ahead, its every minute programmed. The surge of cheering thousands must stop just short of a moving cocoon of security; curtained behind each VIP receiving line is the military aide with the "doomsday" briefcase. Except for that military aide, all of the first lady's travel presents similar requirements for minute care and advance attention.

These massive expeditions are the responsibility of the White House Advance Office. How large a job is this? The table below shows some comparative numbers: [1]

President	Total trips				Total first term	Average trips per year
	Year 1	Year 2	Year 3	Year 4		
Eisenhower	19	30	21	24	94	24
Nixon	22	50	48	38	158	40
Carter	28	62	52	125	267	67
Reagan	25	58	50	111	244	61
Bush I	69	102	77	254	502	126
Clinton	93	111	98	212	514	129
Bush II	110	160	118	284	672	168

The Steps in Trip Planning

If an outside observer assumes that the decisionmaking sequence for a presidential trip begins when an invitation is received and ends with figuring out the message to be delivered, he has got it backward. It is just the opposite: first comes the judgment: what is the message? What is the policy theme that the president wants to publicize? With that in mind, then comes the question: what sort of venue is most appropriate to illuminate the theme: military, economic, academic, political? At this point, the accumulated invitations are reviewed, and if a suitable "matching" locale is not among those being offered, an acceptable invitation can easily be arranged. A trip, then, is actually an instrument of the president's communications strategy, designed to fit the president's priorities rather than merely responding to the priorities of others.

The proper venue having been agreed upon, the "host" is chosen—a company president for instance, or the commander of a military base. The White House lead advance officer is specified and he or she makes contact with the host. Within the White House, careful advance planning is undertaken. Depending on the nature of the trip—its duration, whether overnight stays are involved, whether legislative or political objectives are included—consultation takes place among representatives from the affected White House elements, typically staffers from the scheduling, communications, press, speechwriting, legislative, intergovernmental affairs, political affairs, transportation, social, medical, and public liaison offices plus experts from the White House Military Office and the Secret Service—perhaps also representatives from the vice president's staff or the first lady's office.

For a domestic trip, the advance office supplies the lead advance person, who heads a team consisting of at least three assistants for each individual stop: a press lead aide, a site advance assistant, a press site advance aide, and, if an overnight stay is involved, an RON (Remain Over Night) advance assistant. A trip coordinator stays in the White House and supports the team when it is in the field. (For the considerably more complicated planning for an international trip, see below.)

Most of the recent presidents have codified White House advance work in the form of an advance manual; the most recent editions have built on the preceding ones and on the experiences each administration, in turn, has had. The Clinton advance manual is 121 pages. The Bush administration advance manual is reserved for official use only and is marked "SENSITIVE—DO NOT COPY."

The Effect of Recent New Technology

The Bush White House, and specifically its advance office, has benefited enormously from four innovations in communications technology. "We were all surprised at how primitive we were," exclaimed Todd Beyer, the director of Bush's Advance Office, who had been in the Bush advance office from the beginning and became its director in 2005.[2] Because of technology, the advance team can inspect—without ever leaving the White House—the capacities and layout of rooms, halls, and floor plans of a hotel or a university, for instance, by tapping into the Internet, finding the website of the institution in which the team is interested, and looking at photos of the institution's physical plant. Instead of trying to use e-mails or confusingly complicated (and insecure) conference telephone calls, the team at a faraway site and its White House backup group conducts daily staff meetings via secure video teleconference. This equipment has very recently become secure, portable, battery-powered, and suitcase-sized, which enables members of the advance team surveying a severe disaster area for a possible presidential visit, for example, to check in readily with their White House colleagues sitting in the National Security Council's Situation Room or in one of the several SCIF [secure compartmentalized information facility] rooms in the Eisenhower Executive Office Building. If in Baghdad or Afghanistan the advance group can simply ask the embassy, "Would you mind if we use your SCIF?" and in minutes they will be conferring with the White House.

Every team member, furthermore, has a new, sixth-generation BlackBerry, which allows the owner to send and receive voice and text messages; to take, send, and receive digital photographs, and to use the device as a combination address book and alarm clock. The advance staffer can wake up in the morning in a part of the world that is twelve hours away from Washington and read all the text messages that have been sent to him during the night. The staffer's Black-Berry also has the capability to take digital pictures of a prospective presidential event site and send them immediately back to the White House. The BlackBerry, however, is not yet configured to handle classified information, so some uses of its capabilities are limited; there are also places in the world where signals do not reach it.

Finally, the White House secure computer system has what is called a "shared drive," an electronic library of information about event sites and trip plans including scenarios, schedules, even diagrams. If a trip to North Carolina is being planned, there is a folder in the shared drive labeled *North Carolina*; all the information in it is updated constantly, and everybody in the White House (or aboard *Air Force One*) concerned with the trip can download it to make changes or find out about changes that are being made by others. No more need for e-mails or faxes.

The President's Domestic Travel

If the trip is within the United States, the advance team will go out to the event locale six or seven days ahead of time. An unbelievable panoply of arrangements must be set up; the checklist for one recent presidential trip was twenty-six pages long and contained 485 items. Every planned action, however, is scrutinized and approved by the White House itself. The categories in this panoply include the following.[3]

Types of Presidential Events

Types of presidential events vary greatly; the purpose of the trip may be to give a speech at the United Nations, a commencement, or a dedication; it may be to inspect a disaster area such as Katrina, and to meet and console those who have suffered in it. Presidential trips are often taken for political purposes, visiting several different cities in sequence. "The last day of the 2004 campaign was tough," director Beyer recalled, "we were in nine cities in six states and did seven events. A stop like this is almost unheard of, and it went off without a hitch."

Visits to areas where there has been a natural disaster require special adjustments; the schedule and the series of stops must be exactly arranged to avoid any interference with ongoing relief efforts. Attending the funerals of distinguished notables such as the Pope or Coretta Scott King raises another special caution that Beyer explained:

> For these types of trips the most important thing is not letting the president's involvement overshadow the event itself. We work very closely with the hosts to make sure we don't overstep our bounds and make sure the other groups involved (mostly the Secret Service) don't upset our host with special needs requests. More often than not, however, the host ends up relying on our team (sometimes quite heavily) to help manage the event.

Frequently a trip combines activities where the president is acting in his official capacity with activities where he is functioning only as head of his political party. The White House counsel does the arithmetic to figure out what percentage of all the costs of the trip are official (paid for from federal monies) and what percentage is political—funded by the party or the local hosts. Nonpolitical costs are divided several ways: the White House budget bears only the expenses of the advance teams and of the presidential party; the White House Military Office (all Department of Defense money) pays for aircraft and communications; the Secret Service (Department of Homeland Security) covers its own expenses, including the presidential limousine; the press corps representatives reimburse the White House Travel Office for their travel expenses; and the local hosts meet all event costs including hall and press-riser rentals, banners, signs, tickets, advertising, and motorcade costs for nonfederal VIPs.

Then there are the surprises—sudden emergencies or tragedies when the planning time is hours instead of weeks. "That makes a short fuse even shorter," Beyer observed. Secret Service manpower may be constrained, which affects the trip schedule and changes the advance time for notification. "We don't necessarily announce where the president will be," Beyer commented. "Everyone knows that we are coming to town, but if they don't now exactly where we are going it helps the Secret Service secure the site with limited assets."

Building the Event Site

If the president is coming by plane, the airport itself is an event site. If there is a greeting line, toe-strips will be pasted on the tarmac showing where each person will stand. There may be a crowd at the airport; *Air Force One* itself is a major attraction. In the event site itself, members of the advance team act as diplomats to settle competing demands. Who will sit on the dais? How many chairs in the auditorium? Can some be removed easily if they are not filled? Empty chairs send a wrong signal. Plans can be made for balloon rises or balloon drops (3,000 is the usual number). Beyer recalled an incident in the 2000 presidential primary campaign when candidate Steve Forbes was giving a speech. Someone pulled the switch for a balloon drop, with the result that the entire speech was punctuated by hundreds of pop!-pop!-pop!s.

Technical Requirements

In addition to the hall or classroom where the president will speak, there must be a separate "holding room" to which the president can retreat if he needs to receive or make urgent calls. It is equipped and staffed by the White House Communications Agency using the latest secure communications gear. Author Robert Draper, for example, described what happened on the morning of September 11, 2001, where President Bush was speaking to students in that Sarasota elementary school: "In a holding room outside the Booker Elementary auditorium, Bush spoke by phone to Cheney and to New York Governor George Pataki. He also placed a call to FBI director Robert Mueller, who had been on the job all of a week. 'All right, Bob, this is what we paid you to do,' Bush told him. 'Let's get on it.'"[4]

Other technical requirements include preplanned entry and exit routes specified by the Secret Service.

Building the Local Organization and Working with Vendors

A successful presidential visit is impossible without local sponsors, organizers, and helpers, almost all of them volunteers (unless the site is a military base). A local civic organization may act as host, or the state or local party organization may do so. In any event, there will be hundreds of services that local volunteers can perform and perhaps thousands of dollars in expenses that the hosting group must contribute. Before a trip is approved, a financial agreement is worked out between the host and the White House and signed by the host, specifying who is to do what.

A very close relationship arises between the White House advance team and the local volunteers; the latter are prepared and coached with great care so that no embarrassing mistakes are made. The Clinton advance manual instructed the advance team:

> Game Day Minus 1: Have a volunteer meeting the day before the event. (NOTE: I have seen events with over 300 volunteers.) Assign everyone their jobs, physically walk them to the spot where they will be working and make sure they understand their responsibilities. On game day they can go directly to their assigned positions and be ready to work. Be sure to arrange a location for everyone to gather the next day outside of the mags [magnetometers]. That way you can check then in, give them their Volunteer/Staff credential, and move them through the mags after the sweep.[5]

A presidential visit ignites publicity, attention, and energy in a local community, being thus beneficial as well as financially costly to the local organization.

The advance team has to have business acumen: local hotels and businesses are used for rentals and for purchases of printing, advertising, decorations, food, balloons. The team is instructed to get advance authorization for any expenditures and to keep detailed records of all purchases.

Crowd Raising and Ticket Distribution

Every president, every advance team, wants a big, friendly turnout for speeches and events. It is the advance team's mission to make it big; it is also their objective to guarantee that it is friendly. The advance manual is full of crowd-raising suggestions. During Clinton's time it instructed the team to

Mobilize high school students to help distribute materials; Emphasize the location, day, date and time of the event; Mimeographed invitations signed by popular local figures can be effective in areas of dense population and relatively strong commitment; ... Distribute leaflets at every location where groups of people can be found who would be an appropriate audience. Don't forget movie theaters, shopping centers, shift changes at plant gates, bus stations and stops, sporting events and exhibitions. Be creative, the list is endless.

For indoor events where the president or first lady is to give an address, both the Clinton and the Bush advance manuals have the same rule: admission is only by ticket. "This is possibly the most important thing you will do to build a big and supportive crowd," the Clinton advance manual read. "Ticketing is both a crowd-building and a crowd-limiting tool. If you have a space that only holds a finite amount of people, careful ticketing can ensure a full and happy crowd. Done badly, it can ensure bad stories about little old ladies with tickets who were not able to get in."

The standards for ticket handling are strictly prescribed; both the Clinton and the Bush manuals instruct the advance teams to keep close control over the ticket distribution system. There can be categories of tickets (distinguished only by the color of the ticket), some of them leading to seats closest to the rostrum that are reserved for distribution to "100% loyal groups" (the Clinton language) or to groups "extremely supportive of the administration" (Bush wording). Every ticket has a separate number and the volunteers who distribute the tickets are to collect the names and addresses of the recipients (the Clinton manual tells the volunteers to have recipients produce IDs).

Handling Hecklers and Demonstrators

The Clinton and Bush manuals both deal with this sensitive subject. The Clinton version opens by saying that "it is important to protect the First Amendment rights of those who oppose the views of the President or First Lady." If hecklers appear, the manual continues, an advance team member or volunteer should first "politely ask them to make their statement without affecting the rights of others. If the disruption is vocal you can allow them to be heard, then ask them to be silent so the President or First Lady can respond."

Both the Clinton and Bush White House handled demonstrators similarly. The Bush manual suggests that local police be asked to "designate a protest area where demonstrators can be placed, preferably not in view of the event site or motorcade route." It then goes on to express the hope that volunteers stationed just outside the magnetometers will spot any potential demonstrators, particularly those carrying a sign, and deny them entrance.

As a counter to any demonstrators, the Clinton manual called on advance volunteers to "wave supporting placards in front of opposing ones, or to drown out opponents['] chants with supporting chants of their own." Bush advance leaders are to arrange for the formation of "rally squads" who would "use their signs and banners as shields between the demonstrators and the main press platform. If the demonstrators are yelling, rally squads can begin and lead supportive chants to drown out the protesters (USA!, USA!, USA!)."

The last step is also similar in both manuals: "Local police can be asked to assist with truly unruly persons" (Clinton wording). "Security should remove the demonstrators from the event site" (Bush language). Both manuals stress never to use physical force against the hecklers, the Bush stricture adding that physical confrontation is exactly what the demonstrators are hoping for. "Do not fall into their trap!" it warns, wisely adding: "Before taking action, the Advance person must decide if the solution would cause more negative publicity than if the demonstrators were simply left alone."[6]

Both manuals are firm in reminding their advance teams that Secret Service agents cannot be asked to help control demonstrators unless there is a real physical threat being made to the president or the first lady.

Two Court Cases

One recently resolved and one current court case illustrate the risks advance staffers take when they decide actually to eject protesters from audiences the president is addressing. On July 4, 1994, in Charleston, West Virginia, two demonstrators who were wearing protest messages on their shirts were told by the White House advance staff to cover their shirts or leave. They refused, were ejected, then handcuffed and briefly jailed. Later, local authorities dropped whatever charges they had placed and apologized to the two. The ejectees brought suit, alleging that the federal government had denied them their First Amendment rights. In August 2007 the two reached a settlement with the federal government and were paid $80,000 (but with no government admission of wrongdoing).[7]

In March 2005 President Bush was addressing a public event at the Wings over the Rockies Air and Space Museum in Denver. Two citizens, Leslie Weise and Alex Young, got tickets to the event from a Republican legislator's office. Weise's car had a bumper sticker that read "No More Blood for Oil"—and that attracted the notice of advance volunteers, who surmised that the two "had a viewpoint that was different from the President's."[8] After being briefly detained at the entrance checkpoint, the two were admitted but were warned "not to try any funny stuff." The volunteers consulted with White House Advance Director Greg Jenkins and Deputy Director Steven Atkiss, who instructed one of the volunteers to eject both Weise and Young, which he did.

Two years later, in March 2007, Weise and Young filed a suit against the White House advance officials alleging that Jenkins and Atkiss had "violated plaintiffs' First and Fourth Amendment rights by establishing and enforcing a policy to eject persons, including the plaintiffs, from this event on the basis of their viewpoint."[9] A separate, similar suit was filed against two advance volunteers, who responded by asking the federal district court to dismiss the suit. They argued that they were entitled to "qualified immunity" from suit.

The purpose of the doctrine of "qualified immunity" for federal officials is "(1) protection of the public from unwarranted timidity on the part of public officials, (b) ensuring that qualified candidates are not deterred from entering public service and (c) reducing the chance that lawsuits will distract public officials from their governmental duties."[10] This immunity can be maintained by private individuals only if they are "closely supervised by the government." District Judge Wiley Daniel ruled that the two volunteers had not yet made the case that they were "closely supervised" by the White House Advance Office, denied the volunteers' motion to dismiss, and allowed further discovery.

The volunteers appealed that denial to the Tenth Circuit Court of Appeals, arguing that volunteers in their position might "reasonably believe that the President may lawfully do exactly what he did here: eject Plaintiffs from his speech based upon their contrarian signage. There is simply no clearly established constitutional right that would indicate otherwise."[11]

As of this writing, this case is still in litigation. Whatever the final legal outcome, readers will appreciate the significance of this litigation for the limits that can be put on the actions of White House advance teams anywhere in the country in the future. In fact, the advance office may more recently have changed its policy. When the president appeared on October 3, 2007, before a Chamber of Commerce group in Pennsylvania's West Hempfield Township, a woman was spotted wearing a T-shirt reading "George Bush, your war killed my friend's son." A news account said "she was allowed to remain at the event, and the first question came from a war opponent . . . an usual departure for a White House that likes to keep its events under tight control."[12]

Advancing International Trips

The president's international travel is usually planned around one of the regular summit meetings, such as the G-8 meetings or the Asia Pacific Economic Cooperation (APEC) forum. Bilateral national sessions are scheduled on the way to, or back from, the multinational summit conclaves. For example, Mr. Bush's visit to Iraq in August 2007 was secretly injected into the en route plan on the way to the APEC conference in Sydney, Australia.

The first phase of international trip planning is the discussion, among the president and his national security advisers, of themes and venues; what is the message the president wants to convey to the assembling nations, and to the American people, from this conclave? When these objectives are agreed upon, general instructions are put together that guide the advance party as they review sites and schedules.

The Bush advance office has combined what used to be separate "site surveys" and "pre-advance" missions. One dual-purpose group goes abroad sometimes as early as three months ahead of time (depending on when the whole team can be assembled, and depending on when the host government wants them there). This will be a team of perhaps twenty-five; besides the advance office staffers, it includes representatives from the State and Defense Departments; the National Security Council; the White House scheduling, communications, press, travel, and chief of staff offices; a large contingent from the White House Military Office and from the Secret Service; and if the president plans to host a dinner in the embassy, a group from the White House Mess. In addition, members of the press—technicians and producers as well as journalists—are part of the pre-advance delegation, since for a summit meeting they must make detailed arrangements to support extensive press coverage.

Is the U.S. ambassador in the host capital ready for such an invasion? "No," observed White House advance director Todd Beyer:

> I have found that even if they are familiar with the operation, unless they have worked on an international visit before, they are generally shocked by the magnitude of it all. . . . When you start to go over the number of assets, planes, helicopters, cars, etc., and bodies required for such a visit, you can see their eyes get bigger and bigger and their mouths start to drop open. This goes for the embassy staff as well as the host government—especially those that have never hosted a U.S. president before. . . . I always say: "For those of you who have been part of a presidential visit, you know what you are in for; for those of you who haven't, you're in for quite a ride."

Recognizing that those apprehensions are typical with embassy staffs, the lead advance person schedules a private, one-on-one session with the ambassador, "away from all of his staff," Beyer emphasized. No one needs to be reminded that the ambassador is not a subordinate officer of the State Department; he or she is the personal representative of the president. From that flows an obligation to learn what the president's priorities are for the objective and the "message" of the trip, and to do his or her best to put those priorities first.

"The size for each stop varies a little," Beyer adds, "but we normally plan on about 600 for the advance, traveling staff, and traveling press." The author's estimate is that another 200 come from the Secret Service. (In 1998 President Clinton made a twelve-day trip to six countries in Africa; *fifteen hundred* officials from *fourteen* agencies were needed to accompany and support the president and the sixteen invited members of Congress on that journey.)[13]

"During our tenure," explained Beyer, "we've made great strides to keep the footprint as small as possible. From the staff side, I'm sure that has been achieved, but we don't get involved in the number of security assets [military, intelligence, Secret Service] required to support a visit." The author would add that since 9/11 the security element of a presidential visit abroad has grown to be a very hefty contingent.

The site survey/pre-advance team spends days looking at every possible venue that might be a stopping point for the presidential party. Typically, both the embassy and the host government put forward their suggestions for the ten to fourteen stops they think the president should make each day; the advance team brings them down to earth: three a day is likely the maximum. The team takes digital pictures of each potential "storyboard"—the background scene that would frame the president as he speaks or makes a presentation; they focus on what would be a "mediagenic" picture—and what will be acceptable to the security experts. The military office representatives work out arrangements for *Air Force One,* for helicopters, and for holding rooms for the necessary White House communications gear, and explain why the president will be using only his own limousine and helicopters (because of the communications equipment). The medical unit makes sure that a supply of the president's blood type is placed in each nearby hospital; the Secret Service reviews motorcade routes, vetoing those deemed too vulnerable. The press representatives identify locations for the press rooms, the editing rooms, the satellite uplinks; the hotel advance group finds the nonpublic routes the president can take within the building and begins to draw diagrams for the presidential footsteps.

At least every other day there is a secure video-teleconference staff meeting with the trip coordinator and his colleagues back at the White House. The digital pictures are reviewed, the alternative sites dissected. There will be many differences of opinion to be settled; the advance team looks to the success of this one visit; the ambassador and his staff remind the visitors that they in the embassy must preserve an amicable relationship with the host government for months and years ahead. "We never forget that the embassy staff are the experts on the ground and we rely heavily on their opinions," Beyer emphasized. He reflected on the secretive Bush visits to Iraq and Afghanistan:

> The biggest problem was conducting these major operations with no one on the ground (except for a select few local contacts and the advance team) including the host government knowing about the visit. Both Baghdad stops were especially tricky because they were independent trips. Getting the President off the ranch and Camp David without anybody seeing is complicated beyond belief.... We really leaned on the military side of how to get things done, and for all intents and purposes [these trips] became military operations, with events sprinkled in.

The Pakistan visit in October 2006 was especially challenging because everyone knew the president was coming; special precautions had to be taken to protect the advance team. In fact a bombing occurred in Karachi that killed one embassy staffer.

Once the site survey and pre-advance work has been completed, the advance team returns to Washington, holds endless staff meetings with its NSC and other White House colleagues, and finalizes the schedule for the chief of staff to review and submit to the president. The advance team itself goes out some ten to twelve days before the president departs; it stays on the site right up to the presidential arrival. This is a shorter time period than for previous administrations, an improvement occasioned by the vastly improved communications technology now available. "We are getting a lot more done in a lot less time," Beyer remarked. "Part of that is technology, but it is good stewardship of the taxpayers' money."

The president is presented with a briefing book giving him each day's schedule and background information about each stop or event; the trip director is in charge of the book and the accompanying oral briefing. Policy recommendations and talking points for international negotiations are in a separate briefing book put together principally under the supervision of the national security adviser and the NSC staff.

Stagecraft on May 1, 2003

Saddam Hussein's statue had been toppled; the president wanted to talk to the troops, tell them how proud he was of them. It was up to Deputy Chief of Staff Joseph Hagin to figure out how. Hagin discovered that the huge aircraft carrier USS *Abraham Lincoln* was on its way back from the Persian Gulf en route to home base at San Diego. What about meeting the troops on board, Hagin suggested, in the Pacific, a day away from port? Chief of Staff Andy Card and Communications Counselor Dan Bartlett were enthusiastic. Then the communications office decided to expand the "talk to the troops" into an address to the nation (a decision that would have unintended consequences). The president would have to fly as a passenger on a tactical Navy aircraft and land on the carrier. The deputy chief of staff presented the idea to the president. As Draper recounted it in his book, "Hagin saw a twinkle in Bush's eye. '*He's gonna want to fly it,*' the deputy chief of staff thought."[14]

The president and Card put on inflatable vests and went through a water-rescue rehearsal in the White House swimming pool. "The Secret Service hated the whole idea. POTUS in a dinky S-3B Viking landing on a moving vessel in the middle of the Pacific? Jeez, why didn't they just parachute him into downtown Baghdad?" Draper wrote. Five days in advance, White House aide Scott Sforza arrived on the *Abraham Lincoln,* with a podium, special lighting equipment, and an advanced type of antenna that could transmit to a satellite while being in motion. "Sforza tested the satellite at sea. He studied the variance of the sunlight, the glare off the ocean, and how these would be factored in to the choreography of the ship's inalterable schedule," Draper recounted.

The crew echoed his enthusiasm, came up with idea for sending a happy message to their families and Navy colleagues: a banner that proclaimed "MISSION ACCOMPLISHED." Bartlett and Press Secretary Ari Fleischer were consulted, considered whether the slogan might be misunderstood, finally OK'd the banner, which was produced by a private contractor and unfurled right behind where the president would stand.

The pilot, copilot, a Secret Service agent, and the president took off from the North Island Naval Air Station; not long afterward the pilot invited the president (who had flown as a National Guard officer) to take the joystick. He did and saw Andy Card in the copilot's seat in an accompanying plane—with the joystick in *his* hand. The pilots took the controls again and the two planes landed, the president stepping out and smiling broadly into the worldwide TV cameras. "Hagin and Sforza gaped at this, their best event ever," Draper wrote. "The stagecraft was excellently handled," Beyer commented.

Later the president delivered his speech to the nation from the deck of the carrier, declaring the end of combat operations and victory in the battle of Iraq. The "skittles" in their different-colored uniforms lined up smartly behind the president; the banner was especially prominent. Draper reports, however, that Defense Secretary Donald Rumsfeld "learned of the banner only after the fact, and was not pleased. The final draft of the speech, he would say, 'was properly calibrated. But the sign left the opposite impression, and that was unfortunate.'"

Handling Surprises

President Bush visited Nigeria in 2003, and Beyer described a surprise that took place when he was in the middle of the action:

[Nigerian] President Obasanjo suddenly appeared at one of our events, to great fanfare. Before we had an opportunity to announce our participants onto the stage, he started making introductions. As he mentioned each person—Chief of Staff Card, National Security Adviser [Condoleezza] Rice, Secretary [of State Colin] Powell, etc., I would open the curtain and let them go on stage. Of course the last person he mentioned was President Bush. Our plan was for him to go straight to the podium, but because President Obasanjo was still speaking, when Mr. Bush went to take a seat, all the seats were taken, and he gestured to Andy Card—who promptly stood up, went to the edge of the stage, and jumped off—about four feet. He's an athletic guy, so it wasn't a problem for him, and as always he was a good sport about it. We had a few good laughs about that during our long flight home.

A surprise of another sort came as President Bush gave an outdoor address to a large crowd in Bucharest, Romania, in 2006. "The weather wreaked havoc," remembered Beyer, "and because of the size of the crowd—the estimates were over 250,000—we didn't have an indoor option." When Bush came on stage with President Iliescu, Beyer continued, "it was still raining, but after he was introduced and began speaking, there was a break in the clouds and a rainbow appeared behind him. Needless to say it was a very powerful moment—you obviously can't put a price on a backdrop like that."

The White House Advance Office

In the Bush White House, the travel office, which makes the travel arrangements that the press requires and pays for, was formerly part of the management and administration section; it was merged with the advance office during the Bush administration because of the interrelationships between these two areas of planning. That office has a director and deputy plus a hotel program manager who takes care of the overnight arrangements for all the members of the advance team, including the Secret Service and Military Office representatives. Travel managers take care of the needs of the press.

The advance office is headed by a director and two deputy directors who specialize in long-term planning, one managing the "staff" side of the office and the other the "press" side. Another senior position is the trip director, who travels with the president and briefs him on trip logistics. The advance staff totals twenty-seven plus three interns. The office relies on a list of several hundred volunteers, with some sixty to eighty in regular rotation for international as well as domestic trips. Some of the volunteers are undergraduate and graduate students; a few are grandparents. Several are employees of other federal agencies, but this contingent cannot be used when the trips are political.

The Cost of White House Travel

The General Accounting Office (now named the Government Accountability Office), an arm of Congress, was asked to investigate the costs to the White

House, and to the several other agencies that supported the president's travel, for three international trips President Clinton made in 1998: to China, to Africa, and to Chile. GAO reported that the China visit (which entailed several stops) cost $18,830,000; the Africa trip (also with several stops) cost $42,805,992; and the Chile visit cost $10,540,226.[15] In none of the three expeditions were the expenses of the Secret Service included, so the totals represent a significant underestimate.

Readers will have to wait to see if the GAO is asked to calculate the costs of any of George W. Bush's travel. There is no question that whatever economies have been instituted by the White House, the post 9/11 security, that is, Secret Service expenses, will have expanded greatly.

Looking Ahead to 2009

Asked about the future, Beyer pointed to what he termed "the ever-expanding attention to presidential events." Beyer noted that the "level of scrutiny is . . . high, and just as with a speech, events can be taken out of context. Nontraditional media, such as bloggers, will focus on things the mainstream media won't carry at first, though they will certainly pick up on them." The new president's staff will have to "keep things fresh," he added, "to keep the press interested." That said, Beyer then referred to the challenge of striking the right balance between pulling off "cutting edge" events (such as having the president in a flight suit landing in a plane on the deck of an aircraft carrier) and always preserving the "presidential image" of the chief executive. "Thinking outside the box is one thing," Beyer cautioned. "Taking risks with the image is another. . . . The president is always on the world stage, so we keep this in mind every time he does something."

Achievements versus Activities: The Office of Appointments and Scheduling

What does a President want to do with his years in office? What is his concept of governing? We made up a four-year schedule, anticipating all the major events of Nixon's term. With that, we could plan an overarching program of achievements. Without it, every day would simply fill up with activities.

—David Parker

The only actual test I had was: if you need to see the president, you will see him. If you *want* to see the president, you won't. If a cabinet officer tries to pretend that his "want" is a "need," I scratch his name out and say, "Nice try, but it won't work this time."

—Andrew Card

The deputy assistant to the president for appointments and scheduling, backed up by the chief of staff, is much more then a mere keeper of the calendar. By allocating the president's time, she makes possible—or impossible—the accomplishments by which he is judged: she helps shape his legacy for history.

There is an inevitable progression for a president: from the goals he holds to the themes he emphasizes to the events in which he participates. If there is no long-range plan against which to evaluate the cascade of requests, his day will surely fill up, but instead of achievements there will be only activities. "Time is any president's most precious commodity," emphasized a former scheduler for President Clinton. "How he chooses to spend it will determine what people think of him."[1]

To clarify goals and themes, the Bush White House uses a long-range strategy group that meets once a month under the chairmanship of the counselor to the president, backed up by the Office of Strategic Services and attended by most of the senior staff. "We talk about trends and ideas which will affect the schedule," explained Melissa Bennett, the deputy assistant for appointments and scheduling in the Bush White House. "It's really one of those think-tank opportunities."[2] In addition to planning the president's time in the Oval Office, the deputy assistant is responsible for scheduling public events in the Residence, at Camp David, and at Bush's Texas Ranch.

Bennett heads a staff of twenty-two: twelve full-time White House employees, six interns, and four volunteers. She attends the senior staff meetings, in fact opens them with her summary of what the president is scheduled to do that day.

The Scheduling Process

Requests from the three branches of government for a piece of the president's time flood into the White House at a rate of at least 1,000 a week. Another 250 a week come in from the public. (All of these—to birthday parties, bar mitzvahs, other celebrations—are acknowledged. Even if the answer is a negative, "people are thrilled," commented Bennett, "and their reaction is 'I wrote you, you wrote me back. I can't believe that someone at the White House was responsive to me!'")

Within the White House itself, there is a new and tough rule: no one on the staff may formally propose a schedule commitment to the president unless he or she bears the rank of assistant to the president. The "schedule proposal" must be submitted in writing on a special form designed for just this purpose, be initialed by the assistant and hand-delivered to the Scheduling Office. Proposals for foreign travel, bilateral meetings, summit conferences, telephone calls, or video-teleconferences with foreign chiefs of state originate in the office of the national security adviser; recommendations involving domestic travel or events in Washington are submitted by the appropriate White House policy office or by the deputy chief of staff for policy. Requests from governors come through the deputy assistant for intergovernmental affairs, but since she does not have assistant rank, such schedule proposals must be initialed by the senior adviser for political affairs. The same is true of schedule requests from advocacy groups; the deputy assistant for public liaison sends them through that office.

The nine-person Scheduling Committee meets weekly. It is chaired by the chief of staff and includes the senior adviser for political affairs, the deputy chiefs of staff, the national security adviser (because so many schedule items are in his bailiwick), the head of legislative affairs, a speechwriter, the chief of staff to the first lady, and the deputy assistant for appointments and scheduling. The Scheduling Committee works against a confidential internal calendar from fourteen months to two years ahead; G-8 summits for instance can be planned that far in the future. In the scheduler's office, where the Scheduling Committee meets, is a calendar-forecasting chart consisting of two electronic smart boards, held in a frame mounted on the wall behind winged covers. Each day for four months ahead is depicted as a box, with symbols, checkmarks, and scrawls written with wax crayons but also recorded electronically. While the agenda is always the president's schedule, the attendees also keep the vice president's and the first lady's commitments in mind, but the latter are only potential; it is a firm tradition in the Bush White House that neither the vice president's nor the first lady's schedules go final until the president's schedule for the next day is completed.

When a presidential schedule proposal on the committee's agenda is evaluated to see how it fits with what is doable, a coordinated view is reached and a memorandum is prepared listing the recommended schedule proposals and outlining the issues that may be inherent in each of them. Twenty minutes are reserved with the president each day; called the daily briefing, these sessions include scheduling matters. "Our biggest challenge is to manage requests for time, while protecting private time for the president," commented Bennett.

With the presidential approval in hand, the deputy assistant for scheduling prepares, for each calendar item, what is called an approved presidential activity form and then designates a project officer for each event—always the assistant to the president who signed off on the original schedule proposal. Under the project officer a "working contact" person is specified; that staff person carries the immediate responsibility for seeing that all the listed arrangements are made.

The Bush scheduling office has created an innovation: a special computer program called Timepiece, replacing what had been a somewhat primitive and time-consuming system of making paper copies of each scheduled item, putting them in folders, then recopying and redistributing them every time a change occurred. Timepiece is instant and electronic; it produces a daily presidential schedule; a private daily schedule including off-the-record presidential appointments such as with friends (which has a much more limited distribution); a two-week schedule narrative, a private two-week narrative, a three-month block and, once a week, an annual calendar. A staff officer with proper access rights logs onto Timepiece, enters his or her identifying number, views the constantly updated schedule and prints out a copy. "This narrative is new," Bennett explained, "and the president keeps a close eye on every version of the schedule we produce; he is often the first to raise issues or point out improvements."

E-mails can be exchanged among staff members about individual items on the president's schedule, but the security feature of Timepiece makes it impossible for the full schedule document to be e-mailed anywhere. Other advantages of Timepiece are that it is accessible on the road: in *Air Force One,* at the ranch, at Camp David, and that it automatically creates a historical record of the president's life in office. The staff secretary uses this electronic system in preparing, every night, the daily presidential book of the papers that are on the next day's agenda; each briefing or policy document is matched with the item on the schedule to which it corresponds.

At meetings of the Scheduling Committee, a proposal may judged to be of high value but still unable to be fitted in with all the other commitments of presidential time; it is then referred to the associate director of scheduling for surrogates, known as the surrogate scheduler. This officer may turn to the vice president, the first lady, or other White House senior staffers or enlist the help of the Cabinet Liaison Office (chapter 13) to recruit a cabinet member or an under secretary to take the president's place and speak for and represent the administration. It is not unknown to have cabinet officers consider these refer-rals as importunities.[3] But if the funnel to them is as described here, the poten-tial surrogate can be assured that the request is coming from very high levels at the White House.

Presidential telephone calls are scheduled as well, and one of two forms is used. If it is to be a telephone conversation with a foreign chief of state, a recom-mended telephone call schedule proposal is drawn up, usually by the assistant for national security affairs, and sent to the scheduling office for sign-off by the chief of staff and approval of the president. The scheduling and national secu-rity affairs offices work out the actual timing of the international call; once set the time put aside is close to inflexible, out of deference to the foreign leader's own schedule. For domestic telephone calls, a recommended telephone call pro-posal is prepared by the appropriate policy office and submitted to the staff sec-retary. Once the call is approved by the chief of staff, the president's personal sec-retary fits it in whenever most convenient.

The final step in the scheduling and appointments process is record-keeping, and this is done by the White House diarist (until her recent retirement, the diarist was a woman named Ellen McCathran, a detailee from the National Archives and Records Administration, who served professionally and anony-mously on the scheduling office staff for thirty years). Using the Timepiece entries, and collecting precise information from the president's personal aide, the telephone operators, and the Secret Service, the diarist provides a log of all the president's minute-by-minute activities for both current and future refer-ence. In a statement made in 1998, Ms. McCathran described the log as

> the only complete source of information on the president's activities and meetings. The log lists by time all the activities of the president's day, including incoming and outgoing telephone calls (not his personal . . . calls . . . on his private line), visitors, meetings, conferences, announce-ments, signing ceremonies, recreational and social activities, and travel. The log identifies the president's physical location, individuals with the president (identified by professional title and organization if possible), the length of the meeting and subject matter and purpose of the activity. The diary is compiled of information obtained from source documents, including an Oval Office log kept by the personal aide, and the president's briefing papers. The log traditionally begins with . . . the president receiv-ing a wake-up call . . . or having breakfast and ending with him retiring for the evening. The log accounts for the president's time and activities on a twenty-four-hour basis.[4]

The diarist's computer organizes the log: chronologically from all the source documents and alphabetically by the name of the person or the subject. If a request is made for a given person to see the president, the log can be checked to see whether that person has been with the president before—how often, and on what subject. If the president is to meet a foreign official on an overseas trip, the log can show whether they have met before; it can determine whether topic A was discussed at an Oval Office meeting held two years ago.

For presidential trips, this information is summarized in an activity sheet; if his destination is Ohio, the activity sheet will list the twenty-four other times the president has been in Ohio. Correspondingly, specific data are included in the activity sheets that accompany every international trip. "The diarist is the only person," Bennett said, "who has the complete picture."

The president's daily diary records are available at the touch of a button, through a tightly controlled access code. The diary is, of course, a principal guide for the presidential archives to come: tracks leading into history for the retired president and for authors and scholars in the future.

Looking Ahead

Reflecting about the appointments and scheduling challenges for the next White House, Bennett summarized the lessons learned from the recent past: "Clearly lay out the process to request time on the president's schedule; enforce the policy and procedures strictly; protect private time for the president and first lady; coordinate closely with the office of the first lady, and remember: the White House is not just the president's place of work; it is also his home."

30
The White House Military Office

Few in the public—and few even in the White House—realize the extent to which the president is given hour-to-hour service by men and women of the U.S. military. Since the president is the commander in chief, military support for the presidential office is everywhere in the White House establishment; indeed, the military group is the largest part of the *whole* White House staff family. It is also quiet, professional, and—except on a few occasions—almost out of sight.

The White House Military Office reports to the deputy chief of staff for operations. The director of the Military Office is a deputy assistant to the president, and he is aided in turn by a civilian deputy. Beginning with President Carter, presidents have named a civilian as head of the Military Office, but previous military experience has been considered essential. Under the first president Bush, the director was a retired lieutenant general; under President Clinton, a retired colonel with thirty years of military experience. The White House changed this practice in 2003; since then each director of the Military Office under President George W. Bush has been a Navy flag officer.

Twenty-three hundred military men and women serve the White House daily; large numbers of others support the president and his staff on a less frequent basis. In keeping with the concept of the presidency as a civilian office, uniforms are rarely worn during daytime hours. Understating the presence of military staff is especially important when the president travels abroad; some host nations resent any visible evidence of U.S. armed forces.

Unlike that of the Roosevelt and early Truman years, the military staff of today is not involved in national security policy matters; these are the exclusive province of the national security adviser (chapter 5). The Military Office does, however, review the 400 to 700 letters a week that their commander in chief receives from men and women in the armed forces; Military Office staff help to untangle hardship cases and ensure that the petitioners and their families are treated fairly.

The White House Military Office has fifteen elements under its command, including the director's office. Although all of them function behind the scenes, the principal units deserve a description in any book that aims to give a complete picture of the contemporary White House staff.

The Military Aides

The most visible military personnel are the five military aides: one from each service, including the Coast Guard. Career officers at the level of lieutenant colonel, the five are selected by the director of the Military Office, but it is the president who signs their annual performance evaluations. The aides' White House assignments are, of course, at the president's pleasure.

Each advance team includes a military aide; one is always on duty with the president. It is a military aide who constantly has the "presidential emergency satchel" in hand. Colloquially known as the football because it is passed around, the satchel carries the authentication codes and presidential emergency declarations. The aide who carries the satchel has been trained in emergency drills and facilities and is competent not only to open the bag but also to explain to a commander in chief exactly what each of its contents is and does. The vice president's military aide carries one too. One military aide, when asked by a group of young people what was in the satchel, humorously explained, "Well, let's see—there's the red button for thermonuclear war and the green button for 'more coffee'—or is it the other way around?" Writing in his diary, President George H. W. Bush once asked. "Does Mil Aide need to carry that black case now every little place I go? . . . With the cold war over, I did not think it was necessary for [it] to go everywhere with me. However, Brent [Scowcroft] disagreed."[1]

Some military aides in the past have succumbed to the temptation to elevate parochial service viewpoints into the environment of the White House. Harry Truman's military aide, General Harry Vaughan, so vexed Army Chief of Staff Dwight Eisenhower with intercessions that Eisenhower "had to go right to the President to get who was running the Army straightened out."[2] When Ike became president, he was determined not to have flag-ranked officers as military aides; that tradition continues.

The White House Communications Agency

Communications technology is the lifeblood of a presidency. Joseph Hagin, Bush's first deputy chief of staff for operations recalled a Friday afternoon in March 2001, shortly after the inauguration, when the president had to drive to Camp David. "Because of a snowstorm, he couldn't fly," Hagin said. "He could not complete a single telephone call the entire drive up. On Sunday he drove back. Same thing happened. Couldn't get calls out. And on Monday he had two separate in-town movements. Both times communications in the car were inadequate. He called me in and said, 'Fix it!'"[3]

The Department of Defense was ordered to do an end-to-end review of all presidential communications—secure, nonsecure, voice, data, video. That report, much of it classified, came back in four months, and, said Hagin, "basically it said that the systems were outdated; they were no longer manufactured. The manufacturer no longer supported them and spare parts had to be cannibalized from existing systems."

At no time was the problem with the White House communication system more apparent than in the first hours of September 11, 2001. As the independent commission that investigated the attacks reported, "On the morning of 9/11, the President and Vice President stayed in contact not by an open line of communication but through a series of calls. The President told us he was frustrated with the poor communications that morning. He could not reach key officials, including Secretary Rumsfeld, for a period of time. The line to the White House shelter conference room—and the Vice President—kept cutting off."[4] One observer remembered seeing White House staff members waiting in line to use a secure phone—a totally unacceptable situation.

Little wonder, then, that it has been in the White House Communications Agency (WHCA) that a great many of the improvements and innovations instigated by the Bush administration have occurred.

The Push for Quality Improvement

The communications assessment ordered in the spring of 2001 identified "gaps that were inherent in the support provided to the president." As a result, WHCA instituted a presidential communications upgrade program, fixed the shortfalls, and determined that there was going to be a presidential communications mobilization effort that would maintain and sustain the improvements that had already been made. No more waiting in line to use a secure phone! WHCA has also gone from analog to digital, which has improved voice quality immensely.

Bandwidth is an issue, and WHCA has been able to increase the bandwidth it has available while employing more advanced compression techniques so that more signals can be squeezed into the same or lesser bandwidth. Secure video, such as that being used in the revamped Situation Room, eats up bandwidth, but WHCA has installed new equipment that produces superior pictures with far less bandwidth. The advantage of video is that the users can see one another eyeball to eyeball; what is being conveyed nonverbally is often more important than what is being conveyed verbally—it is a whole new facet of communication that the president did not previously have.

Another measure of quality improvement is the number of WHCA staff who have to go ahead of time to set up a distant site in advance of a presidential visit.

Before 2001 the agency would go out seven days in advance of a trip and have perhaps twenty folks putting in the equipment. Today it goes out six days in advance with fifteen people.

The WHCA Office

WHCA began informally in December 1941 as the White House Signal Detachment and was officially activated in March 1942. Its name was changed in 1954 to the White House Army Signal Agency. In 1962 the secretary of defense designated it as a joint service agency, changed its name again to the White House Communications Agency, and reassigned it from the Army to the Defense Communications Agency, which is now the Defense Information Systems Agency (DISA). WHCA's mission is to "provide telecommunications and related support to the President and Vice President, the National Security Council, the President's staff, the First Family, the Secret Service and others as directed." DISA handles all of WHCA's administrative support, that is, contracting, auditing, budgeting (including testimony before congressional appropriations committees), acquisition planning and review, manpower and personnel management, legal counsel, and functional oversight. While WHCA's commander does not usually testify before congressional committees, Appropriations Committee staffers with the proper clearances do accompany DISA officers on visits to WHCA. This gives them an appreciation for what the agency is doing and needs to do.

While WHCA is under the administrative control of DISA, it is under the operational control of the White House Military Office. The WHCA team is the largest element in the White House: some 880 military men and women plus 28 civilians plus 250 contractor personnel—a ballpark total of 1,200. WHCA's fiscal 2008 operation and management budget was $123.8 million and its fiscal 2008 procurement investment funds were $50.1 million, for a subtotal of $173.9 (up from $79 million in fiscal 1996).[5] The salary costs of WHCA's personnel are paid by the individual military departments; if average pay is estimated at $5,500 per month, the WHCA federal salary expenses would be $79.2 million, making a total WHCA outlay of $253.1 million in fiscal year 2008.

WHCA recruits its personnel from the military services, bringing individuals on board for a period of four years. It maintains a running list of military personnel who are interested in working in the agency and in whom WHCA may be interested, in turn. WHCA does not interrupt a service member's tour of duty but effects the recruitment transfer when the candidate is at a normal time for rotation.

Incoming recruits are first given an orientation and then undergo a rigorous training program. There are also classes for existing staffers to gain upgrades. This provides a level of standardization across the agency. Before the trainees are certified for WHCA service, they must be screened by internal examining boards made up of peers and experienced team leaders. WHCA makes sure that its men and women know exactly what they are doing before it puts them out on the road, because it is a no-fail environment. And if WHCA is not confident that its staffers can perform in that kind of pressured environment, then they go back to the drawing board and start over.

In 1996 WHCA's equipment inventory was 45,624; today it is 13,000 fewer—approximately 32,300. The agency has been able to consolidate and downsize. Electronic equipment is constantly getting smaller and easier to transport. Presidents travel more, and they have the ability to travel more. Even though WHCA has cut back on its equipment, advances in technology allow the agency to keep pace with the needs of the modern president.

WHCA is closely linked into the world of communications research. The agency has many connections with the major companies in the areas of communications and electronic equipment. It has recently instituted a three-person research team that keeps tabs on advanced research and on what the military services are doing, so that they are not too far behind what is going on, including in the academic world.

Supporting a Presidential Trip

When the White House notifies WHCA that a trip is in the works, WHCA has a planning office that starts its analysis of what communications equipment will be needed. Standard templates for WHCA operations are modified to fit whatever may be specialized or unique requirements, and an "op order" is given to a presidential communications officer (PCO). The PCO is the lead for that particular trip, in charge of the WHCA contingent. The PCO is notified of who will be his teammates from WHCA's operational "battle staff," then works with the White House advance "lead" to plot out exactly what the requirements will be on the ground and build a specific "trip kit." Based on the trip kit, the needed equipment is loaded, transported, and installed, and that is not a nine-to-five job. The team's responsibility is to have everything in place at every event site where the president will be—well before he arrives—in order to provide him with that indispensable worldwide communications capability that the American president must have.

For the team that is on the ground, a presidential trip is a 24/7 operation. It typically takes a team a fifteen- to eighteen-hour day to install the initial communications equipment and have it ready for the president's arrival. Then comes the task of maintaining it or making whatever changes may be required—a task that is handled in shifts. As soon as the president departs, there is the immediate job of breakdown; the team has less then twenty-four hours to have the equipment broken down, packed up, and loaded on a truck or plane. From arrival to departure, it is an intense period. A complicated trip such as the one that President Bush took to Australia in 2007—with a stopover in Baghdad—requires fifty to fifty-five WHCA staff. If the president is going to make a speech, the WHCA package will include lighting, mikes, loudspeakers, the podium—everything necessary. At the end of the day, all the president needs to know is that he has a team of people he can rely on; he doesn't need to worry about details because he has the WHCA.

In 2006 WHCA handled 4,166 presidential events, 161 for the vice president, and 422 for the president's spouse. It measured its success rate: 97 percent.[6]

Looking Ahead to 2009

The new president will learn that he has got exceptionally dedicated, professional staffers at WHCA who love what they do, think their work is important, and are very proud to serve him or her. Said one observer: "They are the best of the best."[7]

The White House Medical Unit

The president's personal physician and a group of twenty military colleagues from the armed services (five doctors plus physicians' assistants, nurses, and paramedics) are assigned to duty at the White House. The principal medical suite is in the Residence, and a second is in the Eisenhower Executive Office building. A dental suite is also available for a dentist who makes periodic visits. The Medical Unit's principal patients are the two first families, including the children; staff members are permitted to use the unit's help in emergencies; even a White House tourist who is experiencing chest pains may be assisted.

In Washington the physicians' first objective is to ensure that the president receives specialized care when needed (usually at one of Washington's military hospitals) rather than to provide it themselves in the limited White House facilities. On presidential trips, the medical staff provides support not only for the first family, but also for those who are traveling with the president—for Secret Service personnel, for example, and even for the press. The president's personal physician (currently an Air Force brigadier general) always flies with the president; during public appearances, he takes care not to be anywhere in the president's vicinity to avoid even the remote chance of a bullet hitting him.

Each advance team has a medical staffer who visits nearby hospitals at every planned presidential stop, determining which hospital to use in an emergency and which to use as a backup; finding a backup facility is particularly important if a summit conference involving a number of chiefs of state is being scheduled. The hospital is likely to be asked if a supply of the president's blood type is available, and the president's physician may even dispatch extra medical personnel to that hospital to be on hand if needed. A temporary White House telephone may be installed in the hospital that has the best emergency facilities, but the hospital will be warned against advertising itself as "the president's hospital." The medical unit is in close touch with the Secret Service and runs weekly drills to be prepared for various contingencies. Medical supplies always include breathing equipment and antidotes for biological and chemical agents.

The president has an annual physical and arranges for the results to be released publicly. A presidential illness is not only a medical problem but also instantly injects the president's physician into a tangle of internal strains within the White House. There is likely to be a gritty, three-way tension among the physician, the press secretary, and the president's spouse, as the three struggle to balance the public's need for straightforward information with the protection of the first family's privacy. "We should not be yakkers," commented a former White House doctor. "The public should know if the president is or is not able to go back to work, but they do not have to know his blood count or his urine's specific gravity."[8]

If a president's illness is serious, or his surgery extensive—with general anesthesia in prospect—the most elemental question arises: should the president, pursuant to the Twenty-Fifth Amendment, temporarily transfer his powers to the vice president? In counseling the president, the physician, the president's spouse, the counsel, the chief of staff, and the vice president may all be swayed by different professional viewpoints or personal inclinations. How will the nation's interests be safeguarded from the potential danger lurking in their individual biases?

One observer has proposed that the physician to the president be confirmed by the Senate —to ensure that Congress would have a source of direct information concerning the president's health. In 1981 a pair of physicians suggested that a president's official physicians' panel be established, appointed by a special committee of Congress or a committee of high judicial officers.[9] This proposal was echoed by *New York Times* columnist (and former White House staff member) William Safire, who recommended in 1987 that "the next President should ask a panel of doctors appointed by all three branches of government to check him out once a year, the results to be made public. In his case the doctor-patient relationship might suffer; the patient-voter relationship would improve."[10] Strongly opposing views were put forward in 1988 by a distinguished commission cochaired by a former attorney general and a former senator; the commission argued that "the president's physician must remain a person of the president's own choice. . . . [He] or she should not be subject to confirmation by the Senate or to approval by any other body, medical or otherwise."[11] Finally, a group of former military physicians assigned to the White House including President Clinton's physician, Dr. E. Connie Mariano, asserted that "the office of Senior Physician in the White House should be an entity separate from the White House Military Office."[12]

And where should the line be drawn between safeguarding the president's personal privacy and informing the nation? The aforementioned commission said the president's physician "should abide by the views of the American Medical Association's Council on Medical Ethics regarding doctor-patient confidentiality and those instances when it can be abridged in the national or community interest."[13] The AMA language reportedly says that a physician is "freed from the strictures of confidentiality in the presence of 'overriding social considerations' and when there is the 'need to protect the welfare of the individual or the public interest.'"[14] The physician's necessary involvement in issues of such import is but another illustration of the borderless swamp, in the White House, in which both professional skills and political issues are inextricably submerged.

The White House Staff Mess

Managed by the Navy, the White House Staff Mess consists of three adjacent dining rooms in the lower level of the West Wing that seat forty-five, twenty-eight, and eighteen, respectively, in paneled decorum, for each of two noonday shifts. Some 200 staffers and the cabinet are eligible to dine in the mess. Dinners are now served as well, a reflection of the lengthening White House workday. Private luncheons in their own offices are available from the mess for West Wing senior staff, and carryout trays are provided to harried aides on the run. At the entrance to the mess, hanging noiselessly encased in glass, is a hallowed symbol: the 1790 mess gong from the USS *Constitution*.

Presidential valets serve lunches in the Oval Office and occasionally serve breakfast or other meals in the Cabinet Room. The White House Mess is entirely separate from the first family's kitchen and dining facilities in the Residence. The mess and valets—a staff of fifty—are supervised by the presidential food service coordinator. Those who eat in the mess pay for their food, but the salaries of the Navy service personnel are borne by the Navy. When the president travels, mess assistants prepare some of the first family's meals, and when the chief executive hosts a dinner during a state visit abroad, mess personnel oversee the food preparation.

Camp David

Even though the family quarters at the White House were air-conditioned in 1933, presidential physician Ross McIntire told Franklin Roosevelt that he believed that "a cool mountain retreat would be good for the president's sinuses." In 1942 the National Park Service was commissioned to locate such a site between 1,700 and 2,000 feet in elevation. The Park Service came up with three possibilities: one in Shenandoah National Park and two in the Catoctin, Maryland, Recreational Demonstration Area, "one of about fifty areas established for poor children." It was at 1,700 feet and had a family camp on the site that already had a swimming pool, playing field, and recreation hall. As an assistant secretary of the Navy, Roosevelt had become familiar with the countryside around Frederick, Maryland, and on April 22, 1942, drove up to look at the site in person. He opted for this site, called it Shangri-La, and ordered some new construction, including taking out some trees that blocked the view of the valley. July 18–20, 1942, was his first overnight stay. In all, he paid twenty-two visits to the new presidential retreat. The place was still primitive, however; "the staff stayed in unheated cabins and washed in cold water in metal troughs outside," Margaret Truman wrote. "Deep in the woods, Shangri-La was damp and cold most of the time. I thought it was a terrible place and went there as little as possible." Truman visited it only ten times. Eisenhower renamed it Camp David after his grandson and held at least three cabinet meetings there.

Today, after sixty-six years of refurbishment and development, Camp David has some forty-nine buildings, including seven fireplace-equipped guest cottages, two heated pools, and a glorious view over the Maryland countryside. During President Reagan's years, $1.2 million in private funds were used to build a bell tower and a 130-seat octagonal chapel. George H. W. Bush added family quarters for Camp David's resident staff and new communications and guard quarters. The camp now has a driving range, a five-tee chipping green, a two-lane bowling alley, a sauna, horse stables, a barber shop, a fitness room with exercise equipment, a movie theater, and facilities for sledding, badminton, tennis, archery, skeet, bicycling, and softball.

The fiscal 2007 budget for Camp David was $8.4 million; the fiscal 2008 request was for $7.9 million. In both cases there are classified annexes to the budget requests.

President George W. Bush divides his out-of-Washington days between his ranch in Crawford, Texas, and Camp David, and he is especially fond of Camp David because it is so convenient. As of November 20, 2007, he had visited Camp David 131 times. The Bush administration has instituted three significant innovations at the retreat: the first is the addition of secure video-teleconference equipment, so that Bush can receive his daily intelligence briefing or participate in other important meetings while at the camp. The second is the decision to build a hangar for the new VH-71 helicopter that will soon have the title of *Marine One.* The third is a delightful initiative undertaken by First Lady Laura Bush. She contacted all eleven presidential libraries beginning with FDR's and asked each of them if they could round up some photographs of the respective presidents at Camp David, along with pictures of visiting foreign chiefs of state. Each library sent her a handful of photographs, and she selected one or two from each set. She has had them framed and hung, those of the foreign visitors being placed in the very same cabins where each stayed. It is a thoughtful and charming addition to Camp David's history.

Air Force One

Continuity and innovation being the theme of this book, *Air Force One* is an impressive example.

First, some multiplication: two times one equals two. Sitting side by side inside a cavernous hangar at Andrews Air Force Base in Maryland, just outside of the District of Columbia, are not one, but two enormous 747s; *Air Force One* is plural. The huge building is a hangar combined with a parts and supplies warehouse and office facility. Every kind of maintenance is performed there—even changing an engine—excepting only the kind of work that involves elevating the plane to do underbody repairs. One of the two planes is usually, in fact, undergoing maintenance, with the other ready to fly. The warehouse also has stores of consumables (including a plenteous supply of M&Ms, each one sporting the presidential seal).

Although the planes have been around for a while, they boast many new features. They are fitted with the latest, classified navigational and communications gear. *Air Force One's* regular television sets, for instance, no longer are limited to receiving only whatever local, ground-based signals are on its path; it receives its television signals from satellites. Passengers can now watch national news networks such as CNN or Fox, which, as 9/11 demonstrated, can be a crucially important capability. Another new development is that *Air Force One* now is able to participate in the secure, long-distance teleconferencing network that is anchored in the White House Situation Room and connects the other National Security Council members, wherever they may be, plus other chiefs of state in capitals including London and Berlin. *Air Force One's* equipment also now allows the president to address the nation via television—another crucial capability in a time of crisis and one that so far the president has not had to use.

One can assume that *Air Force One* is also equipped with antimissile systems, since, as reported in the press, "the military already uses such counter-measures on its aircraft."[15] A *Parade* story in July 2000 described the practice of having "pararescue jumpers"—"PJs"—in a C-130 aircraft fly several thousand feet below *Air Force One* whenever it passes over water.[16] Presidential pilot Colonel Mark Tillman commented that while search and rescue teams are alerted about *Air Force One's* flight paths, the reliability of four-engine aircraft now makes such a requirement unnecessary.[17]

Making Trip Arrangements

The Air Lift Operations unit in the White House Military Office is the tasking agency for *Air Force One*. When a trip is being planned, the presidential pilot and his crew are notified so that they can perform the most elementary advance check: can *Air Force One* get in and out of the desired airports? Can the airport handle the plane? (If not, a 757 plane is substituted, as happened for the trip to Virginia Tech, or an even smaller one if need be.) There are seventy to eighty flight experts whom the *Air Force One* crew can call upon to be advance agents, and one of them either goes out ahead of time, or may be resident in the area, to do the advance screening—checking the landing strips, the taxiways. For an international trip, the *Air Force One* agents will be part of the White House initial advance team and then may return on their own for further checkovers. If the airport is one that *Air Force One* has previously used, the data are already on the computers at Andrews. The plane and its crew have to be ready to fly "within minutes," said Colonel Tillman.[18]

Air Force One can be supplemented by one or more of the seventeen aircraft that make up the 89th Airlift Wing, also based at Andrews; these planes can, with the approval of the White House, be used by members of the president's cabinet. Four new C-32A aircraft (Boeing 757-200s) are being purchased for such VIP travel; the cost is $84 million apiece, and each can carry forty-five passengers.[19] The aircraft are replacing older, fuel-gobbling C-137s that dated from the 1960s. A smaller aircraft is also available for the president's use on short domestic flights.

Air Force One has a staff of some 230 men and women, 125 specializing in maintenance and just under 100 crew: pilots, flight engineers, navigators, radio operators, flight attendants, and administrative support. They belong to the White House Military Office and are thus a part of the White House staff family. The operating budget for *Air Force One* was $2.5 million for fiscal year 2008, plus maintenance costs (which are done under contract), plus the salaries of the 230—all part of the appropriations of the U.S. Air Force. The Air Force Requirements Office of the U.S. Air Force defends this budget to Congress; the presidential pilot is not involved with testimony or in congressional contacts. The hourly operating cost of *Air Force One* may range as high as $167,000.

The Flying White House

The presidential plane needs to be looked at with new eyes. It is *not* just transportation for the chief executive; it is a flying White House. It has the flying equivalent of the Oval Office, the first family's residential quarters, an exercise room, the Cabinet Room, the Roosevelt Conference Room, the command center/Situation Room, a reproduction office, and the White House Mess, with space for the working press and the Secret Service. Without ever leaving this facility, the president can view the latest intelligence; hold top secret National Security Council meetings; video-teleconfer, securely, with the vice president, with his combatant commanders, or with other chiefs of state; surf the Internet, address the nation; watch the latest movies; and ride his (stationary) bike. Only the swimming pool is missing. As presidential pilot Tillman put it:

Air Force One is a power projection anywhere you go in the world. All the presidents have done amazing things on *Air Force One*. It's not like the days of old when you jumped on the plane, you fell asleep for six or seven hours, then you started your business on the ground. The plane, right now, is a flying White House; it does have tremendous capability. Due to threats all around the world, it's going to be that most presidents in the future probably may not be able to spend a lot of time in some countries. So *Air Force One* is a kind of its own embassy in the air, a communications platform so that the leaders can be in touch with all the other leaders around the world. *Air Force One* will have to be upgraded to make sure we can do a 24-hour, 30-hour day. Go back and forth. Get them to where they need to go. Everybody's working while they're flying. Do meetings and then let them sleep and eat and carry out their business while *Air Force One* goes back and forth.

The White House and the Air Force are already making up the requirements for new presidential aircraft. The lead time from signing a contract to flying the next model could be ten years—about the time remaining in the life cycle of the two planes currently serving as *Air Force One*. "We are already into the process of looking at different vendors," Tillman said, "whoever are making heavy aircraft these days." But probably not the huge Airbus 3—that plane is too big for many of the world's airports and would severely limit the president's mobility.

Concluded Tillman: "We're the folks behind the scenes; we don't want to do anything that will take away from the message of the president each day he flies. It's the Air Force and *Air Force One*, the crew, I mean—we do tremendous things to make sure this jet is perfect. And everything we do is perfect, because it is a reflection on the president."

Marine Helicopter Squadron One (HMX-One)

Marine Helicopter Squadron One, with a crew of 200, primarily uses Sikorsky Black Hawk and Boeing helicopters. The president's *Marine One,* a Sikorsky VH-3D Sea King, alights on the White House South Lawn and ferries the president to Andrews Air Base or to Camp David. Its home base for maintenance and repair is the Marine Corps base at Quantico, but it operates from the Anacostia Naval Air Station, only minutes downriver from the White House. The White House has contracted to purchase twenty-eight new helicopters for the HMX fleet (chapter 36).

The White House Transportation Agency

Some fifty military chauffeurs, on rotating duty, drive cars for White House staff members on official business. (The former privilege of home-to-office transportation is now rarely, if ever, provided.) The radio-equipped cars, not to mention the BlackBerries that all staffers have, put every staffer within reach of every other one. When presidential trips begin or end, Transportation Agency staffers are the baggage coordinators for the first family, guests, and staff, helping to ensure the security of the cargo and the luggage on *Air Force One* and the accompanying support planes.

The Ceremonies Coordinator

If White House events require the presence of military units such as honor guards, bands, the Herald Trumpets, or other musical ensembles, the ceremonies coordinator serves as the link between the White House and the Military District of Washington in making the necessary arrangements.

Looking Ahead to 2009

Asked what he would tell a future president, a Military Office senior staffer reflected, "To have a feel for this place—to understand what our roles and functions are. A lot of people, especially those new to this place, don't know all of our Military Office components, how we interact with the president's staff to make things happen. We need to have a constant dialogue between the White House civilian staff and the military. The president's personal staff is working to support him; we are working to support him. We must have a rapport."

31

The United States Secret Service

The Secret Service is considered to be one of the premier law enforcement agencies in America, and it has the premier task: protecting the nation's executive branch leadership. The protective units of the Secret Service are extremely close, physically and organizationally, to the president and all of the staff. They are in every corner of the White House; their function is of such importance that no meeting or plan about the president's or vice president's activities takes place without the Secret Service being part of the planning team—be it a visit to the Pentagon or a flight to Abu Dhabi. Every hour of every day is of as much concern to them as to the seniormost officers of the White House staff. Their policies affect the staff's policies, and the staff's policies affect them. It is for this reason that the author judges that the protective elements of the Secret Service are part of the White House staff family and belong in this book.

A Quick History

It is a sad and ironic fact that security for the first family and others has come about only through tragedy. The Secret Service was created in July 1865, as part of the Treasury Department, to hunt down counterfeiters. Only after President McKinley was assassinated, in 1901, was the service given the presidential protective function; in 1908 it was assigned to protect the president-elect. From the ranks of agents in the service was formed the nucleus of what is now the Federal Bureau of Investigation. After President Kennedy was killed in 1963, the Warren Commission investigating the assassination found that the Secret Service's protective arrangements were "seriously deficient" and excoriated the FBI's "unduly restrictive view of its responsibilities in preventive intelligence work."[1]

The Secret Service's protection was extended to presidential candidates in 1968, the day *after* Robert Kennedy was shot. Protection was extended to foreign visitors only after a 1970 incident in Chicago involving French president

Georges Pompidou. Carter White House officials blocked the installation of magnetometers at White House entrances—reportedly claiming that it was not "politically acceptable"—until a man walked in with a gun and said, "Take me to the president!"

It took the bombing of U.S. troop quarters in Beirut before the Commission on Fine Arts relented and allowed bollards (massive concrete posts) to be set up outside the White House vehicle entrances; the gates themselves were heavily reinforced only after a man crashed through the old ones one Christmas morning. The closing of Pennsylvania Avenue, long recommended by security experts, occurred *after* the bombing of a federal building in Oklahoma City in 1995. "That truck-bomb would have flattened the White House," said one Secret Service veteran.[2]

The Structure and Size of the Secret Service

On March 1, 2003, the Secret Service was transferred from the Department of the Treasury to the new Department of Homeland Security. To underscore the determined independence of the Secret Service, the following statutory provision sets the relationship the agency would have with the leadership of the new department:

> The United States Secret Service shall be maintained as a distinct entity within the Department of Homeland Security and shall not be merged with any other Department function. No personnel and operational elements of the United States Secret Service shall report to an individual other than the Director of the United States Secret Service, who shall report directly to the Secretary of Homeland Security without being required to report through any other official of the Department.[3]

The Secret Service is organized into nine offices. The author believes that two of these—Protective Operations and the Office of Protective Research—along with the James J. Rowley Training Center within the service's human resources office, should be considered as part of the White House staff family.

The training center, in Beltsville, Maryland, trains agents and Uniformed Division officers by simulating the environment, the settings, and the day-to-day and threat-based scenarios that they would encounter on the job. The vehicles and equipment used in training are the same as the officers would encounter when on duty. Protective driving is stressed as well as the work of counterassault, emergency response teams, technical security, magnetometers, transportation, K-9, and working protective details. Those USSS special agents who are on any of the protective details participate in training two weeks out of every eight on duty. The center uses mock-ups of *Air Force One* and of the *Marine One* helicopter as part of the training exercises.

Protective Operations is the heart of the Secret Service mission and is described in more detail below. Agents in the presidential protection details serve for only five years at a stretch.

The Office of Protective Research, which includes the technical security and intelligence divisions and information resources management, has devoted a great deal of effort to attempting to determine whether people who are a threat to a protectee can be identified in advance. Is there a "profile" of a would-be assassin? The office helped sponsor a special study on this question, and publishes other research papers on the Internet.[4] After each trip, agents analyze every step of the protective operation, record unusual incidents, and suggest improvements for the future. At any time and almost any place in the world where there is an assassination attempt, the Secret Service tries to collect data, make comparisons, learn new lessons. "We are constantly second-guessing ourselves," said a former official. The division maintains a list of several thousand Americans who are potential threats. Some 400 of them are on a "watch list" of individuals who are known to be dangerous. Some angry or mentally ill people write threatening letters to the president (a felony). The division has a unique computerized system for matching handwriting—the largest database of its kind. As is the case with a fingerprint collection, samples from unknown sources can be compared with known samples on file.

The author does not include another Secret Service office, investigations, as part of the White House staff, but its role is crucial. Present in many field offices throughout the United States, the investigative staffs are focused on enforcing the counterfeiting statutes and, since 1984, on crimes that involve financial institution fraud, computer and telecommunications fraud, and related transgressions. Almost all who become special agents get their start in the investigations area; reciprocally when a protectee visits a local area, investigative staffers from one or more field offices join the protective detail.

There are three categories of Secret Service personnel: special agents, the Uniformed Division, and administrative and technical support. The Uniformed Division, which began as the White House Police Force in 1922, was renamed the Executive Protection Service in 1970 and then renamed the Uniformed Division in 1977; it was codified as a "permanent police force" by public law 109-177 in March 2006.

The Secret Service operates 116 domestic offices and 20 foreign offices, including one in Moscow. It is in daily contact with the National Counter-Terrorism Center, although it does not have a permanent desk there.

As of April 2, 2007, the Secret Service employed a total of 6,463 men and women, of whom 3,306 were special agents, 1,351 were in the Uniformed Division, and 1,806 performed professional and technical support. In the protective offices were 2,215 employees including 631 special agents, 999 in the Uniformed Division, and 585 providing administrative and technical support. This is a somewhat arbitrary calculation; there is considerable flexibility, and so much attrition and turnover that the figures themselves must be regarded as approximations. But of the special agents, 870 have been serving in the Secret Service for between eight and fifteen years, and 503 have been serving for more than sixteen years.

Who Is Protected?

The law authorizes the Secret Service to protect the president, the vice president (or other officer next in the order of succession), the president-elect, and the vice president–elect, and mandates that this protection cannot be declined.[5] Protection is also authorized for the immediate families of the officers just mentioned, for former presidents, their spouses, and their children under sixteen, and foreign heads of state who are visiting the United States. If the president directs, protection can also be provided to distinguished foreign visitors and representatives of the United States "performing special missions abroad." If a presidential election impends, "major presidential and vice presidential candidates" can be protected—and the protection extended to their spouses—within 120 days of the election. "Major" is left to the determination of the secretary of homeland security after consulting with an advisory committee composed of himself, the Speaker and minority leader of the House, the majority and minority leaders of the Senate, plus one other person selected by the members. The homeland security secretary chairs the advisory committee. Any person, except those enumerated in the first sentence of this paragraph, may decline the offer of protection.

An additional category of persons who may be eligible for Secret Service protection has been instituted: the president may, by executive memorandum, identify people who are vulnerable targets because of their duties, their exposure, their location, or other factors, such as whether they may have received threats to their lives, and may accordingly direct the secretary of homeland security to provide protection for them. Examples of persons in this category are senior members of the White House staff.

The level or degree of protection that *any* protectee receives is determined only after a threat assessment is done and a risk analysis is made for each such individual, which will vary with each instance. "We take a very measured approach, and we try to be as efficient and effective as we can in our protection," Mark Sullivan, director of the Secret Service, assured the House Appropriations Subcommittee on Homeland Security in March 2007. "We look at the individual. We look at the threat environment. We will take a look at where they are going, how long they are going to be there for, but we do not look at it, as far as whether it is a political event or nonpolitical event, or whether it is a vacation. We look at the threat environment and we look at the individual."[6]

A provision in the fiscal 2007 appropriations act asks that the Service be reimbursed in full for the expenses of protecting any person other than those identified in the first paragraph of this subsection, for instance a cabinet officer or a senior White House staff officer. To carry out this provision, the Appropriations Committee directed the Secret Service to seek such reimbursement "if these protective assignments create an undue burden on Secret Service protective missions."[7] In fiscal year 2008 these costs total $3.1 million.

The total number of protectees as of mid-March 2007 was fifty-five; twenty-six were in the executive memorandum category. The three principal 2008 presidential candidates (Senators Hillary Clinton, Barack Obama, and John McCain) all received Secret Service protection—although McCain did not accept the protection until April 2008. Senator Clinton was already included because of her status as the spouse of a former president; Senator Obama asked for and was given protection on May 3, 2007, the earliest given a candidate during a presidential campaign (Hillary Clinton excepted). Jesse Jackson was also given early protection when he ran for president in 1984 and 1988 because of threats being made to him.[8]

Providing protection for the major candidates during the 2008 campaign was estimated to require 1,500 agents (who would get special training) and 200 other departmental personnel, trained to be used on a standby basis. They are expected to work for 739 "protective days" (in 2004 it was 454), at an estimated cost of $85,250,000. Some mutual benefit accrues when a Secret Service protective detail guards a candidate during a presidential campaign: the candidate comes to learn why and how the service does its work and how professional the agents are. If that candidate becomes president, the mutual trust and understanding—indispensable between protector and protectee—are that much further advanced.

A 2006 statute expanded the protective responsibilities of the Uniformed Division; they now include "any building in which presidential offices are located," the Treasury building and grounds, foreign diplomatic missions in the Washington area (there are 590), foreign diplomatic missions in metropolitan areas of the United States only if there are twenty of them in one area and there is "extraordinary protective need," foreign consular and diplomatic missions in other places in the United States or its territories and possessions if directed by the president "on a case by case basis," and visits of foreign government officials to metropolitan areas other than Washington if there are at least twenty foreign missions and the visitor is in the United States on government business.

Director Sullivan told Congress that in fiscal year 2006 the Secret Service "provided protection for 4,400 travel stops for our domestic protectees, and 1,875 travel stops for foreign dignitaries." The Secret Service, he said, "experienced a 100% success rate." The director went on to observe that the Secret Service "anticipates that President George W. Bush will be active and maintain a high profile after he leaves office," so it is hiring and training an additional 103 special agents who will help in the 2008 campaign period and then backfill the positions of the more senior special agents who will be reassigned to the Bush postpresidential protective detail.[9]

Sullivan has told Congress that Mr. Cheney, too, will receive Secret Service protection for at least six months, as have other former vice presidents including Hubert Humphrey, Dan Quayle, and Al Gore.[10]

Guarding the White House

Within the White House complex, dozens of officers from the Uniformed Division are on duty (in shifts) at the outer perimeter; others are in the middle perimeter, within the buildings. On the inner protective perimeter are the agents in civilian clothes: perhaps 200 on the White House detail, and a second group with the vice president. A Joint Operations Center (JOC) is the command post for the Secret Service operations in the White House compound. It monitors all the sensors, alarms, gates, and communications centers; tracks the movements of the president and the vice president and their families; and monitors the White House grounds, the surrounding areas, and the air space above them. It permits all of the security elements at the White House to reach one another in seconds; it coordinates emergency actions and the response of Secret Service special operations units stationed on and around the White House. The JOC had been located in the Eisenhower Executive Office Building, but because of the extensive reconstruction of that building, the center was being moved to an alternate location (classified) and was to be tripled in size, permitting representatives from all related law enforcement agencies to maintain face-to-face relationships.

The members of the premier protective details are all professionals; there was neither a "Clinton" nor a "Bush" detail; the agents' assignments vary from three to five years and therefore often overlap a four-year presidential term.

A major unit of the Secret Service in Washington is its technical security division, which provides the physical security for the White House, the Eisenhower Executive Office Building (where the vice president has a ceremonial office), the vice president's residence, and Camp David. This division built the hydraulic gates at the vehicular entrances to the White House, emplaced bollards on the sidewalks around the White House, and installed the video and alarm systems located just inside the perimeter of the White House and the vice president's residence.

On the division's staff are experts in the detection of listening devices, weapons, and radioactive or other materials that could endanger those being protected. "Red teams" practice penetration to make "vulnerability assessments," briefcases and packages are X-rayed, and bomb squads are on call.

Dozens of weapons are detected every year at the White House gates, almost all of them carried by people who have state permits to do so. Unless they are among the very few who have District of Columbia permits, however, pistol packers are taken to local police headquarters where they suffer the embarrassment of arraignment (although the D.C. felony charge is usually reduced to a misdemeanor). Some people who are mentally ill walk off the street demanding to see the president, and about 100 each year are taken to the District of Columbia's St. Elizabeth's Hospital for observation.

The Secret Service has made an addition to its patrols of the White House perimeter: bicycles. In black combat gear, radio-equipped officers use twenty-four-gear mountain bikes to cruise President's Park and keep on the lookout for suspicious lurkers. At the gates, gamma-radiation detectors have been installed to supplement the regular magnetometers that screen the approximately 1 million people who come through the White House gates each year. An innovation that began during the years of the Bush administration has appeared on the security scene: suspicious packages left loose are scrutinized by big, four-wheeled, eight-foot-tall robots.

Handling Protesters

What is the Secret Service supposed to do when a group is demonstrating against the president when he is speaking before a large crowd? Does it create a "free speech" zone or designated area and segregate demonstrators there? Responding to that question during the appropriations subcommittee hearing in 2007, Director Sullivan answered: "It has never been our policy to have a free speech zone. What we will do is implement a security zone. And in that security zone, no one is allowed to come into that security zone, regardless if it's protesters or the general public."[11]

A public event, Sullivan emphasized, is just that: a public event. The Secret Service takes no directions from the White House as to who will or won't be part of a crowd at a public event; all the Secret Service wants to do is to try to ensure that there is no weapon or anything else close by that could hurt a protectee. If agents see threatening behavior, they talk with the person observed and make sure that the person does not move toward the protectee.

As for yellers and hecklers, the Secret Service agents keep an eye on them, but, absent threatening actions, it is up to the host committee to ask a heckler to leave or to seek local police help in handling the removal. The Secret Service does not assist in removals under those circumstances. During an interview with the author, James Mackin, the Secret Service deputy assistant director for public affairs, read aloud an excerpt from an official policy document:

> In the absence of any specific or observable actions that would indicate a demonstration may pose a threat to a Secret Service protectee, protective

facility, foreign mission or the public safety, demonstrators are to be treated as members of the general public and should not be segregated from the public. Secret Service personnel should not initiate any action to segregate demonstration activity from public areas; they should act only in cases when the Secret Service has information that a demonstration possesses a potential risk to a Secret Service protectee, protected facility, foreign mission, or to the general public safety. Should the Secret Service personnel initiate and/or participate in discussions with the demonstration group, or suggest that the group is segregated from the general public area, any meetings or contact with demonstration organizations should include local law enforcement authorities, because it is their jurisdiction.[12]

Nonetheless, incidents involving protesters and alleged Secret Service actions at presidential events inevitably make news, but witnesses and reporters who observe bouncers wearing earpieces often fail to distinguish between Service agents and local volunteers (see chapter 28 for additional discussion of demonstrators). For example, in September 2003 four activist groups sued the Secret Service, claiming, according to a news report, that

in more than a dozen public events nationwide in the past two years, the Secret Service has instructed local police to herd anti-Bush protesters into far-removed "protest zones." They charge that the Secret Service has kept protesters at bay before, but that the practice has increased markedly since Bush took office. . . . They filed the suit in Philadelphia to build upon a four-year-old lawsuit there in which a federal judge issued a restraining order against the Secret Service for keeping anti-government protesters at bay. . . .The judge that day issued a restraining order requiring the Secret Service to allow government critics to demonstrate peacefully as close as supporters.[13]

During a presidential address to the NAACP in Washington in July 2006, "people booed sharply when he [Bush] praised charter schools," according to another press report. "Two men were quickly hustled out of the hall by Secret Service agents for heckling Bush about the Iraq war."[14] In that case the witnesses and the press were in error.

National Security Special Events

In 2000 legislation was enacted codifying an earlier presidential decision directive and authorizing the Secret Service to participate in the "planning, coordination and implementation of security operations at special events of national significance."[15] By this is meant gatherings of people so huge and so densely packed (such as a full stadium) that, regardless of whether or not a Secret Service protectee is present, the assemblage in effect presents a terrorist target. The process is put into motion when a governor or a mayor looks ahead and makes a request that the secretary of homeland security designate the upcoming event as a "national special security event." After considering all the available public and classified information, the secretary makes the call to designate an upcoming event as being in that category.

Between 1998 and September 2007 there have been thirty-two events of this kind (twenty-six formally declared and six treated as such). They have included, for example, State of the Union addresses, Democratic and Republican national conventions, presidential inaugurals, the funerals of Presidents Reagan and Ford, Pope John Paul's visit, presidential debates, the Salt Lake City Winter Olympic Games, and Superbowl XXXVI. For these special events, the Secret Service takes the lead role among the cooperating federal, state, and local law enforcement agencies in a massive enterprise of advance planning and coordinated operations to protect the assemblage. Attacks and medical emergencies are simulated beforehand; extensive field exercises are conducted. This is a recent and truly enormous responsibility laid on the Secret Service.

Mail Screening

All mail and packages being sent to the White House are screened and tested by state-of-the art environmental screening and examination equipment, including specialized chemical, biological, and radiological alarms and sensors, laboratory testing and substance analysis screening systems, X-ray and explosive detection systems, security alarms, and camera systems required to ensure appropriate security. If, for instance, just one piece of mail was found to be contaminated, all the mail in the facility would have to be held until it was conclusively determined that the one piece was not toxic. After 9/11 the screening facility was moved to a temporary location away from town, but the Secret Service is recommending to Congress that that facility be moved closer to Washington by the spring of 2009 at a fiscal year 2008 cost of $26 million. The House Appropriations Committee raised questions about spending this much and has instructed the Secret Service and the Executive Office of the President to work out a joint plan for allocating mail-screening capabilities and reduced the cost to $16.2 million.

Electronic Crime

The Patriot Act of 2001 (Public Law 107-56) increased the Secret Service's role in investigating computer fraud and authorized the director to establish nationwide electronic crime task forces to assist law enforcement, the private sector, and academia in detecting and suppressing computer-based crime. The service has initiated its Electronic Crime Special Agent Program (ECSAP) in which special agents receive basic to advanced computer training and gain expertise in cyber-crime investigations. By the fall of 2007, 770 ECSAP agents were deployed to seventy field offices throughout the world. Why is this important? James Mackin, the service's deputy assistant director for public affairs, explained:

> Having agents trained to perform a forensic examination on a computer or network goes to the core of our investigative responsibilities in financial crimes. These skill sets are essential in the constantly evolving area of network intrusions and other electronic crimes. These same skill sets also have an important role in our protective responsibilities, since almost everything today is run by computers at some level—alarms, cameras, utilities—the ability to monitor and safeguard those systems becomes a priority.

Balancing Protection Operations against Investigative Responsibilities

Since 9/11, a problem for the Secret Service has been fully to discharge its presidential protective responsibilities without slackening its investigative duties—a balancing being made more difficult during 2008 because of the additional task of handling the protection of presidential candidates. In fiscal year 2008 the service requested a total of nearly $1.4 billion, about $123 million more than it had received in fiscal year 2007. The fisal year 2008 request for the presidential protective functions of the Secret Service (including the mail screening and the Rowley Training Center but not including the 2008 presidential candidate nominee protection) came to $837.6 million, an increase of $59.9 million over the previous year. The service said it planned to shift 250 people from investigations to protection to handle the need to protect presidential candidates during the 2008 campaign.

As the House Appropriations hearings began, subcommittee chairman David Price opened the questioning:

> Your protective mission performance is virtually perfect. We really are in awe of that. Your investigatory performance has dropped off, however, according to some measures. Estimated financial losses prevented by Secret Service investigations dropped off by 40 percent between 2005 and 2006, from 556 million to 316 million. Estimated counterfeit currency passed, per millions dollars of genuine currency, increased 40 percent over the last three years, from $58 in 2003 to $81 in 2006. . . . So some of these performance measures are on a downward trend. It does raise the question: Are we devoting enough attention and enough resources to investigations? . . . It seems that there is, very obviously, in this budget, a trade-off between protective and investigatory missions.[16]

In responding, Sullivan pointed to the unusual protective requirement that the year 2008 is laying on the Secret Service, with presidential primaries beginning as early as January. "What we have asked our people to do is prioritize," he said, later adding, "I still would like to work with you on our workforce rebalancing. I do think that that is the answer to a big part of this issue, that we flat out need more people."[17]

The committee voted to appropriate $820.1 for protective services, a reduction of only $17.5 million. But in its report, the committee said it continued "to have concerns about the ability of the Secret Service to manage its agents' and officers' overtime workload. The cost of the Secret Service payroll has increased so dramatically in recent years that budgets for replacing critical equipment, vehicles, and administrative systems have been eroded. Given the rapid evolution of threats, technologies and terrorist techniques, the Committee believes that delaying reinvestment in Secret Service assets is a false economy. . . . The demands of protective operations seem to require more creative and cost-effective solutions."[18]

Summing Up

In the end, the Secret Service must be an adaptable outfit—and always a professional one. If the president rides, the agents will be on horseback; if the vice president jogs, or enjoys super-powered speedboats, they will don sneakers or purchase 495-horsepower engines. They know they must never recount to one president the privileged confidences of a predecessor, nor can an agent ever do the president's bidding: "Please hold my coat for a second." "Can you find me some small bills for the collection plate?" Agent Larry Cockell recounted, "There was never an instance where I overruled the president, but I would find the way to make him see my point."[19] President Kennedy, at Hyannisport, once spotted the agent outside his door. "Why stand out there?" he queried. "Come on in and watch the ball game with us." The answer was no; from the professionals' viewpoint, even new presidents need training.

32 | The President's Commission on White House Fellowships

In 1957 John Gardner, then president of the Carnegie Corporation, had an idea: "If we could take some of the best of our young people and put them in direct contact with the daily functions of government. . . ." He put the suggestion in a memorandum at the time, but nothing happened until 1964 when Lyndon Johnson (who, under Franklin Roosevelt, had been the head of the New Deal's Texas National Youth Administration), was bewailing "the gulf between youth and government." Gardner sent his memorandum to Johnson, who seized upon it and issued Executive Order 11183 of October 3, 1964, creating the President's Commission on White House Fellowships and initiating the White House Fellows Program—an enterprise that is a continuing and highly prized part of the White House environment. The commission comes under the general oversight of the presidential personnel office.

The thirty-one member commission is appointed by the president; the members are to be "outstanding citizens from the fields of public affairs, education, the sciences, the professions, other fields of human endeavor, and from Government service." They serve at the president's pleasure. As of this writing, the chair of the commission is Julie Nixon Eisenhower. The commission annually sends out a call for applicants, who must be U.S. citizens who have finished their undergraduate education and who are working in their chosen professions. The commission seeks exceptionally talented men and women who are not in federal employment (except the armed services), who are near the beginning of their careers, and who also have distinguished themselves in community service. The application form includes requirements that the applicant state his or her "lifetime goals" and must draft a memorandum to the president that, in less than 500 words, makes and defends a specific policy proposal.

Some 800 typically apply. The Office of Personnel Management handles the initial flow of applications. Approximately 100 are selected to be interviewed by one of eight to ten regional selection panels, who in turn select thirty or so national finalists, who come to Washington to be interviewed in person by members of the commission. The commission selects between twelve and nineteen Fellows who are then assigned for a year as aides in the White House, to the vice president, in the Executive Office, or to cabinet secretaries; the receiving agencies pay their salaries; those who are assigned to the White House are put on departmental payrolls and detailed to the White House. Fellows serve for a year (with a possible ninety-day extension); each annual class starts on September 1.

The Fellows' year includes participating in an exceptionally illuminating educational program, including, once or twice a week, lectures and seminars by prominent leaders in and out of government. The president, vice president, the first lady, the spouse of the vice president, White House staff seniors, cabinet secretaries, and Supreme Court justices speak to the classes. President Bush's support for this program is so high that he usually meets at least twice with each class of Fellows, the seminars sometimes extending to almost two hours. The Fellows are also expected to attend class business meetings and are required to make a presentation to class colleagues about their lives before coming to Washington. A further requirement is that each Fellow must participate in local community service in the Washington area.

The educational program for the Fellows also includes up to $8,000 worth of "policy study" travel, such as two four- or five-day domestic trips, one two-week international trip, one to three "military policy" study trips, and one to four one-day policy trips. The Fellows on the international trips often go as members of a U.S. delegation. The Fellows are charged an annual set amount to defray the costs of the food at their many luncheons. A White House Fellows Endowment helps meet other costs of the Washington year.

A class is typically highly diverse—the variety of their life experiences contributing to their education. The class of 2007–08, for instance, included a state trooper and two women fighter pilots.

The commission staff numbers six, is located at 712 Jackson Place, is headed by a director (currently Janet S. Eissenstat), and is funded by the Office of Personnel Management. In October 2005 the White House Fellows celebrated the fortieth anniversary of this program, which began with the class of 1965–66. The commission staff keeps in touch with every one of the more than 600 alumni, including luminaries such as Colin Powell, Tim Wirth, and Sam Brownback.

In meeting with the 2005-06 class, President Bush explained what he believes are the principal goals of the White House Fellowship program:

> First to show people how Government works, so as to inspire people to become involved in Government . . . to recruit people to participate in Government—at any level, whether it be in the Federal Government or the school board. . . . Secondly . . . to teach somebody how to make decisions and how to manage organizations. If a White House Fellow hangs around

the White House, he'll see decisionmaking. . . . And in order to lead you've got to set clear goals that everybody can understand and not be afraid to hold people account[able] as to whether those goals have been met. . . . And thirdly, I would hope the White House Fellowship program takes really smart, bright, capable people and makes them understand that there's always a new horizon, that one should never be complacent if you've been given a lot of God-given talents, that you've got to keep striving for the best.[1]

The words of the application brochure sum up the mission of the White House Fellows program:

It is essential to the healthy functioning of our system that we have in the nongovernmental sector a generous supply of leaders who have an understanding—gained at first hand—of the problems of national government. In a day when the individual feels increasingly remote from the centers of power and decision, such leaders can help their fellow citizens comprehend the process by which the Nation is governed.

*The Physical White House
and Its Environment*

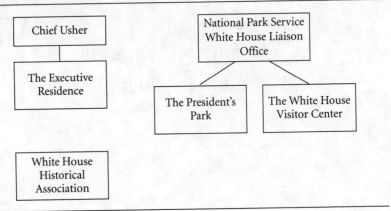

33 | *The Executive Residence*

This book has been describing the White House as an *institution,* the locus of the presidency at the top of the executive branch. As every tourist knows, of course, the White House is also a building, a *home* where the president lives. To clarify the conceptual difference between institution and home, the building is properly identified as the Executive Residence. As a famous building, it has problems: it may be famous for too much. Many competing uses strain its facilities and pressure its staff.

As a Physical Facility

The Residence is a home for president and spouse, children, grandparents, grandchildren, guests and pets (once including a pony). It is also a museum of American history, culture, and presidential furnishings (and has been given accreditation as such by the American Association of Museums); a display center for paintings and furniture; a magnet for tourists; and a secure redoubt. The Residence has seen service as a wartime map and command center, a wedding chapel, a funeral parlor, a nursery, and a church. Today it is at once a backdrop for television productions, a press-conference auditorium, a concert hall, and a banquet center. The White House building serves as a flower stall, overnight hotel, performing arts center, physical fitness emporium, Easter-egg rolling yard, movie theater, heliport, parade ground, carpentry shop, art gallery, library, clinic, office building, conference center, and security checkpoint. (Some reports allege that it is a missile base as well, though officials there deny it.) President Ford added an outdoor swimming pool (with donated funds), Lyndon and Lady Bird Johnson added a children's garden, the Clintons added a hot tub (from donated contributions) and installed a putting green of natural turf and a jogging track.

One of the White House rooms still redolent with not-so-long-ago history is the Map Room on the ground floor of the Residence. In mid-December 1941 Winston Churchill was a visitor in the White House. He brought with him—and set up—his own portable map room in a White House bedroom opposite the Queen's Bedroom on the second floor. As George Elsey recounts, "Roosevelt was a daily visitor to the prime minister's sophisticated presentation of military fronts and vivid displays of allied and enemy naval fleets. Enchanted, Roosevelt told [naval aide Captain John] Beardall, after Churchill's departure: 'Fix up a room like Churchill's.'"[1]

He did, enlisting Lieutenant Robert Montgomery and Ensign George Elsey from the Office of Naval Intelligence. They commandeered the so-called Trophy Room in the Residence.

Montgomery had the paneled walls covered with soft wallboard for their protection and so that the maps could be readily changed. Desks and file cabinets were placed in an island in the center of the room so that the president, in his wheelchair, could study the maps at close range. The maps of battle areas were covered with clear plastic. Grease pencil markings showed the dispositions of enemy and allied troops. Charts of the oceans were studded with colored pins—blue for U. S. ships, orange for Japanese, red for British, black for German, gray for Italian. The pins were of different sizes and shapes to denote the category—battleship, cruiser, destroyer, submarine, or special troop ships such as the *Queen Mary* and the *Queen Elizabeth*. Pins of capital ships bore their names—as did a ship of whatever size on which a member of the Roosevelt family was embarked.

Elsey further observed that "the most important papers" he would be handling "were the exchanges between the president and Prime Minister Winston Churchill, with those between Roosevelt and Stalin or Chiang Kai-shek not far behind. . . . The president doesn't want any place in Washington except the Map Room to have a complete file of these messages."

When the Map Room was closed after the war, Elsey saved the last map that had been posted in April 1945. He intended to give it to Roosevelt, but the latter's death that same month made that impossible. He presented that map to First Lady Hillary Clinton in June 1994, and it hangs, again, in the Map Room today.[2]

The Residence is white—and now stays white longer—because of some special research instigated by the chief usher and undertaken by the National Park Service and by what was then the National Bureau of Standards, in collaboration with the Duron Company, to develop a paint that adheres to sandstone. Beginning in 1986 the chief usher and his colleagues started a comprehensive maintenance project that involved stripping twenty-nine identifiable layers of paint, down to the original sandstone. This in turn revealed cracks and irregularities in the stone that had to be patched or in some cases replaced. Thanks to the new type of paint, the house now needs to be repainted only once every eight years instead of the traditional four years. Congress has provided the funds to extend this maintenance program to the East and West Wings as well. An evaluation is being made to determine whether there should be a repainting before the 2009 inaugural.

Adding to the physical beauty of the Residence are the trees that, following tradition, presidents commission to be planted on the grounds. President and Mrs. George W. Bush have brought in a cutleaf silver maple, a little leaf linden, an American chestnut, and several American elms.

When asked to look ahead at the priority physical needs for the Residence, recently retired chief usher Gary Walters listed a new loading dock, where trucks making deliveries can be screened before they reach the Residence. (Such a facility is included in the comprehensive design plan for the White House and the President's Park, discussed in chapter 34.)

As an Operating Entity

Can the Residence meet all the demands placed on it?

Its staff do their damnedest.

The chief usher (until recently a thirty-seven-year veteran of White House service), with an immediate office staff of seven, is the manager of the Executive Residence. The total Residence staff numbers ninety-five men and women. While all those who work there serve at the pleasure of the president, they are proud of their tradition of being true professionals—and they are expected to continue serving from administration to administration. There have been only six chief ushers since 1891; the average length of service is twenty years; executive grounds superintendent Irv Williams has served for over fifty years.

No staff now lives in the Residence, nor are the employees there responsible for any of the president's out-of-town residences. The first family, of course, has overnight guests at the Residence, but visiting chiefs of state usually stay across the street, at Blair House, the official guest facility for international leaders that is managed and operated by the Protocol Office of the Department of State.

Close to the entrance hall, the chief usher's mini-office is replete with noiseless reminders of both the present and the past. A digital locator box flashes the whereabouts of each member of the first family; computer terminals blink out the details of the fine arts collections, menus, supplies, and budget. On the wall above the monitors hangs a piece of charred wood from the British-set fire of 1814.

In a cement-floored workroom crammed with buckets and buckets of flowers, a florist and her staff of three, plus eleven occasional workers, make up samples of arrangements for the first lady to inspect, then assemble stunning floral centerpieces for every variety of Residence event. All cut flowers are purchased directly from growers or wholesalers; many are flown in from special suppliers across the country. At Christmastime, up to ninety volunteers come in to help arrange floral displays and decorate the Residence.

(While on the subject of flowers, readers will enjoy a story told by Letitia Baldrige, chief of staff to First Lady Jacqueline Kennedy, at a symposium in November 2002 celebrating the 100th anniversary of the building of the West Wing. The indoor White House swimming pool had been installed in Franklin Roosevelt's time. Arrangements were made by First Lady Jacqueline Kennedy for the famous French muralist Bernard Lamont to come down from New York to paint frescoes on the walls and ceiling of the pool room. The work took three months. Lamont brought his own lunch each day, almost always consisting of the worst-smelling cheese, the worst-smelling *choucrout* sausages, pickles, and a bottle of wine. Where did he stash it until lunchtime? In the florist shop's refrigerator. At a state dinner one evening, huge bunches of flowers were brought up to the reception rooms—and the White House suddenly smelled awful. Jackie was horrified; aides and butlers were dispatched to search everywhere to find the cause. Finally Lamont was seen putting his lunch in the refrigerator, and, also, it was learned that cool flowers pick up odors and, when warm, release them.)

When a reception is given, the social secretary and the chief usher, in consultation with the White House counsel, determine ahead of time how the financial arrangements are to be handled. A state dinner for a foreign president is financed by the Department of State. Some events are hosted by the first family but sponsored—and reimbursed—by prominent outside organizations (interest and penalties must be charged for late payment). A third category—political receptions—must be paid for through an advance deposit from the sponsoring party's national committee. (It was in 1998 that Congress, irritated at the practice of very late reimbursements, imposed the advance-payment requirement and penalties for arrears.) At that time Appropriations Committee members put pressure on the chief usher to divulge information about White House parties and the kinds of guests that were being invited.

> They asked me to come up and I went up and talked both formally and informally with members of different committees, including Congressman [Steny] Hoyer and others on the Hill—in order to reach an understanding of the way we operate here, and also to explain the privacy issues that affect the first family. If they had started putting me in front of a desk and asking me personal questions about the family, that would be unfair to the family; there had to be some measure of privacy.[3]

Following strong White House tradition, neither the chief usher nor anyone on the Residence staff testifies before Congress; it is the director of the Office of Administration who is responsible for presenting and defending the budget of the White House Office (chapter 2). Congressional leaders and staff are welcome at the Residence, however, to see for themselves the successful results of their cooperativeness in annually providing the funds for the restoration program. The total fiscal year 2008 budget request for the Residence was $12.8 million, plus an additional $1.6 million for repair and restoration.

The Residence's kitchens are in the hands of world-class chefs, who prepare meals in accord with the first family's preferences for types and styles of menus. A state dinner or other major affair requires bringing in perhaps fifty contract butlers and other part-time helpers to serve the State Dining Room's thirteen tables (the thirteenth table is called Number 14). The Bush family put a stop to the Clinton practice of having extra-large, sit-down dinners—with as many as 1,370 invitees—under enormous tents on the South Lawn. The latest china to be acquired is the Clinton china, which arrived only in 2000; it is pale yellow and is the only china service that carries the image of the White House on it.

Some twenty work-years of overtime is built into the Executive Residence's $14.4 million budget for fiscal year 2008, but many thousands of hours beyond that are gifts to the United States from a staff whose dedication is legendary. "When I hired them," commented one former supervisor, "I said, 'Don't plan on celebrating any anniversaries or birthdays with your family.'" They have no job descriptions, the unpredictable is routine. Are the cut rosebuds not sufficiently unfolded? Some warm whiffs from a hair dryer will get them ready for the party. Does orange pollen from the lilies stain white uniforms? Fetch towels and shake out each bloom before the guests arrive.

There is a chief calligrapher and three assistant calligraphers on the White House staff; they reach out to the Washington Society of Calligraphers for extra help when a big reception impends. Sometimes a friendly competition ensues about what text goes on the menu cards: is there room on one small card for all the desirable data about the courses at dinner, the wines being offered?

The chief usher holds a weekly what-is-going-to-be-happening-this-week meeting among all the Residence staff units to minimize surprises and ensure that everyone is working from the same event calendar. In addition to the meeting, a within-the-mansion-only computer system keeps each segment of the Residence team posted on every event and on every last-minute change that might occur.

"The growing fringe of precedent" is everywhere in the White House, and the old mansion almost trembles under its new uses. The East Room floor, new in 1950, had been nearly worn through by thirty-seven million tourists by the time it was relaid in 1978; it was relaid again in the late 1990s. During a recent musicale, the chief usher counted twenty-seven news teams with minicams. If a presidential press conference is to be held in the East Room, the technical crews jam the stately ballroom with mikes and lights; after the thousands of Easter egg-rollers depart, the South Lawn needs restoration; helicopter blades whoosh the petals off the spring flowers.

Can the new presidency preserve the old graciousness? The loyalties of the Residence staff run in two directions: to serve the current master and mistress of the White House, and at the same time to hold in trust a revered place that belongs to all the American generations.

The Curator

Not only is the Residence the people's property, but most of its furnishings are as well. For nearly 100 years (from 1808 to 1902), outgoing presidents or their families frequently auctioned off their White House china and furniture, or gave them away, with the result that very few pieces of original White House furnishings are left. That practice finally ceased, and in 1961 a statute was enacted that guaranteed the preservation of White House furnishings. Today, once any president declares a White House article to be "of historic or artistic interest," it becomes forever "inalienable" and may be used, displayed, or stored but never sold. Every June, the law requires the National Park Service to undertake "a complete inventory" of all "plate, furniture and public property" in the White House. To perform this duty, Lyndon Johnson, in 1964, established a new position on the chief usher's staff: the White House curator.

There have been seven curators since the post was established. In years past the curator was on the prowl for some of the original paintings and pieces of furniture that had been missing. The curator still accepts an unusual item fitting that category, but the past effort was so successful that the priority now is to broaden the White House art collection and to encourage generous donors to assist in acquiring outstanding paintings of the American West. The curator helps set the standards for accepting gifts that are offered (see box for list of recent acquisitions). "The principal public rooms on the ground and first floors," says the statute, are of "museum character." The curator and his staff of three are there to help them remain so.

The Committee for the Preservation of the White House

In the same executive order that created the position of White House curator, President Johnson established the Committee for the Preservation of the White House under the chairmanship of the director of the National Park Service. The committee's seventeen members are distinguished citizens appointed by the president and include the chief usher, the curator, the secretary of the Smithsonian Institution, and the director of the National Gallery of Art (who also serves as chairman of the U.S. Commission of Fine Arts). Among other duties, the committee advises the president and the director of the National Park Service about what items "shall be used or displayed" at the White House. The first lady is honorary chair of the committee and takes part in its semiannual meetings.

The Family Theater

Like most Americans, presidents enjoy relaxing at the movies, but absent a presidential box, a trip to the local cinema means unwanted disruption. At the

Important Acquisitions 1998–2006

Year acquired	Object	Artist/Maker/Owner
1998	Sinumbra lamps, c. 1820	
1998	Painting: *Captain Richard Shaw,* c. 1815 British soldier credited with setting the White House on fire	Unidentified artist
1998	Papers, c. 1949–52	Charles T. Haight
1999	Pier table, c. 1805–10	Charles-Honoré Lannuier
1999	Five dinner plates, 1778	Royal Porcelain Manufactory, Sèvres Belonging to John Adams
1999	Six soup plates, 1780, 1782	Royal Porcelain Manufactory, Sèvres Belonging to John Adams
1999	Two condiment stands, 1780, 1782	Royal Porcelain Manufactory, Sèvres Belonging to John Adams
1999	Papers, 1900–23	Abby Gunn Baker
1999	Painting: *Fruit in a Chinese Export Basket,* 1822	James Peale
2000	Papers, 1961–63	John F. Kennedy
2000	Desk and bookcase, c. 1830	
2000	Vase, c. 1890	George Washington
2000	Vase, c. 1890	John Adams
2000	Painting: The White House	John Ross Key
2000	Clinton State Service, China Room	
2000	Painting: *The President's House* c. 1814 Shows house after burning	George Munger
2000	Painting: *William Jefferson Clinton (1946–),* 2001	Simmie Knox
2000	Photograph: The Executive Mansion, c. 1860–61	Mathew B. Brady
2002	Painting: *Grover Cleveland*	Victor Dubreuil
2003	Sofa, c. 1810 Belonging to John Adams	James Monroe
2003	Painting: *Three Children,* 1919	George Bellows
2003	Photograph: Red Room, c. 1869–77	Matthew B. Brady
2004	Painting: *Hillary Rodham Clinton (1947–),* 2003	Simmie Knox
2004	Sofa, c. 1850, ground floor hall (pair)	John Henry Belter
2004	Sofa, c. 1850, Lincoln Bedroom	John Henry Belter
2005	Painting: Jupiter, 1994	Andrew Newell Wyeth
2005	Painting: *Asgaard Cornfield (Corn, Oats, Gray Day),* c. 1945–50	Rockwell Kent
2005	Painting: *Barbara Pierce Bush (Mrs. George H. W. Bush) (1925–),* 2005	Charles A. Fagan
2005	Painting: *Tinicum Hillside,* 1931	Daniel Garber
2005	Punch Bowl, 1874, Marion Silver	Tiffany & Co.
2005	Certificate, 1828	John Quincy Adams
2005	Seven plates, 1870 From President Grant's State Service	Haviland & Co.
2006	Painting: *Old Faithful*	Albert Bierstadt
2006	Side Chair, c. 1830	James Monroe

Based on a list supplied to the author by outgoing chief usher Gary Walters during an interview, September 21, 2006.

time of the construction of the East Wing in 1942, the Family Theater was included. When a union operator did not show up one night during the Roosevelt administration, a naval aide commandeered a substitute from the Navy and thus started the practice of having a White House projectionist on call; one aide served for thirty-three years in that role. Currently one of the White House electricians doubles as a projectionist.

The first family makes requests for films from the Motion Picture Association of America; the movies are shown in the White House or at Camp David. President Carter may hold the record for nights at the movies; he viewed 564 showings during his term.

Looking at the Presidency of 2009

Former Chief Usher Gary Walters commented firmly,

> I wouldn't venture to try to give the president advice. As far as what we do here in this House: we know that on January 20, 2009, a new president is going to walk through the door. Our responsibility here is to adjust to that family, and to make this House a home. They will be coming here not knowing what to expect. They will be presented with a staff that has worked here for a lot of years. It is our responsibility to make *them* feel at home . . . to adapt to the new president and to the new first lady, not the other way around. There is not a "White House way" that they adapt to; it's that they have a way that *we* adapt to.

The White House, then, is not empty at the inaugural noon. Through its expectant halls, in its foyers and kitchens, at its switchboards and guard posts, men and women are on duty who will serve tomorrow as they served yesterday. Some have walked taller in the mornings of two, three, or four decades—skilled, committed, and proud—to support the office that they honor and the House that they revere. They will continue to be unknown to their fellow Americans and some of them even to their president, who will eventually depart, as they again remain. Their respectful loyalty is always transferred to each new chief executive, and president after president is rewarded by their service.

Tours of the Executive Residence: The White House Visitors Office

The Executive Residence at the White House is owned by the American people; thousands of them come to Washington and expect to tour the famous mansion. It is almost the only residence of a head of state in the world that is open to public visitation. Before 9/11 the sole requirement for a tour (available 10 a.m. to 12 noon Tuesdays through Saturdays) was to be in line at the White House Visitor Center (chapter 34) early enough to secure a ticket for that day and to pass a magnetometer screening. No fee; no security check. In peak spring and summer months, the available tickets for each day would be exhausted by eight o'clock in the morning; in a typical year 1 million to 1.5 million visitors would have had this very desirable and special opportunity.

Not surprisingly 9/11 changed everything for White House visitation. A stringent reevaluation was undertaken and in September of 2003, after some test runs with school and military groups, an altered system was instituted. Now a member of the public desiring to tour the Executive Residence must first contact his or her senator or representative and request a specific date and time for a tour. Each congressional office now has a staffer who is designated as a tour director. Each congressional tour director forwards the requests to the White House Visitors Office, which is a unit of the White House staff.

The incoming request may be submitted as early as six months in advance. The Visitors Office lays out the tour schedules a month in advance: one tour every half-hour between 7:30 a.m. and 12:30 p.m. Tuesdays through Saturdays, with a practical limit of 2,200 visitors a day.

With schedules laid out, the Visitors Office then can ascertain how many names will fit on each day's series of tours, does its best to match the allocation with the date and time requested, and sends interim acceptances to the respective congressional tour directors. The tour directors send the provisional acceptances to the constituents making the requests, but with the instruction immediately to send in to these same congressional offices the birth dates and social security numbers of each prospective visitor. No later than five days before the visit, this personal data is transmitted to the White House Visitors Office. An innovation was effected in August of 2006: these transmissions are now all on-line.

The Visitors Office forwards the personal data to the Secret Service for the usual background checks. Only when the names receive final clearance is a firm acceptance given to the tour directors and through them to the constituents. If the tours are full (or if the security information is adverse), it is the congressional office, not the White House, that bears the task of notifying the constituent of the denial, but of course the vast number of notifications are the good news of acceptance.

With each acceptance, however, comes what may be an unwelcome warning: no purses, bags, cameras, or other packages are permitted in the White House (wallets, cell phones, and umbrellas excepted), nor is there any storage facility at the White House to park them; they have to be disposed of before tourists approach the White House. This warning has to be communicated to every visitor well ahead of time, and it is the responsibility of each of those 535 congressional tour directors to do so. Failures in communication lead to embarrassment; some unlucky member of the group must stay behind and watch all the bags while others go on the tour.

Members of the White House staff and the White House liaison officers in the respective cabinet departments may send in requests for groups of visitors—

with the same procedures being followed. The tours are self-guided, but members of the Uniformed Division of the Secret Service, who are specially trained in the history of the Residence, are on duty in each room and can answer questions about the furnishings and art work in each place.

The Visitors Office fends off any pressures to favor or ration tour acceptances in the interests of congressional partisanship or vote-enhancing. Former Visitors Office director Sara Armstrong was emphatic: "The tours are for the public and we have to be fair to the public. If they contact a congressional office, we don't know with what party they are affiliated and that's not part of the decision. We owe it to the American public to be fair and not to engage in conferring special favors. If we start doing that, we would be breaking our own rules."[4]

In a typical post-9/11 year, the Visitors Office handles 1,000 requests a week in its spring and summer busy season. The annual visitation from this first category of tours is approximately 425,000 participants.

A second category of White House visitation is the Garden Tours of the outdoor White House grounds. These tours are held on Saturdays, plus one full weekend in April, perhaps one in the summertime, and another full weekend in October. They are free and open to the general public, are ticketed on a first-come, first-served basis, and beyond the routine magnetometer screening, do not require advance background checks, since the participants do not come inside the Residence. Visitors may stroll through the Rose Garden, the Jacqueline Kennedy Garden, and the Children's Garden, which features cemented handprints of presidents' grandchildren. Garden tours are a joint enterprise between the White House Visitors Office and the National Park Service. Staff from the former act as greeters at the gate, pass out information brochures, and arrange for the participation of the military bands, who serenade the visitors from the south balcony; the latter office supplies rangers and ground crews and answers questions from the delighted participants.

"They can walk around, walk up the drive and be that close to the mansion, take their picture in front of it—you can just feel the enthusiasm," remarked Armstrong. "This is particularly helpful to foreign visitors who perhaps have only come to Washington for that weekend and are not able to make a reservation ahead of time—it is a great opportunity for anybody who is here that weekend." In 2006 garden tours accounted for about 76,000 visitors.

The third category of visitorship is the Holiday Open House Tours at Christmas. These are by invitation only—members of Congress, the cabinet, the party leadership, the White House staff; the total number of invitees is some 40,000. During these tours, musical groups from all over the country perform. During the year, dozens of them apply to be selected; they accompany their applications with videos or discs that display their talents. Volunteers or members of the Visitors Office staff listen to the samples and decide which of them will be invited to play.

A very special visitation event comes once a year: the Easter Egg Roll. In 2006, 14,000 kids and their parents were welcomed onto the White House South Lawn; in other years the group has numbered 25,000. Some lucky White House staff member will have donned a rabbit's costume.

Finally there is the category of state arrival ceremonies, where White House staff and several thousand other supporters are invited to gather on the South Lawn to witness the president as he greets the arrival of a foreign head of state. Here the Military District of Washington provides rows of troops to be reviewed, herald trumpets to sound off from the south balcony, military bands to perform, and artillery to fire the proper number of (blank) salutes from the Ellipse.

Making all the arrangements for these cascades of visitors—totaling near 600,000 annually —is the modest-sized staff of the White House Visitors Office. The director and one staff assistant are White House employees; helping them are three detailees from the National Park Service, an intern, and a handful of volunteers. If a big event such as the Easter Egg Roll is in prospect, hundreds of volunteers may be called in to help out with the many youngsters.

Six hundred thousand visitors with no slip-ups—well, except for that Christmastime afternoon when one of the huge, superbly lit and decorated Christmas trees in the East Room broke in half, scattering lights and Christmas baubles in every direction. Quick reaction: screen off the part of the East Room, hoist the broken tree up and out while the tourists gawked, redecorate it in time for an evening holiday reception. Motto around the White House: always be prepared for the unexpected.

34 | The President's Park and the White House Visitor Center

The White House—the Executive Residence and its accompanying staff offices—are of course the eighteen-acre headquarters of the presidency; is not their reason for being, therefore, to help ensure effective top-level administration by the chief executive? Yes, *but* the White House is much more than that. It happens to be the principal structure on the eighty-two-acre President's Park, which also includes Lafayette Park, the Ellipse, the Eisenhower Executive Office Building and grounds, the Treasury Building and grounds, Sherman Park, the First Division Monument Park, and a slice of the Commerce Department building. And as a national park, *its* reason for being, while complementary, is different: its duty is on the one hand to make those places and spaces as completely as possible available to the public (recognizing that some roads or areas may be temporarily roped off for security reasons) and on the other hand to preserve the park's architecture, landscaping, fountains, statuary, and monuments, *"unimpaired for future generations."* Thus, the President's Park encompasses a duality of objectives: within the closed eighteen presidential acres, the goal is absolute effectiveness, security, and privacy for the first family, while, simultaneously, for the other sixty-four surrounding acres—heavily used public areas adjacent to the White House—the park's goal is openness for constant public use (including protest demonstrations) and meticulous preservation of those surroundings for the long future.

The surroundings are unique. The President's Park is more than 200 years old and represents more than two centuries of historic buildings, gateways, landscaping, fountains, sculptures, and monuments. In it are thirty-four separate memorials, forty-one commemorative trees planted by various presidents beginning with Andrew Jackson, a boxwood hedge planted by President Truman, a 1992 time-capsule commemorating the 200th anniversary of the laying of the White House cornerstone, a Children's Garden with cement handprints of several presidential grandchildren, a swimming pool, tennis court, basketball hoop, putting green, running track, and even the remains of a carved, stone trough used in President Jackson's time to cool milk.

Like other national parks, the President's Park is an element in the National Park System and while it is managed by the National Park Service, twelve federal agencies share jurisdictional responsibilities over these eighty-two acres: the Executive Office of the President; the Executive Residence at the White House; the White House Military Office; the U.S. Department of the Treasury; the U.S. Department of Homeland Security; the U.S. Secret Service; the General Services Administration; the National Park Service, the District of Columbia, the Commission on Fine Arts; the National Capital Planning Commission; and the Advisory Council on Historic Preservation.

The President's Park is managed by the director of the ninety-three-person National Park Service White House Liaison Office, located in the Hains Point area. The director reports to the director of the National Park Service through the national capital regional director. The White House Liaison Office is responsible for:

—Providing architectural and design services for the Executive Residence

—Maintaining the grounds inside the White House fence

—Maintaining the grounds of the President's Park outside the White House fence

—Operating the White House museum storage facility (a separate building in College Park, Maryland). This facility, which meets museum standards for storage, houses spare furnishings from the White House collection.

—Performing repair and stabilization work on the collection

—Operating a separate nursery and greenhouse for extra shrubs and plants and bringing them in for special events on the White House grounds

—Operating the White House Visitor Center

The White House Visitor Center

Like other national parks, the President's Park includes a central facility for public information and orientation. It is the White House Visitor Center, opened in 1995 and located in the magnificently renovated Malcolm Baldrige Great Hall of the Department of Commerce (it was once the Search Room of the U.S. Patent Office, where 3 million patents were catalogued). Originally, a principal reason for the Visitor Center was to create a space, out of the weather, where large numbers of people could gather and stand in line to get tickets to White House tours while also viewing some exhibits that would introduce them to what they were going to see in the Residence. 9/11 changed that rationale abruptly. Immediately after 9/11, White House tours were canceled; they were later reinstituted with the somewhat restrictive requirement that tours are to be available only by making advance reservations through the office of one's senator or representative (chapter 33). Many hundreds do this, but the casual, walk-in tourist to Washington is limited to looking through the White House fence from Pennsylvania Avenue and coming to the Visitor Center. The Visitor Center thus takes on an altered purpose; it is no longer an introduction to a tour of the Residence but an enhancement of what the tourist may have studied or read about it. No tickets are needed; the walk-in center is free. In a typical year, 620,000 visitors come through the center; a summer's day brings 3,000.

The center and its staff of National Park Service rangers and helpers (aided by some forty-five Park Service volunteers) responded to this new purpose by organizing educational programs and participatory activities in this massive Great Hall that come as close as possible to creating a "White House experience," not only meeting the needs of visitors from any part of the world and of all ages but exciting their curiosity about the American presidency—its past and its present.

Around the edges of this Great Hall are a series of both permanent and changeable exhibits about every aspect of life in the White House: presidents, first ladies, the design and construction of the Residence, gifts to the president of furnishings and china, White House horses, White House carriages, and pictures of some of the workers in the Residence who have served there for thirty or more years (the record is one who now has been there for fifty-five years). Two television screens continuously play a film about White House history, and there are seating areas for a great variety of lectures and presentations; the Presidential Seal is frequently on exhibit. The interests and needs of families are a high priority at the center. A recent and novel addition is a children's table where tots can color in outlines of White House objects and read "A Funny White House Pet Story."

Even more novel for young people are the special events the staff has designed for three specific days in the year. On Presidents' Day (February 22) a typical young visitor can take the oath of office, be president for a day, go behind a "bully pulpit" rostrum, face an audience, read (with ranger help if needed) a paragraph from a history-making speech of a president—and hear his or her voice amplified to fill the entire hall. A volunteer dressed as Abraham Lincoln answers questions about his years in office and how he saved the Union, while Dolley Madison invites youngsters to sit at her table and learn about being a White House hostess. On July 4th young visitors wear tricorn hats, are photographed against a Declaration of Independence, and are members of the Continental Congress casting a vote declaring independence. On Constitution Day (September 16) youngsters meet George Washington, and wearing tricorn hats, act as members of the 1787 Constitutional Convention voting on the adoption of the Constitution. At any time of year a young person can pick up or ask online to receive a special booklet about the significance of the White House and its neighborhood, read it, "walk in the footsteps of the 43 presidents," complete the booklet, send it in, and become a President's Park junior ranger.

Schools bring students by the busload and park rangers themselves visit schools, give slide lectures and readings. Programs at the center are tailored for every age from kindergarten through high school; nine categories of adult guided tours are given to different areas of the President's Park. The White House Historical Association operates a bookstore at the center where the association's comprehensive sets of publications and other products are sold.

Unscheduled events add to the very visible excitement that the center's staff sees, especially among its younger visitors: a passing presidential motorcade, a helicopter landing or taking off from the White House lawn next door, a drop-by from the White House pastry chef with a tray full of samples of his artistry. The first lady makes unannounced visits, as when she came by in April 2007 to dedicate the center's display of fifty-one elaborately hand-decorated Fabergé-style Easter eggs, one from each state and the District of Columbia.

While the Visitor Center's attractions are impressive, plans are under consideration for future development that will go even further to create a White House "experience" for visitors who cannot tour the actual White House. Lectures and photographs of the Red Room, the Green Room, or the Lincoln Bedroom could be added to the current exhibits; some of the furnishings in the White House, and samples of its artwork, could be loaned to the center; there may be models constructed of the exterior and of the interior rooms of the White House itself.

Massive visitation numbers put a strain on the sod and pathways of the President's Park, especially on the Ellipse, which had been comparatively neglected since 1947. The National Park Service recently completed refurbishing the famous circle with new sod, new irrigation systems, refinished sidewalks, lampposts, signs, and benches.

The men and women who manage the President's Park work full of the same esteem, commitment, and mission for conservation that they dedicate to all the national parks: it is a precious national resource, its grounds echo with history, its structures must be maintained and preserved with immense care, while its spaces traditionally welcome intense public use, including sometimes fervid gatherings of citizens who come with signs and shouts. Accomplishing these multiple goals is a challenging administrative task for the ninety-three members of the extended White House staff family. The fiscal year 2008 budget request for the National Park Service White House Liaison Office for the President's Park was $8.7 million dollars.

A Comprehensive Design Plan for the White House and President's Park

During the 1980s the leaders of the National Park Service became increasingly concerned about the mounting pressures on the resources of the President's Park. Its facilities were inadequate for holding official meetings in the White

House complex, for deliveries to and storage at the Residence, for accommodating increased traffic, for meeting parking needs, for managing state visits and forming up motorcades, for handling protests and demonstrations where citizens assemble to exercise their constitutionally guaranteed right to "peaceably assemble, and to petition the Government for redress of grievances," and for informing visitors to Washington curious to learn about the presidency and its physical and institutional environment. In a typical year the public use areas of the President's Park are the site of 55 special events and 150 First Amendment demonstrations. A 1997 public use survey described typical recurring events, including frequent First Amendment demonstrations (3,000 people each), a *Roe v. Wade* protest (125,000), the once-every-four-years Inaugural Parade (up to 500,000), six to ten state arrivals a year (4,000 each), the annual Easter Egg Roll (25,000), Christmas candlelight tours (33,000), the Christmas Pageant of Peace (270,000), and four-times-a-year parades along Constitution Avenue (up to 100,000 each).

Regulations have been instituted to put some reasonable limits on public use. Demonstrations are allowed only on the Ellipse, in Lafayette Park (a 3,000-person limit) and on the White House sidewalk on the south side of Pennsylvania Avenue (a 750-person limit). Signs not handheld may be displayed so long as they are attended at all times. Nonetheless, pressures on facilities and resources have been mounting. How were these resource issues to be met?

In 1989 the National Park Service put together the beginnings of a comprehensive plan and presented it to the twelve agencies with jurisdiction. In 1992 Congress appropriated money to finance an interagency planning process, and an executive committee worked for seven years, producing a final two-volume document approved by the director of the National Park Service on March 29, 2000, by the Commission on Fine Arts on April 19, 2000, and by the National Capital Planning Commission on May 4, 2000. The plan concluded: "The effect of all these demands is that today many of the resources of the White House and President's Park are at their limits."

The objective of the plan, however, was not to start massive action immediately (although it did point out that the 18-inch steam pipes running under the Ellipse at 400 degrees Fahrenheit under a pressure of 250 pounds per square inch, installed in the early 1970s, had a life expectancy of fifteen to twenty years.) The plan had a threefold purpose: to identify the needs and functions that the site would have to accommodate over the next twenty years; to determine how best to protect the important resources on the site including the White House; and to solve the logistical and management problems that had developed over the years.

The comprehensive plan is a 123-page document, with 74 pages of appendixes, that describes the setting of the President's Park and its historical development, portrays the existing facilities and resources of the Park, and analyzes the serious pressures arising from the intensity and multiplicity of the uses of those facilities and resources. The document then sets forth a comprehensive—and dramatic plan of remediation that preserves existing buildings and landscapes by proposing extensive underground development. The principal recommendations include:

—Constructing a parking garage under the Ellipse and eliminating almost all street parking and all street vending.

—Constructing a visitor-arrival facility and a meeting and conference center underneath West Executive Avenue.

—Constructing a presidential briefing room and media facility underneath the West Wing Drive.

—Constructing an area for diplomatic and business parking and for forming motorcades underneath the eastern half of the now-closed Pennsylvania Avenue. Just east of it an additional underground area would be constructed for general storage of White House supplies. (The plan's originators add a note here: "A long-term design for Pennsylvania Avenue, as well as Lafayette Park, will be considered in a separate planning document.")

—Just north of the White House, constructing one underground pedestrian corridor and one parallel delivery corridor connecting the Eisenhower Executive Office Building on the west with the Treasury Building on the east, with the delivery corridor branching to connect to upgraded loading docks at the New Executive Office Building. These docks and corridors would handle all deliveries to the White House complex.

—Constructing just north of the White House a below-grade, multipurpose recreation space for the first family.

—Constructing an underground pedestrian corridor connecting the Visitor Center to the underground Ellipse parking area.

The following four steps are rated as leading the list of priorities:

—Enlarge the White House Visitor Center into an education center and museum by using two basement levels in the Department of Commerce building and by constructing space under 15th Street.

—Construct an underground pedestrian corridor (with skylights and with moving walkways) leading visitors from the Visitor Center to an on-grade vestibule near the entrance to the East Wing (where a new East Tourist Entrance Building was under construction at the time of this writing).

—Designate the northeast panel of the Ellipse as a special events area, and install electrical connections and structural foundations so that a temporary stage and bleachers could be put up and taken down for performances, concerts, talks, and presentations.

—Upgrade the side panels of the Ellipse with allées of trees, meandering paths, gardens ,and benches. (Those steam pipes are to be rerouted.)

The plan describes and explains each of these proposals fully, accompanying each description with a column headed Problems, Issues, and Concerns.

Demonstrating the intensity of the plan's originators' commitment to meticulous preservation is a second volume entitled *Design Guidelines,* which was issued in 1997. In 124 pages of photographs and of precise drawings, the design of every existing gatepost, urn, staircase, bollard, and lantern is portrayed, so that they can be replicated exactly in whatever new development is undertaken. The plan's appendixes contain the text of the preservation legislation, a detailed listing of the park's existing structures and memorials, a statement of priorities, and an estimate of capital costs, which were put at $303.4 million in 2000 when the comprehensive plan itself was published.[1]

Are the steam shovels on call? No. The White House, watching apprehensively as the costs of the new visitor center at the Capitol have ballooned, is, as of 2008, in no mood to petition Congress to finance such a series of presidential undertakings. The federal budget is in deficit; the Iraq and Afghanistan wars are costly; no appropriation requests have been made to implement any of the plan's principal recommendations.

The plan, then, is stillborn? Quite the contrary. The plan is there. The indispensable research and the examination of options have been done. The agencies that put the plan together have briefed their respective congressional authorization and appropriations subcommittees about it and about its significance for helping set directions for the future. The first two elements of the original purpose of the plan have been accomplished: Agreements have been reached among all the executive branch agencies that have jurisdiction on "the needs and functions which will have to be accommodated at the site over the next 20 years" and "how best to ensure the protection of the important resources on the site including the White House itself."

As the director of the National Park Service White House Liaison Office put it,

> The value of a plan like this is that it is a master plan; the thought process that went into this to identify what were the needs of the site—it doesn't have to be implemented today. It sits there as a framework—for the moment in time when it is necessary and important to take a step. Then the framework is there, rather than reinventing the field. . . . When this administration came in, the president's initiative has been on correcting the backlog of maintenance in the National Park System—and this is part of the National Park System.[2]

More to the point: by making changes in the pavement, sidewalks, fences, and bollards on Pennsylvania Avenue, White House staff have followed the principles and design guidelines outlined in the comprehensive plan. "That document is not a dead document," former chief usher Gary Walters declared. "It is not a document that was supposed to be put on the shelf as being nice to look at; its design guidelines are going to be considered as possibilities for the future."[3]

35

The White House Historical Association: A Private, Independent Organization

Public Law 87-286, enacted in 1961, stipulated that "the principal public rooms on the first floor" of the White House are of "museum character" and that the National Park Service was in effect to be in charge of "all plate, furniture and public property" in the Residence. In the spirit of that statute, the National Park Service in 1961 proposed to First Lady Jacqueline Kennedy the creation of an organization that would be dedicated to "enhancing the understanding, appreciation and enjoyment of the White House" by American citizens and visitors. Mrs. Kennedy enthusiastically supported such an initiative, and the White House Historical Association was chartered in November 1961 as an independent, charitable, nonprofit institution with precisely that purpose.

In July 1962 the association produced and sold its first book, *The White House: An Historic Guide*. This popular publication is now in its twenty-second edition. In the years since its beginning, the association has sold 8 million copies of books covering many aspects of the White House and has produced or sponsored an increasing variety of videos and other educational articles for sale, relating to the public rooms of the Executive Residence.

In 1981 the association developed a new sales product: Christmas tree ornaments, a different one each year featuring artistic depictions of the White House or icons associated with it. These ornaments have been hugely popular, with millions sold since they were introduced. The association's fifty-page catalogue for 2007 also included Christmas cards, framed prints of several of the presidents, neckties, and men's accessories, scarves, jewelry, reproductions of some of the art that is in the White House, bookmarks, and puzzles—appealing to national and international purchasers. A few years ago the association began publishing a biannual, illustrated, scholarly journal, *White House History;* its subscription list is approaching 1,000.

The White House Historical Association uses the proceeds from its sales to underwrite its principal activity—supporting the Executive Residence in acquiring pieces of fine decorative art needed and desired by the White House and in restoring and preserving the furnishings and artwork already there. While Congress appropriates funds for the janitorial services for the Residence and for external maintenance and repair, except for a small acquisition budget each year there are no public monies available for purchases of artwork or for the preservation of internal White House furnishings. For years private donors have been approached on an ad hoc basis and have generously helped out by contributing items formerly in the White House collections of earlier presidents or by financing special conservation efforts.

To put this area of support on a sounder basis, the White House Historical Association has created two special trust funds, managed by separate boards of trustees. The first, created in 1996, is the Acquisition Trust, established for the purpose of purchasing fine works of decorative art that are identified and recommended by the Committee for the Preservation of the White House. The principal of the Acquisition Trust is kept at $7 million but is drawn down as opportunities for purchases arise; at the close of each year, profits from the association's sales are transferred to the trust to restore its original level. The trust financed the purchase of the 200th anniversary china (also called the Clinton china) commemorating the date when John Adams first walked into his as yet unfinished home: November 1, 1800.

(The china is unique; it is the only White House china that has a picture of the White House on it.) Other recent acquisitions include paintings by Andrew Wyeth, Rockwell Kent, Albert Bierstadt, and African American artist Jacob Lawrence. The trust put up the $2.5 million to purchase the Lawrence painting, *The Builders.*

The Endowment Fund was established in 1998, under President and Mrs. Clinton, following the White House Endowment Fund, started in 1991 under President and Mrs. George H. W. Bush. Its name was changed to the Endowment Trust after the $25 million fundraising goal was reached. Its purpose is the restoration and, if need be, the renovation of the public rooms and furnishings in the Residence. The current assets of the trust stand at $43.8 million. Each year a spending level is established for conservation work that equals 5 percent of the assets. In the George W. Bush administration and with Laura Bush's leadership, renovation has been accomplished in the Residence Library (the association's contribution was $207,371); in the Vermeil Room (a contribution of $224,589); in the Lincoln Bedroom and the Lincoln Sitting Room (since the Lincoln Bedroom is not considered a public room, this contribution of $530,084 was paid from the association's operating budget and not from the endowment); and in the Green Room (a contribution of $287,877), where the Lawrence painting hangs.[1] In celebration of the 100th anniversary of the West Wing, in 2002, the association paid for a new carpet for the Cabinet Room; the donation was made to the General Services Administration, which maintains the East and West Wings.

The White House Historical Association is active with other projects as well. It sponsors a program of research grants to university scholars who dig into White House history and produce papers about the White House past. An example: Malcah Yaeger-Dror of the University of Arizona received a grant to do a paper entitled "The Use of Communications Technology in the Kennedy, Johnson and Nixon Administrations."

In collaboration with the Organization of American Historians, the association annually awards three White House History Fellowships, one for a work aimed at the K–12 student level, one for completing a dissertation or doing postdoctoral research, and one that produces exhibits and multimedia projects that "make historical collections available to broad audiences."

The association's library of traveling exhibits and videos, loaned to the presidential libraries and museums, is also offered to other historical and cultural institutions; thousands of schools, universities, and libraries can get them, paying only shipping charges. Among the exhibits is one about White House pets; another, one of a series of Smithsonian Institution Traveling Exhibitions (SITEs), consists of interviews with men and women who worked at the White House, some for half a century.

The association is digitizing the existing libraries of White House photographs, going back to Lincoln, now held in the National Archives, the Library of Congress, and other repositories, into a database that can accessed by the public, the presidential libraries, and other historical organizations.

Beginning in 2006, the association included on its staff a teacher who visits elementary schools in the District of Columbia, Maryland, and Virginia, telling about White House history. In addition, the association guided a group of high school students who prepared a taped audio tour of nine of the various locations where, over the years, protest groups have rallied in the White House neighborhood: suffragists, civil rights advocates, antiwar, pro-life, and so forth; one stop discusses the Truman assassination attempt. Interested groups can take a walking tour while they listen to the tape, or it can be downloaded for playing at home or in school.

March 25, 2008, was the 250th anniversary of the birth of James Hoban, the Irish architect who designed the White House. The association, working with collaborators in Ireland, hosted a symposium about Hoban and his relationship with the White House. On the drawing board are plans, being drawn up with the White House Liaison Office of the National Park Service, to remake the White House Visitor Center (chapter 34).

The association is governed by a board of twenty directors, four officers, and a president; it has a staff of twenty-seven and operates two sales offices, one at the White House Visitor Center and the other at the association's headquarters at 740 Jackson Place—in effect across the lawn from the White House.[2]

Looking to the Future

36

Major Long-Term Innovations by the Bush Administration

During the George W. Bush administration, the White House has been outfitted with an impressive series of changes: organizational additions and physical upgrades.

The three principal organizational innovations have been described in earlier chapters of this book: the Homeland Security Council, the Office of Faith-Based and Community Initiatives, and the USA Freedom Corps Office (chapters 10, 11, and 12). The White House has also dramatically increased its use of the Internet (chapter 18). In the author's judgment these four add-ons will most probably be long lasting; the actual decisions in each case, of course, will be up to the new administration (the Homeland Security Council, however, is statutory).

But beyond the innovations in organizational structure is a category of physical upgrades to the White House campus facilities that the administration of George W. Bush has instituted and that are or will be making significant improvements in the efficacy of the presidency. Some already exist; they already represent important advances in presidential public administration. Others will come into full usefulness only after President Bush has left office; it will be future presidents who will reap their benefits. The American public knows little about these physical innovations, partly because some of them are still only prospective and because certain of them are security-classified. For those reasons the following descriptions are necessarily only partial.

The New Situation Room

As early as 2003 it was clear that the existing White House Situation Room was incapable of handling the most modern telecommunications—especially secure video-teleconferencing—that now are indispensable for the effective functioning of the national security community. With his reelection in 2004, the president felt he could properly make the case for the financial commitment to upgrade thoroughly the old facility.

Since the spring of 1961, when the Situation Room was first set up, only modest improvements had been made: it had been two side-by-side rooms, one especially wired for teleconferences within the Washington area. Near them, in a darkened arc, were TV monitors onto which were sent, electronically, copies of incoming and outgoing State Department telegrams, and other information from the national security community. A few of the NSC staff had their offices in this area also.

Serious planning for the new Sit Room began in 2005; in August 2006 the first office moves were made. The contract for the whole job was given directly to an expert private builder, bypassing what were considered complicated and bureaucratic bidding procedures. There was substantial demolition of existing walls, even extending into the area where, in 1934–35, President Roosevelt had established a sunken garden court, with beautiful columns, a french doorway, and a fountain. In later years, plywood was installed covering up the columns; the demolition uncovered the plywood and the columns. (The latter were carefully removed and have been given to the National Archives for possible auction as White House historical items.) The work included some blasting and very extensive reconstruction. The whole job was completed ahead of schedule and under budget. A ribbon-cutting ceremony was held on May 18, 2007.

The new Situation Room today is actually a complex of thirteen rooms or areas; the entire complex is separated, by special security locks, from the rest of the White House. These thirteen areas are:

—*A reception area.* Tucked into the wall are slots for every entrant to park his or her mobile electronic devices since these items are not allowed in the complex. Mounted on the wall is an agenda screen indicating the groups that are scheduled to be using specific meeting rooms and at what hours. Also built into one of the walls are two glassed-in telephone booths, equipped to handle either secure or nonsecure calls in a private setting.

—*The large conference room.* Up a half-flight of stairs from the Reception area, the principal Situation Room can seat thirty-two participants, thirteen at a central conference table. Its most obvious feature is what is called the Knowledge Wall—a display screen some five feet high and eleven feet long on the end wall at the foot of the table. Up to sixteen images, pictures, texts, photographs, maps, satellite photos, live feeds, and the like can be displayed simultaneously. The room is equipped with an electronic write-board, which permits lines or arrows to be drawn electronically on a map, photo, or computer document. Some eight microphones are in the ceiling, as are sensors for room temperature and humidity—and for detecting the presence of forbidden cell phones. The walls are all coated with a specially soft, acoustical fabric that absorbs ambient sound; they are called whisper walls.

On those side walls are four large flat-screen monitors, each of which can display additional material, such as maps, or faces of individuals or groups who are assembled in any number of remote sites. There is also display of the time in any six cities of the world, always including Washington; the time where the president is located, if not in Washington; Zulu base time at the Greenwich Meridian; and the time in any other three cities of the world, chosen by the participants according to the subject of their discussion. Finally, there is a panel indicating the security classification level of the discussion.

The room has three cameras, one under the Knowledge Wall, aimed at the president, who faces it at the other end of the table; one in the ceiling precisely over the area in front of the president where a document would rest and which can thus transmit the visible text to those participating remotely; and a third in the side wall aimed at the middle of the row of seats on the opposite side of the table, in case the chairperson of the meeting chooses to sit there. In the center of the table is a series of plug-ins where a participant can connect elements of his or her personal workstation: laptop, personal computer, headset and telephone—all handling information up to the highest security classification.

—*The small conference room.* Across from the large conference room is a smaller room that seats seven and has two large flat-screen displays.

—*The executive conference room.* Down the half-flight of stairs on the main level of the complex, this conference room is nearly the same size as the large Situation Room just described. It can seat twenty-one and has six large flat-screen display areas. Its other features—cameras, whisper walls, tabletop plug-ins—are similar to those in the large and small conference rooms.

—*Offices.* There are offices for the director and deputy director of the complex; the director's office has an internal window permitting him to see what is happening in the reception area.

—*The Breakout Room.* A small room, perhaps ten feet square, with a round table seating four and one large flat-screen monitor. This room permits the president to leave a meeting in the main conference room and, conferring with just a few aides, take or make an urgent telephone call, or just use it for very small, private meetings.

—*An equipment closet.* This is stacked floor to ceiling with the electronic equipment needed to support all the functions of the Sit Room complex. There are two duplicate stacks, one used as a backup.

—*A switching center.* This center is used to direct the secure video-teleconferencing to wherever in the world there is compatible equipment: the offices of all members of the National Security Council, *Air Force One,* the forthcoming *Marine One* helicopter, the Roosevelt Room in the White House, Camp David, the ranch in Crawford Texas, all U.S. combatant commands, certain U.S. embassies, and the offices of a select group of foreign heads of state or government.

—The Communications Area. Four consoles send and receive outgoing and incoming messages or e-mails being sent between agencies in Washington and to the combatant commanders overseas. This traffic is passed to the duty officers in the Watch Room.

—The Watch Room. This room is, in effect, the heart of the national security communications structure. Duty officers, sitting at up to six console positions, supervise the process of determining who in the White House is to receive information that comes into the complex. Each of the directors on the staffs of the National Security and the Homeland Security Councils has a "profile" (changeable as needed) that sets out the subjects for which he or she is responsible. The Watch Room's computers are programmed to distribute incoming messages to these officers according to their specific profiles. In addition to, or in some cases overriding the automatic data-handling system, the duty officers constantly make decisions on what should go to the president, the vice president, the national and homeland security affairs advisers and their deputies, and the NSC executive secretary. A low-tech backup to the electronic distribution system is a floor-to-ceiling fixture on the wall of the Watch Room, divided into several dozen slots (president, vice president, and so on) into which actual pieces of paper can be tucked.

The Watch Room also displays the panel that can show the times at any six cities of the world. This room is staffed 24/7.

—A "surge" conference room. This room features a table seating nine, with plug-in capabilities for individual workstations and wall panels for electronic displays. There is the usual panel displaying the time in six cities. This room is typically used when an interpreter is brought in and plugs in a headset to participate in the president's secure telephone conversations with another chief of state.

—A mini-kitchen. This little kitchen is open 24/7. (The White House Mess itself closes at 8 p.m.)

Elsewhere in the White House complex are one or two rooms for cots, in case some staffers must sleep over in order to be immediately available.

On a typical busy day, fifteen or more of the some thirty-two men and women assigned to the Situation Room may be needed to support the continuous cycles of meetings and the never-ending flow of communications. Several of these experienced men and women are detailed from State, Defense, the CIA, Homeland Security, the Defense Intelligence Agency, the National Security Agency, the FBI, and from all the military services.

The Situation Room's usefulness to the intelligence community is obvious. "The new Situation Room is not just a National Security Council tool," explained Deputy Chief of Staff for Operations Joseph Hagin. "We view the Sit Room as really being a support organization for four principal constituencies: the National Security Council, the Homeland Security Council, the advance teams when they go abroad, and the White House chief of staff; those are its four principal customers."[1]

This new Situation Room complex represents a breathtaking innovation in the conduct of America's national security operations. The advanced secure video-teleconferencing system equipment supporting these teleconferences is currently in place in most large American embassies abroad; in addition a few other chiefs of state, including those in London and in Berlin, have it in their own offices. Routinely, the president and his national security aides hold a secure video-teleconference with General David Petraeus and Ambassador Ryan Crocker in Baghdad; once a month Iraqi Prime Minister Nouri al-Maliki comes over to the American Embassy and joins the teleconference. It was during such a session on November 26, 2007, that a groundbreaking level of the process of negotiating international agreements was consummated: President Bush and Prime Minister al-Maliki signed, via secure video-teleconference, a declaration of principles about a "more normalized, long-term relationship between the United States and Iraq."[2] National Security Adviser Stephen Hadley and his colleagues have now started to have regular video-teleconferences with the U.S. team in Afghanistan: the ambassador and the U.S. military commander conferring with the president and his NSC colleagues. With those embassies having this equipment, the president is able to conduct country-specific discussions with the U.S. ambassador and the CIA station chief. A version of this equipment is mobile and battery-powered, enabling White House advance teams to report back to their White House colleagues in the Situation Room.

This mode of communication has exceptional benefits: now not only are papers and voices exchanged, but facial expressions become part of the dialogue; every frown or smile, every furrowing of the eyebrows or tightening of the lips can be seen by all participants. "One of the most remarkable things it does," Hadley commented, "is it gives the president a new tool of diplomacy. His ability to have another foreign leader on the screen, talking face to face, is very powerful. The president uses it to build personal relations, but it also allows you to build a consensus over time."[3]

President Bush and British prime minister Tony Blair engaged for months in this international video dialogue "every couple of weeks on the screen to each other, explaining their views, talking about strategy," Hadley remembered, and it was to this unusual conversation that Hadley attributed the absence of any publicly aired differences between the two men. "Through some very difficult times, such as Iraq, they were always pretty well in sync." Chancellor Angela Merkel of Germany enjoys a similar "video" relationship with President Bush.

But this is not universally the case. Some chiefs of state, friendly allies to be sure, do not like to do business via television. The Saudi king, for instance, does not even want to use the telephone; he prefers to send a trusted envoy to meet with the president in person. These communication arrangements are being handled on a case-by-case basis. A military-to-military link, called the Hotline, has now been set up between Beijing and the Pentagon; a hotline has long been in place between the Pentagon and Moscow.

Every new president-to-president teleconference arrangement, however, raises a separate issue: how is the U.S. ambassador in that country kept informed of what his president has said or agreed to do? If there is a need (and on occasion one or both presidents may want their conversations kept entirely private), the respective ambassador will be accorded a debriefing by the relevant NSC senior director.

It should be noted that while the Presidential Records Act requires all written and electronic communications in the White House to be included in the category of presidential records, neither the president's telephone conversations with foreign chiefs of state nor the recently inaugurated secure video-teleconference sessions are recorded, so no "records" are created on those occasions. The principal reason for this practice is that if foreign leaders knew they were being taped or recorded they would tend to be less candid in their conversations with the president. A secondary reason is that electronic records, such as the many e-mails that *are* stored, take up a great deal of disc space. Video recordings would require an impractical number of gigabytes.

The investment for the Situation Room innovations was approximately $20 million, and included funds for continuous upgrading, in order to keep up, from now on, with the constant improvements in technology.

From Pebble Beach to Stonehenge

On the North Lawn of the White House, the space between West Executive Avenue and the driveway to the northwest gate was being used by news organizations as a place to set up their tripods, lights, and video cameras and do live stand-up interviews with their principal correspondents any time during the day. White House press secretaries would also come out and give live interviews, one after the other, to three or four networks, each of whom had its assigned territory. With heavy use by dozens of technicians, interviewers, and interviewees, what had been grass became mud, and then gravel—from whence came its name Pebble Beach. It was messy, inefficient, and definitely unsightly.

Enlisting the help of the White House Correspondents Association, the Bush White House asked the National Park Service to redesign and reconstruct the area, installing better electrical facilities and utilities, planting attractive shrubbery, and laying down a floor of solid flagstones, which gave rise to a new nickname: Stonehenge. The place now has a professional appearance; the unsightliness is minimized, and the White House Press Corps has gained a significant increase in convenience and efficiency. The transformation was accomplished with the modest investment of $1.4 million.

The Makeover of the Brady Briefing Room

A significant legacy contribution to the White House has been the renovation of the James S. Brady Press Briefing Room (it had been named by President Clinton in honor of Reagan's press secretary, who suffered serious wounds during the assassination attempt on the president in 1981). The existing room was thirty-six years old, and the aging HVAC system, combined with the proliferation of electrical equipment, had made the work environment a difficult one. "It was a cramped, dingy place," commented former press secretary Scott McClellan. The White House Correspondents Association was consulted, and architects and designers were brought in from the General Services Administration.

The room was emptied out for eleven months during 2006–07; the press briefings were switched to temporary space in the White House Conference Center, off Jackson Place. The old press area was gutted—all the way down to the Franklin Roosevelt-era swimming pool. The pool (50 feet by 15 feet by 8 feet) is still there (only a dozen of its wall tiles were removed, and salvaged, to permit installation of steel cross-beams), but it is now full of electronics to support telecommunications and broadcast television. Behind the pool area are revamped booths for the news agencies. The construction addressed problems with asbestos, plumbing, water seepage, and lead paint. A new steel and concrete floor was laid and covered with rubber-backed carpet tiles. The traditional incandescent lights are gone, replaced by low-energy, low-heat-emitting diode fixtures; there are forty-five additional tons of air-conditioning capacity, new pickup microphones over the seats to eliminate the need for boom microphones, and new TV-production workstations in the rear. To the side, up front, are new connections for "cutaway" cameras so that TV viewers can have a front view of their favorite correspondents as they challenge the press secretary at the podium. The forty-nine new press seats are an inch wider, and each seat is wired for the Internet, so a journalist can plug in a laptop and can be miked up and have the audio fed back to the production crew in the rear.

Up front are two different backdrop sets, one for the president, showing the presidential seal, and one for the press secretary (with others available in case a third person is making the presentation). At the side in front, rotating pillars can present two forty-five-inch flat screens able to display pictures, slides, or video. The press secretary for instance could lead off a briefing with a discussion of Congress's handling of the president's budget, then pop up a slide showing the status of all the appropriation bills, or have a two-part display using a split screen. Press Secretary Tony Snow one day was discussing the success the United States was having in getting rid of some of the top leaders of al Qaeda in Iraq; up came the leaders' pictures. All this new presentation technology is controlled by buttons on the podium, and the wiring allows the media to take a direct video feed from those display screens. The cables, wires, and ductwork are easily accessible for maintenance; capacity has been built in for the continuous upgrading that the White House knows will be forthcoming.

The rewiring—that is, the installation of permanent, in-the-wall, fiber-optic cable—has been accomplished in several other key places at the White House: at the Residence, in the East Room and the Map Room, and in the Roosevelt Room in the West Wing. Another innovation was the use of an upgraded mode of television in the Oval Office; in September 2007 the president, for the first time, was able to make a speech using high definition television while sitting at his Oval Office desk. "You'll see a lot more of that," predicted Deputy Press Secretary Scott Stanzel, adding:

> We want to ease into it, because we don't want it to give the impression to the reporters in the room—who are there doing a very serious job—that we are using them as props and we're just giving a speech. We want this to provide more information and tell a more full picture about the news of the day that the press is most interested in. We are thinking ahead and trying to understand: okay, how do we make our points and present the president's policies in a useful way? One of the major purposes of this technology is to help the reporters themselves be more effective—to help them professionally.[4]

The investment in the Brady Briefing Room was roughly $8 million. It is estimated that the press organizations themselves contributed an additional $1 million. As he cut the ribbon officially opening the new briefing room on July 13, 2007, President Bush remarked: "I think it's going to benefit future Presidents and future White House press corps, to be working in modern conditions—conditions where a fellow like me will feel comfortable coming in here answering a few questions without losing twenty pounds. . . . And it's going to make your life better and frankly, it's going to make the lives of future Presidents better as well."[5]

The Reconstruction of the Dwight D. Eisenhower Executive Office Building

On January 31, 1888, the last stone was set in completion of the State-War-Navy building in the block just west of the White House. It had taken seventeen years to build, with its French Second Empire architecture, nearly two miles of marble and limestone tiled corridors, sixteen-foot, eleven-inch ceilings, and solid brick interior walls—making eventual electrification cumbersome and defying central air-conditioning. Harry Truman called it "the greatest monstrosity in America"; a presidential advisory committee in the late 1950s recommended replacing it with a modern White House office building. Preservationists prevailed; its exterior was scrubbed in 1962; in 1971 it was listed on the National

Register of Historic Places. In the Reagan years its grand libraries and the skylit domes above the staircases were restored.

Step by step since the State Department moved out in 1947, White House staff units moved in; by the time of George W. Bush's inauguration, most of the building was given over to White House office space. A statute had also been passed renaming it the Dwight D. Eisenhower Executive Office Building. At a 2002 renaming ceremony, Susan Eisenhower, standing in a White House driveway, recalled "My father spent as much time over there as he did over here."

The tragedy of 9/11 showed that the EEOB had not kept pace with the necessities of a modern office building. It lacked adequate fire alarm, fire protection and suppression systems, and a modern fire escape stairwell. This event provided an opportunity to correct these problems and make the building safer for current and future occupants. Two options were on the table: either keep all occupants off the Seventeenth Street side of the building, or close the street to all vehicular traffic. Consultations by the White House with leaders in the District of Columbia and Congress produced a compromise: keep Seventeenth Street open, but strengthen EEOB's west side to a level of protection that would permit staff to reoccupy those offices. What became clear was this: the building had a great usefulness as a base for modern equipment and technology as well as continuing to be a cherished relic of a bygone era.

President Bush decided, "Let's do this right." He has undertaken a multiyear modernization project of the building's interior. The west side came first: the windows and exterior doors were rebuilt; inside floors, walls, and ceilings were renovated. Much of the original historical fabric was saved, and where possible, as in the ground floor corridor, historically sympathetic replacement material was used. To ensure the safety and security of the occupants, window air-conditioners were replaced by a computerized central air-conditioning system throughout the EEOB, a move that also improved the energy efficiency of the building. In addition, new ductwork and electrical systems were installed. Wood office floors that were not historical were removed and replaced with modern, fire-resistant concrete, raised floor tiles. This enabled placement of all the electrical and communications wiring out of sight, under the floor, allowing easy access for any future electrical or communications upgrades. Several SCIF (secure, compartmented information facility) rooms are being built to handle state-of-the-art communications equipment.

As the modernization project continued, treasures were discovered. Construction workers began scraping layers of old paint off the ceiling of what had been the secretary of war's suite on the second floor (rooms 231 and 232). In doing so, and to everyone's surprise, part of a historical mural was revealed. Old records for that room indicated that an elaborate mural had been painted in room 231. No records were available to indicate what may have been in room 232. The General Services Administration commissioned a conservator to determine the origin and the condition of the mural. In the process of examination, it was determined that twenty-one layers of paint covered the room-sized ceiling mural, which portrayed images of Mars, the Roman god of war, and Victoria, the goddess of victory, in heroic posture riding their chariots.

Since no documentation existed for room 232, it was unclear if any elaborate painting existed on that ceiling. Initial indications were that a mural may have been present. The GSA commissioned the conservators to remove small "windows" in the paint. Some unexpected colors appeared, revealing an elaborate mural, more intricate than the one discovered in room 231. As of this writing, the mural in room 232 is in the process of restoration. Several other rooms in the suite contain elaborate wall and ceiling finishes, called *gesso,* with red and blue glass jewels embedded in the plaster finish. When completed, the entire suite will be restored to its 120-year-old splendor.

As of this writing, the EEOB modernization project has progressed to the building's south section, which originally housed the secretary of state and staff. Following that, the east side will be reconstructed, which was at one time the headquarters of the Navy Department. The entire undertaking will take several years—long outlasting President Bush's term of office—and will add an incalculable treasury of architectural and decorative beauty to the White House environment, not to mention an energy-efficient office building and communications facility of twenty-first century quality. Congress has authorized the General Services Administration to expend $540 million to complete this historic reconstruction.

A New Marine Corps HMX-One Helicopter Fleet

Marine Helicopter Squadron One (HMX-1) was established at Quantico, Virginia, in December 1947, as an experimental unit tasked with testing and evaluating military helicopters when rotary wing flight was in its infancy. In September 1957 President Eisenhower was vacationing in Newport, Rhode Island, when the necessity arose for him to return to Washington on short notice. He flew from Newport to the Quonset Point Naval Air Station on a Marine helicopter— a UH-34. This was the first time an American president had flown in a Marine helicopter. The president recognized the convenience of helicopter flights and continued to fly in the UH-34 for the remainder of his time in office. Whenever the president is on board a helicopter, it becomes *Marine One.*

Successive presidents have used helicopters constantly—for domestic trips and while on visits abroad. The most frequent domestic trips are the flights between the White House and Camp David and between the White House and Andrews Air Force Base. Overseas, *Marine One* has landed in such unusual places as England's Windsor Castle, the Akasaka Palace in Tokyo, Bolivar Square in Bogotá, and the demilitarized zone in South Korea.

Two models of helicopter are used for presidential travel: the Sikorsky VH-3D *Sea King* and the modified Sikorsky UH-60. The former has a cabin seating fourteen (but is limited to ten for presidential flights), a range of 375 nautical miles, and a speed of 115 knots. The latter seats ten but is designed to be transportable, so is more frequently used on international trips. Both have their upper halves painted white, giving them the nickname "White Tops." The Marine Corps purchased nine of the UH-60s in 1988.

As for landing facilities, the White House South Lawn has been configured to be a sometime heliport: portable communications equipment is wheeled out and fire engines stand by at the north edge of the Ellipse. On one occasion, however, the blast from the blades knocked down a tree on the South Lawn, and the flowers suffer. Nonetheless its convenience proves irresistible.

The HMX-One fleet being forty years old (one of them crashed near Quantico Marine Base in May 1996, killing four Marine crewmen), the Bush administration decided to purchase a whole new fleet: twenty-eight helicopters. According to one news account, "Then-White House Chief of Staff Andrew H. Card grew aggravated with the aging fleet's problems in 2002, and he launched the effort to develop a new model with a post-September 11 upgrade."[6]

Long before the actual bidding on procurement began, an intense competition arose as early as 2003 between the traditional builder of presidential helicopters, Sikorsky Aircraft Corp., based in Stratford, Connecticut, and Lockheed Martin Corp., which would use a design by British-Italian consortium Agusta-Westland—a unit of the Italian defense firm Finmeccanica SpA. Prime ministers Tony Blair of England and Silvio Berlusconi of Italy weighed in with letters to President Bush favoring the British-Italian design, while Armed Services Committee member Rob Simmons declared: "This is our president . . . I really don't want to see him flying around in a foreign helicopter."[7] In January 2006 the contract was awarded to Lockheed Martin.

The newly designed plane will be called the VH-71. Sixty-five percent of the aircraft will be built in the United States, in Oswego, New York, in a new facility constructed in March, 2005; the aircraft and its transmission will come from Italy, the blades from the United Kingdom, and the mission systems from the United States. The contract was for twenty-eight helicopters, all for the HMX-One White House fleet. The planes are to be sixty-four feet long and are to carry fourteen passengers and thousands of pounds of additional advanced equipment. According to one news report,

> they must be able to jam seeking devices, fend off incoming missiles and resist some of the electro-magnetic effects of a nuclear blast. They also must have video-conferencing and encrypted communications equipment to allow the president to instantly reach advisers, military officers and foreign leaders. Although the president typically spends only short periods of

time aboard White House helicopters, at times the president can be on board for longer distances. In a crisis, the White House says, minutes can make a difference, so a president should have the full capacity to act no matter where he or she is. In theory, a commander-in-chief should even be able to order a nuclear strike from the helicopter.[8]

Two of the new helicopters will not be delivered for actual flying use; one will be test-crashed, and the other kept in the Naval Research facility at Patuxent as a base on which to try out new communications and other pieces of equipment. The new helicopters will each have three engines and will fly at 150 knots with a range of 300 nautical miles—faster but shorter distances that the currently used VH-3D. The 200-square-foot cabin space will be twice as large as that in the VH-3D. The VH-71's range may be reduced, however, because the weight threatens to be 1,200 pounds in excess of the original estimate.

The original financial commitment for this new helicopter fleet was $6.2 billion; the fiscal year 2007 appropriation for this program was $633 million; the fiscal year 2008 request is for $271 million. The first five were due to be delivered in 2009, with twenty-three, even more sophisticated, models to be ready by 2015.

As of this writing, however, the estimated costs have shot up and the delivery schedule has slipped. Said John J. Young Jr., the under secretary of defense for acquisition, "the Navy and industry teams are having to complete substantial redesign . . . [which] is driving significant cost growth into the program." The new total cost estimate for the twenty-eight planes is $11.2 billion. The first five helicopters are now to be delivered in 2010, but the target date for the completion of the remaining twenty-three is "unknown." In fact, "the problems with the second batch have promoted the Pentagon to issue a stop-work order until it determines what to do and Congress provides more money," he said.

"We took a look at what is the best thing to do for future presidents," explained White House spokesman Gordon Johndroe, "but also looking at it from a cost-benefit analysis. The consensus was future presidents need a new helicopter. The current ones need to be replaced."[9] President Bush will be out of office before even the first new "bird" is delivered; this program is an investment in the presidencies of the future.

In addition, the existing helicopter hanger at Camp David will be replaced with a larger and better equipped hangar to accommodate the new VH-71 helicopters. Its construction schedule will correspond with the delivery of the first of the new airships—about 2010.

The Present and Future Air Force Ones

The two twenty-year-old 747-200 aircraft now used for long-distance presidential travel have just recently returned from a complete overhaul and upgrade at the Boeing plant in Wichita, Kansas. That redo will ensure that the two huge aircraft will be in good shape for another decade, which is what it will take to produce the next version of this remarkable airplane for the president of 2019. The White House has already dispatched a memorandum to the Department of Defense to start the planning for it, a someday investment of probably $1 billion dollars.

Improvements for the Public's Enjoyment

Even under the limitations placed on White House tours after 9/11, some 1 million people come through White House gateways each year. Most of these visitors enter through the east gate. To handle these large numbers efficiently and with proper attention to security screening, a new east entrance building is being constructed, an additional long-term investment in the enhanced efficacy of the White House complex.

Contributions to the Residence Public Rooms

As described in chapter 35, the White House Historical Association sponsors two special trust funds, the Endowment Trust and the Acquisition Trust. These trusts provide contributions for preservation and restoration of the public rooms in the Executive Residence and for the purchase of furnishings and works of art for the White House collection. These are long-term objectives for the benefit not merely of the incumbent first family but for first families in years to come. The total investment from the White House Historical Association for these purposes since the beginning of the George W. Bush administration has been $7,509,449. Of that, $3,432,379 came from the Endowment Trust and $4,077,069 came from the Acquisition Trust.

Improvements to the Grounds

Chapter 34 describes the President's Park in which the White House is located. The National Park Service not only operates and maintains the park and its Visitor Center but has made major capital improvements in the physical elements of the park, especially on the Ellipse. Realizing that the Ellipse had been undermaintained for many years, the National Park Service, energized by its White House Liaison Office, undertook, beginning in October 2004, a four-year program of upgrading the Ellipse. Utilities were reconstructed, new sidewalks and new lights were installed, extensive repairs were made to four fountains. The turf of the Ellipse, and the soil itself, had been compacted by millions of feet over dozens of years; most of it needed to be completely replaced. The work had to be skillfully scheduled to avoid interference with major events in the Ellipse such as the Army's evening tattoo on spring and summer Wednesday evenings, and of course the Pageant of Peace at Christmas. Completion is expected in

October of 2008. The special investment in this long overdue innovative program by the National Park Service cost $14.5 million.

In Summary

Every first family personifies both continuity and innovation at the White House. Harry Truman rebuilt the Residence almost from the ground up; Jacqueline Kennedy called the public's attention to its furnishings; Dwight Eisenhower instituted a staff structure much of which continues today. George and Laura Bush have introduced significant innovations to the physical plant and to the processes of the staff. Above and beyond the annual budgetary outlays for operating and maintaining the White House, and despite being, in effect, a wartime presidency, the president has made remarkable investments in and at the White House that will yield returns to presidencies far beyond his departure date of January 20, 2009, and to the American people for decades to come. The presidency will be a more effective office thanks to those innovations. The author is confident that the first family of 2009 will emulate this example.

The Essence of White House Service

There is always the danger that impulsive, inexperienced aides, puffed up with the prestige of the White House—and emboldened by the absence of personal accountability—will seek to bully the main federal establishments into reckless, ill-considered or improper actions in the service of pet ideological or short-term political aims.

—Jeremy Rabkin

My sense of reality was just altered. I started out being excited working for the president. Then I became arrogant, then I became grandiose.

—Dick Morris

The benefit as a citizen is to understand the glory of this republic and how it works, to have a chance to serve the American people and serve the Constitution and the highest office of the land firsthand, personally; to be there, to be a part of history; to stand in places where history has been made. It's a very uplifting and motivating thing to do. When you walk through the gate of the White House every morning, you have no question of why you're at work. Getting motivated to go to work at the White House was never an issue, never a problem whatsoever. It was a delight to do no matter how frustrating it could be day by day, hour by hour.

—James Fetig

This volume, so far, has given the reader an encyclopedic look at the contemporary White House Staff. It is now time to peer ahead. What can be said about the White House staff of the near future?

The first two epigraphs at the opening of the chapter give rise to the question: Are the White House staff and the cabinet necessarily antagonistic bodies? Is the staff brimming with "impulsive, inexperienced aides," "arrogant" and "grandiose" minions who ply their president's trade, leaving the cabinet out of the loop—or wondering, as former secretary of labor Robert Reich wrote, whether "there *is* a loop" at all? In other words, is staff-cabinet antipathy inevitable?

The answer is yes and the answer is no.

First, as political scientist Charles Jones reminds us, "Presidents-elect enter the critical transition period in a physically and mentally exhausted state, typically dependent on an equally fatigued staff.... However competent on the campaign trail, their aides have been selected for a purpose that is weakly related to governing, if related at all." In 1992 "the lack of Washington-based executive experience among Clinton's advisers was not automatically compensated for by the energy of their youth." As one former aide put it, "the problem with the Carter administration was that there [were] too many people . . . for whom it was the best job they ever had. And that probably is true here [in the Clinton administration] too." Another asked: How can a president "discern [the] governing talent of staff who have never governed?" Jones quotes a Republican aide: "The attack by White House staff on cabinet is a source of bad government. And it is extremely pervasive. There is mutual contempt, but it is much stronger . . . contempt felt by White House staff for cabinet than vice versa. . . . The White House staff, by virtue of physical proximity, feels closer to the president. All White House staffs feel embattled and form deep kinds of bonds, an us-against-them mentality."[1]

Second, with these early mind-sets coloring the perspectives of some if not many of them, new White House staff members will next encounter one of the basic facts of contemporary governance: the reality that the major public policy issues of presidential concern are inextricably scrambled across what were once well-defined cabinet jurisdictions. Preparing for the consequences of climate change, guarding against terrorism, meeting the challenges of economic disparity or immigration, structuring future relations with Russia or China: no "lead" cabinet secretary can marshal the totality of the interagency staff work involved in exploring such issues—nor can even a group of cabinet secretaries inject into that staff work the president's own perspective as to what might be the most desirable solutions.

The preceding chapters have adduced many examples of what fifty-five years of organizational struggles have made clear: the strategic development, coordination, and articulation of major policy initiatives have now become centered in a large and active White House—likely a disquieting notion to the cabinet. So, yes: there is inherent separateness—tension, in fact—between White House staff and cabinet. And in the past there was real hostility—as in the cases of National Security Adviser Henry Kissinger and Secretary of State William Rogers, National Security Adviser Zbigniew Brzezinski and Secretary of State Cyrus Vance, Chief of Staff John Sununu and Environmental Protection Agency Administrator William Reilly, White House policy adviser Ira Magaziner and cabinet secretaries Lloyd Bentsen and Donna Shalala.

In President George W. Bush's first term, the antipathy was not so much between cabinet members and the White House, but, in the Iraq affair, between the Departments of State and Defense—which the White House staff failed to quash. "Throughout the planning process, tensions between the Defense Department and the State Department were never mediated by the president or his staff," concluded one report.[2] After 2006, when Robert Gates had replaced Donald Rumsfeld at Defense and Stephen Hadley had become national security adviser, the antipathies apparently disappeared and much more effective communications were instituted (chapter 5).

What will be the pattern for the future? Will the centralization of policy control also continue? It is the author's belief that the process of centralization will not be reversed, but it is also his apprehension that this recent era of congenial relationships could vanish if arrogance and grandiosity were again to infect the psyche of junior—or senior—White House assistants.

The value of Jones's *Passages to the Presidency* is its advice to new presidents on how to make the transition from campaigning to governing—and on how to avoid the mistakes that have led to such bitterness between the cabinet and the White House in the past. The books stresses, for instance, that a president-elect should choose his White House staff first—to have them in place *as* the cabinet choices are made. A former Reagan and Bush adviser is quoted:

> I have never understood why presidents-elect are so enamored of this idea that cabinet officers matter. They don't matter. You can run a damn cabinet for months without a cabinet officer and nobody will ever know the difference. That's the least crucial item that should be on a presidential agenda. Instead, because of the symbolic value they spend enormous amounts of time on it. They spend very little time on the staff, or how the White House works. It always amazes me that presidents don't understand—even those that have been governors—how much of the real power and decisionmaking in government is in the White House operation.[3]

Dick Morris quotes President Clinton's own rueful retrospection: "I spent all my time before I took office choosing my Cabinet.... It's a great Cabinet. But I didn't spend the time I should have choosing my staff. I just reached out and took the people who had helped get me elected and put them on the staff. It was a mistake." Morris noted: "He [Clinton] would plead for more 'adults' in the White House."[4]

Organizing the Future White House Staff

The structure of the contemporary White House staff is not the mindless burgeoning of willy-nilly empire building; it is a direct consequence of growing presidential needs—step by step, since the 1950s—to have certain tasks undertaken. Elements added to the White House by earlier presidents as useful innovations—the advance, communications, intergovernmental affairs, and public liaison offices, the Situation Room, the weekly cabinet report, the White House photographer, the intern program, for example—have now proven their worth and are standard White House functions. With more and more institutions reaching *in* to the presidency (interest groups, foreign, state, and local officials, political coalitions), and affording additional avenues of persuasion, the White House has organized itself—and grown—to reach *out* to exploit those opportunities. As other authors have so well demonstrated, presidents put great store on "going public"; the "White House bubble machine" is a staff apparatus that no future president will forgo. Governing, as Jones emphasizes, is taking on a style of continuing campaigning. *That is not going to change.*

Above all else, the centrality of the president's personal role in leading and coordinating the executive branch—especially for national and homeland security, detailed in chapters 5 and 10 of this volume—has required the president to increase his own staff resources for policy development. The thirty-two cabinet departments and agencies are every chief executive's proud professional wellsprings, but their disparate capacities have to be marshaled and synchronized, a task that the Constitution itself implicitly assigns to the president.

The tighter and more interwoven the threads of policy issues become—throughout the entire national security community, across all the old boundary lines between domestic and foreign—the more influential and the more numerous may become the White House assistants who must struggle to achieve the synchronization. The more centrifugal are the forces exerted by the inevitable cacophony outside the White House gates, the more potent will become the centripetal strength within.

As political scientist Terry Moe wrote,

> Over time the built-in advantage of the White House will prevail: presidents will incrementally enhance its competence; problems and issues will be increasingly drawn into it for centralized coordination and control, expectations surrounding previous patterns will slowly break down, new expectations will form around a White House–centered system, and the new expectations will further accelerate the flow of problems and issues to the White House—thus enhancing the need for still greater White House competence.[5]

How much flexibility does a new president have to reorganize the White House? The quick answer would seem to be this: almost complete freedom. The Constitution mandates that there shall be a vice president; the law establishes (but does not require the president to use) the National Security and Homeland Security Councils and authorizes—but puts only a modest limit on the number of—highly paid staff. Is the rest a tabula rasa?

No. It is a concluding thesis of this book that most of the seventy-four principal policy offices, the twenty-one supporting policy offices, and almost all of the forty technical and support units in the contemporary White House are so clearly indispensable to the modern presidency that they should be, and in fact are very likely to be, continued in the White House of the future. Not for reasons of tradition, not for reasons of patronage, but because the effectiveness of the presidential office itself depends on continuity of these staff institutions.

A new president certainly can shift the White House offices around somewhat, recombine some with others, decide on a different mechanism for coordinating domestic and international economic policy, pare down or perhaps even strengthen the NSC imperium, decrease (or, as Ike did, increase) the cohort of special assistants for special purposes. A new president will be free to negotiate different roles for the vice president and for the two spouses—but it is, frankly, doubtful that there would be a return to the Alben Barkley or Bess Truman models. Any incoming chief executive—Democrat or Republican—will certainly put new faces in all the policy positions, and he or she could sweep out all the long-termers in the professional posts; but only sheer stupidity would call for replacing, say, the White House telephone operators or the contingent of White House Communications Agency specialists.

Are there superfluous offices in the White House? Only if a president is willing to deprive himself of functions already being performed. While in theory a new president has a clean slate, expectations outside the White House condition his choices. Governors, legislators, state party chiefs, interest groups, and local news media would be the first to decry the "isolated" presidency if the intergovernmental, legislative, political, public liaison, or communications staffs were abolished. Would a new president reduce the Residence staff (and the public tours, and the entertaining)? Cease holding international summits at Camp David? Instruct the first lady to be less active? Return the vice president to isolation on Capitol Hill? Make only the secretary of state the "vicar" of foreign policy? Stay at home more?

A new president might be tempted—but really cannot choose—to transfer the White House counsel's "just-us" function back to the attorney general, to use the House or Senate leaders of his party to manage his relationships with Congress, to delegate the political appointment process back to party headquarters.

In structure, then, the White House staff community is likely to be a continuing enterprise. Whatever changes a new president makes, he may have to make them appear sufficiently dramatic to support a claim that "reform" has taken place—but the changes should not be such as to diminish the powers of governance that the existing system affords. It is the author's judgment that even a "reformed" White House will look a great deal like the one already described in this volume—that there will be continuity as well as innovation.

The Size of the Future White House Staff

The structure of the institution may be reshuffled (even if only cosmetically), but can the actual number of staff be substantially reduced? As shown in the appendix, there are over 6,500 men and women in what the author has defined as the White House staff community. Some 670 of them (aided by about 525 volunteers, 100 interns, and 1 or 2 White House Fellows) are in the policy offices of the White House. Where—and how much—reduction can be made?

President Clinton's promised 25 percent cut in White House staff was in several ways a failure. Out of a touted 350-person "White House reduction," 245 were from Executive Office rather than White House units. The White House offices that bore the cuts were left to carry out their continuing responsibilities with fewer people—adding to the strain on the remaining employees and resulting in a heavy use of interns (an arrangement that had some successes and a few drawbacks).

A new president could ordain that while the core functions would continue, their staffs must be smaller. He might pare his Public Liaison Office, cutting out its policy briefings, for instance, to the Business Roundtable or the Urban League. The president, however, needs the informed influence of just such groups in the halls of Congress. He could delegate subcabinet patronage to his cabinet members, shrinking his presidential personnel staff. President Carter tried that and recognized too late that he had given up too much authority.

The threat of terrorism leaves the president no choice but to require in-depth security support. The president's pastoral role—represented by mail, telephone calls, tourists, hardship cases, messages, cards, and gifts—nearly overwhelms the place. During his first six and a half years, for example, President Bush received over 11 million letters, with e-mails arriving at a rate of 850,000 a month. Does a future president expect fewer? The several hundred volunteers that work in the Correspondence Office that handles those letters and supports the nation's "pastor" have been essential in keeping the staff's heads above the flood.

Size per se is not the true issue in the management of the White House. As former chief of staff Richard Cheney urged,

> I don't think we should place artificial constraints on the president. If the president says he needs 500 people to do the job, give him 500; if he thinks he needs 700, give him 700. It's a minor price to pay for having a president who is the leader of the free world. . . . A $[3] trillion federal budget, 3.8 million federal civilian and military employees—we can afford to give the president of the United States however many persons he needs on his personal staff.[6]

"The president is the best judge of what he needs to do his job," observed a House Appropriations staff officer. "We give him what he asks for—and then, if he screws up, we can criticize him. We have made very, very few cuts in the White House requests."[7] (Of course, however large the total number of people, the inner ring of policymakers is smaller: in George W. Bush's White House there were only 154 White House staff officers with formal presidential commissions. Among these were the members of the senior circle: the heads of the seventy-four major offices described in the introduction and listed in the appendix. Even within that ring, there are, in every White House, a very few who are the president's most intimate associates.)

To be a countervailing magnet to atomizing particles in the polities of the nation and the world, and to be the successful centralizer of the executive branch policy process, the American president needs and deserves all the personal staff resources he can control.

Control is the nub. The limit on White House staff size is the point at which the president senses that he can no longer govern what the least of his staff do or say—and when, because they are not well governed, staff relationships with department and agency heads leave the cabinet chieftains alienated and resentful. This limit can vary: it should not be an arbitrary, imposed figure. The limit on the size of the White House staff depends, in great part, on the internal communications and disciplinary systems that the president builds into the White House.

If information flows readily from the president through the chief of staff to senior staff and to mid-level officers, so that all of them can accurately reflect and relay the president's priorities, a large staff is manageable. As the assistant cabinet secretary attending Eisenhower's cabinet meetings, the author could and did convey to other White House colleagues and to inquiring departmental experts the precise thrust and emphasis of the presidential decisions rendered in those sessions. If there is blockage in internal communications, however, the staff will lack direction.

It is not the number of staff, but their behavior that is key. If White House officers interpret their position as license to minimize consultation with departments or as opportunity to favor their own views when presenting issues to the president, their interdepartmental engagements will be no more than snarling matches—and the staff will be berated. If any of them, of highest or lowest status, let their egos get puffed up by the prestige of the White House title or the privileges of its environment, the traditional acrimony between insiders and outsiders will reappear—to bite them. If any of the two first couples or their staffs treat the experienced press as their enemies, the old battles will heat up—which the White House will lose. If overeager partisanship constantly overcomes the staff's willingness to work with congressional leaders of both parties, the historic tensions will surface, and the staff will be derided as excessive. If the concerns of governors are slighted and skeptical advocacy groups pushed aside, the staff will be excoriated for its haughtiness.

The issue is not how large is the White House staff, but how it is organized and how professionally it conducts itself.

Accountability

Is the staff out of control?

The Iran-Contra escapade of the 1980s certainly gave the public the impression that some members of the White House staff were a freewheeling bunch, pursuing not the president's agenda but their own. It even appeared that some had interposed themselves—the president unknowing—between the chief executive and his line subordinates.

That impression is understandable but wrong—especially wrong in the George W. Bush White House. No major enterprise takes place in the White House neighborhood without the president's knowledge and consent. Those in the seniormost ring of the White House staff are close to the president, and he to them, their confidences intimately shared, the mutual respect intense. The chances that they would keep secrets from one another—especially they from him—are close to zero.

The senior staff are constantly the transmitters of the chief executive's wishes; on occasion they will use—or will be told to use—a directive ostensibly their own to mask the president's hidden hand. Some disgruntled recipients of such orders may mistakenly believe, or may choose to believe, that the instruction emanated not from the president's choice but from the staff's own arrogance. They, too, are wrong. "If Bob Haldeman tells you something, you are to consider it as a communication directly from me and to act on that basis," President Nixon once declared.[8] "If Ham or Stu or Jack calls on my behalf, take their word as coming directly from me," President Carter told his cabinet. "You have been overly reluctant to respond when the White House staff calls you."[9] For their part, rarely does senior staff need the kind of reminder President Johnson often gave: "You make sure you know what I think before you tell [an outsider] what you think I think."[10]

It is the use by lower-ranking aides of the presidential "we" that most quickly provokes cabinet challenges to the staff's reliability. "If you have hundreds of people doing that, there is no way you can keep them out of mischief," commented Kennedy assistant Ted Sorensen.[11] Presidential scholar Richard Neustadt observed: "Only those who see the President repeatedly can grasp what he is driving at and help him or dispute him. Everybody else there is a menace to him. Not understanding, they spread wrong impressions. Keeping busy, they take their concerns for his."[12]

There is however, a sharp, fast antidote to mischief making by the more junior staff, a kind of pruning saw that operates to discipline the White House aide who tries to badger outsiders into believing that he is speaking for the chief executive. Should a query fired back to a more senior White House officer reveal that the original caller was not close to the presidential trunk, but out on a limb of his own, the saw cuts quickly, the limb is severed, and with it collapses the aide's credibility—if not his employment. Whenever cabinet officers, governors, ambassadors, or legislators hear "the White House calling," they may be tempted to test out the pruning-saw discipline through a callback to a more senior officer. At the White House, every mid-level or junior assistant soon learns that he or she operates under that sharp-toothed regimen.

How sharp? Johnson assistant Joseph Califano tells of the evening when he asked his associate, Lawrence Levinson, to pass on a presidential request to Secretary of Labor Willard Wirtz. The secretary doubted the authenticity of the younger aide's request and paid it no heed. The next morning, after explaining his hesitation to an irritated president, Wirtz received the following admonition: "If you get a call from anyone over here, if you get a call from the cleaning woman who mops the floors at three a.m. and she tells you the President wants you to do something, you do it."[13] Johnson, however, followed a very different principle where Secretary of Defense Robert McNamara was concerned. In a 1965 interview Johnson declared: "I've told Bob McNamara if anybody calls him and says he speaks for me, let me have the name of that man right away and I'll fire him."[14]

Accountability—as in "The Buck Stops Here!"—does, however, end in one place: the Oval Office. A White House is organized, and behaves, exactly as the president prescribes: it fits each chief executive's own style. If a Nixon insists that he be guarded—almost isolated—by a "Berlin Wall" of assistants, that is what will take place. If a Clinton, as in his early months, keeps his door open to staffers high and low, he will get just what he invites. If Condoleezza Rice allows the National Security Council to become dysfunctional, as many authors have claimed, the price for what happens in Iraq will be paid by the president.[15]

The White House is the president's house. Accountability runs straight up the line. If a cabinet, Congress, or the country is persistently offended by what a White House staff says and does, there is just one person in whose hands to heap their woe: the president of the United States. Ask not the White House staff to be what he is not. Should a president, fully informed, insist on unwise decisions, it is not his staff who will reverse him. Should he be malicious or dishonorable, it is only the more independent institutions of our nation—Congress, the courts, the press, not the White House staff—who must guard the Republic.

"A Passion for Anonymity"?

Louis Brownlow's 1936 prescription was the original maxim that was to govern the conduct of White House staff: they were to do their work behind the scenes, and stay out of the limelight. This volume has catalogued the assignments that White House staff undertake: gathering information, developing and coordinating ideas for substantive programs, drafting policy option memos, making presentations to the president. These staff activities can breed tension— and possibly conflict—between White House staff and cabinet officers. Such potential polarities are inherent in the methods presidents now use to exercise their leadership over the executive branch.

While the tensions are unavoidable, they would be exacerbated manyfold—so went the old prescription—if a White House staff member were to appear in the newspaper or on television, because that would imply to the public that the staffer was the center point of the action. In the George W. Bush White House, Louis Brownlow's maxim is rather strictly observed.

The Unforgiving Ethical Standard

New recruits may chafe at the ethical demands of government service: conflict-of-interest statutes and financial disclosure mandates. At the White House those are merely the minimum. The White House is a glass house, shot through with floodlights of scrutiny from a skeptical press and a hostile political opposition, watched by a changeable public. It is expected to be a model of public service—and it cannot help but be attacked for even the least of peccadilloes. Its rules of conduct reflect its honored—and vulnerable—circumstance.

The basic ethical standard in the White House is so old and so clear that it comes as a surprise to see any staff officers falling afoul of the rule. Quite simply, the *appearance* of impropriety is itself the impropriety. Will a staffer's acceptance of favors from outsiders, for instance, in fact compromise his or her judgment? No matter; it will look that way—enough to fail the test. The "appearance" rule is not in any law; it is tougher than law. It is the unrelenting standard for men and women who serve near the presidency.

White House staff can have no agendas other than to help the president. Political, professional, and financial ambitions have to be put aside, or one runs the risk of using the office for personal gain and of putting selfish priorities ahead of presidential objectives—instead of the other way around.

Getting Some Help

Before launching any innovations, future White House managers need to know what it is they are reforming. How has the White House been operated in the past? It is of course the author's hope that this work will be of help here. Beyond professional writings of this sort, however, presidential public administration enters virgin territory. With few exceptions, postelection communication between incoming and outgoing White House staff members has been perfunctory at best. Transition briefings are provided for newcomers within the cabinet departments, but conversations among new and old White House office heads have often not gone much beyond handing over the floor plans.

Such communication gaps are harmful to good government. Between election and inauguration, therefore, private forums are needed in which newly designated staff leaders can put their inherent hesitations aside and give a hearing to the observations of those who have preceded them—whether of their own party or not. The White House of the future deserves the seeking rather than the rejection of the experience gained in the course of each presidency.

In 2000–01, thanks to the support of the Pew Charitable Trusts, a group of presidential scholars under the leadership of Dr. Martha Joynt Kumar, created the White House 2001 Project, featuring seventy-five interviews of officials in six administrations, essays in depth about seven of the core White House offices, a library of recent books on the presidency, and an on-line collection of the forms that nominees for presidential appointments would have to fill out for the confirmation process. A book based on this project, entitled *The White House World*, was published by Texas A&M University Press in 2003. Also new in 2000 was an amendment that Congress added to the Presidential Transition Act permitting support for pre-inaugural orientation seminars for incoming White House, Executive Office, and cabinet appointees. (These did not occur in 2000–2001 because of the truncated transition period occasioned by the ballot controversy. Both of these efforts are likely to be replicated in 2008–09.)

Conclusion

What of the future?

As Hamilton would remind us, the raucous pluralism of American society will long continue to be the frustrating environment of those who govern. In a world balancing between peace and the frequent use of force—and in a nation buffeted by competing prescriptions for the division of its resources—parties, legislators, cabinets, and presidents will forever be making their decisions in surroundings that are supercharged with advocacy and pressures.

Can anything bring us together?

John Gardner looks at the White House:

Whatever may be said for the parties and for Congress, the best hope of accomplishing the orchestration of conflicting interests, the building of coalitions and the forging of coherent national policy is the President. It is his natural role. He begins the process long before election as he seeks to put together the constituencies he needs. In this day of media-dominated campaigns, the coalition of constituencies may appear to be less needed to gain electoral victory; but it is as needed as ever if the President is to govern effectively after victory. The President's capacity to balance conflicting forces and forge coherent policy and action should be substantially strengthened.[16]

It is the thesis of this book that the modern White House staff is the necessary part of that strengthening.

After each presidential changeover, the alumni of the years just gone begin to draw together to recall—and celebrate—the unforgettable intensities they shared. Eisenhower administration veterans used to gather in reunion lunch-eons and dinners; the Judson Welliver Society includes all the speechwriters present and past; the 1600 Club welcomes the White House Communications Agency insiders. The Nixon domestic council staffers reunite annually.

Within weeks of inauguration, a new White House staff comes to reflect, as did its predecessor, the president's own policies, priorities, and style. The older core functions continue, juggled perhaps into different hierarchies, adorned with new labels. Faces change, fresh adjustments are made, practices fine-tuned. The White House staff then becomes no more and no less than what the chief executive allows it to be; the instructions it gives are his orders, the procedures it specifies the ones he desires.

The essence of White House service is not the notorious dishonor of a few, but the quiet honor of thousands. The newest intern remembers what the old-est White House veteran never forgets: John Adams's prayer inscribed over the fireplace in the State Dining Room: "I pray Heaven to bestow the best of bless-ings on this House and all that shall hereafter inhabit it. May none but honest and wise men ever rule under this roof."

That invocation reaches the entire White House staff community; few fail to be humbled by the sense of obligation that those words instill. Implied within them is a further admonition: whether high or low in the staff, even in the midst of partisanship, one's duty is not only to the ruler of the present but to the White House of the future—to the president of today and to the presidency of tomorrow.

The true reward of White House service reaches beyond the excitement of the moment, is deeper than the seductive allure of the trappings of office. The ener-getic and intellectually aggressive men and women who make up the White House staff are driven not so much by the thirst for fame in the present as by the prospect of nudging the future—of "hacking a few toeholds on history," in the words of one.

A president is elected to effect a coherent program of change, battling all the while the incoherences of the pluralism beyond the White House gates. The White House staff are his compatriots in this battle, tolerating extreme per-sonal pressure and accepting at least partial anonymity as lesser sacrifices for a larger goal.

Appendix:
Component Offices of the
Contemporary White House Staff

As mentioned in the introduction, by the second term of George W. Bush's presidency, the whole White House staff community, in the author's categorization, was made up of 135 separately identifiable offices: seventy-four are what the author defines as major policy offices, twenty-one defined as supporting policy offices, and forty characterized as professional and technical units. Clearly there are alternative options for making these determinations; the author has leaned on the side of specificity.

For these offices, the number of staffers in each of them has been given here—numbers that must be considered soft because every day brings additional arrivals or departures in the total cadre of White House personnel. The "population" of each office ranges from 1 to 2,300. Also indicated here are the number and assignments of those staffers who are commissioned officers, that is, they have the word "president" in their titles and they carry formal commissions, signed by the president.

While the staffers in the professional and technical units are, in the words of former chief usher Gary Walters, "expected to serve from administration to administration," their tenure at the White House, like the positions of the men and women in all the other offices, is always at the pleasure of the president.

Category of office	Number in office[a]	Number of commissioned officers
Principal policy offices (74)		
The president	3	2
Chief of staff	11	5
Deputy chief of staff for policy	0	0
Deputy chief of staff for operations	0	0
Assistant to the president for strategic initiatives and external affairs	3	3
Counsel to the president	37	20

Category of office	Number in office[a]	Number of commissioned officers
Advance Office	27	4
Counselor (communications)	4	2
Communications Office	14	3
Media Affairs	10	1
Speechwriting	16	5
Domestic Policy Council	14	6
Legislative Liaison	24	14
Management and Administration	4	2
National Economic Council	16	8
Presidential Personnel Office	25	6
Press secretary	12	3
Staff secretary	8	2
Appointments and Scheduling	12	2
Political Affairs	11	2
Office of Strategic Initiatives	11	1
Intergovernmental Affairs Office	9	4
Office of Public Liaison	11	3
Faith-Based and Community Initiatives	7	2
The president's spouse	1	0
Chief of staff to the president's spouse	3	1
Deputy chief of staff to the spouse	2	1
The vice president	1	0
Chief of staff to the vice president	3	1
Deputy chief of staff to the vice president	2	0
Counsel to the vice president	1	0
Counselor to the vice president and press secretary	7	0
Deputy assistant/senior speechwriter	1	1
Legislative Affairs for the vice president	5	0
National Security Affairs for the vice president	17	0
Domestic Policy Office for the vice president	4	0
Homeland security assistant for the vice president	6	0
Spouse of the vice president	1	0
National security adviser	1	1
Deputy national security adviser	4	1
Deputy national security adviser for Iraq and Afghanistan	4	3
Senior director, speechwriting	2	1
Special assistant/senior director, legal affairs	3	1
Special assistant/senior director, legislative affairs	2	1
Deputy assistant /senior director, press	2	1
Special assistant/senior director, intelligence reform	3	1
Deputy national security adviser, regional affairs	7	1
Deputy national security adviser, strategic communications and global outreach	2	1

Category of office	Number in office[a]	Number of commissioned officers
Deputy national security adviser, international economics	3	1
Deputy national security adviser, combating terrorism	2	1
Deputy national security adviser, global democracy and strategy	3	1
Special assistant for Central and South Asian affairs	3	1
Special assistant for international trade and development	2	1
Special assistant for defense policy and strategy	3	1
Special assistant for counterproliferation strategy	3	1
Special assistant for relief, stabilization, and development	2	1
Special assistant for East Asian affairs	2	1
Special assistant for African affairs	2	1
Special assistant for Western Hemisphere affairs	2	1
Senior director for European affairs	2	1
Special assistant, Russia	2	1
Senior director, democracy, human rights, and international organizations	2	0
Senior director, Near East and Africa	2	0
Senior director, combating terrorism strategy	2	0
Assistant for homeland security and counterterrorism	2	1
Deputy assistant for homeland security	2	1
Special assistant and senior director for prevention policy	7	1
Special assistant and senior director for biological defense policy	6	1
Special assistant and senior director for response policy	6	1
Special assistant and senior director for preparedness policy	7	1
Special assistant and senior director for nuclear defense policy	4	1
Special assistant and senior director for cyber security and information sharing policy	4	1
Special assistant and senior director for continuity policy	4	1
Special assistant and counsel	1	1
Subtotal of staff	459	134
Supporting policy offices (21)		
Immediate Office of the president	4	2
Special assistant, cabinet liaison	5	1
USA Freedom Corps Office	4	2
Executive assistant/special assistant to the president's spouse	3	1

Category of office	Number in office[a]	Number of commissioned officers
Press secretary to the president's spouse	3	1
Speechwriter for the president's spouse	2	0
Deputy assistant, director of projects for the president's spouse	3	1
Special assistant and White House social secretary	4	1
Director of advance for the president's spouse	3	0
Director of scheduling for the president's spouse	2	0
Immediate Office of the vice president	3	0
Staff secretary to the vice president	3	0
Advance Office for the vice president	5	0
Scheduling Office for the vice president	4	0
Operations Office for the vice president plus remainder of vice president's total staff of 84	6	0
Executive secretary, National Security Council and remainder of the NSC total staff of 249	118	1[b]
Executive secretary, Homeland Security Council and remainder of the HSC total staff of 48	7	1[b]
Director, deputy director, and immediate staff of the White House Military Office (includes ceremonies coordinator; policy, plans, and requirements; airlift operations; general counsel; financial management/comptroller; security; administrative; and information technology management)	15	1
Experts and consultants not included in the above counts	6	0
Detailees not included in the above counts	9	0
Director, Office of Administration	3	1
Director, United States Secret Service	1	1[b]
Subtotal of staff	213	14
Professional and Technical Units (40)		
Executive clerk	9	0
Special assistant and director of the Presidential Correspondence Office (including Gift and Volunteer Offices)	60	1
Records Management Office	23	0
White House Management Office	9	0
White House Personnel Office	4	0
Photography Office	12	0
Telephone service assistance	17	0
Travel Office	7	0
Visitors Office	6	0
The White House Center Service Team of the General Services Administration	215	0

Category of office	Number in office[a]	Number of commissioned officers
National Park Service Liaison Office and Visitor Center	93	0
U.S. Postal Service, White House branch	11	0
Director of correspondence for the president's spouse	5	0
Operating units of the White House Military Office (including the White House Communications Agency, *Air Force One, Marine One,* Camp David, medical unit, transportation units, food service, five military aides to the president)	2,300	0
Chief usher and staff of the Executive Residence (including the curator and calligrapher)	96	0
Staff of the Commission on White House Fellowships	6	0
Correspondence Office for the vice president	2	0
Military aides to the vice president	6	0
Transportation Office for the vice president	6	0
Photography Office for the vice president	1	0
Administrative Office, National Security Council	12	0
Records and Access Management Office, NSC	20	0
Situation Room and systems, NSC	32	0
U.S. Secret Service: special agents and supporting administrative and technical staffs who protect presidential protectees (including former presidents, excluding dignitaries and 2008 candidates)	615[c]	0
U.S. Secret Service: Uniformed division members serving at the White House complex	914[c]	0
U.S. Secret Service: protective research staff	511[c]	0
U.S. Secret Service: Rowley Training Center staff	257[c]	0
Intern coordinator and White House interns	100[d]	0
Volunteers at the White House (Available pool)	525	0
One-eighth of the staff of the Office of Administration, who serve the White House	28	0
Subtotal of staff	5,902	1
Total offices	135	—
Total number of staff	6,574	154

a. The figures in this column are constantly changing.

b. Statutory.

c. These figures date from early 2007 and shift frequently, so they must be considered as approximations. The Rowley Training Center is also used by other federal law enforcement agencies.

d. Three groups of interns, 100 at a time, serve at the White House, for a total of 300 a year.

Notes

Introduction

1. The Office of Administration is not to be confused with the White House Office of Management and Administration; the latter provides management and administrative services within the White House itself.

2. President Ford bent that tradition himself when he testified before the House Judiciary Committee concerning the Nixon pardon. For a catalogue of the instances since 1970 when White House aides have in fact testified, see Louis Fisher, "White House Aides Testifying before Congress," *Presidential Studies Quarterly* 27, no. 1 (Winter 1997), p. 139.

3. The Presidential Records Act, 44 U.S.C. 2201–2207.

4. The Federal Records Act, 44 U.S.C. 3101–3314.

Chapter One

1. George W. Bush, "The President's News Conference," *Weekly Compilation of Presidential Documents* 43, no. 51 (December 20, 2007), p. 1686.

2. The author is indebted here to Matthew J. Dickinson, *Bitter Harvest: FDR, Presidential Power and the Growth of the Presidential Branch* (Cambridge University Press, 1997), pp. 46, 76, 77.

3. Ibid., p. 84, quoting from Brownlow's book, *A Passion for Anonymity* (University of Chicago Press, 1955–58), pp. 335–36.

4. Ibid., p. 91, quoting from the Merriam memorandum.

5. Ibid., p. 104. Italics added.

6. Ibid.

7. United States Statutes At Large, 1939, vol. 53, part 2, p. 561.

8. The plan effectuated the transfer, into this newly minted Executive Office, of the Bureau of the Budget from the Treasury department.

9. Public Law 107-296 (November 25, 2002), Sections 901–05.

10. 18 USC 3056(a).

11. Public Law 95-570 (November 2, 1978).

12. Public Law 93-270 (June 30, 1994).

13. *Report of the Congressional Committees Investigating the Iran-Contra Affair, Section II, The Minority Report, Chapter 3,* 100 Cong., 1 sess., p. 469.

14. John Lancaster and Helen Dewar, "Congress Clears Use of Force, $40 Billion in Emergency Aid," *Washington Post,* September 15, 2001, p. A-4.

15. George W. Bush, "Statement on Signing the Department of Defense, Emergency Supplemental Appropriations to Address Hurricanes in the Gulf of Mexico, and Pandemic Influenza Act, 2006." *Weekly Compilation of Presidential Documents* 41, no. 52 (January 2, 2006), pp. 1918–19.

16. Ron Suskind, "Why Are These Men Laughing?" *Esquire,* January, 2003, pp. 99, 98.

17. George W. Bush, "Executive Order 13198" (January 29, 2001), *Weekly Compilation of Presidential Documents* 37, no. 5 (February 5, 2001), p. 233.

18. George W. Bush, "Executive Order 13199" (January 29, 2001), *Weekly Compilation of Presidential Documents* 37, no. 5 (February 5, 2001), p. 235.

19. George W. Bush, "Message to Congress on the State of the Union," *Weekly Compilation of Presidential Documents* 38, no. 5 (January 29, 2002), p. 138.

20. George W. Bush, "Executive Order 13354," *Weekly Compilation of Presidential Documents* 38, no. 5 (January 29, 2002), p. 139.

Chapter Two

1. Background interview with the author, December 2006.

2. Whether the president uses this account is at his discretion, and no report to Congress is required.

3. In the formal Executive Office of the President budget request for fiscal year 2008, item 4 is $4,432,000, and it is stated that there are twenty-four people in the vice president's office. But in reality, there are some eighty-five people in that office. Dividing $4,432,000 by twenty-four gives a per-person cost of $184,666. Multiplying the other sixty staffers by $184,666 gets to $11,079,960. The real cost of the vice president's office may be closer, therefore, to $15,511,960.

4. In the formal Executive Office of the President budget request, item 8 is $8,640,000, and it is stated that there are 71 people on the staff of the National Security Council. In reality there are 249 people on the NSC staff. Dividing $8,640,000 by 71 gives a per-person cost of $121,690. Multiplying the other 178 staffers by $121,690 gets to $21,660,820. The real cost of the NSC may, therefore, be closer to $30,300,820.

5. Plus a classified appendix.

6. Using an estimate of an average per-person salary expenditure of $5,500 a month.

7. House of Representatives, 110th Congress, First Session, Committee on Appropriations, Report 110-181 on the Department of Homeland Security Appropriations Bill for FY 2008, June 8, 2007, p. 78.

Chapter Three

Gerald R. Ford was president from August 1974 until January 1977. Andrew Card was George W. Bush's first chief of staff, serving until March of 2006. Scott McClellan was

White House press secretary from 2003 to 2006. The quote is from Scott McClellan, *What Happened* (New York: Public Affairs Press, 2008), p. 84. Joshua Bolten served as George W. Bush's second chief of staff.

1. Richard Neustadt was a special assistant at the White House from 1950 to 1953.This quote is from Sam Kernell and Samuel L. Popkin, *Chief of Staff: Twenty-Five Years of Managing the Presidency* (University of California Press, 1986), p. 142. Italics added. It was in this book that former Carter chief of staff Jack Watson stated: "The image [of the White House chief of staff] that comes to my mind, borne out by some of the stories being told this morning, is that of javelin catcher."

2. This quotation and others in this chapter from former chief of staff Andrew Card were made during an interview with the author, McLean, Va., June 4, 2007.

3. This quotation and others in this chapter from Joshua Bolten, second chief of staff to George W. Bush, come from two interviews with the author on August 29, 2007, and November 21, 2007.

4. Robert Reich, *Locked in the Cabinet* (New York: Knopf, 1997).

Chapter Four

1. This chapter is based on an interview by the author with Staff Secretary Raul Yanes and Deputy Staff Secretary Brent J. McIntosh, Washington, March 27, 2007.

Chapter Five

1. Tenet's book was published by HarperCollins (New York) in 2007. A sampling of other recent books includes Daniel Benjamin and Steven Simon, *The Next Attack: The Failure of the War on Terror and a Strategy for Getting It Right* (New York: Henry Holt and Company, 2005); Sydney Blumenthal, *How Bush Rules: Chronicles of a Radical Regime* (Princeton University Press, 2006); Zbigniew Brzezinski, *Second Chance: Three Presidents and the Crisis of American Superpower* (New York: Basic Books, 2007); Andrew Cockburn, *Rumsfeld: His Rise, Fall and Catastrophic Legacy* (New York: Scribner, 2007); Karen DeYoung, *Soldier: The Life of Colin Powell* (New York: Alfred Knopf, 2006); Lou Dubose and Jack Bernstein, *Vice: Dick Cheney and the Hijacking of the American Presidency* (New York: Random House, 2006); Charles H. Ferguson, *No End in Sight: Iraq's Descent into Chaos* (New York: Public Affairs Press, 2008); Ben Fritz, Bryan Keefer, and Brendan Nyhan, *All the President's Spin: George W. Bush, the Media and the Truth* (New York: Simon and Schuster, 2004); Al Franken, *Lies and the Lying Liars Who Tell Them* (New York: Dutton, 2003); Jack Goldsmith, *The Terror Presidency* (New York: W. W. Norton, 2007); Karen Greenberg and Joshua Dratel, eds., *The Torture Papers: The Road to Abu Ghraib* (Cambridge University Press, 2005); Stefan Halper and Jonathan Clarke, *America Alone: The Neo-Conservatives and the Global Order* (Cambridge University Press, 2004); Stephen Hayes, *Cheney: The Untold Story of America's Most Powerful and Controversial Vice President* (New York: HarperCollins, 2007); Seymour M. Hersh, *Chain of Command: The Road from 9/11 to Abu Ghraib* (New York: HarperCollins, 2004); Michael Isikoff and David Corn, *Hubris: The Inside Story of Spin, Scandal, and the Selling of the Iraq War* (New York: Crown Publishing, 2006); Glenn Kessler, *The Confidante: Condoleezza Rice*

and the Creation of the Bush Legacy (New York: St. Martin's Press, 2007); Marcus Mabry, *Twice As Good: Condoleezza Rice and Her Path to Power* (New York: Rodale, Inc., 2007); Scott McClellan, *What Happened: Inside the Bush White House and Washington's Culture of Deception* (New York: Public Affairs Press, 2008); Frank Rich, *The Greatest Story Ever Sold: The Decline and Fall of Truth* (New York: Penguin Group USA, 2006); Thomas E. Ricks, *Fiasco: The American Military Adventure in Iraq* (New York: Penguin Press, 2006); James Risen, *State of War: The Secret History of the CIA and the Bush Administration* (New York: Free Press, 2006); Frederick A. O. Schwarz Jr., and Aziz A. Huq, *Unchecked and Unbalanced* (New York: New Press, 2007); Ron Suskind, *The One Percent Solution: Deep inside America's Pursuit of Its Enemies since 9/11* (New York: Simon and Schuster, 2006); Ron Suskind, *The Price of Loyalty: George W. Bush, the White House and the Education of Paul O'Neill* (New York: Simon and Schuster, 2004); Tim Weiner, *Legacy of Ashes: The History of the CIA* (New York: Doubleday, 2007); Jacob Weisberg, *The Bush Tragedy* (New York: Random House, 2008); Bob Woodward, *State of Denial: Bush At War, Part III* (New York: Simon and Schuster, 2006).

2. Dick Cheney, interview with the author, Washington, September 25, 2007.

3. These figures come from gleaning through the "Digest of Other White House Announcements" sections of 361 issues of the *Weekly Compilation of Presidential Documents* covering the first seven years of the George W. Bush administration. The author's grandson, Nick Patterson, helped with this endeavor.

4. The 9/11 Commission Report, Authorized Edition (New York: W. W. Norton and Company, 2004), p. 402.

5. This and other quotations in this chapter by National Security Adviser Stephen Hadley come from an interview with the author, Washington, December 27, 2007.

6. Cockburn, *Rumsfeld: His Rise, Fall and Catastrophic Legacy,* p. 178.

7. Tenet, *At The Center of the Storm,* pp. 427–28.

8. Isikoff and Corn, *Hubris,* p. 225.

9. Woodward, *State of Denial,* p. 197.

10. Isikoff and Corn, *Hubris,* p. 200.

11. Italics added.

Chapter Six

Fred Fielding was counsel to Presidents Ronald Reagan and George W. Bush. Lloyd Cutler was counsel to Presidents Jimmy Carter and Bill Clinton.

1. This and other quotations in this paragraph are from off-the-record conversations with the author.

2. Lloyd Cutler, interview with the author in Washington, October 22, 1986. Mr. Cutler attributed this aphorism to former undersecretary of state George Ball.

3. Lloyd Cutler, letter to author, August 8, 1999.

4. See, for example, the agreement with new attorney general Michael Mukasey, summarized in Dan Eggen, "Mukasey Limits Agency's Contacts with White House," *Washington Post,* December 20, 2007, p. A-3.

5. Peter J. Wallison, counsel to the president (Reagan), Memorandum for White House Staff: Prohibited Contacts with Agencies, May 7, 1986 (author's copy).

6. Griffin Bell, with Ronald J. Ostrow, *Taking Care of the Law* (New York: Morrow, 1982), p. 42.

7. Fred Fielding, counsel to President George W. Bush, interview with the author, Washington, October 18, 2007.

8. United States District Court for the District of Columbia, *Judicial Watch, Inc.* v. *U.S. Department of Justice,* Memorandum Opinion of March 28, 2003, p. 3.

9. "National Briefing," *New York Times,* March 26, 2008, p. A-16.

10. Bell and Ostrow, *Taking Care of the Law,* pp. 29–30.

11. Ibid.

12. Public Law 107-40, 115 Stat. 224, September 18, 2001.

13. U.S. Court of Appeals for the Fourth Circuit, *Yaser Edam Hamdi, Esam Fouad Hamdi as next friend of Yaser Esan Hamdi, Petitioners-Appellees,* 316 F.3rd 450 (2003), pp. 30–31.

14. Executive Order 13440 of July 20, 2007, 72 *Federal Register* 40707, July 24, 2007.

15. Attorney General Alberto R. Gonzales, "Legal Authorities Supporting the Activities of the National Security Agency Described by the President," Memorandum of January 19, 2006, sent that day to Senate majority leader William H. Frist, p. 20.

16. *New York Times,* December 12, 2007, p. A-27.

17. Jonathan Weisman, "Bush's Challenges of Laws He Signed Is Criticized," *Washington Post,* June 28, 2006, p. A-9.

18. *Weekly Compilation of Presidential Documents* 41, no. 52 (January 2, 2006), pp. 1918–19.

19. Carl Hulse, "Lawmakers to Investigate Bush on Laws and Intent," *New York Times,* June 20, 2007, p. A-16.

20. Ibid.

21. Walter Dellinger, Opinion Memorandum for Hon. Abner J. Mikva, counsel to the president, November 2, 1994. The Supreme Court case cited is *Freytag* v. *Commissioner,* 501 U.S. 868 (1991) at 906.

22. Fielding, interview with the author, Washington, November 28, 2007.

23. Adam Liptak, "Plainly a Pick of Like Mind: Bush Nominee Backs President on Powers," *New York Times,* October 20, 2007, p. A-1.

24. Jed Rubenfeld, "Lawbreaker in Chief," *New York Times,* October 23, 2007, p. A-29.

25. Jim Rutenberg, "Clinton Plans to Consider Giving Up Some Powers," *New York Times,* October 24, 2007, p. A-14.

26. Robert E. Gilbert, *The Mortal Presidency* (Fordham University Press, 1998), p. 242.

27. Lou Cannon, *President Reagan: The Role of a Lifetime* (New York, Simon and Schuster, 1991), p. 198.

28. Gilbert, *The Mortal Presidency.*

29. Testimony of Fred Fielding before the Miller Center Commission on Presidential Disability and the Twenty-Fifth Amendment, as printed in the report of that commission, White Burkett Miller Center of Public Affairs, University of Virginia, Lanham, Maryland, 1988, p. 7.

30. Ann Devroy and Ruth Marcus, "Clinton Team Follows Bush 'Road Map' on the Transfer of Presidential Power," *Washington Post,* June 14, 1993, p. A-17.

31. Oxford University Press, 2006.

32. 418 U.S. 683 (1974) at 708–09.

33. See Michael Abramowitz and Amy Goldstein, "Bush Claims Executive Privilege on Subpoenas," *Washington Post*, June 29, 2007, p. A-12; and Paul Kane, "West Wing Aides Cited for Contempt," *Washington Post*, February 15, 2008, p. A-4.

34. It was the case of EPA official Rita M. Lavelle. See Louis Fisher, *The Politics of Executive Privilege* (Carolina Academic Press, 2004), p. 129.

35. Ibid., p. 130. The OLC memo (8 Op. O.L.C 101, 1964), however, cautioned that its analysis was done in connection with the Lavelle case and "should be applied in other contexts only after careful analysis."

36. Adam Cohen, "Congress Has a Way of Making Witnesses Speak: Its Own Jail," *New York Times*, December 4, 2007, p. A-34.

37. Dan Eggen, "Mukasey Refuses to Prosecute Bush Aides," *Washington Post*, March 1, 2008, p. A-2.

38. "Text of Miers's Letter to President Withdrawing as Nominee," *New York Times*, October 28, 2005.

Chapter Seven

1. This and other comments in this chapter by Matthew Kirk, former deputy assistant for legislative affairs, 2001–04, were made in an interview with the author, Washington, March 9, 2007.

2. This and other comments in this chapter by Candida Wolff, assistant to the president for legislative affairs, were made in an interview with the author, Washington, June 1, 2007.

3. Helen Dewar, "Bush, Allies Scramble for Tax Cut Votes," *Washington Post*, April 6, 2001, p. A-12.

4. Jeff Zeleny, "Bush Meets with Democrats on Their Turf," *New York Times*, February 4, 2007, p. 24.

5. Michael Abramowitz, "Bush's Relations with Capitol Hill Chilly," *Washington Post*, May 13, 2007, p. A-5.

6. Andrew Rudalevige, "George W. Bush and Congress in the Second Term," in *The Second Term of George W. Bush: Prospects and Perils*, edited by Robert Maranto, Douglas M. Brattebo, and Tom Lansford (New York: Palgrave/Macmillan, 2006), p. 80 and figure 5.1 and p. 88 and figure 5.3.

Chapter Eight

Clay Johnson III is former director of the Office of Personnel Management in the administration of George W. Bush.

1. Of the 557 nominations sent to the Senate since 2001, 255 were nominees whose names were submitted two or more times.

2. This number is the total that exist. Most are filled multiple times during an administration, due to turnover.

3. National Commission on the Public Service, *Leadership for America: Rebuilding the Public Service* (Washington: 1989).

4. Clay Johnson III, "The 2000–2001 Presidential Transition: Planning, Goals and

Reality," in *The White House World,* edited by Martha Joynt Kumar and Terry Sullivan (A&M University Press, 2003), p. 311.

5. For details, see Bruce Adams and Kathryn Kavanagh-Baran, *Promise and Performance: Carter Builds a New Administration* (Lexington, Mass.: Lexington Books, 1979), p. 64.

6. This and, unless noted, other comments in this chapter by Clay Johnson III were made during an interview with the author, Washington, February 21, 2007.

7. This and other comments in this chapter by Chase Untermeyer, director of the Office of Presidential Personnel under George H. W. Bush, were made during an interview with the author, Washington, September 4, 1997.

8. Richard M. Nixon, *The Memoirs of Richard Nixon,* vol. 2 (New York: Warner Books, 1978), p. 285.

9. Paper from Dwight Ink and others in support of an amendment to the Presidential Transition Act of 1963, Spring 1999, author's personal collection.

10. The Presidential Transition Act of 2000, Public Law 106-293, signed by President Clinton on October 12, 2000.

11. This material was published in Kumar and Sullivan, *The White House World.*

12. Brian Faler, "Confirmed Fun for the Spouses of Appointees," *Washington Post,* March 25, 2005, p. A-17.

Chapter Nine

John D. Ehrlichman served as Nixon's principal domestic policy affairs assistant. Ted Sorenson was Kennedy's principal domestic policy counselor and speechwriter.

1. This and other comments in this chapter from Joel Kaplan, deputy chief of staff for policy, were made during an interview with the author in Washington on August 9, 2007.

2. This and other comments in this chapter from Allen Hubbard, then assistant to the president for economic affairs, were made in an interview with the author in Washington on March 19, 2007.

3. This and other comments in this chapter from Keith Hennessey, then deputy assistant to the president for economic affairs, were made in an interview with the author in Washington on May 1, 2007.

4. Tevi Troy, deputy assistant to the president for domestic affairs, in an interview with the author, Washington, May 20, 2007.

5. George W. Bush, "Remarks on Election Day and an Exchange with Reporters in Crawford, Texas," *Weekly Compilation of Presidential Documents* 40, no. 45 (November 2, 2004), p. 2790.

6. John Bridgeland, George W. Bush's first domestic policy assistant, interview with the author, June 11, 2007.

Chapter Ten

1. Executive Order 13286 of February 28, 2003, Section 8(a), subparagraph g. *Weekly Compilation of Presidential Documents* vol. 39, no. 10 (March 10, 2003), p. 268.

2. Executive Order 13228 of October 8, 2001, Sections 2, 3(l), 3(g) and 5. *Weekly Compilation of Presidential Documents* 37, no. 41 (October 15, 2001), p. 1434.

3. Entitled "Organization and Operation of the Homeland Security Council," February 29, 2001.

4. George W. Bush, Homeland Security Presidential Directive Number 1 (October 29, 2001), *Weekly Compilation of Presidential Documents* 37, no. 44 (November 5, 2001), p. 1568

5. George W. Bush, "Message to Congress," of June 18, 2002, *Weekly Compilation of Presidential Documents* 38, no. 25 (June 24, 2002), p. 1037.

6. Public Law 107-296, Sections 107(d) and 901.

7. This and other comments in this chapter from Joel Bagnal, deputy assistant to the president for homeland security, were made during an interview with the author and David Trulio, executive secretary of the Homeland Security Council, the White House, July 17, 2007.

8. Executive Order 13286, Section 8-a of February 28, 2003.

9. George W. Bush, Homeland Security Presidential Directive No. 5 (February 28, 2003), *Weekly Compilation of Presidential Documents* 39, no. 10 (March 7, 2003), p. 280.

10. National Commission on Terrorist Attacks upon the United States, *The 9/ll Commission Report* (New York: W. W. Norton & Company, 2005), pp. 402 and 406.

11 David Trulio, executive secretary of the Homeland Security Council, interview with the author, the White House, July 17, 2007.

12. President George W. Bush, quoted in letter from Frances Fragos Townsend, assistant to the president for homeland security and counterterrorism, to the president transmitting report entitled *The Federal Response to Hurricane Katrina: Lessons Learned,* White House, Washington, February 2006.

13. *The Federal Response to Hurricane Katrina: Lessons Learned,* Report to the President from Frances F. Townsend, February, 2006, p.1.

14. Public Law 109-364.

15. Statement of North Carolina governor Michael F. Easley before the Senate Judiciary Committee, April 24, 2007.

16. Statement of Senator Kit Bond before the Senate Judiciary Committee, April 24, 2007.

17. Homeland Security Council, *National Strategy for Homeland Security,* October, 2007, p. 29.

18. Excerpt from a July 2007 National Intelligence Estimate on "The Terrorist Threat to the U.S. Homeland," quoted in the New *York Times,* July 18, 2007, p. A-6.

Chapter Eleven

Rev. Gaddy is president of the Interfaith Alliance. Kuo served for a time in the Office of Faith-Based and Community Initiatives.

1. The Personal Responsibility and Work Opportunities Reconciliation Act of 1996, Section 104, Public Law 104-193.

2. Anne Farris, Richard P. Nathan, and David J. Wright, "The Expanding Administrative Presidency: George W. Bush and the Faith-Based Initiative," *The Roundtable on Religion and Social Welfare Policy,* Nelson A. Rockefeller Institute of Government, State University of New York, Albany, N.Y., August, 2004, p. 4.

3. Ibid.

4. George W. Bush, "Executive Order 13199 of January 29, 2001," *Weekly Compilation of Presidential Documents* 37, no. 5, p. 235.

5. Ibid.

6. George W. Bush, "Executive Order 13198 of January 29, 2001," *Weekly Compilation of Presidential Documents* 37, no. 5 (February 5, 2001), p. 233.

7. White House Office of Faith-Based and Community Initiatives, *Unlevel Playing Field: Barriers to Participation by Faith-Based and Community Organizations in Federal Social Service Programs,* August, 2001.

8. Farris, Nathan, and Wright, *The Expanding Administrative Presidency,* p. 10.

9. George W. Bush, "Executive Order 13342 of June 1, 2004," *Weekly Compilation of Presidential Documents* 40, no. 23 (June 7, 2004), p. 980, and "Executive Order 13397 of March 7, 2006," *Weekly Compilation of Presidential Documents* 42, no. 10 (March 13, 2006), p. 417.

10. George W. Bush, "Remarks to the Knights of Columbus Convention, Dallas, Texas," *Weekly Compilation of Presidential Documents* 40, no. 32 (August 9, 2004), p. 1433.

11. Jay Hein, director of the Office of Faith-Based and Community Initiatives, interview with the author, May 2, 2007.

12. Religion News Service, "In Brief: Interfaith Group Wants White House Office Closed," *Washington Post,* April 29, 2006, p. B-9.

13. David Kuo, *Tempting Faith: An Inside Story of Political Seduction* (New York: Free Press, 2006), p. 168.

14. The Supreme Court of the United States, *Jay F. Hein, Director, White House Office of Faith-Based and Community Initiatives et al., Petitioners* v. *Freedom From Religion Foundation, Inc., et al.,* Opinion of Alito, S., June 25, 2007, pp. 4, 5.

15. Ibid.

16. Ibid., p. 14.

17. Ira C. Lupu and Robert W. Tuttle, "Legal Update: Americans United for Separation of Church and State (and others) v. Prison Fellowship Ministries," *Roundtable Letter,* Roundtable on Religion and Social Policy, Rockefeller Institute of Government, State University of New York, December 11, 2007 (mdtbl@socialpolicyandreligion.org).

18. Ibid.

19. Ibid., p. 9.

20. Paul Singer and Brian Friel, "Leaps of Faith," *National Journal,* January 8, 2007, p. 14.

21. Ibid.

22. *New York Times,* January 29, 2008, p. A-27.

23. Ann Farris and Claire Hughes, "White House Touts Faith-Based Achievements in Report," *E-Newsletter,* Roundtable on Religion and Social Policy, Rockefeller Institute of Government, State University of New York, February 26, 2008 (mdtbl@socialpolicyand religion.org).

24. Ibid.

25. Ibid.

26. Ibid.

27. Barry Lynn, executive director of Americans United for Separation of Church and State, copy of letter of February 25, 2008, supplied to the author by Americans United for Separation of Church and State.

28. Alex J. Luchenitser, senior litigation counsel, Americans United for Separation of Church and State, who sent a copy of this letter to the author.

29. Anne Farris, "Obama Would Keep Faith-Based Office at White House," *E-Newsletter*, Roundtable on Religion and Social Policy, Rockefeller Institute of Government, State University of New York, April 25, 2008 (mdtbl@socialpolicyandreligion.org).

Chapter Twelve

Foreword by George W. Bush in brochure entitled *"USA Freedom Corps,"* Washington, January 2002. The second epigraph comes from Sheryl Gay Stolberg, "Bush's 2002 State of the Union Volunteerism Initiative Is Seen as Sputtering," *New York Times,* January 27, 2008, p. 18.

1. George W. Bush, "State of the Union Message to Congress" (January 29, 2002), *Weekly Compilation of Presidential Documents* 38, no. 5 (February 4, 2002), p. 138.

2. George W. Bush, "Executive Order 13354 of January 29, 2002," *Weekly Compilation of Presidential Documents* 38, no 5 (February 4, 2002), p. 139.

3. Off-the-record interview with the author, February 2008.

4. George W. Bush, "Executive Order 13285 of January 29, 2003," *Federal Register* 68, no. 22 (February 3, 2003).

5. George W. Bush, "Executive Order 13401 of April 27, 2006," *Weekly Compilation of Presidential Documents* 42, no.17 (May 1, 2006), p. 808.

6. Off-the-record interview with the author.

7. VfP was established by Executive Order 13317 on September 25, 2003, *Weekly Compilation of Presidential Documents* 39, no. 39 (September 29, 2003), p. 1266.

8. David Mervin, *George Bush and the Guardianship Presidency* (London: Macmillan, 1996), p. 106, quoting C. Gregg Petersmeyer, who was the director of that office.

Chapter Thirteen

1. Ellen Nakashima and Dana Milbank, "Bush Cabinet Takes Back Seat in Driving Policy," *Washington Post,* September 5, 2001, p. A-1.

2. This and other comments from Ross Kyle, director, Cabinet Liaison Office, were made in an interview with the author, March 14, 2007.

3. Robert B. Reich, *Locked in the Cabinet* (New York, Alfred A. Knopf, 1997), p. 179.

4. John Podesta, Clinton chief of staff, interview with the author, July 9, 1999.

5. Andrew Card, Bush chief of staff, interview with the author, June 4, 2007.

Chapter Fourteen

The quote from Balz and Allen can be found in "Four More Years Attributed to Rove Strategy," *Washington Post,* November 76, 2004, p. A-1. Green's quote appeared in the *Atlantic Monthly,* September 2007, p. 72.

1. Dana Milbank, "Serious Strategery": As Rove Launches Elaborate Political Effort, Some See a Nascent Clintonian 'War Room,' *Washington Post,* April 22, 2001, p. A-1.

2. Mike Allen, "Rove Trims Sails but Steers for Victory," *Washington Post,* October 17, 2004, p. A-1.

3. Richard W. Stevenson, "Top Bush Strategist Adds Another Big Hat," *New York Times,* February 9, 2005, p. A-19.

4. Peter Baker and Michael A. Fletcher, "Rove to Leave White House Post," *Washington Post,* August 14, 2007, p. A-1.

5. Richard W. Stevenson, "With Bush Safely Re-elected, Rove Turns His Intensity to Policy Issues," *New York Times,* March 28, 2005, p. A-14.

6. Charles Babington, "Fragile Senate Coalition Set to Pass Bill on Immigration," *Washington Post,* May 25, 2006, p. A-3.

7. Excerpt of an interview with Rove by Martha Joynt Kumar on May 8, 2002; printed in her book, *Managing the President's Message* (John Hopkins University Press, 2007), p. 85.

8. Dana Milbank, "Serious Strategery."

9. Dan Balz, "Resident Thinker Given Free Rein in White House," *Washington Post,* December 13, 2004, p. A-19.

10. Ibid.

11. Ibid.

12. For Clinton White House relations with the RNC, see Bradley Patterson, *The White House Staff: Inside the West Wing and Beyond* (Brookings Institution Press, 2000), pp. 211–12.

13. Adam Nagourney and Jim Ruttenberg, "Rove's Word No Longer Gospel," *New York Times,* September 3, 2006, p. 1.

14. Dick Morris, *Behind the Oval Office: Winning the Presidency in the Nineties* (New York: Random House, 1997), p. 338.

15. Kathryn Dunn Tenpas, "Words vs. Deeds: President George W. Bush and Polling," *Brookings Review* (Summer, 2003), p. 33.

16. Sara Taylor, former director of the White House Political Office, interview with the author, August 20, 2007.

17. "Cheney on the Polls," *Washington Post,* March 20, 2008, p. A-7.

18. Tenpas, "Words vs. Deeds," p. 34.

19. Ibid., p. 35.

20. Ben Feller, "Well-Timed Funding in Tight Races: One Perk of Incumbency Is Cabinet Officials Bearing Checks," *Washington Post,* October 27, 2006, p. A-21.

21. Dan Balz, "In New Hampshire the Spotlight Is on Rove," *Washington Post,* May 8, 2003, p. A-1.

22. Off-the-record interview with the author.

23. Ibid.

24. Dan Balz, "GOP Aims for Dominance in '04 Race," *Washington Post,* June 22, 2003, p. A-1.

25. Off-the-record interview with the author.

26. "Excerpts from Former Justice Dept. Aide's Statement on Attorney Removals," *New York Times,* May 24, 2007, p. 17.

27. Stephen Labaton and Edmund L. Andrews, "White House Calls Political Briefings Legal," *New York Times,* April 27, 2007, p. A-18.

28. Robert O'Harrow Jr., "Bush Is Asked to Discipline GSA Chief in Hatch Act Inquiry," *Washington Post,* June 12, 2007, p. A-7.

29. United States House of Representatives, Committee on Oversight and Government Reform, Majority Staff, *Interim Report: Investigation of Possible Presidential Records Act Violations,* Prepared for Chairman Henry A. Waxman, June 2007, p. 7.

30. Peter Baker, "Rove to Leave White House Post," *Washington Post,* August 14, 2007, p. A-1.

31. Anne E. Kornblut and Michael D. Shear, "A Mixed Legacy: 'Architect' Envisioned GOP Supremacy," *Washington Post,* August 14, 2007, p. A-1.

Chapter Fifteen

Maggie Grant is director of the White House Office of Intergovernmental Affairs; Ray Sheppach is executive director of the National Governors Association.

1. Dwight D. Eisenhower, "Message to Congress Transmitting Final Report of the Commission on Intergovernmental Relations," *Public Papers of the President, 1955,* June 28, 1955, p. 641.

2. Bradley Patterson, *Ring of Power: The White House Staff and Its Expanding Role in Government* (New York: Basic Books, Inc., 1988), p. 220.

3. This and other comments in the chapter by Maggie Grant were made during an interview with the author in Washington, May 18, 2007.

4. This and other comments in this chapter by Sheppach were made in an interview with the author in Washington, September 20, 2007.

Chapter Sixteen

Sorenson was a top aide to President Kennedy. Mike Meece is former deputy director of the Office of Public Liaison in the George W. Bush administration.

1. Tim Goeglein memorandum to Karl Rove, shown to the author.

2. Jim VandeHei, "Pipeline to the President for GOP Conservatives," *Washington Post,* December 24, 2004, p. A-15.

3. Sheryl Gay Stolberg, "Bush Aide Resigns After Admitting Plagiarism," *New York Times,* March 1, 2008.

4. Internal public liaison office memorandum, shown to the author.

5. This and other comments by Lezlee Westine, former director of the Office of Public Liaison in the Bush administration, were made during an interview with the author in Washington, October 31, 2007.

6. This and other comments in this chapter by Michael Meece, former deputy director, Office of Public Liaison, were made during an interview with the author, Washington, September 28, 2007.

7. This and other comments in this chapter by Rhonda Keenum, former director, Office of Public Liaison, were made during an interview with the author, Washington, June 21, 2007.

8. Conversation with the author, his White House associate, in the 1970s.

9. The author considers this series of contacts of Ms. Westine's to be an ideal model

for transitions at the White House from one administration to another, especially when there is a change of party.

10. List of 2006 events shown to the author by Keenum during an interview in her office, June 21, 2007.

Chapter Seventeen

Torie Clarke is a former Department of Defense spokeswoman and the former assistant secretary of defense for public affairs under Donald Rumsfeld. She was press secretary for George H. W. Bush's 1992 reelection campaign and was a close adviser to Senator John McCain during his early congressional career. She is the author of a book entitled *Lipstick on a Pig: Winning in the No-Spin Era by Someone Who Knows the Game* (New York: Free Press, 2006). The quotations are from pages 171 and 234 respectively.

1. The figures in this paragraph are from Martha Joynt Kumar, *Managing the President's Message* (Johns Hopkins University Press, 2007, p. xxxi). The author draws liberally on the research, wisdom, and insights in that book in composing this chapter and is accordingly greatly indebted to Professor Kumar for that privilege.

2. Ibid., p. xv.

3. Ibid., p. 80.

4. Ibid., p. 81.

5. Mike Allen, "Hughes Keeps White House in Line," *Washington Post*, March 19, 2001, p. A-1.

6. Kumar, *Managing the President's Message*, pp. 89–90. Karen Hughes was communications adviser to Governor Bush in Texas, then became counselor to the president at the beginning of the Bush administration.

7. Ibid., p. 3.

8. Ibid., p. 82.

9. Ibid., p. 31.

10. Al Kamen, "The USDA on Iraq: Everything's Coming Up Rosy," *Washington Post*, May 8, 2006, p. A17.

11. Robert Pear, "Buying of News by Bush's Aides Is Ruled Illegal," *New York Times*, October 1, 2006, p. A-1.

12. Kumar, *Managing the President's Message*, pp. 293–4.

13. Ibid., pp. 30–31.

14. David Barstow, "Behind TV Analysts, Pentagon's Hidden Hand: Courting Ex-Officers Tied to Military Contractors," *New York Times*, April 20, 2008, p.A-1.

15. Ibid., p. 24.

16. Ibid.

17. Howard Kurtz, "Retired Officers Still Doing the Pentagon's Work on TV," *Washington Post*, April 24, 2008, p. C-1.

18. Barstow, "Behind TV Analysts, Pentagon's Hidden Hand," p. A-24.

19. Editorial, "The Tarnished Brass," *New York Times*, April 26, 2008, p. A-26.

20. David Barstow, "Pentagon Suspends Briefings for Analysts," *New York Times*, April 26, 2008, p. A-11. The author cannot help commenting that this Pentagon "key influencer" initiative is hardly in keeping with the final lines of the second Torie Clarke quote at the beginning this chapter.

21. "Military Public Relations Effort Faces Inquiry," *Washington Post*, May 25, 2008, p. A-11.

22. Dana Milbank, "Bush Courts Regional Media—President Aims to Bypass Large News Outlets' 'Filter' on Iraq," *Washington Post*, October 14, 2003, p. A4.

23. Dan Bartlett, counselor to the president for communications, interview with the author, June 1, 2007.

24. Kumar, *Managing the President's Message*, pp. 98–99.

25. Elisabeth Bumiller, "Keepers of Bush Image Lift Stagecraft to New Heights," *New York Times*, May 16, 2003, p. A-1.

26. Kumar, *Managing the President's Message*, p. 100.

27. Ibid., p. 101.

28. Bartlett interview.

29. Kumar, *Managing the President's Message*, p. 137.

30. Ibid., p. 142.

31. Ibid., p. 143.

32. Ibid., p. 29.

33. Ibid., p.112.

34. Ibid., p.111.

35. Ibid., p. 304.

Chapter Eighteen

David Almacy is the White House Internet director.

1. See Martha Joynt Kumar, *Managing the President's Message: The White House Communications Operation* (Johns Hopkins University Press, 2007).

2. George W. Bush, "Remarks on Launching the New White House Web Site and an Exchange with Reporters," *Weekly Compilation of Presidential Documents* 37, no. 35 (August 31, 2001), p. 1247.

3. This and other comments in this chapter from David Almacy were made during an interview with the author, Washington, August 16, 2007.

4. Dan Bartlett, former communications director, interview with the author, June 1, 2007.

5. Michael Abramowitz, "President Reaches Out to a Friendly Circle in New Media," *Washington Post*, September 16, 2007, p. A-2.

Chapter Nineteen

Marlin Fitzwater served as press secretary to Ronald Reagan and George H. W. Bush; these quotes are from his book *Call the Briefing!* (Times Books, 1995).

1. For a brilliant and exceptionally thorough discussion of the White House press secretary and the functions of that office, see *Portraying the President: The White House and the Media* (Johns Hopkins University Press, 1981) and *Managing the President's Message* (Johns Hopkins University Press, 2007), both by distinguished presidential scholar Martha Joynt Kumar, who has had an observer's seat in the White House press quarters since 1995.

2. This quote from Terence Hunt, chief White House Correspondent for the Associated Press, and others attributed to Hunt in this chapter come from an interview with the author, September 26, 2007.

3. Scott McClellan, *What Happened* (New York: Public Affairs Press, 2008), p. 124.

4. Patrick Buchanan was special assistant to the president during the Nixon administration; he wrote speeches for both the president and the vice president.

5. McClellan, *What Happened,* p. 121.

6. This and other comments in this chapter from Dana Perino were made during an interview with the author, Washington, April 2, 2007, when Perino was deputy press secretary.

7. This and other comments in this chapter from Alexis Simendinger, *National Journal* White House correspondent, were made during an interview with the author, March 1, 2007.

8. McClellan, *What Happened,* p. 226.

9. Ibid., pp. 154–55.

10. Kumar, *Managing the President's Message,* p. 225.

11. Ibid., p. 229.

12. Ibid., p. 242.

13. McClellan, *What Happened,* p. 197.

14. For a full table of all presidential press conferences from 1913 to 2007, see Kumar, *Managing the President's Message,* p. 261.

15. Dan Bartlett, interview with the author, June 1, 2007, when Bartlett was director of communications.

16. Martha Kumar, interview with the author, January 31, 2007.

17. Kumar, *Managing the President's Message,* p. 181.

Chapter Twenty

Sorensen was John F. Kennedy's speechwriter; McGurn was chief speechwriter for George W. Bush.

1. If there is no podium on hand, or no press present, the event is almost certainly an extemporaneous occasion, with briefing material, if needed, prepared by other staff units.

2. This comment and others in this chapter from William McGurn were made during an interview with the author, May 18, 2007.

3. For example, President Bush's address to the Hispanic Chamber of Commerce, before his departure for an extended trip to Central and South America, *Weekly Compilation of Presidential Documents* 43, no. 10: 256–62.

4. George H. W. Bush and Brent Scowcroft, *A World Transformed* (New York: Alfred A. Knopf, 1998).

Chapter Twenty-One

1. Lyndon B. Johnson, "Remarks of the President upon Signing of the Ratification of the Convention with Mexico for Solution of the Problem of the Chamizal," The Treaty Room, December 20, 1963.

2. Don Bonafede, "Vice President Mondale—Carter's Partner with Portfolio," *National Journal*, March 11, 1978, p. 376.

3. Unless otherwise noted, remarks from Vice President Richard Cheney quoted in this chapter were made during an interview with the author in Washington, September 25, 2007.

4. Bill Sammon, "Bush Lauds Vice President Cheney for Helping Him Govern," *Washington Examiner*, April 12, 2006, p. 15.

5. As quoted in United States District Court for the District of Columbia, *Walker* v. *Cheney: Memorandum of Points and Authorities in Support of Plaintiff's Motion for Summary Judgment*, Civil Action No. 1: 02CV00340(JDB), April 11, 2002, p.17.

6. U.S. District Court for the District of Columbia, *Complaint for Declaratory and Injunctive Relief, Walker* v. *Cheney, Civil Action No. 1:02cv00340*, February 22, 2002, p. 2.

7. Richard Cheney, Letter to the House and Senate, reprinted in U.S. District Court for the District of Columbia, *Memorandum of Points and Authorities in Support of Defendant's Motion to Dismiss and in Opposition to Plaintiff's Motion for Summary Judgment, Walker* v. *Cheney*, May 21, 2002, p. 3.

8. 31 U.S.C.717(b)(1) & (3).

9. U.S. District Court for the District of Columbia, *Memorandum of Points and Authorities in Support of Plaintiff's Motion for Summary Judgment, Walker* v. *Cheney*, April 11, 2002, p. 4.

10. *United States* v. *AT & T Co.*, 567 F 2d (D.C. Circuit 1977).

11. U.S. District Court for the District of Columbia, *Walker* v. *Cheney*, Civil Action No. 02-0340 (JDC), *Memorandum Opinion*, p. 29.

12. In a Congressional Research Service report to Congress, *Walker* v. *Cheney*: District Court Decision and Related Statutory and Constitutional Issues, March 8, 2004, legislative attorney T. J. Halstead observed: "If interpreted broadly, the holding in *Walker* could greatly limit the ability of GAO to compel production of information from the Executive Branch," p. CRS-6.

13. *Washington Post* story quoted in Stephen F. Hayes, *Cheney* (New York: Harper Collins, 2007), p. 409.

14. Commission on the Intelligence Capabilities of the United States Regarding Weapons of Mass Destruction, *Report to the President of the United States*, March 31, 2005, pp. 50–51.

15. *Meet the Press*, September 16, 2001, quoted in Hayes, *Cheney*, pp. 479–80.

16. Hayes, *Cheney*, pp. 199–200.

17. U.S. Code, Title 18, Section 2340A.

18. *Washington Post*, June 11, 2004, p. A-6.

19. Goldsmith, *The Terror Presidency*, pp. 149, 158.

20. Ibid., pp. 88–89.

21. Hayes, *Cheney*, p. 484.

22. Ibid., pp. 491–92.

23. Bradley H. Patterson, *Ring of Power: The White House Staff and Its Expanding Role in Government* (New York: Basic Books, Inc., 1988), p. 293.

24. See chapter 2, note 3.

25. Patricia Dane Rogers, "The Vice President's Residence: A Fast-Track Makeover Opens the Mansion to Light and Art," *Washington Post,* November 15, 2001, p. H-1.

26. Ibid.

Chapter Twenty-Two

1. *Association of American Physicians and Surgeons, Inc., et al.,* v. *Hillary Rodham Clinton,* United States Court of Appeals for the District of Columbia Circuit, case numbers 93-5086 and 95-5092, June 22, 1993, p.11.

2. Public Law 95-570, 95th Cong., 2 sess. (November 2, 1978), sec. 105(e).

3. Carl Sferrazza Anthony, *First Ladies: The Saga of the Presidents' Wives and Their Power,* 2 vols. (New York: William Morrow, 1990–91).

4. George W. Bush, Address before a Joint Session of Congress on the State of the Union (February 2, 2005), *Weekly Compilation of Presidential Documents* 41, no. 5 (February 4, 2005), p. 121.

5. Interview with Jim Lehrer, *The News Hour,* WETA, February 17, 2005.

6. George W. Bush, "Remarks on Helping America's Youth Initiative" (October 27, 2005), *Weekly Compilation of Presidential Documents* 41, no. 43 (October 31, 2005), p. 1607.

7. This and all other comments in this chapter from Anita McBride, chief of staff to Laura Bush, come from an interview with the author, Washington, May 2, 2007.

8. Linton Weeks, "National Chapters," *Washington Post,* September 10, 2001, p. C-1.

9. Charles Lane, "Attacks Led to 'Dialogue' for Justice Kennedy," *Washington Post,* January 26, 2002, p. A-11.

10. Ann Gerhart, "The First Lady's Second Reading," *Washington Post,* January 25, 2002, p. C-1.

11. Ibid.

12. Jacqueline Trescott, "White House Seeks Raise for the Arts," *Washington Post,* January 31, 2004, p. C-1.

13. Jacqueline Trescott, "National Design Awards Presented at White House," *Washington Post,* July 19, 2007, p. C-9.

14. *Weekly Compilation of Presidential Documents* 42, no. 18 (May 8, 2006), p. 830.

15. Jacqueline Trescott, "Green Room Makeover Incorporates a Colorful Past," *Washington Post,* September 20, 2007, p. C-1.

16. Lynne Duke, "In Laura Bush, World's Women Gain Powerful Rights Advocate," *Washington Post,* March 9, 2002, p. C-1.

17. Ann Gerhart, "At the Wheel, Laura Bush Shows She Can Shift Gears," *Washington Post,* May 15, 2002, p. C-1.

18. Ann Gerhart, "Mrs. Bush's Prague Pilgrimage," *Washington Post,* May 21, 2002, p. C-1.

19. Keith B. Richburg, "U.S. Rejoining U.N. Agency after 19 Years," *Washington Post,* September 30, 2003, p A-1.

20. Carlotta Gall, "Laura Bush Carries Pet Causes to Afghans," *New York Times,* March 31, 2005, p. A-12.

21. Ibid.

22. Jim VandeHei, "First Lady Lobbies for Women's Rights in Mideast," *Washington Post*, May 22, 2005, p. A-20.

23. Jim VandeHei, "First Lady Says Mideast Change Will Be Slow," *Washington Post*, May 25, 2005, p. A-15.

24. Eugene Robinson, "Mideast Mission Unaccomplished," *Washington Post*, May 31, 2005, p. A-17.

25. Jacqueline Trescott, "Cultural Diplomacy Gets a New Worldview," *Washington Post*, September 26, 2006, p. C-2.

26. "Laura Bush Criticizes Burma's Military Rulers," *Washington Post*, January 5, 2008, p. A-4.

27. Michael Abramowitz, "First Lady Calls for U.N. Resolution over Ongoing Strife in Burma," *Washington Post*, September 6, 2007, p. A-12.

28. Dan Eggen, "First Lady Condemns Junta's Response to Storm," *Washington Post*, May 6, 2008, p. A-15.

29. Faiza Saleh Ambah, "Lifting the Veil from a Deadly Disease; Laura Bush Speaks with Saudi Women about Breast Cancer," *Washington Post*, October 25, 2007, p. A-13.

30. "Power Profile of the Week," *The Examiner*, Maryland ed., October 29, 2007, p. 16.

31. Sheryl Gay Stolberg, "First Lady Raising Her Profile without Changing Her Image," *New York Times*, October 15, 2007, p. A-1.

32. Deb Riechmann, "Laura Bush Spotlights Signs of Hope in Afghanistan," *Washington Post*, June 7, 2008, p. A-11.

33. Ann Gerhart, "Laura Bush, Out of the Garden and into the Fray," *Washington Post*, May 19, 2004, p. C-1.

34. Michael Fletcher, "First Lady a 'Critical Asset' at Republican Fundraisers," *Washington Post*, August 16, 2006, p. A-4.

35. Peter Baker, "First Lady's Influence Goes Global," *Washington Post*, October 15, 2007, p. A-4.

36. Elisabeth Bumiller, "First Lady Has Husband's Ear Even about Staffing, She Says," *New York Times*, March 25, 2006, p. A-10.

37. Baker, "First Lady's Influence Goes Global."

38. Lois Romano, "Laura Bush: A Twist on Traditional," *Washington Post*, May 14, 2000, p. A-1,

39. This quotation and others in this chapter from Lea Berman, former social secretary to Laura Bush, come from an interview with the author, Washington, April 26, 2007.

Chapter Twenty-Three

Steve Bull was a presidential aide to Richard Nixon; the quotation is from an interview with the author in Washington, July 25, 1986.

1. This and other comments in this chapter from former presidential aide Blake Gottesman were made during an interview with the author, at Harvard University, May 31, 2007.

2. Unless noted, comments by former Clinton presidential aides Steve Goodin and Andrew Friendly were made during a joint interview with the author, Washington, D.C. January 17, 1998.

3. Andrew Friendly, quoted in Peter Baker, "The President's Loyal Shadow," *Washington Post*, December 29, 1997, p. A-15.

Chapter Twenty-Four

Quoted in Martha Joynt Kumar and Terry Sullivan, *White House World* (Texas A&M University Press, 2003), p. 305.

1. Reagan White House assistant John Rogers, as quoted in Kumar and Sullivan, *White House World*, p. 285.

2. Background interview with the author.

3. Ibid.

Chapter Twenty-Five

1. This quote is from a paper on "The Office of the Executive Clerk," written by the executive clerk in January, 1992, p. 9, and is in the author's personal collection.

2. "Reagan Vetoes Saudi Arms Sale Ban," *Washington Post*, May 22, 1986, p. A-31.

3. Shana Judge, "Ronald Geisler: A Walking Encyclopedia of Presidential Information," *Government Executive*, October 1989, p. 74.

4. Kirk Semple, "In Twilight of His Life, A Former Moonshiner Finds Mercy," *New York Times*, December 13, 2007, p. A-27.

5. He acts pursuant to 4 USC 7(m).

6. The words in the Constitution are "consent" and "make." Apparently the noun "ratification" is used to denote the whole process described in this section.

7. G. Timothy Saunders, executive clerk, interview with the author, Washington, June 12, 2007.

8. Shana Judge, "Ronald Geisler."

Chapter Twenty-Six

Robert Dallek presented remarks before the Committee on Oversight and Government Reform, House of Representatives, 110th Cong., 1st sess., Report 110-44 *Presidential Act Amendments of 2007*, p. 4.

1. 44 U.S.C. 2201–07.

2. The records of the Council on Environmental Quality, the Office of Management and Budget, the Office of National Drug Control Policy, and the Office of Science and Technology Policy are not presidential records but are federal records and are governed by the Federal Records Act (44 U.S.C. 3101 et seq.). A U.S. district court decision of June 16, 2008, has affirmed that records of the Office of Administration are governed by the Presidential Records Act, not the Federal Records Act, and are not subject to the Freedom of Information Act. This decision is being appealed, so litigation is pending on this question (Del Quentin Wilber, "White House May Keep Documents in E-Mail Flap Private," *Washington Post*, June 17, 2008, p. A-3).

Although the papers of the vice president come under the definition of presidential records, they are not commingled with the papers of the president but are kept separately. If a vice president never becomes president, his papers may be preserved elsewhere at a place of his choosing; if he wishes, the vice president may donate his papers to the presidential library of the president under whom he served.

3. George W. Bush, Executive Order 13233, *Weekly Compilation of Presidential Documents* 37, no. 44 (November 1, 2001), pp. 1581–84.

4. D.C. District Court, Civil Action no. 01-2447, *Memorandum Opinion of October 1, 2007.*

5. "Records under Wraps," *Washington Post*, November 13, 2007, p. A-18.

6. Phillip Droege, director, Office of Records Management, interview with the author, Washington, July 20, 2007.

7. 44 U.S.C. 2112.

8. Sharon Fawcett, assistant archivist for presidential libraries, interview with the author, June 26, 2007.

9. U.S. House of Representatives, Committee on Oversight and Government Reform, *Interim Report by the Majority Staff: Investigation of Possible Presidential Records Act Violations*, June 2007.

10. Peter Baker, "White House Ordered to Keep E-Mails," *Washington Post*, November 13, 2007, p. A-4.

Chapter Twenty-Seven

1. This and other quotations in this chapter from Darren Hipp, director of the White House Correspondence Office, were made during an interview with the author, Washington, November 6, 2007.

2. Frederick E. Fox, "The Pastoral Duties of the President," undated memorandum, author's personal collection.

3. This reporting requirement is laid on all senior employees of all three branches of the government, including PAS nominees, and presidential, vice presidential and congressional candidates as specified in Section 101 of Title I of the Ethics in Government Act of 1978.

Chapter Twenty-Eight

1. Emily Charnock, James McCann, and Kathryn Dunn Tenpas, "Goin' Mobile: Assessing First-Term Presidential Travel from Eisenhower to George W. Bush," paper presented at the 2006 annual meeting of the American Political Science Association, August 30–September 3, 2006, p. 20.

2. This and other comments in this chapter from Todd Beyer, director of the White House Advance Office, were made during an interview with the author, Washington, March 2, 2007.

3. The subheads in this section are taken from the table of contents of the 2002 *George W. Bush Presidential Advance Manual.* That manual is not a public document, but its cover sheet, table of contents, and six specific pages were released to the American Civil Liberties Union under subpoena as part of the discovery process in a lawsuit initiated by the ACLU. The ACLU has made those eight pages public.

4. Robert Draper, *Dead Certain: The Presidency of George W. Bush* (New York: Free Press, 2007), p. 137.

5. The author's personal collection of presidential papers includes two editions of the Clinton advance manual, given to him by a Clinton White House advance staffer. They are not marked as classified or sensitive, and do not carry any other restriction. The quotations here are from page 76 of the most recent of the two manuals, published under the sponsorship of Clinton advance director Dan K. Rosenthal.

6. Peter Baker, "White House Manual Details How to Deal with Protesters," *Washington Post*, August 22, 2007, p. A-2.

7. Ibid.

8. U.S. District Court for the District of Colorado, *Complaint and Jury Demand*, filed March 15, 2007, p. 7.

9 Ibid.

10. U.S. District Court for the District of Colorado, Civil Action No. 06-cv-02355-WYD-CBS, *Order*, October 30, 2006, p. 6.

11. U.S. Court of Appeals for the Tenth Circuit, Cases No. 06-1504 and 06-1516, *Appellants' Opening Brief*, p. 20, filed February 26, 2007.

12. Sheryl Gay Stolberg and Carl Hulse, "Bush Vetoes Health Bill Privately, without Fanfare," *New York Times*, October 4, 2007, p. A-17.

13. General Accounting Office, "Presidential Travel: Costs and Accounting for the President's 1998 Trips to China, Chile, and Africa," GAO/NSIAD-99-164, Washington, September 21, 1999.

14. Robert Draper, *Dead Certain*, p. 194. The author drew extensively on pp. 191–96 of the Draper book in recounting this episode.

15. General Accounting Office, "Presidential Travel."

Chapter Twenty-Nine

David Parker was a scheduler for President Nixon; Andrew Card was President George W. Bush's first chief of staff.

1. Billy Webster, interview with the author, Spartanburg, South Carolina, October 6, 1998.

2. This and other comments from Melissa Bennett, deputy assistant to the president for appointments and scheduling, were made during an interview with the author at the White House, May 11, 2007.

3. In his book *Locked in the Cabinet* (New York: Alfred Knopf, 1997), pp. 107–08, former secretary of labor Robert Reich recounted a diary entry:

April 29

"The White House wants you to go to Cleveland," [Reich's secretary announces]. . . .

"Houses don't make phone calls. *Who* called?"

"I don't know. Someone from Cabinet Affairs. Steve somebody. I'll schedule it."

"How *old* is Steve?" . . .

"What difference does it make? They want you to go to Cleveland. You're going to Cleveland." ...

"I'll bet he's under thirty. . . . Some *twerp* in the White House who has no clue what I'm doing in this job. Screw him. I won't go. . . ."

Orders from twerps in the White House didn't bother me at the beginning. Now I can't stomach snotty children telling me what to do. From the point of view of the White House staff, cabinet officials are provincial governors presiding over alien, primitive territories. Anything of any importance occurs in the imperial palace, within the capital city. The provincial governors are important only in a ceremonial sense. They wear the colors and show the flag. Occasionally they are called to get their next round of orders before being returned to their outposts. They are of course dazzled by the splendor of the court, and grateful for the chance to visit.

4. U.S. Senate, *Final Report of the Committee on Governmental Affairs,* deposition of Ellen M. McCathran (March 10, 1998), 3: 4418.

Chapter Thirty

1. George H. W. Bush, *My Life in Letters and Other Writings* (Scribner, 1999); quoted in Scott Sherman, *Washington Post Book Review,* November 21, 1999, p. 13.

2. Evan P. Aurand, naval aide to President Eisenhower, Oral History 127, Columbia Oral History Project, Eisenhower Library, p. 4. Used with permission.

3. Deputy Chief of Staff Joseph Hagin, interview with the author, Washington, July 25, 2007.

4. The 9/11 Commission Report, Summer, 2004 (New York: W. W. Norton & Co.), p. 40.

5. These figures are from Appropriations Committee sources.

6. Background interview with the author.

7. Ibid.

8. Author's interview with a former White House physician.

9. R. S. Robins and H. Rothschild, "Doctors for the President," *New York Times,* April 7, 1981, p. 25.

10. William Safire, "The Operating Room," *New York Times,* January 5, 1987.

11. White Burkett Miller Center of Public Affairs, University of Virginia, *Report of the Miller Center Commission on Presidential Disability and the Twenty-Fifth Amendment* (Lanham, Md.: University Press of America, 1988), p. 25.

12. *Disability in U.S. Presidents: Report, Recommendations and Commentaries by the Working Group* (Winston-Salem, N.C.: Bowman-Gray Scientific Press, 1997), app. 2, p. 22.

13. White Burkett Miller Center of Public Affairs, *Report on Presidential Disability and the Twenty-Fifth Amendment,* p. 26.

14. Robert E. Gilbert, *The Mortal Presidency: Illness and Anguish in the White House* (New York: Fordham University Press, 1988), p. 275.

15. Del Quentin Wilber, "Police on the Lookout for Terrorists with Missiles Near Airports," *Washington Post,* September 9, 2006, p. A-3.

16. Jane Ciabattari, "The President and His PJs," *Parade,* July 9, 2000.

17. This and other comments from presidential pilot Colonel Mark Tillman were made during an interview with the author at Andrews Air Force Base, September 27, 2007. The author also received a personal tour of the plane.

18. Background interview with the author.

19. Jackie Spinner, "Plane Cleared for Takeoff," *Washington Post,* July 23, 1998, Maryland Section, p. 4.

Chapter Thirty-One

1. Miriam Ottenburg, "Time to Revise Security Plans," *Washington Evening Star,* September 28, 1964.

2. Background interview with the author.

3. Public Law 109-177 of March 9, 2006, Section 607, which amends Section 3056 of Title 18 of the U.S. Code.

4. From 1992 to 1997, in conjunction with the Bureau of Prisons and the National Institute of Justice, the service undertook the Exceptional Case Study Project, which investigated the "thinking and behavior of . . . 83 persons known to have attacked or approached to attack a prominent public official" in the United States during the years 1949–96. What did they find? The researchers discredited three myths: that there is a single profile; that assailants are mentally ill; and that attackers threaten targets directly in advance. They did find, however, that two-thirds of the attackers "did tell family members, friends, colleagues and associates about their thoughts and plans, or they wrote down their ideas in journals or diaries. These findings clearly pose an extremely complicated challenge to those who are protectors. If the government had total intelligence about everyone's private comments and writings, then it might know who is dangerous. But that is not the kind of government the nation would ever want.

5. 18 USCS 3056, of 1913.

6. 110 Cong., 1 sess., *Hearings before the House Appropriations Subcommittee on Homeland Security,* March 13, 2007, p. 670.

7. 110 Cong., 1 sess., *House Appropriations Committee Report 110-181 on the Department of Homeland Security Appropriations Bill, 2008,* June 8, 2007, p. 79.

8. Jeff Zeleny, "Secret Service Guards Obama, Taking Unusually Early Step," *New York Times,* May 4, 2007, p. A-19.

9. House Appropriations Subcommittee hearings on homeland security, pp. 642, 645.

10. Christopher Lee, "Cheney Could Keep Security Detail," *Washingon Post,* April 8, 2008, p. A-17.

11. House Appropriations subcommittee hearings on homeland security, pp. 681–82.

12. This and other comments from James Mackin, deputy assistant director for public affairs, were made during an interview with the author, in Washington, January 7, 2008.

13. Carol D. Leonnig, "Lawsuit Criticizes Secret Service: Anti-Bush Protesters Are Kept at Bay, Advocacy Groups Say," *Washington Post,* September 24, 2003, p. A-27.

14. Darryl Fears, "At NAACP, Bush Tries to Mend Rift: Applause and Boos Punctuate Speech, His First to Group as President," *Washington Post,* July 21, 2006, p. A-6.

15. The Presidential Threat Protection Act, Public Law 107-544.

16. House Appropriations subcommittee hearings on homeland security, p. 663.

17. Ibid., p. 667.

18. House Appropriations Committee report on homeland security, p. 78.

19. From a National Geographic Society DVD entitled "Inside the Secret Service."

Chapter Thirty-Two

1. George W. Bush, "Remarks on the 40th Anniversary of the President's Commission on White House Fellows," *Weekly Compilation of Presidential Documents* 41, no. 43 (October 28, 2005), pp. 1617–19.

Chapter Thirty-Three

1. George Elsey, *An Unplanned Life: A Memoir* (University of Missouri Press, 2005), pp. 19–21.

2. Ibid. See picture on p. 113.

3. This and other comments from former chief usher Gary Walters were made during an interview with the author, Washington, September 21, 2006.

4. Sara Armstrong, director of the White House Visitors Office, interview with the author, Washington, Summer 2007.

Chapter Thirty-Four

1. The comprehensive plan and the design guidelines were printed in limited edition. Readers who want more detail should contact the director of the National Park Service Liaison Office, Room 344, 1100 Ohio Drive, Washington, D.C. 20242.

2. Interview with Ann Smith, director of the National Park Service's White House Liaison Office, December 14, 2006.

3. Interview with former chief usher Gary Walters, at the White House, September 21, 2006.

Chapter Thirty-Five

1. See Jacqueline Trescott, "Green Room Makeover Incorporates a Colorful Past," *Washington Post,* September 20, 2007, p. C-1.

2. The author thanks Michael Melton, chief administrative officer of the association, for his helpful interview, September 25, 2007.

Chapter Thirty-Six

1. Joseph Hagin, deputy chief of staff for operations, interview with the author, Washington, July 25, 2007.

2. Peter Baker, "Bush, Maliki Sign Pact on Iraq's Future," *Washington Post,* November 27, 2007. p. A-12.

3. Stephen Hadley, national security adviser, interview with the author, Washington, December 27, 2007.

4. Scott Stanzel, deputy press secretary, interview with the author, Washington, October 12, 2007.

5. George W. Bush, "Remarks at a Ribbon-Cutting Ceremony for the Renovated Brady Press Briefing Room," *Weekly Compilation of Presidential Documents* 43, no. 28 (July 16, 2007), pp. 938–39.

6. Peter Baker, "Cost Nearly Doubles for Marine One Fleet," *Washington Post*, March 17, 2008, p. A-1.

7. Renae Merle, "Looking to Fly the Flag: Rivals for New Marine One Contract Promote Their US Credentials," *Washington Post*, June 17, 2003, p. E-1.

8. Baker, "Cost Nearly Doubles for Marine One Fleet."

9. Ibid. The Young and Johndroe quotes are included in the Baker article.

Chapter Thirty-Seven

Jeremy Rabin was professor of government at Cornell University, now professor of law at George Mason University, and author of several books on law and the presidency. Dick Morris was a presidential assistant in the Clinton administration. James Fetig was liaison to the press office from the National Security Council in the Clinton administration; the quotation is from Martha Kumar and Terry Sullivan, eds., *The White House World* (Texas A&M Press, 2003), p. 96.

1. The quotations in the paragraph are from Charles O. Jones, *Passages to the Presidency: From Campaigning to Governing* (Brookings, 1998), pp. 107, 40, 106, 107, and 112, respectively.

2. RAND study on planning for postwar Iraq, quoted in Michael R. Gordon, "Army Buried Study Faulting Iraq Planning," *New York Times*, February 11, 2008, p. A-1.

3. Jones, *Passages to the Presidency*, pp. 104–05.

4. Dick Morris, *Behind the Oval Office: Winning the Presidency in the Nineties* (New York: Random House, 1997), p. 98.

5. Terry M. Moe, "The Politicized Presidency," in *The New Direction in American Politics*, ed. John E. Chubb and Paul E. Peterson (Brookings, 1985), pp. 244–45.

6. Richard Cheney, interview with the author, Washington, D.C., April 27, 1987 ($1 trillion edited to $3 trillion to reflect current size of government).

7. Background interview with the author.

8. H. R. Haldeman, interview with the author, Santa Barbara, California, April 16, 1986.

9. Joseph Califano, *Governing America* (New York: Simon and Schuster, 1981), p. 411.

10. Ibid., p. 50.

11. Quoted in Samuel Kernell and Samuel Popkin, eds., *Chief of Staff: Twenty-Five Years of Managing the Presidency* (University of California Press, 1986), p. 106.

12. Richard Neustadt, "Presidential Leadership: The Clerk against the Preacher," in *Problems and Prospects of Presidential Leadership*, ed. James Sterling Young (Lanham, Md.: University Press of America, 1982), pp. 1–33.

13. Califano, *Governing America*, p. 412.

14. "An Interview with LBJ," *Newsweek*, August 2, 1965.

15. For a list of books on the Bush administration and Iraq, see chapter 5, note 1.

16. John W. Gardner, *Toward a Pluralistic but Coherent Society* (Queenstown, Md.: Aspen Institute for Humanistic Studies, 1980), pp. 20–21.

Index